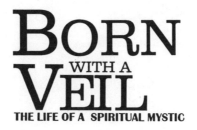

BORN
WITH A
VEIL
THE LIFE OF A SPIRITUAL MYSTIC

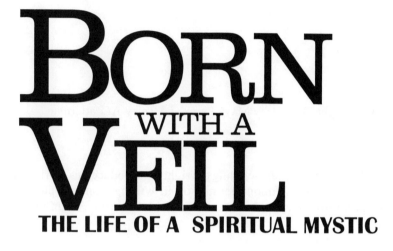

BORN
WITH A
VEIL
THE LIFE OF A SPIRITUAL MYSTIC

By Maya Perez
with Terry Latterman

HAMPTON ROADS
PUBLISHING COMPANY, INC.

Hampton Roads Publishing Company, Inc.
891 Norfolk Square
Norfolk, VA 23510
Or call: (804)459-2453
  FAX: (804)455-8907

To receive a catalog of other Hampton Roads books, write or call toll-free 1-800-766-8009.

ISBN 1-878901-04-4

10 9 8 7 6 5 4 3 2

Cover design by Patrick Smith

Printed in the United States of America

An Introduction

by Jess Stearn

Maya Perez is a remarkable psychic. I have never met anybody quite like her. She introduced me to the metaphysical field when I was a young newspaper reporter, and didn't even know there *was* such a field. And she made a believer of me. For as the days, months and years rolled by, every prediction she had made for me, however fanciful it seemed at the time, materialized in every detail. With her uncanny insight, at this first meeting, she picked me out as a newspaperman, but said I wouldn't be one much longer. "You shall write many books," she said. "Your third book shall be a bestseller, and your eighth book shall spread around the world." I remember laughing to myself, at this time, at the ridiculousness of it all. I was very happy with my job as an investigative reporter for the largest newspaper in the country, and had no thought of any other career.

"I have no intention of leaving newspaper work," I said. "Even as a boy that was all I ever wanted to be."

She smiled, and the smile lit up the dark swarthy face, with its inscrutable eyes. "It is right that you not now leave this job, "she said. "For you will write stories, and the publishers will read them and ask you to do books about the subjects you wrote about. And because of this, you will leave your newspaper work."

Two books were written, as she said, and neither was successful commercially. But other predictions she made have materialized, such as a broken engagement and a subsequent marriage to somebody she has perfectly described. And so I had hopes for a third book, which I wrote on my own time while I was still a newspaperman.

By now I had enough confidence in this South American soothsayer to tell my editor at Doubleday, "Have no fear, the next book will be a bestseller." And I really believed it, which, I supposed, as I look back, was some form of wishful thinking.

My Doubleday editor laughed. "If you're right, we'll put you on our executive committee."

My third book was *The Sixth Man.* It was a study of male homosexuality. I had researched it diligently, confining myself to the

i

homosexual's impact on society and society's impact on him. The etiology of it, the causative factor—for that I relied on the renowned psychiatrist, Doctor George Henry, who made a lifetime study of the subject. Remembering Maya Perez' prediction, I thought I had done all I could do.

I had been away on a trip, and had come back to my New York apartment a few days after my book had come out, without realizing it was now in the stores. There had been no advertising, no publicity, and little excitement about it in the publishing house.

I was at a gym, planning to work out, when I got my first word of the book. Over a battery of lockers, I overheard a gymnast say, "I guess we won't see Stearn around here any more, not after that book report in the *Saturday Review* (of Literature)."

I looked over the top to the lockers and saw two men whom I knew slightly. "Oh, I'll be back," I said. "I'm paid up for four months."

It was a Saturday afternoon. On the way home, I picked up a copy of the *Saturday Review* and turned to the report. I soon understood what the two men had been talking about. In a review of my second book, on juvenile delinquency, the reviewer had extolled the book and its author—me. I think "brilliant" was one of the lesser superlatives employed. Now, as they discussed *The Sixth Man,* I found that I had become a dolt, a dunce, unable to understand the complex subject I had undertaken. I got a zero for effort. I had tried, but to no avail. With a heavy sigh, I threw the magazine in the nearest trash can. That for Maya Perez, and her predictions. No more of that junk for me, and no more books. What publisher would want me after that review? And now back to being a newspaper reporter, if I could land a job. The future looked dreary indeed. I didn't blame Maya. I just blamed myself for being such a fathead. A man trained as a reporter believing what a psychic had to say. How absurd. So she had a couple of lucky hits. I might have done as well on the law of probabilities. I made a mental note to begin calling the various city editors I knew on Monday morning. I not only felt sorry for myself. I felt sorry for the Great Maya as well. How embarrassed she must be.

My hand was on the phone Monday, immediately following breakfast, when it rang with a curious insistence. I picked up the phone. It was Lee Barker, my editor at Doubleday. His voice rattled with excitement. "The strangest thing is happening," he said. "People are trooping into the bookstores on Fifth and Madison Avenues and buying fifty copies of *The Sixth Man* at a time."

On Wednesday, he called with an advance report on the Sunday *Times* book review section. "Your book is on the bestseller list," he said. And there it was for nearly a year, and as Maya had said I had become an established writer of books. For quantity, I soon discovered, ruled a world where quality was often secondary.

I called Maya to tell her the good news. Her voice carried a certain measure of indignation when she replied: "Why should you be surprised? Didn't I tell you that?"

I had a string of successful books after that, *Yoga, Youth and Reincarnation, Door to the Future,* etc, and then with a start I remembered Maya's prediction for my upcoming book. It would spread around the world. In other words, in the language of my friend, novelist Taylor Caldwell, it would be a whopping success.

And it was. *Edgar Cayce — The Sleeping Prophet* immediately rose to the top of the bestseller lists, and was published in every corner of the globe. The Great Maya had done it again. What more could I say for her?

There would be other books, and motion pictures, and I would be writing the scripts, and even directing.

I could hardly believe it, for I had no desire to be a screenwriter. And as for directing, that was better left to the likes of John Huston and Steven Spielberg.

"I can't believe it," I told a feisty Maya Perez, still peering into the future, still telling people things they didn't believe at the time.

"Why can't you believe it?" she cried with her usual indignation. "Didn't I tell you it would happen?"

And so she had, this most remarkable of psychics, and a remarkable lady, with all that.

CONTENTS

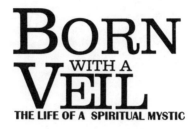

BORN
WITH A
VEIL
THE LIFE OF A SPIRITUAL MYSTIC

ONE
Early Childhood

My life started just before midnight in Guyana, South America, during a blinding rainstorm on August 2, 1905. Over my face was a film-like substance. This is called a caul or veil. It is known to be valuable as a good-luck omen. In the olden days sea captains paid as much as $500 for one, in order to keep their ships safe from a shipwreck.

There are many ancient tales about the caul, but my experience is: when a mystical individual is ready for higher experiences, one of these veils is lifted in order to allow the mortal freedom to delve deeper into the secret chambers of the subconscious, to open certain secret doors where the masters of light reside, thereby enabling the individual to obtain wisdom from the soul teachers. When we are ready to be initiated, then we are given various problems that can sometimes be most difficult. How we handle these problems is important, as it tells the inner teachers whether we have learned our lessons or failed to conquer them.

At birth I was named "Mable" after a cousin of my Father who, at the time, was staying with my family. Later my baby brother, Cecil, could not pronounce the name and called me Maya.

Reminiscing about my childhood, I realize my Mother really had her hands full with me. Certain incidents stand out in my memory, beginning with when I was eighteen months old. On this particular day, my family was not home except for my Father and he put me on a potty. I sat there wondering, "Why did Father put me on the potty? And where are Mother and my nurse?"

The next incident I can remember happened just before my third birthday. I was playing with my dolls when a whirling light came over my head. I looked up at the light and said, "I do not wish to live this life because I am going to be bad, and I do not wish to be bad."

The light disappeared and I went on playing with my dolls.

When I was three my eldest sister Ruby took me to school. She was thirteen years old. I sat on the baby stool which was designed for visiting children and looked around the room. The nine or ten children in the private school, who were taught by Miss Amy Humphrey, did not interest me. I was much more interested in Miss Humphrey. I studied her, then asked, "Miss Humphrey, why aren't you married?" Poor Miss

Humphrey looked at me speechless. The children were shocked and so were my parents when Ruby told them.

That evening when my Father came home, he took me into his private office. He looked sternly at me and said, "Mable, your sister Ruby informed your Mother about what happened in school today. You should not ask personal questions. You will not be given permission to go to school until you have learned not to ask such questions."

Six months later I was sent to a Catholic school. All went well until I was around five years old, then one day I came home and announced, "Sister Mary has a lover." My parents were not amused. Some time later Sister Mary ran away with an Englishman. A year or so later, Ruby took me once more to Miss Humphrey's school.

"What is your name?" Miss Humphrey asked me.

I remained silent and she looked over at Ruby who answered, "Her name is Mable, and Cecil, our younger brother, calls her Maya, but she does not care for either name."

Miss Humphrey studied me for a few moments then asked, "How would you like to be called May?"

I smiled and nodded my approval.

That summer my family planned a party, which was to be held at the Tapacooma lake. This was about six or seven miles into the interior of Henrietta, Essequibo. I heard the plans and wanted desperately to go with the group, but my Father did not want me to attend because I was too young. I was to be left with the nurse.

Mr. Varder, an Englishman, who was an overseer at the sugar factory, saw me crying. Wiping my tears with his handkerchief, he whispered, "Meet me at the boat landing tomorrow morning at five a.m."

Of course I was there promptly at five. He hid me under a tarpaulin at the back of the boat. After we had passed two locks, I came out and put my feet over the side of the boat into the water.

Looking at me in amazement, Father asked, "May, how did you get here?"

"Oh, I hid under the tarpaulin," I replied smiling.

Needless to say my parents were shocked, and so were the twenty or more guests who were riding in the two boats.

We arrived about ten-thirty a.m. at the Lake house. It was owned by the Pires family. They were South American Indians, called Bucks. I believe they were related to my Father.

About eleven thirty several friends and relatives went off to explore the pineapple fields and areas surrounding them. Several couples went off by themselves. One couple looked at me and said, "Go with your brother Albert."

I ran about looking for him, but could not find him. I walked deeper and deeper into the pineapple fields, when suddenly I realized that I was near the forest. The forest was full of wild and dangerous animals.

I started to pray. "Please God, please help me find my way back to the Lake house. Please let my Father and friends find me."

It was noon when all the guests returned to the Lake house for lunch. That's when my Father realized I was not with the group.

He immediately left with some workmen, who had come to manned the boats. Rudy, a young South American Indian boy, who was about twelve, was in this group of men. He was psychic and said to my Father, "Come, I know where she is."

I was found around four in the afternoon. I had remained in the boiling sun all afternoon and had fallen into my outer-consciousness. I could not speak and was in a trance-like state.

Adolph, one of my Father's workers, put me on his shoulder and brought me to Father, who was now ready to whip me, but Adolph said, "No, Master, she is in a trance."

Yes, God and his Angels had put a cover over my head and held me in a trance-like state until I was returned to the Lake house.

I later heard that Mr. Varder was an alcoholic and had drunk almost a whole bottle of rum. He became so drunk that two men had to hold him up when it was time to leave.

Shortly after my experience in the pineapple field, Father and Mother planned to go to a bicycle race in the next town. The morning of the race, I asked Mother, "Can I wear your gold nugget earrings?"

"Yes, May, you can, but first you will have to get your ears pierced."

Mother left the room and I ran to the kitchen. I got a piece of ice and a needle. Putting ice to my ears, I pierced both ears and then put the earrings in. Since they were gold, I was protected from infection.

That afternoon, my Mother and Aunt May were sitting in the grandstand watching the races when Aunt May looked over to me and noticed my earrings. She asked my Mother, "When did May get her ears pierced? She is wearing your earrings."

Mother looked at me and gasped, "Child, what have you done?"

With a big smile, I answered, "I pierced my ears."

Mother looked horrified and nothing more was said.

Father was speaking to a Dutchman, a Mr. Muller. I went over and asked Father for a schilling. Father ignored me.

Again I asked, "Can I have a schilling?" Again I was ignored.

Then Mr. Muller looked at me and asked, "What are you going to do with a schilling?"

"I will play the races and if I win five dollars, I will give your little daughter Georgie half." Georgie was seven.

Immediately he pulled out a schilling from his pocket and handed it to me.

I won five dollars and gave Georgie half. Many years later, I told Georgie, "If I had not promised your Father I would give you half, I would never have parted with the money."

When we returned home, that day, the first thing Mother did was to snatch the earrings out of my ears, leaving me with a scar for life.

I remember one afternoon, that same year, around my sixth birthday, I happened to be sitting on the veranda overlooking the street. Mother came out and pointed to an old lady who was part East Indian and black, called Dougla.

"May," my Mother said, "see that woman? Never go near her house. She is a witch."

I looked at the woman full of curiosity.

A few days later, I went to the woman's house and swung on her gate. She was busy advising a woman. When she finished, she noticed me and came out and walked over to me. She looked at me, then put her hand on her chin and asked, "Little girl, what is your name?"

I replied, "May."

She looked puzzled, then remarked in a quiet tone of voice, "Little girl, you will one day do my work."

I walked away wondering, "How can I do her work, she is a witch."

Later, I learned Old Lady Fortune, as she was also called, was capable of becoming a fireball and could travel throughout the countryside, bringing utter destruction to those who had upset her in any way.

A few months after my visit to Old Lady Fortune's home, my Mother caught my Father and a young woman called Sweet Rose in an empty house next door. Sweet Rose was Old Lady Fortune's daughter, and she also was adept in black magic.

The next morning, Mother took Ruby, Cecily, Clarice, whom we called Clara, Albert, whom we called Bertie, Cecil, Randolph, whom we called Rannie, baby Alfred and me to Georgetown.

It was 1912 and a plague was killing many people. It also killed my little brother Alfred, who was fourteen months old.

The night he died, I was visiting my friend Olive, when we suddenly heard footsteps coming upstairs. We both listened and we both became apprehensive. Suddenly at the top of the stairs, a cloud in the form of a man appeared. It stood there, then disappeared. We were both in a state of shock, when again we heard footsteps and Airie, Olive's older brother, came in and asked, "What are you doing here, May? Your brother just died."

I could not speak. It was Olive who said, "Yes, we just saw him."

Two years after Alfred's death, my sister Amy was born. June 15, 1914. In numerology, the number 6-6-6 designates a strange destiny.

I remember my Mother watching over Amy when she was three and praying as she slept. Amy was always sick with strange ailments. At the time I did not understand what was wrong, but later I was told by my spirits, Mother was sent a condition while Amy was in her womb. I also realized it was Old Lady Fortune who had given my Mother this condition.

Throughout the years, I have gone back to 1913 when Amy was conceived and sent light pouring into my Mother's womb. Every time Amy was ill, I would do this rite. I would also speak to Old Lady Fortune asking her to heal me and all my loved ones, and I would tell Sweet Rose to heal us and dissolve the curse that was sent through negative thoughts. (I do not advise anyone to do this rite unless they are pure in spirit and working with God.)

I can remember my Mother telling us tales about our lineage. She was named Ella Maude Randall Mackintosh. Her grandfather, Henry Randall, was from England. In 1845 he visited Barbados, then a colony of the British West Indies. There he married a nurse named Louise and they had a son, Henry Jr.

Louise died when Henry turned fifteen, and he was sent to live with an aunt in Guyana where he met my maternal grandmother.

My Father's grandfather, George Mackintosh, was from Scotland. He married a girl who was half-Portuguese and half- South American Indian. They had two sons. One was educated in England and settled there.

My grandfather Mackintosh owned a large estate about seventy miles from Georgetown, called Reliance in Esseguibo.

Grandfather disliked my Mother because she was a spiritualist and encouraged my Father to sit in on her weekly seances. All went well until a lady in the group died. In a seance that followed her death, a knock was heard on the door. A young man in the group opened the door and saw her spirit standing there. He fainted and after that experience the seances stopped. Grandfather felt that God had answered his prayers.

In 1912 Father went to Scotland, England and France. While in Paris he had his palm read and was told, "You have come across many bodies of water for two pieces of paper that you, a thirty-third-degree Mason and metal engineer, have on your person. You have several children, but one little girl who is seven years old will one day be a famous author."

Father repeated this prediction to Mother, then turned to me and asked, "May, what would you like to be when you grow up?"

I quickly replied, "A famous author."

Just before Father returned from England, my mother was talking to aunt May, Victor Pires' wife. They were really not my aunt and uncle, but Victor was almost like a brother to Father and we called them aunt and uncle.

On this particular day, aunt May came over to see my Mother. She was greatly upset because Uncle Victor had beaten her. I was seven years old and it was about eight or eight-thirty when my Mother, not wanting me to hear any more of this conversation, asked me to go to bed.

I answered, "No!"

"I'll whip you if you don't obey," she threatened.

"You are always saying you are going to whip me. Why don't you do it?"

Mother went to a tree and broke off a few small branches and really gave me a sound whipping.

The next morning I had welts on my arms and Mother didn't want me to go to school. "You are not well and will stay home today," she announced.

"I'm not sick and I will go to school," I answered.

I went to school and Miss Humphrey saw the welts. She was shocked and at lunch time she sent her maid over to my Mother's and told her that she was going to keep me until Father returned from Europe.

My Mother immediately packed my clothes and gave them to the girl. That afternoon, Miss Humphrey changed my clothes and took me for a walk. We passed our veranda and my brother Albert was there, along with Clarice and Cecily. Miss Humphrey bowed to them and I did the same. Albert thumbed his nose at us and I thumbed my nose back at him.

"Young ladies do not thumb their nose," Miss Humphrey said primly.

On our walk back, Albert again thumbed his nose only this time I did not.

I stayed with her for about ten days.

The employees who worked in the foundry for my Father made flags and filled balloons to welcome him home. There was a big celebration in our front yard and I came up to my Father and said, "Mother beat me."

Well, of course, after talking to my Mother he realized I deserved it.

I also recalled being called Little Miss America because my clothes were ordered from the Montgomery Ward catalogue. I did not like the clothes available in my country and I loved parading about in my American clothes.

As a little girl, I was terribly afraid of the dark. It was in the dark that I saw ugly faces floating about, which I instinctively knew were not of this world. In the bright sunlight, I always saw little spirits which were friendly and exceedingly beautiful. These I would welcome as my little playmates. I truly loved them and referred to them as my very favorite people. I did not, at the time, realize that I was a mystic child living in two worlds. Neither did I know that it was fear of the dark that created the evil-looking demons that rested in my lower consciousness and in the bright sunny morning, when I was not afraid, the thought-forms with spirits were lovely and happy.

Mother was beside herself many times when I would predict things that were about to happen. As a child, I was really most difficult.

In this book, I will endeavor to give in great detail my true purpose in this life, but for now I will say that my purpose in this life is not to exploit demons but rather to purify them, in order for them to become our true and faithful servants. Please believe me when I say that with positive thoughts, we mortals are able to do great work in order to fulfill our greater destiny.

TWO

The Sinking of the Uberaba

In 1918, when I was thirteen and Ruby twenty-three, she married Culbert Kennedy. Cecily was twenty-one and Clarice nineteen. They went to New York with Aunt Ida. Later, that year, my Mother took Albert and me to New York to visit my aunt and my two sisters. Cecil and Randolph stayed with Father and Amy went to visit Ruby. New York was exciting, but there were problems. Mother became ill.

I went to school for awhile, then stopped to take care of Mother. Through my prayers, Mother was able to regain her health.

During the summer of 1919, Father arrived in New York. He had to be operated on for gall bladder problems. The operation was successful and the doctor advised Father to live in a warm climate. Father decided on Barbados. He went on ahead of us to get settled into a house and position and when it was time for Mother to join him, she decided to take me to Barbados with her.

I felt a chill go through my whole being and cried out, "Oh, Mama, no! Not Barbados! I don't want to go there. Please let me stay in New York. I can go to school here and my sisters will take care of me."

I had an amazing premonition of the sinking of our ship, the *Uberaba*. It was so vivid that I have never forgotten the experience.

Mother turned a deaf ear to all my pleading. She smiled, knowing full well that I had not gone to school for the past year. I had lied about my age and had found a job, telling her I was going to go to night school, which I had failed to do.

She told me I would learn to like Barbados. The weather was wonderful. I could go swimming every day if I wanted to.

Finally the day of departure came. I asked Mama if I could go and buy a few gifts for the family. She looked at me and hesitated, but gave her consent. As I left, the thought came to me to run away. I didn't want to go to Barbados and the ship would probably sink. This thought alarmed me. I stopped to have an ice cream soda to give myself courage but that failed. The drink was left on the counter.

On my way back to the apartment, I went into a store and picked out some gifts with a heavy heart. Turning the corner to our apartment I saw my Mother, Aunt Ida, my two sisters, and several friends standing on the steps. I became fearful because I knew they were waiting for me.

I quickly slid into a doorway, but I was not quick enough. A friend who saw me, pulled me back to the house.

I cannot describe the quarrel that erupted when my Mother and family realized that I really did not want to leave New York. After much sorrow and tears, I was somewhat comforted by finding that the ship, which was a Brazilian luxury liner, had a swimming pool and other fun things.

That night my Mother became seasick and could not leave the cabin. I was left under the watchful eye of the stewardess, but most of the time she could not find me. The second day out she simply gave up and I enjoyed myself going all over the beautiful ship and doing as I pleased.

I met Mary, an eighteen-year-old girl, who was traveling alone. She was going to visit her brother who was a doctor living in Brazil.

Mary advised me to say I was sixteen because I could easily pass for that, but I looked her straight in the eye and said, "I am already passing for eighteen so why should I say sixteen?"

She introduced me to a Brazilian millionaire, who was an inventor. He was traveling with his secretary, a handsome young man about twenty-four or five. Mary liked the secretary, and the inventor, a man in his late thirties, was soon attracted to me.

As we toured the ship one afternoon, the stewardess who had been sent to look for me found the four of us together. She returned to the cabin and told my Mother I was being entertained by two gentlemen and a young girl friend. She assured my Mother that one of the gentlemen was old enough to be my Father, so that I was sure to be safe. After that I was not annoyed.

One day the inventor informed us some of his inventions were on board the ship. He had gone to Washington to have them patented. One invention was a screen-less movie. I listened to him describe the invention and thought how wonderful a movie would be without a screen. To me he was the most brilliant and wisest person I had ever met. I was enthralled by his personality.

One morning, rather early, I got up and went on deck. The night had been stormy and the ship had reeled from one side to the other. Neither my Mother nor I had slept. I saw a man standing by the rail looking off into the far beyond. He turned as I passed him and said, "This ship almost went down last night. The captain was up all night."

He was quite disturbed. They were getting the life boats in order. "I'm afraid it's a very old ship and can't stand any more storms," he remarked.

I looked at him amazed, remembering my premonition of the ship going down. I was indeed concerned. As I seemed interested to listen to his story he went on to explain why he was sure the ship would not last many more trips. When he finished I ran to tell my Mother what he had said.

"Mama, Mama," I screamed running into her cabin, "the ship almost went down last night. The man said he was happy that we will be arriving in Barbados tomorrow. He said he will never take this ship again because it is too old. I must tell Mary and those nice men to get off at Barbados."

Rising to a sitting position, my Mother glared at me.

"Don't you dare give advice to Mary or anyone else. As a matter of fact, I would rather you did not see those two men again. Mary is a nice girl, but you are too young to be in the company of older men. Soon you will be telling me that one of them is proposing to you."

"Why, Mama, how did you know?"

This remark made Mama get up immediately and she started dressing. She was too angry to say anything.

Finally her curiosity got the better of her and she said, "That man is ten or eleven years older than you, child. You are only fourteen! Did you tell him your age and that you have to finish your schooling?"

"Mama, it was the older man and he is thirty-eight, but don't worry, I still want to see Barbados and this man is a millionaire and has inventions on this ship. One is a screen-less movie. Wouldn't it be dreadful if the ship did go down?"

By now my Mother was dressed. Some mysterious power had suddenly made her almost well. Even though the ship was still rocking, she went up to the dining room and had a big breakfast.

All that day my Mother watched me very closely and I was unable to contact either Mary or the two Brazilian men.

Toward evening, while Mama was taking a nap, I ran up to Mary's room. She excitedly told me that my admirer was becoming concerned about my real age and he had asked her exactly how old I was. Under a barrage of questions she had told him I had just turned fourteen. He appeared shocked and just walked away.

The next day turned out to be beautiful and sunny, so all thought was forgotten about the possibility of the ship going down.

Around three o'clock we saw the beautiful island of Barbados. Mary and I were leaning over the side of the ship watching the native boys dive for coins when our two admirers approached. The older man looked sad and told me he realized I was quite young, but he would like to write to me if my parents would not object.

"Oh, no, I have wonderful parents. They are most understanding." I smiled because I too wished to continue our friendship.

"My Father is almost as young as you."

The moment I spoke, I knew I had chosen the wrong words for he was looking off into the hills of Barbados and sadly remarked, "That's the trouble, May, I am too old and you are too young, yet you have such understanding. I feel you are ageless, my dear, and I would very much like to continue our friendship. Here is my address. Please let me hear from you once in a while, and I shall write to you."

"Oh, yes, I will and I do want you to meet my Father."

Their meeting was disastrous. Mother walked away from him leaving my Father and me alone with my friend. Father glared at him in complete silence.

"As soon as John, my helper, takes the trunks off the ship, we are leaving," he remarked.

And that was how I said good-by to Carlos. Leaving in the motor boat for shore, I threw a kiss to Mary and could see the two men leaning sadly over the rail.

Five days later, as I came home to dinner, my family were already seated at the dinner table. Under ordinary circumstances I would have received a scolding from Mama for being late. I was surprised when she did not speak. Instead, my brother Cecil, said, "I will tell her, Papa."

"No, Cecil, let her eat her dinner first," my Father answered softly.

Looking over at my Father I asked in a positive tone of voice, "What is it I should know? I won't eat until you tell me, Papa."

There was a tense silence for a moment, then my Father answered sadly, "The *Uberaba* went down off the coast of Brazil today. I'm sorry, May."

Suddenly my whole world stopped. Thoughts reeled in my head. What does one do when the inevitable happens? If only I had tried to warn them. I went to my room, fell on my bed and sobbed.

My Mother came in and sat on the side of the bed trying to stroke my hair, but I pushed her away.

She sat beside me for a few minutes in silence then said, "Please forgive me, dear. I did not understand. I wish I had been kinder to your friends. If only we had invited them here."

I did not answer Mama and she quietly left me with my grief.

Later my Father learned that some of the passengers were saved, but we never knew how many. Definitely the inventions all went down, and with it the screen-less movie.

THREE
Francis

My fifteenth birthday found me attending a private school for girls and teaching Sunday school in our Methodist church on Bay Street in Bridgetown, Barbados, British West Indies.

In October, the church gave a concert. Five-year-old Kathleen Brayson was in my Sunday school class. She was extremely shy. I encouraged her Mother to let Kathleen recite at the concert. She was reluctant to let her do this. I assured her that I would sit in the audience and give Kathleen the necessary power to recite and overcome this shyness.

My Mother, my thirteen-year-old brother Cecil, my eleven-year-old brother Rannie, my six-year-old sister Amy all attended. I sat with my Mother and the younger children took seats near the stage.

Just before Kathleen was to appear on the stage, I overhead two girls whispering behind me.

"Look out of the window," one of the girls whispered to her friend, "two young men are looking at this girl in front of us. Who is she?"

"I don't know," her friend answered, "I am not sure. I think she is from New York. She is going to school here."

The first girl stopped for a moment then continued her whispering. "The blond young man is Francis Lord, Reverend Lord's son. The other dark-haired young man is Neville Taylor. They are close friends."

Mother and I immediately looked out of the window. Two young men were standing there staring at me. Suddenly I felt a warm feeling flow through me as if a blanket of love were sweeping through my whole being. I was filled with ecstasy that I had never experienced.

I had promised Kathleen's Mother that I'd raise my hand when her daughter went on stage, thereby giving Kathleen the power to perform. The time for raising my hand had come. Kathleen was waiting on stage for the signal but I was unable to lift my finger, much less my hand. All my power had vanished, I was like a person who has been hypnotized. The young blond man with the deep blue eyes penetrated my innermost being with his mesmerizing stare. Poor Kathleen stood frightened and frozen on stage unable to open her mouth. Finally, she was led backstage.

From the moment I turned my head away from the young man's hypnotic eyes, time stood still for me. I remember nothing until much later when I found myself running home down Constitution Road, looking for shelter from a sudden tropical rainstorm.

My Mother, unable to run, had taken shelter with my two brothers and sister under a shop awning three blocks behind me.

The storm became so violent that it became impossible for me to reach my house so I, too, had to take shelter under an awning.

I soon realized that someone was watching me. Turning, I saw the man with the piercing blue eyes.

I turned my eyes away. He reminded me of John Boles, a popular film actor of that time, only this man was much younger and very handsome. He appeared to be about twenty years old, five feet-eight inches tall.

We stood there in silence when he spoke.

"I would like to introduce myself. I am Francis Lord, my Father is Reverend Lord, the head of the two Methodist churches."

I held my tongue. Drawing closer, he pleaded, "May, please speak to me."

Defiantly I answered, "You seem to be well informed about me, however, I am not in the habit of speaking to strangers."

Smiling, he exclaimed, "Oh, I am not a stranger. We have mutual friends. My friend Neville Taylor has a sister Esther. She is a friend of yours."

I relaxed a little, saying, "Yes, I have met Esther Taylor through mutual friends. She passes my home on her way to Queen's College. I hope to go there some day."

The rain stopped and the moon was out in all her glory. I began to walk down the street towards home. Francis followed me saying, "Please allow me to escort you to your gate. I live on this same street, about half a mile down the road."

I did not reply and he kept pace beside me. Strangely I had a feeling that we had walked together many times before and would walk together many times in the future.

We strolled in silence until reaching my gate. Then he asked, "Will you meet me in the park tomorrow at five p.m?"

"No," I answered, "I do not go out with men to whom I am not formally introduced."

He continued speaking as I walked away. "I will be waiting near the bandstand."

I smiled to myself as I opened the door to my home. Later, in bed, I found myself wondering about his strange mysterious powers. The thought came to my mind, "I bet he made me run to that shelter by causing the rain to become violent."

Although at the time it was a frivolous thought, I have since become aware that there are, in fact, individuals who have the power to cause such situations. These people are able to send thought patterns to their subconscious minds, which then contact the individuals they wish to control. To develop defenses against these people, it is advisable to pray and read the Biblical Psalms. You will then be able to lift up your consciousness and become immune to the widespread psychic manipulations of powerful individuals.

The next afternoon I arrived for our rendezvous a few minutes after five. Francis was waiting near the bandstand. He rose smiling and greeted me with a warmth that I was to remember the rest of my life.

We sat on a bench overlooking the park, and he handed me a box of chocolates. He fed me two pieces then took a piece for himself.

"Do you have a friend? Someone that you care about?" he asked.

"No, of course not," I answered, "I'm only fifteen. My parents would not allow me to keep steady company."

He held my hand and said with a smile, "Your parents are wise. I agree with them that you should not keep steady company; of course, in my case, it is different."

We both laughed. I was silent for a few minutes then asked," Francis, how old are you?"

He thought for a moment, then answered, "I am twenty-one and old enough to be your advisor and teacher."

At that we both laughed happily. Nevertheless, those were very prophetic words that I was to remember all of my life.

After that conversation, I became serious for a few moments and carefully selected my words before asking my question.

"Francis, last night you stared at me through the church window. Why? Did I look different from the other girls?"

He was silent a long time as he held my hand; then he answered with a great deal of hesitation as if afraid to say something that might disturb me.

"Yes, you are different from all the other girls that I have ever met. Not that you look different—only from the way that we met."

He stopped for a moment then continued. "Neville and I had some work to do in the big church where my Father preaches. I had a sudden urge to pray and asked Neville to pray with me. When we finished, we sat in silence and I received a message. It was quite clear: *Go to the church on Bay Street. There you will find a young girl dressed in white. She is not a native of this island. She is very important to your spiritual and divine destiny as she is from the past and was connected to you in many lives.* "

We both remained silent after he finished speaking. Needless to say, I was too shocked to tell him that I also had powers that I had found could be used for myself and others.

In a few moments he continued again. "May, I have strange powers. It is because of these powers that I have not followed my Father into the ministry. It is his greatest desire for me to become a minister, but I have been afraid to become involved with the church. I would love to stand in the pulpit and preach the word of God, but instead I am a manager and bookkeeper in the Red Store."

It was odd, I thought, that I had never seen him there since I shopped in the store often. He answered my unspoken question.

"I started working there a few weeks ago. Usually I work at the back of the store. My work as an accountant is to keep a record of the books and see that all is in order."

We sat there quietly, then I asked, "Francis, do you have someone that you care about?"

He looked deeply into my eyes and replied, "Yes, there is a young lady. Tita White. My family wishes me to marry her, but I am not in love with her. Oh, there is an attraction, but I've been told that she is not for me."

"Who told you that Tita is not for you?" I asked, wondering who his advisor was.

He paused before he spoke. It was as if he would like to avoid giving me the answer.

"The same voice that told me you were connected to me from a past life."

I did not question him further. We sat quietly while he held my hand tight as if he was afraid that I would disappear.

He quietly said, "It is so good to hold your hand again."

I laughed and asked, "Again? Where have you held my hand before?"

Pressing my hand close to his heart he answered, "Yes, I have held your hand many, many times. Oh, it is so good to have you with me. So wonderful."

I realized suddenly that it was getting quite dark. Looking at my watch I exclaimed, "Francis, it is after six o'clock and my dinner hour is at seven. I must leave you."

Kissing me gently on my cheek, he asked, "Promise me that you will see me again? Please promise that you will see me again and again?"

"I promise, Francis," I replied seriously. "I promise to see you again and again."

"Very well, then I will let you go," he answered smiling happily as he got on his bicycle, then turning to me whispered softly, "Good-by, dear one from the past. Good-bye for now."

The next Sunday I met Francis at church. There was a new minister from England and everyone had come to hear him. While my Father was speaking with the minister and his wife, both Francis and Neville came over and spoke to me. I agreed to meet him in the park on the following afternoon.

This time I arrived first. When he got off his bicycle, he greeted me with a happy smile and handed me a small package. I opened it and found it to contain an expensive bottle of French perfume. I thanked him, but knew that I could never use it because my Mother would be suspicious about where I had obtained such an expensive gift. Later I gave it to a friend.

A strange phenomenon occurred that afternoon while we were walking in the park. I was looking down at the shimmering water in a large pond when I suddenly looked up at Francis and discovered a strange light glimmering all around him. I did not know it at the time, but now I realize it was his aura that was shining so strangely.

Impulsively I exclaimed, "Francis you are shining like a god! Oh, dear Francis, you are a god walking here on earth."

He pulled away from me as if I had struck him. His voice sounded astonished as he cried out, "Don't say that! It is sacrilegious!"

Disturbed by his angry tone of voice, I replied with some hesitation, " Oh, but I didn't mean it that way. There was a light shining all around you. It must have been the light of God shining through you."

My innocent explanation humored him and he gently took my arm in his and led me to a seat nearby.

We sat peacefully for a short while, then Francis said, "May, tonight I will see Tita. Since I have met you I have seen her only once and today she called me at the store."

"Well, do you wish to marry her?" I asked, intuitively sensing that his desire was to be with me. Yet the tone of his voice was suspicious and demanding.

"No, I do not," he quickly answered.

"Then why not explain that you don't love her and would like to just be friends," I asked, wondering why he was disturbed about a childhood friend.

"May, a voice within me keeps saying that Tita has given me great trials in another life, and it is important for me to be diplomatic with her or she could again cause me great sorrow."

As he spoke these words, I felt a strange sensation in the pit of my stomach. It was an omen of evil for both of us.

"Francis," I cried out, "see her, but do not admit that you do not care for her. If you do she will try to destroy us. I, too, get messages. God tells me what I need to know so that I can be protected."

Francis pulled me towards him and whispered in my ear, "Please believe me. No harm will ever come to you if I can help it."

The next year was a happy one. Everything went by as if we were living on a magic carpet. Francis and I had many wonderful talks about psychic phenomena. We would talk about the Bible and the many miracles that were manifested in God's name, also of evil that was created by negative thoughts. I was not aware of it then, but he was playing an important role in the web of my destiny as a teacher of deep occult and mystical secrets. He brought his Bible with him and taught me the meaning of the Psalms. He was indeed my teacher, but I was too young to realize it until years later.

Then, shortly after my sixteenth birthday, my whole life changed. Father and Mother had gone to the theater with some friends. Amy was in bed with a cold. Cecil and Rannie were on the back porch studying for an examination.

It was a bright moonlit night and after finishing my homework, I went down to the front gate to watch the people in the tram car or those on the street as they passed by our home.

Out of nowhere a voice asked, "Who are you waiting for?"

It was Francis. In a joking manner I replied, " I had a feeling you would be out on this bright moonlit night. They say when the moon is full one must be careful. The witches and warlocks are sure to be out."

Many nights we had chatted by this gate, but this time it was different. I invited him in and we went to the back porch where Cecil and Rannie were studying. Francis spoke to the boys about their studies. When they mentioned their school, Combermere, he became interested because he had also attended this school.

We left the boys and went into the garden. We watched the fish swim in our large pond in murky moonlit water. It was beautiful and eerie. He took me in his arms and the rest of the world disappeared for us.

About an hour later we were startled when we heard Cecil's voice saying, "Mother and Father are home. It's best that you leave, Francis. May is not allowed to have young men in our home."

Francis and I started to walk toward the front of the house when Cecil pulled him back and exclaimed, " Francis, leave by the back gate. Father might see you and May could get into trouble if he finds out that you have been here. Come with me."

Cecil quickly unlocked the gate that led into an alley and Francis, who by now was quite disturbed, rushed away as Cecil and I went into the house.

I thought no more about it until a letter arrived a week later. The envelope was burned and as I tried to open it my hands trembled. Mother entered the room and became suspicious over my behavior and pulled the letter out of my hand. After she finished reading it she handed it to me with a shocked look on her face.

From that day on, the words in that letter were imprinted on my soul: *We know you entertain men in your home when your parents are out. We hope you are not pregnant, but if you are, you are getting what you deserve. The man that you entertain is engaged to someone else. Curses are being sent to you.*

Mother spoke calmly as she asked, "Are they referring to Francis Lord? Did you at any time have him here while we were out?"

I was frightened, so I told the truth. "Yes, Mother, it was Francis. I did invite him in, but both Cecil and Rannie were home. Believe me, there is nothing wrong. Francis is an upright and godly young man."

"May, I believe you," she answered quietly, "but someone must have seen him come in and got the wrong impression. I'll speak to your Father about this matter."

That night, after dinner, Father called me into his private den and asked me to sit down.

I waited impatiently for him to speak. Then he said, "May, your Mother has informed me about a very malicious letter that came to you in the mail and that the envelope was burned. Is the accusation true and was one of the young men Francis Lord?"

Taking a deep breath, I answered, "Yes, Father, I did invite Francis to come in one night last week, but Cecil and Rannie were here. Believe me, my friendship with Francis is not the sordid affair that the letter implied. Francis is a wonderful and very spiritual young man. Like his Father, he is man of God. Believe me, no harm will ever come to me through him."

He shook his head sadly and replied, "This could very well be true, dear, but I'm afraid you have attracted a lot of jealousy from someone who is evil and malicious. This person could easily try to destroy my reputation as well as yours. I hold an important position here. One which many natives would be happy to step into. This is a small island and gossip could travel over the whole town. Try to remember that we are strangers here. Also, I understand the letter stated that Francis is already engaged. Even if he were not, you are too young to be keeping steady company. I would like you to promise me that you will not see this young man again."

"Father," I replied, shocked, "how can I make such a promise? We both belong to the same church and sometimes we're bound to meet. How can I possibly ignore him?"

He got up and kissed me and answered, "Try to use your discretion. This situation could be very difficult."

A few days later, I noticed the girls in school whispering behind my back and purposely avoiding me. I felt hurt, and when I tried to speak to one girl, she just walked off and snickered with the other girls. I was lonely and extremely troubled, but I could do nothing to help myself. When the tide of life's flow is going against you, you must learn to go with it. One must be still and realize that like all things, it will soon pass away.

The evidence was piling up against me. Instinctively I sensed it was Tita who sent that dreadful letter. Also, she was spreading evil lies about me.

I told Mother what was happening at school. She was quite disturbed and spoke to my Father about getting a lawyer, but he explained that we couldn't prove who had written the letter or started the ugly rumors.

Because of the ugly rumors and the snubbing in school, my Father took me out of school, at my request, and found a private tutor who was willing to give me lessons three afternoons a week. It was rather boring to stay home, but it was much better than going to school and being snubbed and gossiped about.

Now that I was not in school, I had time to really explore and appreciate the beauty of this tropical island. It was populated with blacks, mulattos, quadroons and octoroons besides the English, Canadians and tourists from many foreign lands.

There is a great deal of black magic practiced on this island since the natives are extremely superstitious. They believe that someone could "image" and send evil to them. To ward off these strange darts of poison, they perform many ceremonies after dark or by the light of the moon. These rites are usually performed by men or women who have studied magic from childhood.

The letter that was sent to me, with the burnt edges on the envelope, had been tinged with island magic. This my Mother was well aware of and she advised me to burn the letter and pray for the sender.

Six weeks passed and I had not seen or heard from Francis. One evening Cecil said he had something to tell me. We went to his room and he said, "May, I saw Francis this afternoon. He asked me how you were and I told him about the letter and that you had left school. He was very disturbed and asked if you could ever forgive him?"

Cecil was silent, waiting for me to answer, but there was a lump in my throat and I could not say a word.

After a moment of complete silence Cecil continued. "He looked terrible. I felt sorry for him. Why don't you give him a call?"

Finding my voice I exclaimed, "Oh, Cecil, why did you tell him about the letter and school?"

He looked at me, not quite understanding why I was upset and answered, "Well, he would have found out anyway. Look, May, I know you and Francis are innocent, so have a heart and phone him."

"I can't," I answered with tears in my eyes, "Father has asked me not to see him because gossip may hurt his position here."

Shrugging his shoulders and patting my head, he kindly remarked, "Well, if this is the way you feel then let us say no more about it."

Three weeks passed. Then one Sunday afternoon after my Sunday school class, I saw Francis with Marie Johnson, a mutual friend. Marie and her Mother were visiting Barbados. They had come to spend a few months in the tropics for their health. The warm climate had proved to be a good tonic for both of them and they had decided to stay a year. The Johnsons lived in a large house overlooking the bay.

Francis smiled as he said, "Hello." Marie greeted me with a happy embrace saying, "Come home with us for a cool drink. My Mother has been asking for you. We all miss you."

I hesitated, but changed my mind when I saw the unhappy look on Francis' face.

"I will be happy to come and visit you and your Mother. How is she?"

"Mother is better now, but last week she was in bed for two days with a virus."

Mrs. Johnson greeted us and I was happy that I had come. Both she and Marie had traveled extensively and could talk about most countries. Mr. Johnson had passed away.

I enjoyed the cool drink and ate a small piece of cake and seeing Francis after our unfortunate episode gave me a strange feeling in the pit of my stomach. He did not relish the cake because, I surmised, he was feeling the same way as I was feeling.

Mrs. Johnson excused herself and Marie told us to walk down to the beach since she had some work she had to finish.

There was a stairway down to the beach and Francis helped me down. My feet slipped and for a moment I found myself in his arms.

We both felt the strange feelings of electric waves passing through our bodies, but neither of us said anything.

After such a long absence, it was good to be alone with Francis. We walked silently along the beach; both of us were happy as we listened to the waves and the pounding of our hearts.

The silence was broken by Francis.

"May, you know how deeply sorry I am to have caused you so much unhappiness," he whispered pulling me over to him, "if I had spoken to your parents, then everything would have been all right. Now, everyone thinks we are having a sordid affair."

We again sat quietly and I placed my head on his shoulder as tears flowed down my cheeks. I wept as if my heart would break while he tried to console me.

"Cecil told me about the letter you received. Do you still have it?"

"No, I burnt it and prayed for the person who sent it."

"If you had that letter then I could find out who wrote it by the handwriting," he said putting his arm around me.

"I know who sent it," I replied in a positive tone of voice. "it was Tita! But God knows that I have forgiven her and am praying for her every day."

"I understand you are not going to school. Please explain why."

I knew Cecil had spoken to him about it, but I explained how intolerable school was for being snubbed and gossiped about.

"What was the contents of the letter? Can you remember it?" he questioned, still holding me close.

I repeated the letter, line by line, and he sat as if turned to stone.

Five minutes passed and then he said, "May, this is a serious matter. I had no idea it had gone this far. Let me speak to your Father. I'm sure he will understand."

"No, no," I exclaimed, "please Francis, don't do that. Father would understand but Mother would not. She dislikes anyone who causes me trouble. No, never do that."

He was silent for a long time then spoke softly, "May, do you understand about soul mates? My love for you is something like that. I love you very much. It is not the ordinary type of love that I feel for you. It is as if you are a part of me, the other half of my soul. This is the way I love you."

I did not speak, and the tears were streaming down my face. Francis wiped them away with his handkerchief. I felt cold and shivered. Francis held me close for a long time, but an eerie feeling of impending disaster surrounded me, until we re-entered the house.

Three months after the incident of the letter, Mother took me to see a doctor. I had not been feeling well so I thought nothing about going for a checkup. I soon realized this was no ordinary checkup. It was an examination to find out if I were pregnant.

While I was putting my clothes on, I heard the doctor say to my Mother, "Madame, I am quite positive that your daughter has never been touched. She is a virgin."

Mother thanked him and we left. I was quiet on the way home. I thought over what the doctor had said and was distraught. How could my own Mother do this terrible thing to me? Why didn't she ask me? She must certainly have realized the embarrassment that she had caused me. Dear God, if my own Mother does not trust me, then why should strangers believe me that I am a good girl?

Mother must have sensed what I was thinking for she said, "May, I know you are a good girl, but I had to definitely find out."

I did not speak, I was deeply hurt. All at once my life had become terribly complicated. I was not the happy carefree girl that had come to Barbados a little over a year before.

That night I could not sleep. I finally got up and threw a robe over my shoulders and walked out to the front of the house. It was a bright moonlit night, and the stars were bright, but I was not at peace. Kneeling down on the soft grass, I held up my arms to the heavens and cried out to the Lord God of the heavens, "Oh Lord God, help me. Do not let these evil people crucify me. God, you know that I am innocent of these dreadful accusations. Send me help so that I may be vindicated."

After I had prayed, I felt peace within myself and may have gone into a hypnotic state when suddenly I heard a voice say, "May, what are you doing out there at this time of night?" I glanced up and saw my elderly neighbor leaning out of her window. She was staring down at me.

I quickly rose and ran into the house. The prayers may have healed my aching heart because I was sound asleep as soon as my head hit my pillow.

Just before my seventeenth birthday, Father announced we were going to move to Hastings and I was to find a four-bedroom house on the seashore.

I found a beautiful house which was usually rented to vacationers. Everyone loved the house. It was large and had a lovely garden and a small house in back for servants. It was called "Carville."

Cecil and Rannie went to Bridgetown on the tram car to school and Amy to a small private school near by. I still had my teacher.

Once a month my Mother and I went to church in Bridgetown and it was then I would see Francis for a few minutes. Nothing unusual happened until I was seventeen. During this time I would meet mutual friends and see Francis at their home or at church affairs.

One morning my friend, Marie, called me and told me that Francis was leaving the colony and wished to bid me good-by. I arranged to visit her the next afternoon. She lived only one half mile from Hastings.

I arrived at 5:30 p.m. Soon after Francis arrived and we immediately went down to the beach to talk.

"May," he said, "I am leaving for New York next week." He was quite nervous.

Holding his hand, I exclaimed, "Oh Francis, I will miss you."

Smiling he replied, "No, May, I have a plan. If you follow this plan you will be in New York before Christmas."

"Oh Francis," I replied, ecstatic, "I will do whatever you say. Please tell me what to do."

For a few moments he was quiet while he held my hand, then said, "May, I have strange powers which I do not always use and this is the reason I have not studied for the ministry."

He stopped for a moment, then continued. "May, when the moon is young, light a white candle, then read the 91st Psalm. This must be done every night until your desire has been manifested. By December you will be in New York. Neville is there. Here is his business address and phone number. Call him. He will know where I am."

We sat and prayed, asking God to grant us our desires.

This was in the month of June, 1923. In August I turned eighteen and in September, Father asked, "May, how would you like to go to school in New York?"

"Oh, Father," I exclaimed in a shocked tone of voice, "you know I would love it."

That night I thanked God and the angels for granting me the desires of my heart.

I said good-by to my mother and family with an ache in my heart. At the last moment I felt it was wrong for me to leave. When I kissed Mother and Cecil, I sensed a strange feeling of deep sorrow. Something inside told me that all was not well.

Father kissed me and said that I should go to school and study so that he would be proud of me. I nodded without a word. I was afraid that the tears would come full blast.

The captain told my parents that he would take good care of me and see that I was put into my sister's care when the boat arrived in New York.

I happened to be on deck the second day out to sea, when I heard someone playing a piano. I looked into the salon where the music was coming from and saw one of the passengers sitting at the piano playing "The Blue Danube Waltz." He was tall and blond with deep penetrating blue eyes and appeared to be about forty years old or more. Standing next to the piano leaning over the top of the baby grand, with her head resting on her arms, was a blond woman. She was smiling down at him. I listened to him play for a few minutes. He seemed oblivious to either the woman leaning on the piano or of me.

Later that evening, at dinner, I saw the man and looked around for his companion. She wasn't there.

I walked up to him and asked, "Where is the round-faced blond lady that I saw with you in the music salon while you were playing the piano?"

He looked at me in surprise as he introduced himself as Mr. Walters.

"There is no other lady on the ship. You are the only one."

It was now my turn to be surprised and I immediately looked at the captain for verification of his reply.

"Yes," the captain answered smiling, "you are in full charge. Fifteen men and one girl."

No more was said of my apparently illusionary lady.

After dinner three men, who were passengers and a couple of stewards, sat out on deck. It was a warm night and the moon was out in all its glory. Mr. Walters moved over and sat next to me. For a few moments he just sat in silence looking inquiringly at me. The conversation was light, then he said, "I am interested in hearing more about the lady. What did she look like?"

I described her height and looks and he exclaimed, "That was my wife Helen. She died a year ago. She loved music and always leaned on the piano when I played. You must be very psychic."

I laughed and replied, "Yes, I am."

The rest of the trip was uneventful and I was happy when the New York shoreline became visible and I knew we were soon to dock and I would be seeing my beloved Francis again.

FOUR

Back to New York

I arrived in New York three days before Christmas. My sisters Clarice and Cecily greeted me with hugs and kisses. I introduced them to Mr. Walters and he left. I never saw him again.

My sisters had a two-bedroom apartment in Washington Heights. Since I had lived there before, I still had several friends. As soon as I was settled, I phoned Neville. A girl answered the phone. I asked for Neville and she replied, "I'm sorry, he no longer works here. I think he left his home number. If you will hold a moment I will look."

"Of course," I replied.

She returned to the phone and remarked, "I can't find the address. Can you call tomorrow? I'll look for it later."

"Thank you," I answered deeply disappointed, "I'll call tomorrow."

When I phoned the next day, she answered in a tone of finality. "I'm sorry I can't locate the address, and no one around here seems to know where he lives."

I thanked her and hung up feeling depressed. I had come a long way only to find a stumbling block in my path.

A few days after Christmas I felt like the most unhappy girl in the world. Then the doorbell rang. A young Gypsy woman about twenty-five years old stood there. She asked if I wanted to have my palm read. She must have sensed the deep sorrow that was in my heart because she took my hand and clasped it tight.

She looked into my eyes which were filled with tears and said, "You have come across the ocean to meet a blond man. Is it not so?"

I was amazed at her keen sense of perception. Quickly I replied, "Yes, but how did you know that?"

She smiled and answered with a look beyond her years, "It is my business to know the secrets of the soul. Do you want this man? If so, give me some money."

I went into my bedroom and returned with three dollars. She looked at the money and asked, "Is this all you have?"

I was ashamed but had to confess that I was short of cash.

"Then give me some clothes."

This I could do and immediately went into my sister's closet. I brought out two skirts, some blouses and one dress which, when discovered later by my sister and much to my sorrow, made her extremely angry. She had no patience with me and my psychic powers.

The Gypsy, however, was pleased because she pulled me into the kitchen and asked for some salt and an egg. I gave her the salt and she sprinkled it into the fire. Then she asked for the egg. This she broke over a pan of water. She said some mystical words and passed her hand over the egg. More salt was thrown into the fire and again she spoke mystical words. As she was doing this, I was standing quietly by in a semi-trance. I could not say a word even if I wanted to. I felt hypnotized.

Turning to me, she asked, "Did you try to call this blond man?"

"Yes, I did, twice. But his friend has moved and they do not have his address."

Holding my two hands in hers and looking deep into my eyes, she answered with authority.

"Go back and call the number again."

I interrupted her saying, "But I have already called twice."

"Then call it again and you will get the address."

With these words she rolled up the clothes into a bundle and left.

I went out to make the call since we had no phone. The same girl answered. This time she said, "Just a minute."

A man came to the phone and gave me the address. I contacted Neville who gave me Francis's phone number and address and I wrote to him.

Around January 5th, Francis arrived at my sister's apartment. I introduced him to both my sisters and also to Clarice's friend, Teddy Martin. Francis asked me if I would like to attend a movie. I accepted and we left.

On the street he spoke with great concern. "May, be very careful with that man Teddy. He has evil eyes. I'm afraid, my dear, he may cause you great harm. I have never seen such evil around anyone. His aura is absolutely black."

"Oh, Francis, he is a friend of my sister Clarice. She has known him a long time. I just met him tonight."

"May, I feel he will cause you to have deep sorrow."

"Francis dear," I laughingly replied, "I am so happy to see you. Let us not worry about Teddy."

"Very well, my dear, but I just wanted to caution you. Please be careful."

He was quiet for awhile then blurted out, "May, as long as you are a virgin I will never take advantage of you, remember that. Some day I would like to write to your father and Mother."

"I know, Francis, I know."

Later I was to recall his words as Teddy did cause me great sorrow.

I enrolled in night school to study English and creative writing. I enjoyed these courses very much.

I saw Francis many times until he went to Canada in March to see his sister.

Cecily was a dressmaker and she introduced me to Madame Marie, a French dressmaker. I worked for Marie for several months and we became close friends, until my automobile accident, the following year, 1924.

Clarice worked in a hotel as a maid, but was promoted to housekeeper and had several girls under her supervision. (She eventually owned her own hotel in Connecticut.) Albert worked in a restaurant and learned to became a bartender.

In April of that same year, Father wrote and told us he was returning to Guyana to help Victor Pires build a factory to make pineapple juice, which he wished to export. Victor was like family to us. We called him Uncle Victor and his wife Aunt May. Uncle Victor contacted all of the people he knew about this plan to build this factory, but his dream never materialized. It nearly broke his heart because he had Father quit his job in Barbados to return to Guyana for nothing, but Father was an engineer and had owned his own foundry in Henrietta Essequibo and later sold it.

In September, 1924, we received a cable informing us our beloved Mother had died. Later we learned she had died from a fever that lasted nine days. No, it was not malaria. The doctors could not understand why this fever took Mother in nine days.

I did not know it then, but learned that when a condition of evil is sent, it takes nine days to destroy the soul of that victim. Mother was a victim of someone's evil powers. We all grieved and I could not get over my grief.

In early October of 1924, I met Carlos, who had just bought a car. One Sunday afternoon, he came to my home and invited me to go for a ride out into the country. Clarice urged me to go. She thought the diversion would help heal my grief.

Carlos was a new driver and he was not familiar with driving laws. We came to a corner and he turned, without stopping to check for traffic, and smashed into another car. I was thrown from the car. Two young men picked me up and took me to a hospital. Carlos had run away and was nowhere to be found.

The car was towed away, and I remained in the hospital for a week. Clarice came with Teddy to take me home and Teddy paid the hospital bill.

I lay in bed for a month.

One night I dreamed of Francis, and he again warned me. "Be careful. There is danger ahead."

I wondered what he meant in this dream. Some months previous, I had called Neville Taylor to inquire about Francis. A woman answered and informed me that Francis had returned to Barbados.

In November, I began to feel better. I was now able to walk again, but had to sit on one side because my coccyx had not healed and I would feel a stabbing pain shoot up my spine if I did not sit properly.

One afternoon in early December, Teddy came by to visit me. My sisters were both working and I was alone. He offered to massage my back and I didn't think it was anything evil and allowed him to do it. I became very relaxed and fell into a hypnotic state. In this semi-trance condition, and without me being aware of what was happening, he had turned me over and started to have sex with me.

I was shocked into full consciousness and I screamed, "No, Teddy, No!"

He ignored me and continued. I burst into tears. My tears did not stop even after he left. I felt humiliated and ashamed. How could such a thing have happened to me?

I prayed to God, "Why God? Why did this man do this. Why? Why? Why?"

The answer was, "You have great work to do. Others will come to you with this problem and then you will understand."

When my sisters came home they saw my red eyes and asked, "Why are you crying, May? What is wrong?"

I gave them some excuse, but never told them. I was too ashamed to talk about what had happened.

Toward the end of December, 1924, a new friend, Ivy, came by and invited me to have dinner in her husband's restaurant. They served Spanish food which I loved. After we finished dinner, Ivy said, "I spoke to Teddy and he is very sorry he took advantage of you and wants to ask your forgiveness. Let's go to his home."

"No, Ivy, no!" I cried, "this man is wicked and I don't trust him."

"Come now, May, you are a big girl and you can take care of yourself. Teddy truly loves you."

As I listened to her, I thought, yes, Teddy did pay for my hospital bill. Maybe he is sincere.

We arrived at his apartment to find he had been expecting us. His table was set with his best white tablecloth. His best china and silver were beautifully placed along with flowers. He had wine, ice cream and cake and it looked lovely.

He kissed us both on the cheek and asked, "How are you, May?"

Without a smile, I replied, "I am well, thank you."

The evening went well until 10 p.m. when I said to Ivy, "It's time to go."

Teddy had taken my shoes off and refused to give them back to me. By eleven o'clock Ivy said, "I must go or my husband will be angry. Please give back May's shoes."

With a strange smile he said, "No, May will stay here. I will call her sisters in the morning and tell them we are going to get married."

I was shocked and shouted, "Teddy, give me back my shoes or I will leave without them!"

"No, May, you can't. It's snowing. You can sleep on the sofa. I promise I won't harm you." I reluctantly stayed.

The next morning, Saturday, Teddy called Clarice and informed her that we were getting married and he would have the license by Monday.

Sunday, Teddy gave me a large sum of money and told me to shop for new clothes. I did as he asked. The next Saturday, he gave a large dinner party for relatives and friends at a large restaurant on Broadway to celebrate our up-coming wedding.

Three weeks passed. I was still in Teddy's home. No license. No wedding. Many friends came by to congratulate us.

On January 26th, a young girl named Delores came by. She was a friend of Teddy's. We offered her dinner, but all she wanted was to speak to Teddy alone. I began washing dishes and did not pay any attention to her.

The next evening and many evenings that followed, Teddy gave me excuses that he had to go out to appointments. He never returned until ten or eleven o'clock. I was left alone.

I spoke to an old friend, Alvena, who felt I should call my sister Clarice and explain that Teddy did not get a license and had no intention of marrying me. Instead, he was going out every night leaving me alone. I was too ashamed to call Clarice, instead I gave my next door neighbor, a boy of twelve, five dollars to follow Teddy. He found that Teddy was going to Ninety-Sixth Street and Broadway to Delores's house, where she lived with her parents.

As soon as I learned this, the stress I had been under for many days finally made me take action. I phoned Clarice and she came over the next afternoon. She told me to immediately leave the apartment and we packed my clothes. Everything purchased with Teddy's money, dresses, a new coat, shoes were left. I wanted no part of his finery.

We left Teddy's apartment and went to Delores's home and spoke to her Mother. She was shocked and could not believe that Teddy would do such a thing. She didn't believe us, even when we showed her his apartment house keys.

Clarice and I went to the elevated train station and waited. About 6:30 p.m., both Teddy and Delores came down the stairs. Clarice went up to Teddy and scolded him for treating me in such a shameful humiliating manner.

Teddy did not answer. It was Delores who said, "Let's go to the police station and settle this matter."

Teddy looked sheepish as he followed us all to the police station.

The police captain listened to our story. Clarice spoke up and told him I was eighteen and that Teddy had kept me in his apartment against my will for over one month. Now he was leaving me home alone nights and going out with Delores.

The captain looked at Teddy and asked him if this were true. At the time I thought Teddy was in a trance-state. He replied, "Yes, sir, it is true."

Then the captain asked, "Is this girl a virgin?"

Teddy answered, "Yes."

The captain looked at an officer and announced, "We'll have to book him."

Teddy was in a state of shock. Delores started to cry. Clarice handed Teddy his keys and we left.

Teddy was incarcerated for a week. Delores did not have the thousand dollars for bail. Her Mother would not give the money, neither would his sister or his brother.

The next week, when the case came up in the Washington Heights Court, the judge listened to the case and asked if I were pregnant. I answered, "No."

Then he asked my age, and by this time I had had it so I replied, "Nineteen."

The judge shook his head and said, "Case dismissed."

In looking back to that episode in my life, I know that Teddy had powers of darkness that were partly demonic. Francis was aware of his negative vibration and warned me twice. I was too young and innocent to realize what was happening. I was very confused and it was as if I were being taken over by some negative force and I did not have the power to protect myself.

It was interesting that Teddy's first wife died in childbirth and Delores died a few years after she had a child. A young lady in my home town in South America had been in love with Teddy since she was a teenager. Her Mother was known to have demonic powers. Many people, even my sisters, were afraid of her. Teddy eventually married this young woman. If I had married Teddy, I feel that perhaps I, too, would have died.

I moved back in with my sister Clarice and Cecily. They did not charge me for rent or food. About two weeks later, Cecily took me to where she worked. She was a finisher of women's dresses. She did all the little finishing touches to them. She had heard about a job opening for twenty dollars a week. I think I started at fifteen and worked up to twenty. It was my job to bring the dresses to women who examined them, and then place the perfect dresses in one pile and the irregulars in another.

More sorrow was soon to follow. In South America, my brother Cecil got a job in the gold fields and soon contracted malaria. He returned home to Georgetown and died in 1925, just after my twentieth birthday. Father again thought it was from a curse.

His death was a shock to the whole family, especially to me.

Several nights after his death, I was awakened by strange knockings on my bedroom door. This door led out to the kitchen. I opened the door and found no one there. Going back to bed, I sat and pondered about the strange knocks, then heard them coming from the bathroom door. I opened that door and no one was there. I sat down and tried to figure out the reason for the strange knocks.

Three more knocks came from the door leading to the kitchen. Now I was sure it was Cecil trying to communicate with me. An eerie feeling came over me and I picked up my robe and ran to my older sister Cecily's room. I whispered to her what had just happened and she told me to lie down and calm myself.

The next morning, I was sitting in the kitchen having coffee with my sister Clarice when Cecily came in, followed by her tiny little girl, Bette. The child took one look at my bedroom door and screamed. She pointed her finger saying, "Mommy, Mommy, look man standing in front of the door!" With those words she ran out of the kitchen and refused to return to the kitchen for several days.

After Cecily and Bette left the kitchen, Clarice looked at me and said, "I had a very strange dream just before Cecil died. It appeared as if I was standing on the pier in Georgetown. I saw a small boat coming down the river. A little boy was in it. As it got closer, I saw it was Cecil lying in the boat. The boat passed me and the boy just looked up with haunted eyes. I thought, how could Cecil be here? Where is he going? Why doesn't he speak to me?"

Clarice stopped speaking for a moment, then continued, "I cried out, "Cecil, Cecil, come back!" He answered, 'I can't,' and the boat disappeared into a fog or something that looked like mist."

That night, again I felt Cecil was in my bedroom. I jumped out of bed and ran into Cecily's room saying, "Let me sleep in your bed, Cecily. Cecil is in my room."

I laid down beside Cecily and finally went to sleep.

The next morning, I remembered my dream. I found myself in a small room. Cecil was lying on a bed. I leaned over and touched his forehead. It was burning hot. Immediately, I ran into the kitchen and found a towel. I poured hot water over it and placed it on Cecil's head and said, "Cecil I wish to stay here with you."

With deep sadness in his eyes he replied, "No, you can't stay with me. Go back home and in 1956 you will be with me in spirit."

The next morning I told my dream to my sisters, which was a vision. I did not realize that I could still be in the physical body and be with those who have passed over into the spirit world.

I worked for Madame Marie for two years until I met Mable. She taught me how to read palms and also cards. In 1927, my psychic powers found me advising friends and relatives about business and personal affairs. I had my own apartment in Washington Heights and I got a job in a tea room. I met women, people who played the numbers game. I gave them numbers and they reimbursed me.

In the later part of that year, I felt it was very important for me to go to Guyana to see my father and his new wife, Gladys. I had a premonition that my father would only be here for a few more years. I had strange fears about my father. I wished with all my heart to visit my family. I prayed and asked God to give me the money for the trip.

The need to be with my father never left my mind. I dreamed of him. One of the dreams took vivid form and because of it, I took the action which gave me the means with which to see my father and his new wife and family.

In this dream I saw my dead Mother arguing with my father. She rebuked him for marrying Gladys, who was not much older than my oldest sister Ruby. I listened to my father while he sheepishly tried to placate her. Suddenly I thought, why not ask Mama for a winning number and play the lottery.

Now it may be there are those who look with abhorrence upon this, but the practice of playing the lottery has always been part of one's life in British Guyana, and while I am no longer a young impressionable woman, I still feel winning a lottery ticket was the only means for me to earn the fare to my old home.

"Mama, please give me a winning number," I asked.

My Mother pulled away and demanded that my father order me to stop my pleading. I could see Father was relieved to have me intervene, for he scarcely could justify one living wife to a dead one.

I continued my request and I still remember the impatience with which she tossed a number to me.

"Very well, play 011."

A dream? A vision? 011.

I played the number with great anticipation and good money. I failed to win. The following day, with a great deal less money, I played the number again. But this day I was less sure and turned to God. I reached out to Him, letting Him see I knew I should not seek money from Him, but I opened my heart to Him in agony and longing to see my father. I knelt for hours. I did not pray in vain. 011 was the winner and I thanked the Lord for His blessed understanding and merciful kindness.

The next day I went to see my sister Cecily and told her of my good fortune. She asked, "May, are you going to see Francis?"

"Why do you ask Cecily? I haven't heard from or seen Francis since February of 1924. Why should I look him up?"

With a sad look on her face she said, "May, I have a confession to make. Francis did come to see you in early April of that year and I told him you had returned to Barbados. He also wrote you a letter and I tore it up."

"Why, Cecily? Why did you do this? It was wicked of you!"

"Oh, May, I was going through a dreadful time. I gave birth to Bette that year and I had no husband. I was jealous of your happiness."

I left my sister with sadness in my heart. I arrived at my studio apartment, in Washington Heights, and knelt down and asked God to forgive her and also to help me to forgive her. This apartment had been very fortunate for me. I had many clients who came to have me read the cards for them and give them advice.

That night I decided I would take the *Lady* and stop off in Barbados to see how Francis was and if he had married.

I arrived in Barbados December 14, 1928 and stayed at a friend's home on Bay Street in Bridgetown.

One afternoon around 5:30 p.m., I saw Francis riding past the house on his bicycle. The next afternoon, I went down a few blocks and waited for him.

A few minutes after 5:30 p.m. he again came by and I said, "Hello, Francis. How are you?"

He got off the bicycle, looked at me and did not recognize me. He rode off without a word.

I went home got undressed and went to bed. Shortly after, Edna came up. She heard me sobbing and was anxious to know if I was upset or had heard bad news.

Between sobs I said, "Oh, Edna, I saw Francis and he did not recognize me. Oh dear God, how could he forget me?"

Embracing me, she kindly answered, "May, the last time you saw Francis you were very young. You have now matured. Of course you are different. I can understand Mr. Lord not recognizing you."

I remained quiet but the tears were still flowing down my cheeks.

"Would you care for some hot soup or tea?"

"No, dear, I just wish to be quiet."

The next Sunday was Harvest Sunday and Edna insisted that I go with her. The church was filled with people and Francis was assisting the minister.

As he came down the aisle with some boys who were singing, his friend Oscar pulled him to one side and pointed to me. I saw a look of utter astonishment on his face when he realized that it was I who had spoken to him the previous day. Edna and I left shortly after.

The next afternoon, I went into Bridgetown to purchase some gifts for my family, because I was leaving in a few days for Guyana. Bridgetown is quite small and someone must have told Francis that I was there shopping. He followed me with his bicycle when I was on the trolley, which was pulled by mules in those days. As I got off in front of my house, I saw Francis coming up the street on his bicycle. I quickly opened the door and went up to my room.

In a few minutes Edna came up and knocked on the door. Between sobs I cried, "Come in."

I was lying in bed and she came over and stared down at me.

"May, Mr. Lord is downstairs. He would like to speak to you."

"Oh, Edna, I can't. I can't. Something tells me I will never see him again."

She left and later told me, "May, he is very sad. I feel you should see him."

I did not answer. My spirit had told me I was not the same girl that he remembered. Teddy had hypnotized me and taken my virginity. I was on a different plane of consciousness. Francis was still pure. I was not.

I left for Guyana two days later.

FIVE

The Skeleton Key

I arrived the 22nd of December. It was wonderful to be home and even more so renewing acquaintances and opening up memories.

One day, I went to visit Miss Humphrey. She brought back many wonderful memories and she surprised me with one of her own memories.

"May," she asked, "do you remember what you asked me on your first day of school? You were three years old and wanted to know why I was not married."

"Of course," I replied with an amused smile. "My parents were horrified and I was not allowed to return to school for six months."

She looked at me sadly and said, "I can explain that to you now. My mother died and I was an only child. I had to take care of my father and his sister, who was an invalid. Even though I had several proposals of marriage I had to remain with my family. They needed me to take care of them."

Miss Humphrey was truly a good person. Strange that she had never forgotten my question and felt she had to answer it, after all those years.

Subconsciously I was always reminded of the reason for my visit. It was all like a dream. But the dream I remember most had a vision-like quality about it, since it was to begin a period of trial for all of us. It happened, in February, some six weeks after my arrival.

In this dream I met a beautiful lady dressed in the fashion of the Regency period. Her long white, flowing gown had a huge pink sash about her waist, and her lovely leghorn hat was the typical floppy confection of flowers and streamers tied beneath her chin. For a moment I was a child again, for this was my mother as I remembered her.

"How are you, Mama?" I greeted her admiringly. She was so young, so beautiful and so vibrant.

"I am well and happy, child," she said.

Then she extended her hand and there in her palm I saw an odd key which was shaped from a hairpin. It looked like a skeleton key.

"Look, child," this lady urged, "I have a beautiful home and a delightful garden and all these flowers are of my own planting. This key is for you. I want you to come and stay with me."

"No, Mama, I do not want to come with you." I felt fear for this eternal young being who had been my mother. But she continued, "I will be waiting for you with open arms." Her smile hurt me and her extended arm was like an electric jolt.

"No, no," I heard someone cry out. That someone was me. I realized this as I sprang from my bed. The full moon of the tropical night cast an eerie silver light over the garden. I looked upon an enchanted fairyland and felt sad. It was the hand of death that had touched me.

Because my father was a thirty-third degree Mason, I felt he knew magic. I mean magic in the sense of a mind in tune with the higher forces. I thought when he learned of my experience he would comment upon them and put my mind at ease. Imagine my consternation when he listened in silence and left me sadly, for he was unmoved by what I had told him.

I suppose I should have been warned by my father's sadness but I forgot all about it when I cycled to town that day. Without a doubt, my wheel actually was caught by the tram railing and I plunged to the ground with such force that I lay stunned and half-conscious. A trades-man and his helper picked me up and carried me and my wheel into a store. They revived me, then plied me with questions, which I saw were to help them take me home. Because of my clothes, they asked if I were American. I found strength to tell them of my visit and was pleasantly surprised to hear my father and the kindly storekeeper were lodge members. He immediately decided to send me home with his chauffeur, but I protested. Under no circumstances did I want my family to know of this mishap through strangers. I knew in a few moments I would be able to cycle home on my own.

Once home, I explained to my stepmother I was not feeling well and wanted to go to bed. She administered a sedative and saw that I was made comfortable in spite of the heat.

Morning found me in a weakened condition, to my dismay, for I now knew I would have to tell the family of my mishap and the thought bothered me. However, my father returned from town with the whole story from the tradesman. He demanded to know why I had not told him of the fall. "Because I did not want to worry you," I said, becoming petulant. "I'm all right, I tell you."

"But you may be injured internally, daughter." His eyes examined me carefully. "I think that we should call the doctor." But I protested with all my strength. I did not want him to sense my own worry about the lethargy I felt. As I raised my hand he saw the bruises, which naturally led to the disclosure that I was also bruised on my leg and thigh.

"But it doesn't hurt," I cried, "I only want to rest. Don't worry, please. Just let me rest."

Three weeks later found me still lethargic and without any good reason for it. The doctors had examined me without finding the cause for my weakened condition. By now I was discharging a watery flow whenever I made any prolonged effort to move. I barely had the energy to move about the house. No longer was I sure that I would be all right. Why couldn't the medical men help me?

One afternoon I became aware of excitement in the air. At first it was my wonderful stepmother whose voice I heard excitedly calling to my father. They met in the music room and whatever she told him sent him flying to my bedroom. Eagerly they told me of a report of a fine native doctor. She was a Hindu healer who treated spells and curses. My family had come to the decision that since medicine could not help me, it had to be something evil. We were ready to take any means to make me well and strong again. The next morning my stepmother accompanied me to the native healer.

She had an occult-like beauty about her, which was enhanced by her penetrating dark eyes and the coronet of braids of black hair which she hid with a red bandana. She was silent and aloof but intent upon her examination of my body.

She looked at me with her deep penetrating eyes and said, "You are in love with a blond man."

I answered, "Yes."

"Don't go back to his home. Go on to the United States. If you marry him you will not continue with your work."

I looked at this woman and knew I had special work to do and that I would never see Francis again. My eyes filled with tears.

She ignored my stepmother until she was through with me. Then she spoke to her. Fortunately, I heard all that the healer said to my step-mother for, as the years have passed, that dear little lady has all but forgotten what transpired, except for a vague description of that very formidable healer.

"I find the patient suffering from psychic tampering by someone not of this life. She is being pulled toward the other side and her life-energy is being sapped from her astral body. I do not know how much of this you understand, Madam, but I nevertheless advise you to send your stepdaughter away. Let her cross salt water. When she does, this spell will be broken. I find nothing physically wrong with this girl. Her fall was caused by disembodied spirits and she will die if she remains in the colony. This is the decision you and your husband must make." Her voice stopped, but I sensed her eyes on me for the moment and then her quiet melodious voice reached us, "God bless you both."

Whatever else may be said of native doctors, my family felt there was wisdom in what I had been told. The *First Lady,* a ship out of Rio de Janeiro in route to New York and Canada, was to give me passage out of the colony. I protested, because I did not want to leave my father. I felt I could overcome evil vibrations and spells. But my father was firm. He reminded me of the bicycle mishap and of my ensuing lethargy.

"My dear, whether we want to believe in phenomena or whether we scoff, let us both face the fact that you are not getting better. So let's try something. It's carnival time in Trinidad and with your Aunt Lil ready to put you up, why not go there for enjoyment? Then you may return to New York and find a doctor of your own choice to look into your strange condition."

"But I don't want to leave you, Papa!" I was disheartened by his apparent agreement with the native healer. "Let me stay with you. I came here for a year. I just know I'll be all right."

"No, dear," he made his decision. "You must leave, for I feel your mother is trying to take you with her." His eyes were on the garden as he told me this thought of his. It was as if he expected to see the wraith of the beautiful woman who used to be my mother. I was stunned to hear my wise father say this to me. Yet because he did say the words, it helped me to accept the thought my illness was unnatural, and I accepted the inevitable.

A week later, my father placed me in the care of the ship's doctor, who readily accepted the mission. The doctor and I were to be comrades on the trip. I reached over the railing to better wave good-bye to my beloved father as he stood below on the pier. I felt a wave of cold premonition envelope me. As his eyes looked up at me I knew I would never look upon his beloved face again. My eyes filled with tears which were blinding me as I tried to control them.

"Now, now," chided the doctor. "You are too big a girl to cry like this."

Between convulsive sobs, I unhappily blurted, "Oh, I know I shall never see my father again." I shall never forget the doctor's perplexed face as he reminded me, "But, my dear, you are only going to Trinidad. Surely you may visit your father whenever you wish?"

I told the kindly doctor I would only visit Trinidad during the carnival, but my destination was New York.

By this time, he had seen me to my cabin and prescribing a sedative to be given to me by the stewardess, he left me. I must have slept all night without awakening. Morning found me refreshed and for the first time in many days, energy flowed through me. When I met the good doctor during breakfast, I could see his gratification with my apparent recovery.

With this awakening, all that had happened for weeks before seemed like an unhappy dream. A nightmare with momentary bits of happiness.

Carnival time in any country is fantastic, but especially in the tropics, one can truly appreciate the glamor of the mixed nationalities and the native music and singing.

I arrived in Trinidad and Freddy Smith and his wife came to meet me because my Aunt Lil had become ill and she had arranged for them to take care of me for the two or three weeks I had planned to stay.

Mrs. Smith was from Venezuela, South America, which was just a few miles from Trinidad. Her husband, Freddy, was a native of Trinidad. They had friends who owned houses on the small islands around Trinidad. Several of these islands were just big enough to hold a house or two.

One Sunday we went to one of these houses. We had lunch and went swimming in the bay. I was amazed to see several large ocean liners sailing by within speaking range. Some of the passengers waved as they passed and one man shouted that he was going to return and swim with us. I loved every bit of it; especially as my illness had completely vanished. Just as it had appeared from out of nothingness and into nothingness it had disappeared.

A few days after this exciting Sunday, the Smiths took me to see a haunted house about fifteen miles out of Port of Spain, the capital of Trinidad. No one lived in the house. I had confided to them about my supernatural powers, therefore they were interested in seeing what would happen. The whole house was all right except for one room upstairs. I got to the door and just could not enter. It was as if a block of matter was standing in front of the open door. I did not try to enter and we left.

After lunch in a rather unique restaurant where they served spicy native food, we went to visit a friend who was psychic. He had one name, Bacchus. He was part East Indian, part English and part black. When it was my turn to speak with him, I entered the room and immediately felt his power as he stretched out his hand to clasp mine. A strange feeling came over me. As he spoke waves of electricity penetrated my whole being. He had an English accent.

"You have come out of a death cycle. Someone from the spirit world has been trying to take you out of the body but you were saved by your inner angels. They say that you have great work to do." He hesitated for a brief moment then continued. "No, do not contact the blond man.

He is from the past, but if you marry him then you too will be blocked as he is. A woman has cast a spell over him and is very powerful." Looking straight into my eyes he asked, "Do you recognize who this blond man is?"

As if in a trance I answered, "Yes, I do."

Passing his hand softly over my hair, as if giving me power, he said, "There was a tall dark man who caused you great trouble. He took your virginity, then tried to trap you into living with him. He too was under the spell of a woman from your home. Had you married him then you would have died as two others who married him did. Do you recognize this dark man?"

Again, I answered, "Yes."

"You have come through many strange experiences," he continued, "many more are ahead, but God and your spirit forces will see you through. In the end, you shall conquer, for you shall lead many others to God. Just as I do."

When I left Trinidad, the energy was flowing through my body freely. I was a little wiser, for several situations had been cleared up in my mind.

Arriving in Barbados, Mrs. Mary Brown met me at the pier. She was surprised to find me looking so healthy. My father had written to her saying that I had not been well. I informed her of the Trinidadian healer and the fantastic time that I had had at the carnival.

Nothing unusual happened the six days that I waited for *The Lady*, which was returning from Brazil and which was to take me back to the States.

Oscar came down to the ship to see me off and I told him to tell Francis goodbye. I never saw Francis again.

I sailed for New York remembering the wonderful family I had left in British Guyana and the good friends who had been so thoughful during my visit. I returned to New York completely well with no need for a doctor. So for the moment the vision that had started the round of experience was forgotton; or did it lie dorment within the confines of the subconscious?

SIX

The Dividing Line

$\mathbf{M}$y return from British Guyana was to be highlighted by romance, marriage, and motherhood. I had forgotten during this period the nightmarish malady I had experienced while in my father's house and certainly no thought remained in my mind of the circumstances which led me to tear back to New York months earlier than I had intended.

I met a man named Vincent Blair and we started dating. This was in April of 1929. It was time to go on with my life and around 1930, Vincent and I moved into an apartment together, just a few blocks from where I had been living. We were very happy and in April of 1932, I gave birth to a daughter, Yvonne.

Every time Vincent spoke of marriage, I would feel fear and a cold chill in my heart. I learned years later, on a trip to Egypt, that I had had a cosmic marriage. This type of marriage represents a mortal making vows to God and I could not ever marry in this lifetime.

It was in August of 1932, the morning of my father's death. As I lay in bed, I had the following inner journey where my father and I were to meet once more. I gazed at a beautiful garden and decided to go in. As I came to the gate it suddenly opened and I walked into a paradise of flowers and plants. They seemed to be different than anything I had ever seen.

I cannot say how long I lingered in the garden, but it must have been just a few minutes as we gauge time here on earth. All at once I felt an unusual force drawing me to the other end of the garden and as I turned the path I saw a house ahead of me. It was brightly lit and I was drawn inside, as if by an unknown force. There were many people crowded in the large room and I felt a hand on me.

Turning away, I heard a woman's voice say, "I tell you I touched her, come and see for yourself." I tried to walk fast but I was outnumbered and many hands were upon me.

"Please leave me alone," my voice seemed to thunder throughout the room, making it vibrate as if with an earthquake. The people sensed power and immediately made way for me to pass through their midst. Coming to the end of the room, I glanced over to the far end and saw a tall, handsome blond man standing in the corner with folded hands. He was silently surveying the unusual happenings. I felt that he was a friend and returned his smile and nod.

Again a door opened and I walked in to find an empty room. In the middle of this smaller room was a man sitting on a stool. At first I thought he was a small man until I saw that he was sitting on a stool that was meant for a child. His head was bowed and he seemed tired and depressed. As he looked up, I recognized my father.

"Oh, Papa, what are you doing here?" He smiled a wry smile as if he was forcing himself to smile and with an effort answered me.

"I have come a long way. I am happy to see you, my dear."

"Papa, what is the matter with your forehead? It is bruised and there is some blood on the wound."

"Yes, dear, I fell down and struck my head, but I could not wait to have it taken care of, it was such a long journey and there was not much time."

Looking down at his feet I saw that they were swollen and I bent down to rub them, asking how this had happened?

"I walked across some rough country. It was a long walk and I am tired, but God has answered my prayer and I am able to see you once more."

At these solemn words I started to cry. Something inside told me that he spoke the truth, this was the last time I would see my beloved father. At this thought the tears flowed again. He put his hand on my head and patted me as if sympathizing with my grief, but I felt nothing.

"Papa, why did you walk? Why did you not come by boat, or car?" I had still failed to grasp the situation. My father was not concerned about mileage, nor were his feet swollen because he had walked physical miles, but because a psychical distance between us caused him pain.

"My child," he said, "this is the way it must be. I prayed that I might see you once more, and the wish is granted. I did not want to die alone." At these words a previous vision flashed through my mind and I remembered a hospital room that looked very much like this one.

My father continued. "My darling child, our hearts and minds are as one. From this moment think of me as happy and free."

"Time for the visitor to leave." I clung to my father, but a woman, gentle but firm, led me to the door and into the foyer. I saw several groups of people speaking different tongues and they spoke to me. From one of these groups the woman who had first "touched" me called attention to me. I tried to slip away but my tormentor was faster.

"Don't touch me." I spoke quickly and recoiled from this woman. "Dante's inferno" came to my mind. Before I could say more, my father came to me, took me by the hand and led me past these people. His strength and force was a protective light for me and we soon were looking at the garden. He opened the door for me and smiled happily when I blew him a kiss of farewell,

While in the garden, I sensed that the tall blond man was close by and turned as I heard his voice. "You came to see your father." He continued, "You are fortunate to have been permitted to come into the dividing line. Yet I see that you have the power, a rare gift indeed."

I did not understand all that he told me at that time, for I was still ecstatic with the overwhelming beauty of the garden. He spoke of the silver cord which still held me to the physical body and of the privileged knowledge that the cord could still bind while I walked into the territory of the in-between.

I was reluctant to leave this magnificent man, but I knew that he was right. I had to return. I believe that he was the "Keeper of the Watch." It was his destiny to guide those who had separated from earth and were to be prepared for their next consciousness. Indeed my father was in good hands, as I would be when I came again.

He walked off into a violet mist and I found myself at a bridge. Hundreds of ethereal people came towards me from the other side. They walked in sound, so I waited until a young woman came up to me.

"Please tell me to which planet I would come if I crossed the bridge?" The girl looked at me without understanding. An older shadowy woman came up to us, and quietly sent the younger on her way. Then turning to me she ordered, "Go back. Go to the archway where you left your friend. There you will meet the woman who will guide you homeward."

But I repeated, "Tell me which planet I would reach if I crossed this bridge?"

Brusquely she told me. "This is not for you to know. Do as I say! There is not much time." I reached out to hold her back, but she became one with the mist. I thought, "Why can't I find out for myself? Who is there to stop me?"

I must have taken six steps along the bridge when a stronger will than mine forced me to about-face. Against my will, I retraced my steps and came to the archway where the Keeper stood with an unsmiling woman. I sensed that we were not in rapport, yet this was her way to fulfill her destiny. I ignored her, but the Keeper read my mind. He smiled sadly at my humanly dislike and his eyes chided me for my spiteful thought, for he knew that I felt that I could learn about the other side of the bridge from him. Still I had to try.

"Tell me, friend, where would I find myself if I crossed the bridge?" He rebuked me. "Do not try to learn more than you already know. To know the answer is to remain here in this area which separated your physical life and your true life. Go home. This friend waits patiently to guide you. Trust her. There is very little time."

He put my hand in hers and immediately I felt a soaring sensation. We were high in the sky and rivers and mountains and land masses moved below us. Within my mind there seemed to be a necessity for me to win this woman, for I believed that should I win her friendship, then she would tell me abut the bridge. Oh, how clever I thought I was to put the question in another form. Surely she would answer me.

"Tell me, friend, are you from Earth and may you come back at will? May you cross the bridge, too?" I wondered what her answer would be.

She smiled for the first time. She had seen through my efforts and the so-called leading question fell with a thud. She must have thought me very young, for she answered me in terms she thought that I would understand.

"If you lived in a dirty house and left it to live in a lovely clean one, would you return to your dirty one?"

So she had chosen to answer my question with another. I could only say, "No, I would not."

Suddenly we were before a golden door and I felt myself pushed through. My husband's voice was asking, "What is wrong, dear?"

I blinked my eyes looking up at the bright sunlight, suddenly realizing that I had been dreaming. Yet my heart felt as if leaden bands were tied around it. Then a little inner voice said, "Your father is dead."

I looked at my husband with tears in my eyes, saying, "My dear father is dead. I just had a vision of him in a strange place." I then described my vision to him. After a few minutes he said soothingly, "Oh, he is all right, it was just a dream, my dear. Don't worry. Is he still ill?"

"Oh, yes, don't you remember? I told you that he was going into the hospital for a checkup. That was the last I heard."

Just then the baby started crying and my day began. That afternoon I had friends over for a bridge game and at five o'clock the door bell rang. I opened it and there stood my cousin Lance. He seemed disturbed so I asked him to come in and have a drink.

He took me into the kitchen so we could be alone and pulled out a telegram from his pocket and handed it to me. I didn't take it. All I can remember was laying my head on the table and saying, "Oh, dear God, my father is dead." And so it had happened.

A week later I received a letter from my older sister, Ruby, telling me that my father was found, the morning of my vision, on the floor with a bruise on his forehead. A patient in the next room heard him fall out of bed and went in to help. My father said, "Oh, my God, am I going to die alone? Oh, God, no!" Those were his last words on earth. Nevertheless we were given the privilege of talking to each other before he entered the spiritual plane.

Some will say that this is nothing but an illusion, but isn't all life an illusion? If so, why can't we make it a beautiful illusion, through the power of the inner being and the mortal thought? Yes, I am sure that we could make this miracle of a beautiful life come true. But it was not to be, Vincent and I separated. The separation was inevitable because of his drinking problem. One night he came home drunk. He almost fell on a switch-blade knife and I knew that marriage was not for me.

SEVEN

Beyond the Dividing Line

Shortly after my father passed, the anguish of the separation and the empty loneliness made me contact a medium, the Reverend Betty Cox. It is a natural and understandable reaction at such a time for one to wish to recall the departing relative, hence many people try through various methods to communicate with their loved ones. Sometimes with success, more often with failure. It is not wise to try to hold these souls here on earth, as I learned through an appalling experience.

I had been crying incessantly for several weeks when a close friend told me of Reverend Cox, who was considered to be an amazingly gifted psychic. She gave readings which consisted of "messages" as she called them, or mental impressions she received from her clients as she talked to them. She was also well known for her materialization work. When I heard this, a surge of hope stirred in my aching heart. I felt it was important for me to see and speak with Reverend Cox; therefore, I wasted no time in making an appointment with her.

The reading she gave me was very accurate, especially in the details of the death of my father. At the close of our session, she asked me if I had a question. This pleased me, for it gave me the opportunity to bring up the real reason for my visit.

"Oh, yes," I cried eagerly, "I do hope you can help me. Reverend Cox, please help me to contact my beloved father." The words came out in a rush of emotion, as tears came to my eyes.

"I see," said the medium. She remained silent for several moments while she studied me intently. There was an expression of sympathy on her face. At last she spoke, "Well, there is a certain method that I use to contact departed spirits. You may try it, but I must say, I can never guarantee success in these matters. I know, however, that you are a medium of the first water and it would be all right to teach you how to contact the spirit world. In any case, be prepared to face disappointment just in case nothing happens."

"Oh, thank you, Reverend Cox," I replied seriously. "I will do as you advise."

"It will take a lot of discipline and a great deal of meditation and sincere prayers. Are you willing to do this?" She asked, looking at me closely.

"Oh, yes," I answered quickly, "I'll do everything, just as you say."

"Very well then," she said softly. "Now the first step is for me to teach you how to make the entrance within." She consulted a calendar on her desk before saying, "The third Friday of this month will be perfect, as that is the day of the full moon. You come here on Wednesday before and I will instruct you in the ritual and give you all the things you will need to bring about this manifestation to your outer world. You must make arrangements to be home alone that Friday night. Also see that you have a photograph of your father. One that was taken just before he passed over, for it is necessary to have it in front of you the night that you are going to perform the manifestation."

On the designated Wednesday, I again went to the medium's house. For some minutes she talked to me about the seriousness of what I was about to attempt, but I assured her I wished to go ahead regardless of the consequences. On her desk was a beautiful white carnation resting in a glass of water.

"You are to take this flower, my dear," she said. "I have blessed the water by reading the Lord's prayer over it and I've also put in some other important things that I would rather not tell you at this time."

Next she handed me a candle, saying, "You will need this too." I remembered the candle for it was a beautiful long white one, showered with little gold specks.

"Friday you are to fast all day. You must be absolutely certain to do this. Don't forget. No food at all, but you may take liquids."

With deep sincerity, I said, "I will do as you say, Reverend Cox."

"Good," she exclaimed seriously, "Now listen carefully to these instructions." She needn't have cautioned me. I was devouring every word she spoke.

"Friday night have the picture of your father near the flower and the candle. Make yourself comfortable, for you will be sitting a long time. At ten o'clock light the candle, read aloud the 23rd Psalm and follow this with a prayer for God to guide you throughout the ritual. Continue praying for God and His angels to bring you light. This is the method for going deep within your soul consciousness."

After taking my hand in hers, Reverend Cox said, "I must impress you that prayer is important. Keep praying. Do not allow fear to creep in. If so, you will be blocked from going within. Good luck and God bless you."

By Friday evening, I was in a state of ecstatic happiness. Long before the appointed time I had everything arranged. I had decided to sit in bed for the rite. Although I told myself to remain calm, and that no harm could come to me, my hand shook as I lit the candle at precisely ten o'clock. Determined not to be afraid, I closed my eyes and repeated the 23rd Psalm aloud. After that, I prayed earnestly for God to guide and protect me as I went within the door of the subconscious. The prayers began to relax me and little by little my nervousness faded until at last I was immersed in deep tranquility. For some time, I have no notion of how long, I enjoyed this beautiful feeling of peace.

Suddenly, I felt myself moving outward, forward, as if a part of me, the *thinking* part, *knowing* part had become separated from the mass of matter that was my physical body. I felt free. I was freed from the little *ME,* sitting upright in bed.

I was no longer bound to the gross physical body. I was now free to explore an enchanted and unknown vastness and I now moved in a universe of color that was unbelievably beautiful. Faster, faster, I sped into limitless space. Far ahead of me was a point of light. I knew that I must reach that light. All at once the light disappeared and I could feel myself returning slowly to the world of matter. I was back on the bed, but the room was in total darkness. The candle was out. I was abruptly startled back to complete awareness.

I thought to myself, "I thought I had closed the windows. I must have forgotten one." I felt for the matches and lit the candle. Then I got up to check the windows to find I had been right, they were closed. Again, I thought, "Perhaps something is wrong with the candle." After a few moments of tense concern, I went back and sat on the bed.

I prayed for a few minutes, trying to get back into the feeling of deep, peaceful relaxation, but again the room was in darkness. For some moments I remained sitting on the bed. I was now aware of a tingling sensation at the back of my neck. But still I could not believe that anything out of the ordinary was wrong.

"Oh, this is ridiculous!" I thought, "there's bound to be a logical explanation."

Again I lit the candle and glanced about, looking for some source of a draft or some sudden shift in the air currents. Thinking something was wrong, I sat on the bed and waited to see what would happen next. After about five minutes, I heard a great rushing of wind, and I saw the flame of the candle bend to one side as if someone were trying to blow it out a third time. I knew then no shift of air currents was to blame. Something of the supernatural was in my room. I felt it.

Then it happened! The incredible happened! A form materialized at the foot of my bed—not a form resembling the physical, human body—but a form of fluffy, airy substance, like the pictures of ectoplasm seen in psychic books. Yet, there seemed to be eyes. Eyes that penetrated into my very soul. I was transfixed with fear. I could not speak, but silently, I began to pray. "Oh, God, have mercy on me! Oh, my God, protect me from this Being, whoever it is."

Suddenly, the atmosphere in the room became even more charged, as the Being of ectoplasm spoke, not with sound nor with a voice as we know it here on Earth, but in electrified thought waves.

"Never do this again! If you do, I may not be able to come through to you and another may come in my place to try to destroy you. Because of your great love for me, we forgive you. But remember that we are sleeping and you have disturbed us. Again, I say, because of your great love for me, you are forgiven. God be with you now and always. Good-bye!"

The form was gone as it had come, with a rush of cold wind. Horrified, I remained where I sat, staring at the spot where the apparition had been only moments before. Could this Being, this white vaporous form, be the man I knew as "Father?" Had I contacted another spirit? The real spirit of physical man? Overcome with emotion, I sobbed like a child. Then I got out of bed and knelt down in prayer to ask God to forgive me for selfishly disturbing a soul that was resting in another plane of consciousness.

"Forgive me, Father," I pleaded, "I did not know. I did not understand. Never again will I do such an evil thing. If it is God's will to send an angel to speak with me and if that angel is my earthly mother or father, then and only then will I allow myself to be contacted by the spirit world."

Let me say that many souls have contacted me throughout the years, but only then, is it right to contact our loved ones—at God's will, not ours.

EIGHT

Back to Work

In 1935 I went back to work in a tea room. I was going to use the knowledge of reading cards and palms, which my friend Maria had taught me. My hours were from 10 a.m. until 5 p.m. and my sister Cecily took care of my daughter, Yvonne.

Four years later, I met Juan Valdez, who told me I could get a job in a night club reading palms. This was on Broadway, a place called The Havana Club. He introduced me to the owner who said, "I know someone who would enjoy and appreciate you working for him. It's Cerrutti's restaurant. I got the job and worked there until early 1942.

Later that year, I was working at a large hotel near a beach. A friend informed me of the Versaille club on 50th Street, in New York City, now called The Round Table. She had gone there to ask for Miss Doris, a palmist, and was told she was on vacation until September.

"May, why don't you go there? It's a large club with music, dancing and entertainment. I know the Greek owner. He owns the club with his brother, Nick.

It was a hot July and I felt that God had given me this information and it was important for me to go.

I returned to New York at the end of July and phoned the Greek owner, a Mr. Otto. I introduced myself and told him I worked during the winter months at Cerrutti's Club.

"Yes, Madame Perez, I have heard of you," he answered in a friendly tone of voice, "come in tomorrow."

I thanked him and the next afternoon I arrived around 5 p.m. Mr. Otto offered me a cool drink and asked me to read his palm. Before reading it, we talked of many things, then I exclaimed, "I see two partners with you. Soon you will be the only manager. Both your partners will leave and you will be alone to run your business."

"Oh, Madame, I'm here with my brother, Nick, and another gentleman, Mr. Arnold. I'm never alone."

"Oh," I replied smiling, "but I see you here alone."

With that we had a few more words and I said good-bye and left.

I had some business to attend to on Tuesday and did not return to the seashore. On Thursday, I received a call from Mr. Otto. He sounded extremely excited.

"Madame Perez, you gave me a reading on Monday. At that time you said I would be the sole manager here. I must say I did not believe you, but today, I am the sole manager. My brother is in Greece and Mr. Arnold has had a heart attack. You have the job."

I worked at the Versaille Club until the Spring of 1942, when I was told Armondo would be interested in having a palmist during the luncheon and afternoon hours. This was a good arrangement because I never left my daughter Yvonne alone, and had been paying a sitter five nights a week.

There was another reason for me to leave the Versaille Club. Besides Miss Doris, there was another reader, a Miss Annabelle. Both of them came in during the afternoon and left around seven-thiry or eight. I came in around 9 p.m. until midnight. I felt Doris was jealous of me because I not only read palms, but also danced with the men who were alone.

One night four men came in and asked me to give them readings. One young man, in the group, had just started working with them. They were CIA men.

I looked at the young man, who was about twenty-seven years old, and said, "You must be careful because your work will involve great danger. I advise you to do more prayers. Later you will be sent out on a dangerous assignment and I see an accident to your leg. Be very careful."

In a sharp tone of voice he cried out, "How do you know?"

One man interrupted loudly, "Shut up! Don't admit to anything."

The young man looked ashamed and I felt sorry for him.

I had a grave problem working at Armondo's Club, because Anna, who worked nights and whom strangely enough I had never met, was quite disturbed about me. In late 1944 she became ill and Armondo asked me to come in and work nights. She died in early 1945. Her whole body was riddled with cancer.

About a month after she passed over, I was coming down the steps that led from the restroom to the dining room and felt someone push me. I held on to the railing and saved myself from a bad fall. I knew it was Anna and started to pray for her. I felt more at peace and my readings became even better.

Another strange incident happened to my cousin Renee's brother Felix. I loved him dearly. He was like my very own son.

Felix joined the army and I gave him a farewell party. It was a sad affair because all through the whole evening, Felix kept saying, "It's my last party because I won't be coming back."

These remarks were very upsetting to me and his sister, Renee, and even more so, when his friend Larry told me they had walked down

Broadway and all Felix kept saying was, "This is the last time I will see Broadway. I'm not coming back."

I tried to speak to Felix, but he just laughed and replied, "May, you always say that 1956 will be the last year of your life, now why do you scold me?"

These words were like a slap in my face, because all through the years, because of my dream with Cecil, I kept saying God wanted me in 1956 and I hoped to fulfill my destiny by then.

In late 1943, I met Eddy and we started dating. He was from Puerto Rico and lived a few blocks from my apartment on 108th Street, near Broadway. He was an engineer and was handsome enough to be taken for a movie star.

I usually came home around 6 p.m. and cooked dinner for Yvonne and myself. Sometimes Eddy would eat with us, and other times we ate with him at his home. He lived with his mother, Carmen.

One afternoon I came home early and Eddy and I went shopping. We passed a store run by Gypsies, and we went in for a reading.

There were two Gypsies giving readings. The older one read me and the younger gave Eddy his reading.

The older woman looked at me and said, "You have great work to do. You, too, can see into the souls of man. I see a great star over your head and lots of light. Within a year, you will leave New York and go to the West Coast. There you will have greater success. Your daughter will marry early and have many children. It is her destiny to take care of children, but late in life she, too, will do your work. I see much traveling in and out of the country."

I thanked her and gave her some money. When we got home, Yvonne was there with a young friend and I told her what the Gypsy had said.

It was Yvonne who asked Eddy, "What did she tell you?"

He was silent for a few moments, then exclaimed, "It was a young girl who gave me the reading. I don't believe her. She saw only bad luck and a dark cloud over my head. An evil cloud. Then she asked me for my ring. She needed something to ward off the evil. I hope she returns my ring."

He left shortly after, and I could feel his angry vibrations.

I didn't see him for a few days, then the weekend was upon us and he came over looking deeply depressed.

I asked, "What is wrong, Eddy? Why are you angry?"

"May, I had the Gypsy girl arrested. She wouldn't give me back my ring and the police made her return it."

" Eddy, You didn't! You didn't!" I cried, "you didn't arrest that nice girl?"

"Yes, I did! I paid fifty dollars for that ring and I liked it."

We had a few words and he left, still quite angry.

Monday afternoon I went to the Gypsy store and spoke to the older woman and her husband.

She recognized me and asked, "Are you the same women who came in with a tall handsome man?"

"Yes, I am and I want to give you some money. My friend told me he had your daughter arrested and I'm sorry. Really sorry."

"Lady, you are like my sister. You do the same work and I see great success for you, but your friend, who looks like a movie star, has an extremely dark cloud over him. Yes, I see evil coming to him. He has an evil soul. We Gypsies work hard and we have much trouble. This man brings us more trouble. Lady, leave him or you, too, will have curses over your head. Do not see him. Leave him. Go away. He has a death curse over him. Go away soon."

I listened to her and knew I must never see Eddy again.

I avoided Eddy for two months and was now working nights. A friend, Jean, was now living with Yvonne and I, in my apartment. Jean told me that Eddy kept phoning, but I did not return any of his calls.

One night, I was leaving the club and a friend walked outside with me to help me get a cab. It was snowing and he had offered to help.

We were waiting for the cab when Eddy arrived. He walked up to us and said, "This is my fiancee. I will get a cab for her."

I stood as if turned to stone. I felt heavy. It was indeed a strange feeling. After a few moments, I was able to speak. "Please, Eddy, leave me alone."

The cab arrived and I went home.

I did not see him for several weeks, then in March, I was just walking into my doorway when Eddy came up.

"May, I wish to speak to you. I walked away and he pulled my coat. Again the heavy feeling swept over me and I cried, "For God's sake Eddy, leave me alone."

He started to pull me by my coat and I pulled away and ran. He was quick and again grabbed my coat. Two men came up and grabbed Eddy and held him. He fought them, and other men arrived and we were surrounded by people. Some were strangers and some were neighbors. It was an Irish neighborhood and Eddy was Puerto Rican.

Yvonne came running out and pulled me away. I don't know how we got to the police station, which was just a few blocks away. It may have been fifteen or more minutes. When we went into the station, the captain was sitting alone at his desk.

I told him I lived at 108th Street and there was a man I wanted arrested.

The captain quickly answered, "Lady, I can't help you now. There's a riot on 108th Street and I just sent some men there."

Then Yvonne spoke up, "The man we want arrested is the one who started the riot."

"Oh, then give me your names and address."

We gave him the information and he said, "You will hear from us soon."

When we returned home, it was quiet. The cops had picked up Eddy, but later I heard he had been released that same night.

From then on, Eddy called Armondos every day. He asked for me, complaining I had had him arrested. I knew it was the Gypsy curse and if I ever went back to him, I, too, would be cursed.

In October, of that same year, Armondo said I would have to stop Eddy from calling or I would have to leave my job. Since he would not stop calling, I was forced to leave.

I had no alternative. I had Eddy served with a summons to appear in court.

The day of the court session, Eddy's brother came over and said he was sorry that I had lost my job. It was he who told the judge that Eddy had caused me to lose my job. The judge warned Eddy that if he ever bothered me again, he would put him in jail.

I never saw Eddy again, but a friend of Yvonne told her that Eddy had returned to Puerto Rico to have a woman do some work for him, to release him from the strange curse.

Felix left for the service in 1944, and in early 1945, I received a letter from Renee telling me Felix had died. A friend of Felix had been in danger and he had gone into the line of fire to help him. It was very sad news.

In November of 1945, I put Yvonne into a Catholic convent on Staten Island. She was thirteen and it was a lovely school. I sold my furniture in my apartment and gave the lease to a woman who answered my ad. I left for California.

There, I got a job at Ciro's, a famous club frequented by the movie stars and those with important positions in the film industry and, of course, tourists who came to see the stars.

Early in 1946, I met Harry, who worked at Macambo, across the street from Ciros.

He asked, "How would you like to work in Palm Springs? My boss is building a club there. It's called The Stables. I also have friends who own the Casa Del Camino. You can live there."

Immediately I said, "Yes."

After many telephone calls and letters, I arrived in Palm Springs, California and spent the winter there.

Many famous people came to Palm Springs. I used to see Howard Hughes, but did not give him a reading at that time. He used to come in after riding his horse and looked pretty dirty. Even his hands were dirty.

In 1947 I got an offer to work in the Fairmont Hotel in San Francisco. I arrived there in August. The owner, Mr. Dave Long, hired me to entertain the guests with palmistry reading. It was a rage in those days.

Prior to my getting this job, I had met a charming couple, Mr. and Mrs. Dalion. I had met them in Hollywood, while I was working for Ciro's. Mrs. Dalion had been impressed with my analysis of her character. She was gifted with a singing voice and I persuaded her never to give it up.

After the reading was over, she asked me if I had ever visited San Francisco. I informed her I had never been there and I would love to work there. She then gave me the name of a Mr. Bob Young and told me he was in the Fairmont Hotel, up on the hill. I thanked her and they left.

I wrote to Mr. Young and soon received a letter with glowing accounts of my readings of the Dalions. They were his favorite guests and would I care to come to San Francisco to talk to him and his lovely wife.

This was my connection with San Francisco and I truly felt God was guiding me and it was important for me to take the offer. I prayed over the matter and the answer was good. I answered and said I would arrive in San Francisco in August.

In a few weeks time, working at the hotel, I came in contact with many famous people. Some of them leaders in San Francisco. Others were from towns around the Bay area. It was interesting how quickly I became popular among these people and was invited to go places with many prominent leaders.

I remember one day when Bob came to me and said, "Madame Perez, a very important man would like you to come up to his room in the Hotel. He would like a reading and he is offering you one hundred dollars.

I startled Bob by saying, "Bob, the gentleman will have to come down here. I am not going up to his room."

"But Madame Perez, he is giving you one hundred dollars."

I still nodded my head no.

Later on, Bob talked it over with his wife, who told me, "May, if you don't feel like going to this gentleman's room, then he will have to come down."

So it was arranged for Howard Hughes to see me after closing hours. The bar was left open. He appeared, immaculately dressed. I remembered how dirty he had looked in Palm Springs, but now he was immaculate.

There were three men waiting at the bar as I greeted him.

I thanked him for the amount he had given me and started the reading. He talked about his business and an appointment with the government, also about a boat that was in the harbor, both a big problem.

He was at times trying to hide. I could see him running. All at once times changed and I now saw him as a high Priest in the Temples of Lemora. He was running in the desert, away from the Temple. He came to a large gate, which immediately opened up. He entered and the gate closed. He was saved in that life but again, he was trapped in this lifetime. I explained to him the experience of the past and told him to pray. Holding his hand, I prayed for him.

As he walked away, I felt strange and nervous. Something was not right. I had not done enough prayers, neither had I told him how I felt about him running away from his problems. I felt very strange and for about a half hour could not get up. Later on, I decided to pray for this man. As we all know Howard Hughes lived a strange life. He was blocked and he died a strange death. I always wondered about Howard Hughes and his strange karma.

It was in October when I became extremely unhappy, because many of the people I associated with, would reveal to me many mysterious and unusual secrets. I discovered that Bob was not sincere and was a student of black magic, which he used for his own selfish purpose.

He used his power to obtain political gains for himself and other people. At first his employees and customers brought these problems to me and I tried not to believe them. However, one night, Fran the cashier, told me a story that was unbelievable. I could understand how a layman, such as Fran, would believe that her experiences would cause her to lose her mind. She acted like a lost child until I told her that the bad dream she was having was, in reality, the truth.

She told me that the night before, she had awakened to find Bob leaning over her bed. His face was distorted and his smile was like one possessed with the devil. She had screamed and the apparition had disappeared.

While listening to her story, I had decided to leave this horrible place. It would soon be Christmas and a good time to leave.

A few days before Christmas, I returned to New York. I wanted to see my daughter Yvonne and my family. I also decided to write to Bob and tell him I had found another position and would not be returning to San Francisco. Before I could mail it, I received a letter from Fran asking me to return, as she was on the verge of a nervous breakdown.

I never mailed the letter to Bob and returned to San Francisco against my better judgement, but with the feeling that Fran needed me. In some way, I was being compelled to go. I arranged with the convent that Yvonne was to come to San Francisco the next year, 1948; but Yvonne wanted to stay in the convent.

My first night back at work, I tried to explain to Fran about good and evil forces and how one can send thought forms out to another person through concentration. I made her promise not to tell anyone what we had discussed, or what we would be doing. It had to be done secretly. I felt sure her problems would be resolved. I spent many hours in prayer and meditation to help Fran and in a few days, she told me she was feeling much better.

Everything was fine until a morning in April. Fran came to my apartment. Her eyes were red from crying and she was nervous and hysterical. She was in the same state as she was a few months previous.

Although she had not been feeling well, she had gone to a party with Bob. During the evening, she had gone into one of the rooms for a short nap. She woke up hearing a man and woman talking in an adjoining room. She recognized Bob's voice. The woman he was talking to, spoke with a foreign accent. Fran was sure she was the Egyptian woman who worked for Bob, but had to leave because the customers could not understand her. Later on this woman became ill.

Fran heard Bob say, "I don't understand it, I had Fran in the palm of my hand and now she's changed. I can't get through to her."

The woman spoke, "It's Madame Perez. She understands and knows how to change the stream of power that is sent to another person."

As they left the room, their voices were drowned out by the music from the party.

A few nights later, Bob came to my table and sat down. He had a strange expression on his face, which he usually wore when he wanted something from one of his customers. With superficial charm he asked, "How are you tonight, Madame Perez?"

I was immediately on my guard. He knew I was aware of what had been happening to Fran.

"I'm fine," and without waiting for his reply, I got up and excused myself. He put his hand out to stop me and said, "Just a minute, I have an interesting story to tell you."

I sat down, more out of curiosity than interest. Then he began to tell me the story of his life.

One incident caught my attention. It happened a few weeks after his marriage, when he met an old lady from Mexico. It was she who taught him the art of inner magic. Through these rites he was able to elevate himself to being not only a man of means, but also looked up to in his community.

Suddenly he asked, "Madame Perez, do you believe in the arts of manifesting conditions? In other words, the white and black arts?"

For a few minutes I remained silent. Thinking carefully I answered in a low voice, because I did not want the people in the next table to hear me.

"Yes, I do, but these rites should be used only for constructive purposes to release those who are caught in traps and cannot help themselves."

Without another word, Bob rose and left my table.

Shortly after this episode, I began to feel tired. At times I felt as if my life was being drained out of me. Someone was tampering with the cord of my life. My personality was completely changed. I was irritable and could not concentrate on anything for very long.

One night, just before midnight, I went into the employees' lounge. I needed to be alone and rest for a short while. Mary, one of the waitresses, came in and when she saw me asked, "Are you all right?"

Before I could answer she continued, "I know Bob is trying to put a spell on you, Madame Perez. He had done this to Fran and me, too. I felt his unearthly powers. Do something. Just don't sit there and go to pieces."

At that moment, someone entered and I told her I would contact her later.

A couple of nights later, after Mary had spoken to me about my condition, I was sitting at a corner table, near the entrance. It was during my break period and I was enjoying a cup of hot tea. Mary came and paced back and forth, near the entrance. I thought she was looking for one of her boyfriends. Shortly after, I saw a distinguished looking woman come in. Mrs. Young, Bob's mother, who was hostess for the evening, rushed over to greet her.

Mary, who was standing near my table, ecstatically announced, "Now we will see what will happen."

A waiter was hurriedly sent to summon Bob and his wife. I could see, by the expression on his wife's face, that she was frightened. For a moment, I wondered who this woman could be.

Mary said, "She's the Union official, who is here to see about the Mexican help in the kitchen. They are not registered with the Union."

I continued to watch, with neither joy or malice, just pure amusement.

Suddenly Bob came in and with a flourish greeted the smiling woman. He asked if she would care for a drink. She shook her head and I heard her say, "Thanks, but I do not drink during business hours."

Bob looked furious and I knew what he was thinking, "This is not going to be easy."

Mary and I both assumed what was going to happen, but were both wrong. Much to my disappointment, a customer asked me for a reading. Reluctantly, I left and went to their table, which was in back of the room.

About forty-five minutes passed before I could return to my table near the entrance. I glanced over to see what was happening with the Union Card conference and almost fell out of my chair in sheer surprise.

In front of the Union woman was a plate of flaming ice cream. It was perfectly beautiful, but the woman looked entirely different. Her hat was askew, her feather dangled over Bob's face and she was saying, "Dear boy, I knew everything was all right." At this remark, Bob kissed her hand.

Mary came flying over to me exclaiming, "My God, he's giving her ice cream with a whole bottle of brandy poured over it!"

I felt sorry for Mary. It was she who had called in the Union, trying to get even with Bob. Apparently there was no way she could stop this man and his evil ways.

One hour later, Bob with the help of another man, took the woman home. How he accomplished this, I will never know, as it looked like a major project. As she went out the door, the woman wobbled all over the place. I did notice she and Bob were hilariously happy.

The later part of September, 1948, I had a terrible human ailment, which I cannot describe, except to say it was the aloneness. It would almost drive me mad, even though I was with many people every night. I still had a great longing for someone or something. I was anemic and constantly catching cold and often felt as if someone was trying to take over my body.

One night, I had a disagreement with Bob's mother. As I look back over the years, I can see how silly my phobias were. At the same time, I felt Mrs. Young was taking unfair advantage of me, and without giving any reason for my behavior, I went on strike. Bob tried to make me see how ridiculously I was behaving, but I refused to listen. My ego had been hurt. Possibly he was activating negatively and was trying to control me, which caused our outer vibration to clash. Not able to retaliate with Bob, I naturally took it out on his mother. A few days later, Bob's secretary phoned and informed me that Mr. Young wanted me to take a vacation. I quickly answered, "I will take a vacation, but it will be a permanent one from that hotel."

In December I was still out of work and was giving a few readings at home and at private parties.

One afternoon, a lady called and asked if I would give her an appointment for a reading. She gave me the name of a person living at the hotel, where I had been working. I hesitated at first, but then decided I would have her come to my apartment. She gave me her name, which was Leni Jones. I was surprised when I learned she was Egyptian by birth. While I was reading for her, I had a feeling that there was some connection between her and Bob. As she was leaving, she said, "I would like you to meet my mother. She has great powers and can do miraculous things. Her English is not good, so if you would like to meet her, call me evenings so I can translate for you."

"Yes," I answered, "I would be interested in meeting her and have her demonstrate her amazing powers for me."

I knew Leni's mother was the foreign woman, with the accent, Fran had overheard speaking at the party with Bob.

I telephoned Fran, who had left the hotel and was working in a restaurant in North Beach. She verified my feelings, as she had seen Leni many times with her, while her mother was working at the hotel.

Fran was worried about my association with these two women and told me to be careful. I liked Leni and was curious about her mother's strange powers. I therefore felt that someday I would like to meet this woman.

Yvonne turned fifteen and wrote she wanted to remain at the convent and become a nun. I immediately took her out and brought her to San Francisco to live with me. This was the spring of 1948. She started going to school and everything was going along fine, until she met Jack. It wasn't too long before he proposed marriage to her. I tried to stop them, but realized how silly I was to fight destiny. Once the pattern is created, no mortal can change it. At sixteen, they married and returned to New York.

Now several weeks had passed and I had not heard from them, so I called Leni and asked her if her mother would look into the akashic record to find out what had happened to my daughter and her husband.

"Yes, May," Leni answered, "my mother is in deep mediation, but you can come over at four this afternoon."

When I arrived, Leni's mother, Moni, was ready. She said Yvonne was with Jack's family in New Jersey and she was trying to adjust to the great change in her life. Soon she would visit my sister, and I would hear from her.

After the meeting, Leni asked why I had allowed Yvonne to marry so young. Before I could answer, Moni remarked, "It was her destiny. May could not change it."

I verified Moni's statement, and yes, when Yvonne was five years old, I had had a vision that she would marry at fifteen.

Several weeks passed before she called to tell me she had been visiting Jack's family and was trying to adjust to the marriage.

In January of 1949, I went to work for Ricky's Town House, in San Francisco. For a short time, I was happy there, then one night, Alice, one of Bob's hostesses came in with a girlfriend. I was pleased to see someone from the hotel and told Alice to give my regards to all my friends there. We talked about all the strange characters we all knew. Many people believed in coincidences, but through the years, I've come to the conclusion that everything that happens has either been manifested by us or by outside forces who engineered it.

In the spring, I moved across the Bay, to Oakland, to break the evil spell.

One Sunday afternoon, I was out walking in downtown Oakland and saw a beautiful restaurant, called Murfees. My inner spirit told me to go and apply for a position. I went in and was told a Mr. Murfee was not in, but was expected shortly. I told the waiter to bring me a drink and while sipping my drink, I happened to look in an alcove and I saw a man sleeping. I thought, "This has to stop. If I'm going to work here, everything must be in order. I'll speak to the manager about this."

About fifteen minutes later, the sleeping man woke up. He went into the back and I saw a waitress speaking to him. It was Norman Murfee. As he walked over to me, I saw he was tall, handsome, with blond hair and a charming smile.

"You wished to speak to me?" he asked, sitting down next to me in my booth.

With a surprised look on my face, I answered, "Are you Mr. Murfee? I stopped in to apply for a position as a palmist, I'm Madame Perez. I worked at several restaurants, including the Fairmont and Ricky's in San Francisco. I saw you sleeping in the booth and made a note to speak to the management about it." That was how I met Norman Murfee, who became one of my best friends.

"I heard of you from several customers. Yes, we could us a good palmist. When do you wish to start working? We are closed on Monday, why not come in on Tuesday."

I told Norman about my connection with Bob Young and mentioned about his magic, also mentioned about the incident of losing my job two nights after Bob's hostess came to see me.

Norman smiled and said, "That wasn't a coincidence. Don't worry I promise not to listen to any gossip."

I worked there for two months, meeting prominent and wonderful people. One couple, a Mr. and Mrs. Monty, I remember well, because they played a part in my life in the following two years. All went well until June, when Larry Cain, a columnist, came in with a young lady. Norman told me they were in, but I had not noticed them. Both Norm and I felt we were in for some trouble.

A few days later, the mayor of Oakland phoned Norman and told him I could not work there, as palmistry was not allowed.

Three weeks after I left, the restaurant went into the hands of a receiver. I could not believe that Bob Young closed the restaurant. That was giving him too much power, and I believe only God can determine destiny. Yet, it seems strange. I began to realize that no one can run away from anything. I decided to go back to San Francisco and face the music, come what might.

I found a nice apartment in downtown San Francisco and went to work in a tea room. Again, I felt I had to tell the proprietor that I seemed to be a marked woman. I told her of the incidents at Ricky's and about Norm Murfee. She also knew I had worked for Bob Young. She was a caring person and seemed to understand the natures of man. She felt whatever forces were working against me, would still be trying to understand and undermine me one way or another. Calmly she assured me not to worry, because no one could influence her mind against me.

I worked for her for two months, starting in July. Two months later, my cousin Renee arrived from New York to live with me. We often talked until the wee hours of the night. I would try to advise her about the forces of evil in this city and encourage her to read books on subjects of phenomena and malpractice. I told her about my experiences with

Bob Young and what had happened to me since I left the hotel. I introduced Renee to Fran, who was now living a few blocks away from my apartment. Fran and I warned Renee never to apply for work at The Fairmont Hotel. San Francisco is a big place and no one need know that we are here. Everyday I would remind her, so she would not forget.

One afternoon we passed the hotel and I again said, "Renee, work any place in San Francisco, but never here." She promised to respect my advice. Renee was sincere and felt her eyes were being opened to the hidden danger of life, but I feared for her when she would return each day and say she could not find work.

One day, she came home with a happy and perplexed look on her face. I waited for her to tell me, but I knew she had found just what she wanted at the hotel I had warned her against. It even happened on the second night that she would work in the same room where I had given readings. Something within me said this is the hand of destiny. You cannot fight these forces. They are too strong. Be calm and know everything will be all right. It was inevitable that Renee would be attracted to this hotel. I was fearful and concentrated so strongly to keep her from going there, that it could have been my mind guiding her to do this thing which I was afraid of. Usually what you are afraid of, will in time, be manifested.

Renee was happy with her job as a cigarette girl, and I took her news calmly. She, however, was thinking that I was going to send her back to New York. She later told me that she definitely felt I would strongly disapprove and ask her to leave.

One thing I insisted was that Renee should never tell anyone that she lived with me, or that she was my cousin.

One afternoon in early October, I was sitting with a friend in the restaurant where I was working and I noticed a lady that used to come to the hotel. She spoke to me and asked about my health. I mentioned this to the proprietor, because I believed she was one of Bob's friends. She made a joke of it and laughingly said, "Now the fireworks will begin."

Little did we realize she had spoken the truth.

Two weeks later, a woman came into the little room where I gave readings. She asked if I would give her a reading, but as I was about to start, I saw the bartender jump over the bar. I called the hostess, who immediately signaled me not to give the reading. I excused myself and went to talk to the hostess.

"Madame Perez, don't read this woman. She's here with two plainclothes policemen. They are sitting at the bar and we feel they were sent in here to get you."

I went back to the woman and told her I was informed not to read for her. She was aware of the fact that I knew her identity and asked if I was afraid. I felt the cards were stacked against me and I replied, "No, I'm not afraid. I gave readings in prominent hotels for over a year in San Francisco, including the mayor and his wife, who knew I was reading here. As a matter of fact, policemen use to take me home when I worked late." She listened to this and lifted her eyebrows. I knew she doubted what I was saying.

I started to read for her and the hostess came over and said, "Madame Perez, if you want to read for her, it's up to you, but no money is to be given to you. This woman is a detective."

The woman looked at me and her eyes said: still afraid?

Thoughts were going through my mind, "God, why do we do things when we know we are doing wrong?"

The answer came, "You have no alternative. Keep calm. All things will work for your benefit."

Most of us look back on our lives and realize that we are nothing, but problems with a force greater than us drive us on to do its will. When I was through, the woman got up and asked me, "How much?"

I answered, "No charge."

She angrily got up and threw two dollars on the table. One dollar fell on the floor. I bent down to pick it up and a man immediately appeared with a badge in his hand. I was ordered to go with them.

On the way to court, one of the detectives rode in back with me. His name was Frank.

He said, "Madame Perez, we don't like to bother people like you, but we couldn't help it. Quite a few phone calls and letters have come about you. Who do you know who dislikes you so much?"

I smiled and answered, "An old acquaintance."

This answer got me a sympathetic look. When the car stopped at the station, Frank helped me out of the car. Once we were inside the building, the others left me alone with Frank. They seemed happy away from us. You see, most people are afraid of those who are acquainted with psychic friends. Frank treated me nicely. As we passed through the outer part of the station, I noticed a tall handsome man standing in the middle of the room. He nodded to Frank and he went over to speak to him. As they were talking, they both looked in my direction. In a few minutes, Frank came back saying, "This is Mr. George Cristapher, the supervisor. He would like to meet you."

I looked at Frank with astonishment and said, "Not him! I don't want to meet the supervisor at this time!"

Frank could not understand my reaction.

He answered, "Come now, he can help you."

Stubbornly, I insisted, "I don't want any help and I don't want him to know who I am." How stupid can one be?

Frank decided to appease me by giving me another name. "I want you to meet him," he replied, "he is a good man."

Mr. Cristapher was not as interested in my name as he was in the charges brought against me. I told him a business acquaintance was causing me trouble.

"I'm sorry he brought a nice-looking lady like you in here."

He waited to hear what I would say. I, too, was sorry and looked at him with interest.

He remarked, "Good."

My bail was set at one hundred dollars. By chance I had just this amount in my apartment. I called Renee and she brought it to me.

Renee arrived and when she looked at me, I knew what she was thinking. "It's all my fault."

The bail was paid and we went to see a friend of mine. De De Macarrie. When I told her what had happened, she could not believe it. She agreed it was the work of a diabolical mind and knew Bob Young was capable of such a deed. Immediately she called her friend, Alfred Del Carlo, an assistant district attorney of San Francisco. He told her he would come and see me the next day. Now, mind you, there was nothing wrong or illegal with palmistry, it was the power that Bob had with top people in high office that enabled him to give me so much trouble. There was no getting away from this man's power.

The lawyer arrived at the appointed time and listened to my story. He told me there would be an investigation.

After the investigation, he called me and said the investigation had shown someone did not like me. His associate, Pat Brown, had also heard of me. The lawyer became one of my best friends. It was he who took me to the doctor, whenever I needed to go to one, and helped me on many many occasions over the years. We remained the best of friends and years later, Pat Brown became governor of California.

A few weeks later, the case was called and it was dismissed.

After the case, I became alarmingly ill with a fever. For one week I could not go out or do anything.

One day, Mrs. Marlin came by to see me and immediately called a doctor. When he heard how I was feeling, he advised that I should be brought in immediately. As she was helping me dress, a spiritual friend came in to see me. She said I did not need a doctor and insisted my ailment was of the spirit. I didn't know who was right, so I went to the doctor. As we left my apartment, my spiritual friend called out, "You will be sorry. The doctor will only make you worse."

My friend said, "I've seen a lot of funny characters visit you, but this one is the craziest of them all. What did she mean You are not sick in your physical body?"

I told her I would explain some other time. Right then, I felt sick all the way through me, physically and spiritually.

After we left the doctor's, we stopped at a grocery store and bought two large lamb chops, salad greens and vegetables. The general opinion was I would benefit from a good meal. The doctor gave me an injection and I did feel better.

I sat and watched as dinner was being cooked. Renee came home and was surprised to find me out of bed and sitting up waiting to eat dinner, as I had not eaten anything but soup and juice for one week.

Fran stopped in to see me that evening. She had heard that I was not feeling well. She had been discharged from the hospital two days previous, and she, too, was feeling weak.

I appreciated the effort, on her part, to visit me, but by nine o'clock I had to go to bed. Renee had gone upstairs to visit a friend, Rita. I woke about eleven and realized I was very ill. I phoned Rita's apartment. The two girls came down and found me having convulsions. Renee tried to reach the doctor and when she could not, she called my friend who had taken me to the doctor that afternoon. She came over immediately. They made me as comfortable as possible. With their tender loving care, the convulsions were brought under control.

The next morning, my spiritual friend called and asked me how I was feeling. I told her I was sick and I had had convulsions. She came over and prayed with me. She advised me to call the Church of Religious Science in Los Angeles or write to them. I was to ask for their prayers, this I did.

Dr. Ernest Holmes, the founder of this church, answered me himself. Within a week, thanks to the prayers from his church, I was better and shortly thereafter, I recovered.

One morning, Norman phoned me. He said, "May, I told my brother Emerson about you. He will be happy to meet you." His brother owned the Villa Chartier in San Mateo, which is a few miles south of San Fransisco.

This was 1950. I worked for Emerson for a year, then went to another restaurant for several months. In 1952, I returned to New York and again worked for Armondo.

NINE

Jess Stearn:
The Metaphysician

It was in the fall of 1952 when I first saw Jess Stearn. I was working at Armondos. The impact of my subconscious, as Jess passed me on his way to the men's room, was as if an electric ray had come into contact with my whole being. I responded immediately to this innerself, held out my hand to him and said, "Would you care to have a consultation?" He looked at me skeptically and smiled, "What sort of a consultation?"

"A life reading," I told him.

"I don't believe in all that," he answered.

I looked beyond the man and saw his inner emotions, then said, "I don't blame you because you have just come through a very trying time. You are divorced."

He sat down immediately with an expectant look of a little boy who wants candy but does not truly believe he will get it.

We talked of his marriage, his children, a little girl, age six, who loved horses; a boy of seven, who would one day be taller than his six-foot-two dad, and, of course, about his divorce which had taken place a while back, and of his grandmother, whom he adored and for whom he grieved deeply when he lost her.

Jess brought many people to me for analysis. The most important was Dr. Harold J. Reilly, who later saved my life.

I had no idea, when I met Jess Stearn, what a dynamic part he would play in my outer life, and the purpose for me, which was to help him reconstruct his inner life. We seemed to fit completely into each other's lives. Jess had the practical knowledge of the outer world, whereas I lived more on the inner planes. I understood the Masters of the inner planes, who permitted me to call upon them to help Jess and the many friends he brought or sent to me for analysis and assistance. It became routine for Jess to come into the club late at night, either alone or with friends, and to wait until I was through working and take me home.

Jess and I would talk for hours about our mutual problems. His biggest problem, at that time, was that he felt blocked, as if he were going nowhere. He wanted to get out of the newspaper field. At one session I saw him writing many books and told him that this was his true destiny. Later, I saw that he would really become famous and that his third book would be a big success. This book was *The Sixth Man.*

My problem was that I was thinking of dying and I wanted to die. I began thinking of taking a space in Carnegie Hall. I still believed the vision I had of Cecil, that in 1956 I would die, and I wanted to give the last year of my life to God by helping people.

I wondered at the time how anyone could not believe in evolution. Dust to trees—animals to man—now, man evolving to higher spiritual levels of consciousness.

I told Jess, "You are in your fifth cycle. That means greater illumination. It means great success for money, wealth and power which must be used for good. You will be in the cycle of big business and greater freedom will be yours this year than you have ever had before."

A vision came through. I was in a lecture hall. The intellectual man was still melding with the mystic. Who would win? Of course, Cayce. Soon all of Jess's characteristics will be changed and many will wonder why. In fact, a few nights ago at a dinner party given for Jess, the hostess, a long-time friend of his, commented on his physical, mental and spiritual change.

"It must be the yoga, don't you think, Maya?" I agreed, but knew that beyond yoga is an over-all pattern—God's pattern—and know now that Edgar Cayce was the spirit that was to seep into the man called Jess.

Through the years, I have wondered about the "radar" feeling that I received when I first met Jess Stearn, but it was not until 1986 that I became aware of why Jess made me nervous when he called on the phone.

There were many times when Jess and I were at cross purposes, and it was Dr. Reilly who would take me out to dinner and try to make me understand that I was wrong. Even now, I can hear him say, "You and Jess must always be friends. It is most important that you are mentioned in his new book *The Door to the Future,* so that the world will know what Jess and I think about you."

Then I would agree to call and make up with Jess, who would be waiting for my call the next morning. After I called him, a complete feeling of happiness seeped into my innermost being, and I was at peace with the world. It is strange but true: when one is connected to your Soul Path you cannot be at cross purposes with that person.

There was something within Jess Stearn that was great. An indefinable sensitivity I could not really pinpoint until the night I saw him on the platform speaking of the Edgar Cayce group.

Words fail me as I try to express the spirit taking over the mortal man and giving to this man a new way of life and the power to inspire the many spiritually-hungry people of the world.

As I sat looking at this phenomenon, my consciousness projected the future of things to come and I saw Jess speaking before thousands and I knew that he had unlocked a giant, a being so great that Mother Nature had seen fit to imprison it in him until the time was ripe. Now is the time for all mankind to learn the many truths—and it will be through the conscious mind of this man who had been one of the world's greatest skeptics.

Jess spoke of Edgar Cayce as naturally as if it were Cayce speaking, as indeed it was. He told of the astounding mystical readings that helped all manner of men and how through these truths many thousands were able to see the light for the first time.

Then he brought out the shocker—Cayce, at first, did not believe in reincarnation and neither did Jess.

In deep meditation a message came through. "Maybe, you were Jess's mother. He was a prince and at age twelve a magician taught him magic. Jess was able to control many people. You told his father, the king, and he chastised Jess, who resented you. This is the reason for your love-hate relationship in this life, also for your nervousness and worry about Jess." This message alerted me to the true fact of our relationship. I also remembered that Jess had a very negative relationship with his own mother in this life, and I sensed that he had had many mothers that he had not loved.

Kneeling down, I asked God to help me heal Jess. After a long prayer and meditation, I heard a voice saying: "The God Force within me greets the God Force within Jess, healing all thought forms that he has created since the beginning of time and may this God Force also heal me, Maya, since the beginning of time and forever."

I repeated these words aloud and suddenly, I felt a feeling of peace seep into my being. I knew that God had answered my prayers and the dark shadows would be fulfilled with light and love.

I was eighteen when my brother Cecil died. It was a shock to the whole family and especially to me. It was he who told me that I would be in the world of spirit in 1956. Not understanding his message, I naturally thought that I would have to die in order to be in this world.

I told this vision to Jess and he tried to reason with me not to believe that I was going to die, but I would only smile and say, "Jess, I am quite ready to die." Sometimes he would say, "I think you are wrong, Maya." At other times he would look at me with sadness in his eyes, wondering what he was going to do when I was gone.

I met many famous people while working as a palm reader. It was always more than just reading palms. My psychic powers always came through and I could see the person's problems and thus was able to advise him or her.

One of the famous people that came into the club was Margaret Mitchell.

I was working in Cerrutti's restaurant and it was late in the afternoon, about four o'clock, when the waiter called me over to her table. I recognized her immediately. I took her hand and received a vibration of great disappointment. Upon closer examination of the lines of her hand, I knew she would not accomplish her deep desire to write a second book. My psychic impression was centered around some mystery connected with the publishing of her first book and I could not see another book. It was not until months later I learned the true facts; however, on this particular day I read her palm.

"Your mother is happy about your success and your grandmother is here. She is also happy and wants you to pray for her."

I spoke of various other incidents in her life and then she asked, "Don't you see anything in connection with my business affairs?"

I looked at her right hand. The line of destiny was broken and had a cross on it. No matter where I looked in her palms I could not see what she really desired.

Finally I said, "I know you are hoping to write another book, but at the moment, I do not see the fulfillment of this wish. Perhaps as time goes on your destiny will change."

She hesitated as she rose from her chair. I knew what she wanted to ask, so I said softly, "There could be a change soon. Pray, I'm sure you will in time succeed."

A friend came over to me as Margaret Mitchell left and asked, "Did you know that was Margaret Mitchell, the author of *Gone with the Wind*?"

"Yes, but I'm afraid she was disappointed. I did not see another book." I smiled as he walked away shrugging his shoulders.

Margaret Mitchell lived in the South. Later she was killed in an automobile accident on Peachtree Street in Atlanta, Georgia.

A mutual friend confirmed my strange feeling about her book. Margaret Mitchell had great aspirations to write, but every manuscript was rejected until in desperation she brought out her grandmother's true diary of the Civil War era. It had been in a dusty old trunk in the attic. She showed it to her agent friend who immediately saw the potential of the diary which became *Gone with the Wind*.

It was Margaret Mitchell's destiny to bring one important book to the world. I had seen fame, but not real happiness for her. Only an ephemeral mark and a cross on her line of destiny.

Many great people came in for readings. Some I have never forgotten because they left their mark on world history.

Two young men, in particular, came in for a reading. One of the men, Wernher von Braun, had a head line but no heart line in the palm of his hand. I predicted that he would be connected with a great invention.

A few days later, an older man came in. He looked about fifty-five or fifty-six years of age.

"I came to see you alone because my son said you told him he would be connected with a great invention."

Father and son had the same palms. A head line but no heart line. I knew he would give up love of family and travel for his work - a work he was presently involved in.

"Madam, will my son's invention be used for destructive purposes?" he asked with great concern.

I went into deep meditation, looked up at him and sadly answered yes.

He placed his head in his hands and exclaimed, "Oh, my god!"

He really suffered because of the destructive power of the V-2 rocket. Wernher, however, was given the opportunity to work on his great love. Rockets for space travel. His work helped put men on the moon, but he also designed and helped build the first U.S. ballistic missiles. He died in 1977.

Arlene Dahl came into Armondos one day. She is a famous movie star and was delighted to sit for a reading. She was born on August eleventh, 1928. In numerology she is a three life path. Anyone born on the eleventh day of any month, especially in August is a philosophical master come back to do a great work, especially if that soul is a three life path. We became good friends and I saw her on many occasions. Arlene starred in thirty movies and eighteen plays. Over the years she has written sixteen best-selling books on astrology, health and beauty.

Arlene came down with Melchizedek who became David, then Jesus. She was a high priestess and astrologer in a past life.

In 1991, Arlene will start her year of miracles. She will open up and work with the Inner Masters of Light. There's a grandmother (from a past life) who could help her. She will be one of her guides. Several more books will be written by her or about her. I felt she was a great soul in a past life. She will eventually do greater work and the future holds many miracles that she will manifest. She will do God's work.

Jess introduced me to Marilyn Maxwell. This introduction, however, was a few years later, when I was working at Ciro's. She invited me to be a guest in her house and we became close friends. I felt like we had been sisters in another life-time. She was a very special person, quite attuned and psychic. She was always ready to meditate and pray, and was one of the most spiritual people I have ever met. During my stay with her, we meditated many times. When we meditated, the Masters came through and gave me messages to give to her. She always became very relaxed after meditation. We were both born in August and were Leos. Her favorite name for me was Leo. I knew her for several years and spent many beautiful days at her place. She and Rock Hudson were close friends. Before she died she told her friends that she wanted to contact me, but I missed her and she passed away. She had a heart condition which we both knew about, but her death was due to a pulmonary condition.

Of all the people who came into the club, it was Jess who has remained, over the years, as my dearest friend. For love and support he is always there for me, and I for him.

TEN
Ten Dollars and Faith

On January 3, 1955, I woke up with a pounding heart. I had had a strange vision.

In this vision, I saw myself in a large room. I was on a platform speaking to a large group of people. Many people were seated below me. Some were waiting expectantly, some yawned in boredom, others just waited—for me.

While dressing, I was interrupted by the insistent ringing of my telephone. It was my good friend, Lynn, saying, "Hello, dear, what are you doing today?"

"Oh, Lynn, "I replied, "I just had a vision in which I was in a large hall giving lectures to many people so now I am going to Carnegie Hall to rent space."

I didn't mention that my brother Cecil had told me in a dream that I would join him in Spirit next year, and the reason I wanted to rent space was to devote this year to God, by helping people with my psychic powers. It would be a way of giving myself to others and to God.

"Oh, dear," she exclaimed, "I was in meditation and your face came up to me. Whatever you are going to do today will be very important, but do not rent space, rent a studio."

With a laugh I replied, "Lynn, I have only ten dollars. How can I rent a studio with ten dollars? I thought I would rent a space for a few hours a week for consultations and lectures."

"Maya, dear, if God wants you to have a studio, he will give you the money for it. Go and get a studio."

"Very well, Lynn, I will follow your advice."

I was still not sure as I thoughtlfully put down the receiver and doubt began to argue with me in earnest. How could I possibly rent a studio in Carnegie Hall, of all places, with exactly ten dollars to my name?

I had begun to think constantly of dying and was in fact quite ready to die. It was important to devote this last year to God, by helping people, but how could I do it with only ten dollars?

Then a soothing voice overcame my doubt and I heard it say, "Do not be afraid. Believe! All good things are possible with God."

I smiled gratefully, for even with the doubts, I knew my vision was going to be fulfilled. Now I must take the first material step. I would walk across town to Carnegie Hall on this January day in 1955 and prove my vision true.

The day was dark and foreboding, but I was not aware of the cloud-filled sky. It "felt" beautiful to me. I felt the wind upon my face as I looked into the heavens. I was feeling very near to All Good.

"Heavenly Father," I prayed, "Let there be a place for me —high in the heavens—with the sun shining in its beautiful windows."

Immediately, as though I were already there, the sun spread its brilliant rays across the heavens and I knew that God had answered my prayer.

Then—there was Carnegie Hall, the home of so many triumphs and so many defeats. But I would not think of failure.

STUDIO FOR RENT. *My* studio—that was what I thought as I saw the sign. I was so excited I entered the wrong door, but a nice young man, a guide, directed me toward the administration office.

I was walking on air. I didn't need the door sign to invite me to enter. Wasn't this to be *my* place for some time to come?

A charming lady nodded and smiled as I entered. She motioned me toward the seat opposite her desk. "Pardon me," she said, "but I must finish this report. I will be with you in a moment."

I studied her pleasant, middle-aged face. Clear-eyed, with straight even brows beneath a high, smooth forehead, a firm chin and a nice strong nose, not too large. Her lips slightly compressed as she expertly completed the report before her.

"There," she said finally, "that's that." She raised her brows questioningly. "Now what may I do for you, Miss—Mrs.?"

"I am Maya Perez," I introduced myself.

"And I am Leonore Sheer." She smiled encouragingly, but her voice was all business. "you are interested in having a studio in Carnegie Hall?"

"Yes, Miss Sheer, I am considering a studio in which I can give lectures of a metaphysical nature."

She studied me closely for a moment, and then, as though satisfied, said, "I have just the right studio for you. It was just vacated and I am sure it will fill your needs. It consists of two rooms: the larger of the two will hold fifty people and the rent is $2400 a year, three months rent in advance." Then as an afterthought, "I should not forget to mention, however, that one of its nicest features is a large terrace which you would enjoy."

"I am very much interested, Miss Sheer," I confessed, "but I do not have the money at the moment."

A look of astonishment crossed her face as I made this statement. I knew that she was thinking, if you don't have the cash, why are you wasting my time and yours?

"Please don't worry, Miss Sheer," I tried to assure her. "If the studio is suitable, I will have the money."

She relaxed, reflecting my own confidence, smiled and got up. "Come with me," she said, motioning for me to follow. She led the way to the available studio.

Opening a large, panelled, brightly varnished oak door, she waited for me to enter.

There it was! The studio of my vision! I gazed around the spacious room and exclaimed, "Indeed, this is the haven which God wants me to have."

"My" studio was beautiful. Five large picture windows let the north light diffuse through it, illuminating even the darker corners of the room. The adjoining terrace afforded an entrancing view of the city, and the inner rooms suited my purpose completely.

At one end of the larger room there was a platform. Upon it was a stand, for music and for books. There were growing plants and two chairs on the dais. Again I felt myself back in the vision, which had been just as vivid as this room now was. It had to be, for *this was the same room I had seen then.*

"How do you like it, Madame Perez?" Miss Sheer's voice brought me back to the world of reality.

I could not answer her at once. I was studying the intriguing pattern in the floor covering. There was a crescent moon, a long sunbeam pointing to a silver star and other mystical signs. Such beauty had had to be created by a mystic. Yes, this studio was exactly the right setting for my mystical teachings.

"Well, Madame Perez?" Miss Sheer looked at me expectantly, then noted my study of the floor pattern. "Interesting, isn't it? A Countess had the studio for many years. After the Countess released it, another tenant took over the lease. Now there is illness in his family and he has gone back to California. I've already accepted a deposit from a man and his wife, with a small child—contingent upon their finding other living quarters. If it isn't possible for them to arrange things satisfactorily, you may have the studio."

She frowned, as though puzzled, and said, "I don't know why I say this, because I do have a long list ahead of you."

I smiled to myself. She did not know, but I did.

We returned to the office and I gave her references and other information which she required. That taken care of, we began discussing the world of mysticism. I took the opportunity to explain why I was prompted to seek a studio.

She listened intently, then graciously said, "I will gladly help you in any way that I can."

I knew then that she now understood her reason for moving my name from the bottom of the list to second place.

I thanked her for her kindness and left feeling more elated than I had been about anything for a long time. The peace within me promised that all would be well. It would work out as the vision had foretold.

But doubt and fear, the dark twins, again began to haunt me that night. They were determined to test me.

"Where are you going to get the money for the lease?" one would ask. "How can you be so impractical? Aren't you putting the studio before the money-cart?" The other chimed in. And the more I prayed, the more it seemed an impossible dream.

Then I remembered my walk across town, and the skies, first gloomy then flooded with light—God's Light—it had to be.

Reassurance came once more. A voice deep within me whispered, "Do not be afraid. You shall have your studio and you will be notified in the morning. You will be shown the way. Be grateful to Him who showeth you the way."

Faith had won the victory. I thanked God for the message of guidance and went calmly into a deep and restful sleep.

Late the following morning, I was aroused by the ringing of the telephone. It was Miss Sheer calling.

"Madame Perez," she said cheerfully, "do you still want the studio? If so, please bring your deposit over."

Did I still want the studio? Did I still want the studio! The demonstration of my prayers and my vision was all I could think of.

"Of course I do, Miss Sheer," I laughed, with a deep happiness thrilling through me. "I will be in to see you between four and five o'clock this afternoon. Thank you so much for calling, and God bless you."

I rubbed my eyes, seeing the ten-dollar bill, my only money.

I was panic stricken for a moment. Where was I going to get the money to make the deposit for my new lease on the studio? I recalled the message I had been given the night before. My mind, now alert, searched for possibilities. A few telephone calls and a fast trip to a pawnshop and I found myself $40 richer. At least temporarily, this was every cent I had in the world.

Hesitantly, I entered Miss Sheer's office. But if I had had any doubts about her accepting the money to bind the lease, they vanished as I found myself signing a statement promising to pay the balance on or before the middle of January.

I could hardly wait to get home to begin calling my friends. When I rang Jess, he said, "This is great, May. I am deeply happy for you. I've felt the night clubs were not for you. I will help you all I can, you may depend upon it."

The last call I made was to a friend who was then out of town. Breathlessly, I told him of my vision and my plans.

"That's great, May," he enthused. "Don't worry about the money. Just how much do you think you will need to get under way? Around a thousand you say? Well, you go to my bank, give them my name, tell them what you want, and I will send the bank the necessary credentials."

The days following were hectic. At his bank, at every bank, the answer was the same. "No, we are sorry, but since your friend is out of town, it is not possible to negotiate a loan. Perhaps your friend can get a loan himself for you, and you can arrange to repay him."

Time was flying. I had only five days left before January 12th the day I had hoped to move into my new home. I called my friend and told him what I had learned at the banks.

"Don't get excited, May," he said, trying to soothe me. "Be patient. This is only Friday. Give me time to think and I'll call you on Monday."

Anxiously I awaited his call. When it finally came, I pressed the receiver to my ear as I recognized his voice.

"All right, May," he said, "I will arrange a loan for you here."

Great! Wonderful! My troubles are over.

Tuesday morning, humming softly to myself, I dressed carefully and made plans to go shopping for furniture and various items I would need in the studio.

On my way, I stopped at the hotel desk and found two letters waiting for me. One was from a friend, congratulating me, with a $25 check enclosed. I gleefully opened the other letter. It was from my out-of-town friend.

"Dear May," I read. "I am so sorry, but after discussing the matter of the loan with you last week, I find I am unable to get it for you. My affairs are not in good order at the moment. I am sorry, but I did not realize this at the time I made you the promise, but conditions make it impossible at this time."

I slowly read the letter through again, my steps growing heavier and heavier as I walked. The depths of the pit into which I had suddenly fallen appalled me. Subconsciously I believed, but consciously I was extremely disturbed. I feebly hoped this was not the end of my dream. I was in shock. "And after he promised," I thought. Numbness crept through my body.

Again I thought of Jess. Why not call him?

I tried to call Jess, but he was not in his office. Wandering aimlessly, I lost track of time. Once again, I tried to reach Jess at his office, but had no luck.

I returned to the street and the crushing throng of people—the endless mass of humanity forever pushing, hurrying, with never enough time to fully accomplish anything. My mind seemed to mingle with them then, out of the mire of despondency, I determined *not* to become a part of that awful turmoil.

I walked on and on, still not heeding my direction, but gradually there arose in me a feeling of peace. I began hearing an inner voice saying, "Stay calm, and call Lola."

"Call Lola?" I heard myself answering aloud. "Oh, no, not Lola. I still owe her a hundred dollars of the money she loaned me last summer. Please God, not Lola. I am ashamed to ask her. Please God." I prayed, "not Lola."

I had observed people talking to themselves many times and had invariably concluded that they were either crazy or perhaps counting their money. I had no money to count, but who knows, I thought, perhaps I was really cracking up.

Again the voice implored, "Call Lola." It was insistent, even sounding a little impatient as I continued to procrastinate. I reflected for a while, then the thought came, "You did not wait for guidance before as to the source of the needed money. Will you never learn?"

Lola was a Jewish friend that I had helped. She had had a tiny store on East 56th Street when I met her in 1942, selling dresses at two for fifteen dollars. Now, in 1955, she had a very large store on Madison Avenue near 72nd Street and her dresses were selling from $50 to $250.

After doing some yoga breathing in order to release my mind, body and soul, I called Lola. She immediately told me to come down and have dinner so that we could talk over any problems.

I went to her store and while I was waiting for her to finish with her customers, I began to cry. One of her employes came over and said, "Madame Perez, Lola does not like tears. Dry them, and whatever your problem, she will help you."

That evening Lola decided to donate $700, but it was to be done through her bank.

When we went to the bank, Mr. Clark, the manager said, "Why are you interested in this woman? She's not even in an orthodox religion." Lola replied, "If Maya Perez wants this money, she will have it." In three days I had the money and had signed the lease, and on the 12th of January, 1955, I was in Carnegie Hall.

I was happy with my studio. Lola came in several times and brought friends from out of town.

One night, Jess brought in Dr. Reilly at one of our message meetings. After the usual session, H.J., which is the way I referred to Dr. Reilly, asked if I would give him a private consultation. I consented and we went into the little back room that I used for that purpose when there were other people present. Several times, we were interrupted by Irvin, a crippled seeker of information who was always hoping to find someone that could heal him. Irvin knew Dr. Reilly and had gone to see him at his health club in the RCA Building, trying to get the good doctor to give him an appointment.

Politely, H.J. would say, as Irvin interrupted us, "Please call me up at my office."

Irvin came in several times as I was about to go into trance, and finally H.J. locked the door to the small room.

After a few moments of prayer and silent meditation, I saw a vision of a very sick woman with several doctors around her bed. I described the woman and the scene to H.J., who listened intently but said nothing. Suddenly the woman appeared to me again, but this time she was well and standing with a tall man. There was a ring over her head, and she appeared to be smiling as she stood in the sunlight. There were blossoming oleanders surrounding her and the tall man.

Again I described the scent to H.J., and he blurted out, "Why, that is my sister Vi. She was very ill a few years ago and needed an operation. The doctors opened her up and found her to be full of cancer. They simply closed the incision and told me they could do nothing for her as she was too far gone. Later I took her down to Florida to recuperate.

"One day, as I was walking along the streets of Miami Beach in deep thought, searching for a way to help my beloved sister, I saw an old man eating something that looked like green cactus. The old man looked so vital and alive that it aroused my curiosity. I asked him what he was eating.

The old man smiled and was, "It is Alo Vera Cactus. I had ulcers but this has cured me."

"Where did you get it," I asked.

"Oh, it grows here in Florida, Arizona and California.

I went home and meditated about what the old man had said. He was almost ninety years old but looked wonderful. He could easily pass for sixty-five or seventy. That night I dreamed I was in a hot house and the cactus was growing in large pots. The next morning, I found a shop that carried the plant and immediately ordered some large leaves and sent it to Vi. She was instructed to put six inches of a large leaf in boiling water. Let it stay overnight, then drink three cups of the water evey day. It has been two years and now Vi is well.

"If the doctors had operated on Vi, it would have thrown poisons into her blood stream and she would have been beyond human help. It was a blessing that they had decided not to continue with the operation."

"Now," said her brother to me, "Vi is considering marriage to the tall man you have seen in your vision."

To say the least, H.J's story had been surprising to me. I had seen Vi at the health club and had been amazed at her wonderful look of vital energy. She was now living a beautiful and fulfilling life, helping her brother in the club.

After that, we talked about his personal life. I told him there was another marriage in his destiny.

He looked disturbed and asked, "Is my wife going to die? Because that would be the only way. I would never divorce my wife."

I remained silent. Then he continued, "Is my wife ill? Can you see anything wrong?"

After a few moments, I said, "Your wife has problems. She should come to the club and get treatments. I see an emotional problem that she has brought in from another life. This causes her to worry about things that may never happen. She needs massage and colonics to clean out the spleen, as that is our lower consciousness. The spleen takes in all negative vibrations. In our dictionary, it is said the spleen is full of spite. It is full of all negativity." He looked worried and exclaimed, "You are right. I can't get my wife to come in and take the treatments regularly. What can we do?"

"The only answer is prayer," I replied.

"Oh, she prays but she is very stubborn. I will try to get her in for some treatments."

Shortly after, another sister, Dorothy Reilly came to see me. She was a tall striking red head. I had never met her, but I was quite impressed and felt a strange sense of kinship. Later, I learned through a vision, that she had been my mother in a past life. Her birth date and year added up to an 11 life path. I knew she was not only a very attractive and striking individual, but also a very intuitive and powerful soul. We talked about Vi, who had been to see me and also of her mother, Lucy Bell, that had come through in the readings, as a very dynamic vibration. After that, I tuned in to Dorothy and said, "You have been a high priestess and a healer in many of your past lifetimes and in this life, you will be put through many difficult tests. However, I see you overcoming them and later working with your spirit guides."

"Oh, my dear!" she exclaimed, with a happy smile, "this is exactly what I want. I have dreamed of healing and am now giving massages at my brother's health club in Rockefeller Center. I only do this with my special friends, but later, I wish to work with others."

I looked at her chattering and then at her palm for I was concerned about a block in her vibrations. Yes, there in her palm was a square which showed that in time she would be spiritually ill for a long time. I did not mention this to her but asked that we pray together. For awhile, there was total darkness around her aura, and then the light appeared. I knew then, there would be a time in Dorothy's life where we would be very important to each other. Through the years she was able to do astral projection and come to me in California and advise me where to go and find an apartment. Then there were other times when she would call me and ask, "When are you coming to New York?" I would reply, "I don't think I will come this spring. I do not have a place to stay."

"Wait, let me call you back." In a few minutes she would call again and say, "I have a beautiful apartment on East 86th Street. It will be ready in June."

In 1965, Dorothy was having worry problems. She felt insecure. This is usually caused when an eleven life path is not doing the true healing work and is vibrating as a lowly two.

It was her brother, H.J. who sensed that Dorothy was very insecure and asked me to take her to California and ordain her into deep spiritualism. I agreed, and Dorothy stayed with me six months. It was at that time I changed her name to D.D. Reilly which gave her an eight vibration and the powers of a queen. It also opened up her power to manifest greater supply. There were times when Dorothy was making the transition to D.D. that she would forget everything. I had to watch her carefully as she would leave her bank book and other things in the bank or in stores. After a few months she was able to make the step and it was in April of 1965 that Dorothy became the Reverend D.D. Reilly. (D.D. passed in April of 1988 and is now one of my most powerful guides.) Not long ago, she came to me in a vision and said, "Maya, you are going to have a meditation center in the mountains. She then introduced me to a spirit who would manifest this miracle for me. The spirit was very old but appeared to be a three year old. She then introduced me to one of her co-workers, a tall, well-built man, who told me to visualize my desires. Later, I had another vision. I was taken into a room where two Masters were sleeping. As I entered, they awoke and one Master asked, "What is your desire?" I answered, "I wish to work with God. I do not wish anything that is material. I wish to help God and I want to heal this world. Oh, God, I want to help you. I want to have a center to teach people how to become God realized. I want to do God's work. The Master smiled and I woke up. I believe that God will open up the doors for me to have my center of light.

Shortly after I moved into Carnegie Hall, an invitation arrived for me from John Conte, a T.V. producer, who had just married Ruth Harris, the actress. They invited me to their wedding reception which would be held at the Borgois's residence on East 61st Street.

I had met this charming couple a few weeks before when Jess Stearn, my good friend, called asking me to preside over a mystical class to be held at a mutual friend's house. I arrived around ten o'clock and found all the guests sitting in a circle with the lights dim. Later I learned that this had been arranged so I would not recognize anyone. The last person that I gave a message to that evening was John Conte. His vibrations were very strong and the clarity of the message was amazing. Visible in his vibrations was a large letter H. Part of this H was a vibrant color red, another part green and the remainder pure white. I interpreted this to mean that someone with the initial H in their name would be very close to him. This person would be involved with him through the emotions. The green meant vibrations of money and the white the spiritual. Close contact with H would bring about a total change in the inner concepts of John's thinking. These changes would either make him or break him. Yes, this was an important and dynamic vibration.

John could not place anyone with the initial H, who could possibly have such influence over him.

A friend in the group called his attention to his companion of the evening, a girl he had met only a few days before who had accompanied him to the meeting. Shortly after, while returning from a visit to Ruth's home, he proposed marriage and she accepted.

The reception was a very elaborate one. Many famous actors and actresses were there. I particularly remember Rudy Vallee, as he was a Leo like me.

After greeting Mama Borgois, Ruth and John, I went over to a corner of the room where Mama Borgois's oldest son and his charming wife were engaged in conversation with a dark handsome young Indian about twenty-six years of age. They spoke on various subjects and Romash, the dark young man, was especially informed on world events, politics and the mystical side of life. He had traveled extensively and was associated with the United Nations. He was Nehru's highly intellectual and extremely interesting nephew, Romash Nehru. He and I discussed names after the others had drifted away. He told me his wife's name was Coundash.

"How wonderful," I exclaimed, "your names sound like fairy book names."

Politely Romash asked me my name. When I replied, "May," he said, "Oh, but May does not become you."

I laughed and asked, "How do you like the name of Maya?"

"Ah-h-h-h, yes, Maya," he answered with a sweep of his right hand, "Maya is more becoming. It fits you better. The name Maya is mystical and means illusion. It is significant for it goes back to the beginning of life itself. I like that."

"Well," I said pensively, "at the age of three, my younger brother called me Maya. He could not say my name of Mabel, but I did not care for the name, probably because it does mean illusion. No one wants to be merely an illusion."

Just then my attention was drawn to a lovely lady who had entered the room. The most beautiful girl I had ever seen. She looked about twenty-three or-four years old and was dressed in a colorful Indian sari, with many jewels around her neck and arms and even her sandaled feet were bedecked with rings. On one toe was a magnificent ruby ring. In her ears she wore fabulous diamond earings. I gazed with admiration at this girl who walked with the grace of a goddess.

"Who is that lovely creature?" I inquired of my companion.

"That is Coundash, my wife." he answered. "Come here Coundash and meet Madame Perez." He motioned to her to join us.

She looked over and smiled, as she literally glided over to us. As she stood in front of me, I looked deep into her eyes and saw dark pools where joy and sorrow intermingled.

"Oh, Madame Perez, you are just the woman I have been wanting to meet. John and Ruth have told me so much about you. I am dying to talk with you. Tell me what do you see of my past and future?"

Listening to her soft lilting voice and looking into her innocent face, I said "You are a lovely princess, I am enchanted by your child-like beauty."

"Oh, that John, he has told you all about me. Where is he?" Turning around she left to find John, her lovely mouth pouting in childish anger.

"Maya, may I call you Maya? I think the name is right for you, much better than May. The vibrations are higher. Please forgive Coundash, she is a lovely child but lives forever in a dream world." Romash said, and I detected the wisdom of the ages in his eyes. I knew this young man was born to do big things and told him some day he would be an Indian potentate. This intrigued him and we talked about it until Coundash returned.

Convinced that John had not been my informer, Coundash coaxed, "Come, Madame Perez, can you see anything of my little son and my mother?"

Looking off into the far beyond, I answered, "Your son was born to be a ruler. At a tender age he will appear to be unmanageable, but bear with him. Try to understand his unruly whims. You will never be able to control him with the whip. This is a big test, but through helping your son you will in time grow. Your mother is surrounded by great unhappiness. There is a feeling of being completely alone in the world. She is seeking happiness, but it is like a mirage always beyond her reach. Yes, it is as if there is a curse in her subconsciousness. She, too, needs help and it is for you to give her this. Through helping others, in time, you, too will be helped. Over your head I see a rainbow. This is significant of divine help that is in the far off future."

As I spoke tears came to Coundash's eyes, and holding my hand she guided me to the far corner of the room, where we could talk alone. Motioning me to a vacant sofa, she sat on the floor at my feet.

"Yes, my son is a great problem," she said. "He has fits of temper and neither Romash nor I know how to handle him. My mother is very unhappy, since my father died. She seems to be aimlessly searching for him hoping— always hoping that someone may be able to open the door to the spirit world.

"She goes from one holy man to another but no one has been able to solve her problem." I thought silently, "Her mother should try to help others to solve their problems and in time she will learn to solve her own."

Shortly after the wedding reception, the newlyweds came to my studio with Jess Stearn and a few other friends, bringing some wine, records and a record player. We were all enjoying ourselves, dancing to the music when Reverend Almo, my neighbor, came to the door. When I invited her to come in and join us in celebrating the occasion of my new studio, she looked in through the open door, saw a few of my friends dancing and having a happy time, and turned to go, exclaiming, "Heavens, no! We don't do this sort of thing here in Carnegie Hall. I am surprised they allow it."

As she walked away, I felt a strange weird fear sweep over me, and knew that in the future this woman would cause me grave trouble.

The following day, Frances Parker, a metaphysical teacher, who shared a studio in Carnegie Hall, called me. She asked if I would be willing to share my studio with Rev. Andrew Choike, two evenings a week. I said, yes, I would be happy to meet the good Reverend. Later that afternoon, she brought him to talk the matter over with me. He was from Trinidad. Rev. Choike was a teacher of metaphysics and a medium. A refined and well-mannered man, who appeared to be well versed in the field of deep mysticism.

I liked this man of God immediately, and did not hesitate to accept his offer. He was willing to pay a good price for using the studio, and he played a large part in the drama unfolding at Carnegie Hall.

In early February, I received a phone call from a gentleman who gave his name as Mr. Roberts. He requested a consultation and I invited him to come up. As we talked on the telephone, I felt an unexplainable chill go through me. The appointment was arranged and I put the receiver down with a sense of foreboding. He was to arrive within the hour. Lowell Edison, a mystic song writer who was visiting me, felt my fear and offered to remain, although he had an urgent appointment elsewhere.

Mr. Roberts was about forty-five, tall and extremely thin, with dark brown hair. His deep-set eyes bored through me and seemed to penetrate the very depths of my soul. He nodded to Lowell, sitting in the waiting room, and introduced himself to me with a vain attempt at a smile. It was the cold, frozen smile of a dead man.

I asked him to sit down at my desk and immediately went into the consultation. I didn't want to be in this man's presence any longer than was necessary. While I talked to him he seemed to come from another world, and an eerie feeling again encompassed me. Waves of fear engulfed me. My tongue was very heavy and my eyes were blurred and hazy. I tried to pull myself together, but I was unable to do so. I felt weak and excusing myself, I got up and went into the adjoining room.

"Lowell, please do not leave me alone with this strange man," I whispered. "I can't explain what is happening, but I don't like it. I have never been so frightened."

Just then, the door bell rang. Going to the door I was surprised to see my daughter, Yvonne. She stood there and for the moment I felt that she was the angel God had sent to help me. I kissed and hugged her, then explained the situation, asking if she could stay for an hour or more. I told Lowell it was all right, that Yvonne would stay with me. I asked Yvonne why she had come. "Mama, I felt you were in danger," she answered.

Leaving my daughter in the waiting room with a book, I put all my powers to work and went back to Mr. Roberts. I sensed a powerful hypnotic vibration all around this man. I knew that he had an unusually strong vibration, not for good, but for evil.

I do not recall the words I used, but I remember that I pleaded with him to use his dynamic powers for the good of mankind instead of its destruction. We spoke of the cosmic powers and discussed unseen entities that at times took over the mortal consciousness in order to destroy God's creations.

"Madame Perez," he said softly, with a tremor in his voice, "All that you say is true. Can you help me, can you do anything for me?" He stopped for a moment as if overcome, then continued, "Please release me from these demonic forces of darkness!"

"Only if you are sincere in your desire to be healed of these powers of darkness," I replied. "It is up to you to make this decision. Then God can heal you through me. These are your karmic vibrations, the vibrations that your thoughts and actions of the past have created."

I still could not escape the eerie feeling as his sunken eyes continued to stare at me as if trying to undress me. I felt that this man was not only insincere, but a fiend, ready to destroy me if ever he could catch me alone.

Asking for the second time to be excused, I hurried to the waiting room.

"Please, Yvonne, don't leave me," I begged. Yvonne, seeing my obvious distress, asked, "Do you want me to call the elevator man?"

"No," I replied hastily. "Just don't, under any circumstances, leave me alone with him."

I returned to the large room almost in a state of panic. I tried to calm myself, "This is a test," I told myself, "and I must not fail. I must try to help this man, even though he is a sex fiend and a murderer. Oh, dear God, give me the strength and the wisdom to rise above this problem."

The aura of death that surrounded this man was extreme. I knew this was to be a battle of two minds. Looking him directly in the eyes, and with what I hoped sounded like confidence in my voice, I said, "Mr. Roberts, we must pray, for you cannot go on like this. The things that you do in your moments of darkness will not only destroy others, but yourself as well. It is for your soul we must pray. If we do not pray for you, the consciousness now yours will be dissolved forever."

In a voice of utter despair, he exclaimed, "Madame Perez, I have no soul. I am like a dead man. A man that walketh the earth, but with no will of his own."

With these startling words he held out his hands and I clasped them. They were cold and clammy. All the warmth of the life force was gone from him. Nevertheless, I prayed for him, asking God to come to his aid. Then he laid his head on the table and cried. It was the frightened sobbing of a little child hopelessly lost.

Finally, he looked up and smiled, but this time his eyes had a faint glimmer of life in them. After a few moments of silence, while he pulled himself together, he got up and bowing his head, kissed my hand. At the door he asked if he could come again. I smiled but kept quiet. Thanking me for my prayers, he left.

Returning to Yvonne, I said, "How did you know I needed help?"

"Mama," she replied, "I was in meditation when suddenly a voice said, "Go to your mother, she is in danger."

All I could say was, "Thank you, God, thank you."

In mid-February, I contacted Reverend Rose Erickson. I told her I had left the nightclubs and was currently in Carnegie Hall. She asked me if I would care to give some messages the following evening at a meeting to raise funds for the General Assembly of Spiritualists. Many ministers were coming from all over the country. It sounded exciting so I agreed to participate.

When I arrived, I found over two hundred people gathered there. Rose met me at the entrance and checked to see if I was properly attired to make an appearance on the platform. After adjusting the neck of my dress, she gave a nod of approval and motioned me up to the platform where several ministers were already seated on about seven or eight rows of seats.

I went up to the top row and sat down. "How did I ever get involved in this?" I thought, "but I can't back out now. I'm trapped."

I felt, somehow, as if the hand of destiny had planned it as a test and I had to prove to these people that I was ready for acceptance as a bona fide medium. I tried to be as inconspicuous as possible.

On my right was my friend, Rev. Frances Parker and on my left was Renado, who turned and looked at me. Not recognizing me, he inquired, "Who are you?"

Quietly, I gave my name and very quickly he replied, "Don't know you."

I smiled. Only a few minutes before, I had inquired of my neighbor as to who he was. At that moment, two ministers arrived and sat in the only two vacant seats in the front row. They both turned to survey the many ministers and teachers sitting on the platform. They gazed up at me in astonishment, as if not believing it was me. They were the Reverends Almo and Brown.

Reverend Brown and I were old friends. She and I had worked in the same club at different times. She had asked the manager to put a screen around her so that any church attendants would be unable to recognize her if they happened to come into the club.

Reverend Brown found her voice. "Why, Madame Perez," she snorted, and turned away. For the moment she chose to forget our past friendship.

Immediately Renado looked at me, realizing there was an alien in camp, but his attention was diverted as a cold stream of air wafted up on the platform. Everyone asked where the cold air was coming from. They checked the windows and even a back door, and not finding them open, wondered bewilderedly where the cold breeze was coming form.

Renado looked at me (I was praying with all my might) and asked, "Aren't you cold?" "No," I replied. I was aware of the importance of surrounding myself with the protective white light of God. I knew where the cold wave was coming from—from those two minds down front, and it was being directed at me.

Faintly I could hear the speakers beginning their messages. One woman was saying, "Spirit says this and Spirit says that." Suddenly I heard Renado say, "Spirit says this and Spirit says that. Why doesn't she speak for herself?"

I was in a trance state and did not hear my name called. It was Renado who said, "I think they are calling you." Still in a trance-like state, I went down to the platform and gave ten messages. One was to Dr. Holloway and after the messages he called me over and asked if I would give him a private consultation. I agreed and told him I was in Carnegie Hall. Looking around us we both noticed a group of ministers speaking in hushed tones. They were looking at me in an angry manner.

I had visited Dr. Holloway in Steinway Hall, but I had not seen the good Doctor since 1952 when he had seen the symbols of doves around me. He had interpreted the message as meaning I would give spiritual messages of love to the world through the body I now occupied. Now that God had blessed me with a studio and had brought to pass what Dr. Holloway had seen so many years ago, I felt that he should know about it. Dr. Holloway was surprised and pleased about my news, but he had forgotten that he had given me the message.

Now Dr. Holloway said, "I have a very big problem. Can you give me some advice about the matter and help me to solve it?"

I held his hand and prayed for a few moments, then said, "Your problem lies in the emotional area. You are making a very dynamic change. I see a separation and broken ring."

"You are right, you are right. May I come to see you Monday morning? Let's say around eleven."

The following Monday morning, Dr. Holloway came in at exactly eleven o'clock. He looked around the studio and smiled, saying, "Reverend Perez, you are not only a spiritual medium, but you have the power to visualize also. This is a remarkable manifestation." Sitting down in the chair opposite me, he asked, "What can I do for you? Do you need a church charter?"

I looked at him in amazement, and stupidly asked, "Why, how do you know?" He smiled at me and said, "I can arrange to get you one. I have very good connections with Dr. H.J. Fitzgerald whose headquarters are in Oakland, California. I was extremely impressed Saturday night with your messages. You spoke as a true mystic would. It would give me pleasure to assist you in your ministry. Yes, I will write Dr. Fitzgerald right away."

I was elated and amazed at the way Spirit worked. This was indeed the voice of God speaking through this good man. I thought the charter would probably be manifested through Rev. Rose Erickson, but if it was God's plan to bring it to me with Dr. Holloway's help, then so be it.

"I would appreciate your getting a charter for me," I said, "I would be eternally grateful."

ELEVEN

The Lull

In March, 1955, I received my Charter and was ordained by the Universal Church of the Master. Reverends Parker and Johnson and several others attended the ordination and participated. Dr. Gilbert Holloway had assisted me in all the details in obtaining the Charter. Dr. Fitzgerald had advised me in connection with the ordination. I was indeed grateful to both men.

A few days after the ceremony I started advertising in the section for churches in the Sunday *Journal-American*. Mr. Pollett, a very nice gentleman in charge of the advertising, assisted me. I felt I could tell him my problem. I needed to rent space in my studio, for I still had a few nights available. I asked if he knew of anyone who might be interested. He was very considerate and thought for a moment and remembered Eunice Parker, the "Lady of Light" who had just returned from California. He informed me as to how I might contact Reverend Parker.

He began questioning me about psychic phenomena. He had experienced visions and strange situations that had amazed and puzzled him. He thought it best not to mention his experiences before the general public as most people just scoffed and ridiculed.

Throughout his conversation he had insisted on calling me "Pastor," even though I referred to myself as Maya Perez. I thought it might be his polite way to address ministers, or, on the other hand, he could be secretly laughing at me. I finally dismissed the whole incident and blessed him. He was too sincere and genuinely interested in psychic matters to be laughing at anyone.

I called Reverend Parker and she was delighted to hear of the available nights in my studio. Unfortunately, she could not take advantage of it as she had paid in advance for the nights she needed in Steinway Hall and would not be able to make any changes until next month. She would definitely contact me as soon as she was free of her current obligations.

Leaving no stone unturned, I telephoned Jean McGafferty of the *Enquirer* to see if she knew of anyone that would be interested in renting space. She thought perhaps a friend of hers might be interested and she would let me know. I thanked God for this ray of light and the many blessings that I had already received, but my heart had grown heavy.

Going over to a large painting of myself hanging on the wall, I spoke to the woman in the painting. "Tell me, Maya, how did this happen to you? What is wrong? They only come for the classes. All your friends from the nightclubs have forgotten you. Only Jess and the Contes have stood by you. All the doors have suddenly closed. Why?"

Turning away from the picture, I started to leave the studio when the phone rang. It was Ruth Conte. She wanted to come up for a consultation.

Ruth came breezing in and gaily greeted me with, "Maya, dear, how are you? How is everything going for you?"

I hesitated for a moment not wishing to burden anyone with my problems but I just had to talk to someone. "Frankly, Ruth, not good. Only you and John and, of course, Jess and H. J Reilly have stayed with me. All my other friends have turned out to be fair weather friends and have left me."

Looking me full in the eyes, Ruth explained, "Maya, Jess and I have talked this matter over. You surely must realize that in coming into Carnegie you are going to attract an entirely different type of people. People that frequent the night spots go there to drink and have fun, but the ones that come to you here are those in trouble. They are either physically ill or in desperate need of spiritual counsel. I personally believe that you have the gift of power, although John does not believe as I do."

"Ruth, I know that you believe in me and because of this I can help you. I will make a chart for you and John. I only do this for those I love." Ruth leaned over and kissed me.

"Thank you, Maya, thank you very much and God bless you."

"Now," I said quickly for I was tuning in on the Spirit within, "First we will manifest a good job for John in California. Then we will get a big house with a swimming pool for you."

Ruth looked at me in utter astonishment. "Do you really think we will go to Hollywood and have a house with a pool?"

Feeling quite complacent, I said, "Yes, Ruth, did not the Father say, 'Ask and it shall be given unto thee'? We sat in silence. Ruth was too filled with emotion to speak.

"Ruth, I am really grateful for all the things you and John have done for me. If it were not for you and Jess, I would truly be alone."

Preparing to leave, Ruth commented, "Yes, Jess is a wonderful man. John and I are grateful to him for bringing us together, and you, dear, for seeing such a happy sailing ahead for us.

"Tell me, Maya, will we ever have a child?"

"Of course you will have children, why ask me such a silly question? Ruth, did Jess introduce you to John, because I did not see that?"

"No, another friend did, but it was through the psychic meeting Jess arranged that really hit the ball on the head."

I laughed at her funny way of saying things and I was still laughing as she left me.

The next morning, John called. "Maya, I'm really delighted with the chart, but I still cannot believe these things can be brought about just by prayer and faith. You have these changes scheduled for July in the delineation, and the Father will open the door for these events to happen. Oh, well, we will have to wait and see. Believe me, honey, if we get that house with the big pool in Hollywood, you will have to come and visit us."

A little annoyed at John's disbelief, I too, thought, "Yes, John, we will have to wait and see. "I did not understand why people could not comprehend God and the way he manifested good. For did he not say that all I have is thine. All one had to do is read the story of the "Prodigal Son" in the Bible to know the truth.

I still had John on my mind when Jess called. "Maya, Ruth tells me you need help. I would like to help you but my East Side friends are not going to come to Carnegie Hall and listen to you tell them the Father will manifest for them. Furthermore, you have started advertising in the *Enquirer* and now I hear the *Journal*. What are you trying to do, bring in the entire police department?"

For a few seconds I hesitated and then I slowly told him, "Jess, I think the world of you. This I believe, that some day you and all your East Side friends will follow me. Believe me, too, when I say I did not like the nightclubs. Many times when I held someone's hand during our prayers, I was not my true self. Now God has given me a place to pray and since I have only one more year to live, I must do all I can. Why do you, of all people, criticize me? Please try to understand and go along with my program."

For a few moments Jess, too, was silent, then he replied, "Maya, I believe you and want to help you if you would let me do it my own way. This is too much, you have to be more subtle with your approach. Many of your friends are laughing at you. After all, is it not better to have a lot of customers than to sit and look at an empty studio? For instance, Mama Borgois would have sent many people to you but she, too, feels that you should operate with secrecy."

A long painful silence followed before Jess continued. I sensed that he was well aware of the resentment I was feeling.

"I hear John and Ruth are two of your converts. Ruth thinks you are remarkable and comes to see you quite often."

I still did not answer. He could not help knowing how displeased I was that he did not understand what I was trying to accomplish.

Making a vain attempt to console me he said, "Maya, I believe you are going to be here with us for a long time. I wish you would stop saying you have only one more year to live. If you persist in this fantasy, the little men in their white coats will have to come and get you."

At this last statement I blew up. "Jess, if you really believe I am insane, why do you come to see me? What are you trying to prove? I cannot help but believe my own brother. Why should he lie to me?"

"Maya, I don't think you are insane. I know you have a great gift but why not use it to the best advantage? Oh, well, arguing with you is getting us nowhere. I talked to Bob Sylvester about you and he is willing to give you some publicity, perhaps that will help you."

"Thank you, Jess," and as I hung up the receiver, I wiped away my tears. I thought, "Jess is really a good man and I should not be impatient with him Please, dear God, let him understand."

In mid-March, Jean McGafferty called to inform me that Reverend Christenson was going to be ordained at a church in New Jersey. If I wished to attend, I could go with her. We had much in common as Jean handled the advertisements for the spiritualists and was in contact with many wonderful mystics. Jean was a highly illumined soul. She sensed impressions of people and situations to such an intense degree that it was quite fantastic.

As we walked down the street I recognized a friend who was interested in all things pertaining to the occult world.

"Jean, would you mind if I invited my friend Irvin to accompany us to the ordination?" She agreed and I introduced her to Irvin.

We three arrived just in time for the elaborate banquet. After the speeches and the ordination, the Bishop who presided over the ceremony asked me to give a few messages. I consented and started with the Bishop, calling the name of his uncle who had passed over a few years ago. He gave profound advice on matters concerning the church and the Bishop's family. The Bishop was quite impressed and thanked me profusely. I talked to several others before I noted a longing look in Irvin's eyes.

"My friend," I said, "you are only looking on now but some day you, too, will be on a platform giving messages, just as I am doing now."

This was too much for Irvin. He asked, "Really, Maya, do you think so? How do you know?"

"Irvin," I said, "I am positive, for your mother, God bless her, just said it would be very shortly."

The next day Irvin came to me for a consultation. We both went into prayer, to my sorrow, for all during the prayer he insisted on putting his knees firmly against mine. He said he could not function without making contact. Secretly I thought, "Oh, Father, what price must I pay for spirituality?"

As she had promised, Eunice Parker called me the last week of March. She made an appointment with me for the next afternoon. I was pleasantly impressed by the tall girl with the flaming red hair who entered my studio at five o'clock that afternoon. The young lady introduced herself as Loretta, manager of Eunice Parker, "The Lady of Light." Immediately I sensed this girl had unusual powers and if properly channeled would be very dynamic.

Mrs. Parker following Loretta was equally striking in appearance. She, too, had red hair but was more on the slender side, giving an impression of ethereal quality. She was very quiet and just listened while Loretta and I talked on various psychic events that had occurred during our lives. There seemed to be a great rapport between us so we made tentative plans for the future.

Loretta asked me to give both of them a message. Eunice Parker looked up at me expectantly. I said to Eunice, "Your inclinations are toward the healing side of work. Someone in your life, possibly your husband, does not approve of what you are doing. This is a thorn in your side."

Turning directly toward Loretta I told her, "Your husband or partner is not right for you. The sooner you part from him the better. Your thoughts do not blend and your paths in life are going in opposite directions. You are doing the right thing with regards to work. You are very good in helping others climb upward."

Commenting to Eunice, I said, "Loretta has a very strong power, but you have the healing rays, which could be developed to a great advantage. Possibly your determination to succeed in life and your strong urge to help others will in time bring you this force of healing light."

"Maya, Eunice wants to put on a singspiration and she needs a piano for this. Can you arrange it?" Loretta asked me. My reply was, "I am sorry but it would be impossible. They do not allow music or singing in this studio, for unfortunately my place is right over the air vent and I am restricted as to noise."

"Reverend Perez," said Eunice in her soft voice, "I am planning a health lecture, but not until this fall." It seemed as though we could not work anything out for the present that would be profitable for all concerned. I was greatly surprised to see Loretta when she returned a half-hour after they had left me. It seemed she wanted to discuss a few matters alone with me.

Loretta, hesitant to reveal the reason she had returned, began by discussing Eunice. She told me Eunice had started her career as an Evangelist at the age of fifteen. Her father was a minister and she grew up with religion in her home. She had given up the church to work in nightclubs and hotels. Her daughter was presently singing with the Amie Semple McPherson choir.

Suddenly she blurted, "Maya, would you be interested in our working together?"

"Really, Loretta, I can't say. What do you have in mind?"

"Well, dear," she said confidently, "I would give the lectures and you would give the messages. Most people want to hear messages. This gives them hope to carry on. I have some very unusual experiences of ESP. One particular situation happened not so long ago over in New Jersey. A man had died in the house and his spirit came back and broke dishes or anything else that got in his way. After considerable prayer we were able to exercise some control over his spirit and communicate with him. The spirit later informed me that there was hidden treasure there. I would like to buy the property and search for this treasure. Of course, the property is very expensive."

I was amazed at Loretta's story. Did she not know that under practically every piece of property was hidden treasure? If one had the patience to look long enough for it, they would discover it, but I did not want to upset her by telling her this was so.

"Loretta, the greatest treasure of all is the little cell of God that is buried within our innermost being. We should concentrate on discovering and uncovering this treasure."

I had given thought to her suggestion and decided to try working with her. "Now let me see, I have four nights open. I think Friday would be the best. It may work out well for both of us, let us see what develops."

The first week of April, Reverend Christenson and Dr. Kaplan suggested they share the studio with me. Reverend Christenson would give messages as I had been doing and Dr. Kaplan would heal. All the money derived from these proceedings would go to pay the rent, until we cleared expenses.

I did not like this arrangement but I had little choice as I was badly in need of financial assistance. I reluctantly agreed but with a sense of foreboding. I would wait and see how it worked out.

The evening of the first session had only a handful of people in attendance since this was not my regularly scheduled class night. Dr. Kaplan came early, but by eight-thirty, Reverend Christenson still had not arrived so we proceeded with the class.

At nine o'clock, Reverend Christenson, looking very disturbed, entered the studio. She nervously whispered to me to continue, and not wishing to disrupt my class, I waited to question her.

After the session had ended and the last person left, Dr. Kaplan and I sat in silence when suddenly Reverend Christenson blurted out, "Look here, this is too much for me. It is too far for me to come every week, and furthermore, I do not feel it is time for me to start this work."

Dr. Kaplan looked at her in amazement and it was evident it took considerable effort on his part to control himself. Finally, he said, "I am shocked by your sudden change of mind, why did you not call us and tell us of your decision?"

Reverend Christenson, still extremely nervous, looked appealingly at me. I was concentrating on this new turn of events trying to ferret out the real meaning. In a voice that seemed to me to be far away I commented, "Possibly she has just thought it over."

Dr. Kaplan got up from his chair and walked over to the window. He was extremely angry. After a few moments he regained his composure, for he came over to me and said, "Reverend Perez, if you will have me on the night you have your own class, I will be happy to come and heal the people."

I sensed that the doctor was battling his frustration. I knew that for a long time he had been unable to find an outlet for his work. He had succeeded in healing Reverend Christenson and a few others not in our work, but he had not had any real opportunity to reach the people.

Feeling a wave of great compassion for this sincere man who had a desire to be helpful to mankind, I answered, "Dr. Kaplan, I would be happy to have you help me on Thursday nights."

A short time afterwards I learned that the news had traveled along the grapevine and the Reverend Christenson had been ordered not to associate with me or my "organization."

Realizing what was happening to me, I cried out, "God, why are these people who call themselves Christians, why are they against me? What have I done to them? Oh, God protect me from the arrows that flieth by day and the evils that cometh at night time." Suddenly, I felt a strong urge to go outside. Getting up, I went out into the hall and came face to face with my neighbor, the Reverend Almo. She gave me a curt nod and I said, "Hello." It was as if the Masters wished me to know who my enemy was. Going back into the studio, I lit a candle and prayed, but this time I was calm and strong. God had given me the power to pass the test.

TWELVE
Friends or Foes

Early one morning I received a call from a Professor Martin, who informed me he had been at a meeting that Rose Erickson had given for the General Assembly of Spiritualists a few nights before. He requested an appointment, as he wanted to see me on an important matter. I told him I would be free that afternoon.

Professor Martin had a soft soothing voice and felt that I had known him before in a previous life. He was tall and fair, with deep penetrating eyes and brown hair sprinkled with gray. His problem was two-fold: material and spiritual. He wrote books and gave lectures on mystical experiences of this world and the next. His wife did not approve of his work and was a great hindrance to him. "Reverend Perez," he said, "can you help me to get released from my marriage?"

Bowing my head and praying for a few moments for guidance, I replied, "I feel that if you are released from this marriage, you will continue the same pattern. Why not try to make a success of this marriage?"

Sadly he said, "You have no idea how hard I have tried, but without success. It has become unbearable, as well as humiliating to have a wife who is like a stone around my neck. There is only one answer and that is to free myself."

"I will help you on one condition, that you do not remarry." I said. "God wants you to evolve from within. There are some people who should not marry for this reason. Marriage blocks this type of Soul growth."

He was indignant, "My dear lady, God teaches that men and women should be together."

"Very true, Professor Martin, but only if they are in tune." I realized that there was no point in pursuing the matter any further. I did not wish to argue with the man, for it is only through mistakes that we find the right path. He would have to realize this for himself.

"I will pray for the right action, Professor Martin," I said as I proceeded to give him a reading.

After much discussion in other areas of his present and past lives, he suddenly informed me, "I write under the name of Martin. Some day I will give you my real name."

He studied me for a moment. "I am amazed how you can see my sister, who has passed on, my children by my first marriage, and my mother, who is not well. You have indeed a rare gift. Now let us discuss you. Who are you? Where did you come from? How did you ever come to take this studio? I can see it is very good for you. You are now at the crossroads of your world. All types of people will come to you, some out of curiosity, others because they feel as I do, that you can help them."

I thought of all the questions that he had fired at me in such quick succession and wondered why he was so interested. Suddenly I knew he felt as I did, that we were old friends of long ago.

"Well, where should I begin, Professor, at the beginning? I was born in South America. My mother brought me to the States when I was thirteen. A year later, we went to the British West Indies, where I remained until I was eighteen years old. Then I returned to the States to finish my schooling. I have a daughter who is married. I have always wanted to do this work, so I went into nightclubs as a palmist, where I entertained for many years.

"All my life the cosmic Masters have contacted me. The first time, I was just three years old. I saw a great wheel of light. It did not frighten me, I seemed to understand the meaning, for I spoke to the light saying, "I do not want to live this life. I will be bad and I do not want to be bad." As young as I was I knew I had powers that would be difficult for me to control and I would at some time use them destructively. This frightened me.

"I haven't the time to tell you of my whole life, which has been quite unusual. I've had many experiences which would be very difficult to explain. To sum it up, on the morning of January 3rd of this year, I had a wonderful vision that has changed the course of my whole life. It is because of this vision that I am here. Mystical lives are difficult to understand and most people do not believe in them."

"My dear lady, not only do I believe you, but I will help you in every way possible. I understand you for I, too, have had a vision which led me from the business world to the exciting world of mysticism. I know this is the real world, for the world of materiality is only a temporary abode until we rise to a higher level." Glancing at his watch he bade me good-bye and left.

One snowy night in February, while I was conducting a psychic class, I looked up and was startled to see Mr. Roberts sitting opposite me in the circle (the man who I thought had some demonic influences). Among the others present were Professor Andrew, my good friend, and Lynn and Lowell Edison, my staunch protectors in my previous encounter with Mr. Roberts.

Immediately I gave Lowell the signal to take over and give a few messages. When he came to Mr. Roberts, Lowell said, "You are in need of psychiatric treatment for your emotions." There was a slight pause, then Lowell continued in a lower tone of voice, "There are times when you feel like ending it all."

This statement surprised Mr. Roberts, but he said nothing. Later he said, "Is there any hope for me?" Lowell replied, "Yes, help will be given to you if you ask in the proper manner."

After class Mr. Roberts took me aside and asked, "Would you like to go out and have a bite to eat, or a cup of coffee?"

"Thank you no, Mr. Roberts. The weather is so bad and it is snowing so heavily that I would prefer not to venture out," I replied.

"Perhaps we could go to the restaurant here," he persisted.

I consented reluctantly, but made a firm mental note to leave him downstairs after we had eaten.

As we left the studio, Lynn whispered in my ear, "Be careful, Maya, he seems so strange."

Everything went smoothly until the waiter paged me for a telephone call. As I went to the telephone, I wondered who could be calling at this time of night.

It was Lynn. "Maya, don't let that man come back upstairs with you. A strange fear crept over me while I was riding home in the cab. He knows you're alone, so why don't you tell him I called to say I lost my key and I'm locked out. Tell him that I am coming back to spend the night with you. Get rid of him, Maya, I'm afraid for you."

"Calm yourself, Lynn," I said, "I am well aware of the danger. I was alerted the first time I heard his voice over the telephone. I, too, am deathly afraid of him and I do not intend to go back upstairs with him. But, have no fear, I am protected."

Going back to the table, I told Mr. Roberts that Lynn was coming to stay the night with me. As he looked into my eyes I tried not to flinch. I sensed that he was aware of my fear—that he would try to hurt me if given the opportunity. I think he knew that the phone call was not as I had reported it to him.

"I must leave you now, Mr. Roberts, "I said, "Thank you. If you will give me your phone number, I will call you when we have another class."

"Sorry, Madame Perez, I cannot do that. I am married and my wife would not approve." I knew full well that he lied, and he was aware that I knew it.

I wondered at the nerve of this man. Trying to reason with his better self, I made another attempt. "Then give me the phone number or address of a friend. It is only fair that I should know something about you. You know all about me."

As I spoke, the knuckles of his bony hands stood out like ropes, his face tensed, then turned stony. He really looked like the madman he was.

Then he became perfectly calm. The hidden power that was not his, this entity that took over his physical body, had left him. I was amazed at the transformation. The thing that he and I were fighting came from a world of demons.

"Madame Perez, you know how the cosmic forces work. Why do you bother trying to help me? Of myself, I would never hurt you. Not only would I not hurt you, dear lady, if anything, I would defend you with my life. You have given me the only happiness I have known in a long, long time."

A feeling of compassion swept over me. "I wish, for your sake, I could believe you, Mr. Roberts. It is my great desire to help all who are distressed, as you obviously are. But let's face it, you have hurt others—why not me? There is an evil power beyond your control that prompts you to do these things. I have been praying for divine power to help and direct you on the right path. I have not had your full cooperation, so it is impossible for me to help you. I must ask you never to call or try to see me again."

As I made a quick retreat, leaving him sitting alone at the table, I glanced at his eyes and remembered the comment made by my cousin, as we were leaving the studio that evening. "He is a dead man, a ghost come back to haunt the Earth." I had hushed her, so he would not hear. I did not dare look back. The last glimpse of the ghastly, weird, indescribable look in his eyes, I knew would always remain in my consciousness. A few months after that, I saw him standing outside a stage door. No, I did not wait to speak.

As I rode up the elevator, I felt my defenses had been shattered and asked the operator if it were at all possible for anyone to gain entrance to my studio through the adjoining terrace.

He reassured me, saying, "Madame, that is virtually impossible, unless he had wings, and if you are worried, there is a policeman who walks through the halls every hour of the night."

The next morning, Bertha called and came in to see me. It was Bertha who had told me of Carnegie Hall. For a little over a year, she had been renting space from an artist in the building. She gave psychic readings and advice. Bertha had great emotional problems in her life which were overwhelming her. Often, she would come in to have a cup of coffee with me and to ask me to pray with her.

This morning she had some news that had come via the grapevine. It seemed that someone in the building was telling everyone that I was operating without a charter. This would affect both of us as she, too, did not have her charter. I told her I did have my charter, and was too busy to become unduly concerned about what my neighbors in the building were planning. What could I do at the moment but pray? God had placed me here, and he would open the way for me to stay.

That afternoon, Professor Martin came to see me. I had seen him a number of times since we had first met. He was coaching me in the art of lecturing and giving instructions in phases of deep occult study. He had also given me advice on other matters. I told him about the call from Bertha.

He meditated in silence for a few moments, then said, "It is your friend and neighbor, Reverend Almo. I know her. Although she is a wonderful psychic, she has failed to see the truth in her efforts to reach the heights. Her mind is closed to right thinking. She feels that you are an imposter and that you should be put out of the building. Maya, this woman is sick. I want you to go and knock on her door. Tell her you know what she is doing."

I stared at him in amazement. Suddenly I realized that he must be a special agent of the higher realms and also of the state.

He looked at me, paused, and then continued. "I know that you do not want to do this, but don't you see, this is the only way? This woman is vindictive. In the past, she has caused a lot of trouble for many others. She not only writes to the Police Department, but she gets groups to chant, creating evil for various mystics throughout the country."

"Professor Martin, I know this to be a fact. Why should I go and beg this woman, who is not only evil, but actively working against the Father? Anyone who tries to hurt another person by bringing about his or her downfall walks with the destructive forces of evil, the devil."

"Sometimes we must stoop to conquer, Maya, my dear. This woman got your predecessor out of here because she had a California Charter. There seems to be some discrepancy in the out-of-town Charters. Hate is setting the stage for your downfall. You had your vision, the money came, but now you have a California Charter. But Maya, I see trouble; however, you will overcome it."

"I do not know what I am going to do, Professor. I have been taking one step at a time. I feel as if I were dreaming sometimes and a great big hand is pushing me forward. Yes, I realize it is fate, but I must not forget that God is on my side. The stage is set too perfectly for it to be mere chance. To believe is not enough, we must know that we know."

"Why don't you get married?" he asked softly, "stop fighting the fates. It is an empty sacrifice, trying to help people. Most of the time they do not want your help. In time, they will tear you apart to succeed in rising out of the pit. To help them rise, we must first teach them right from wrong. This they do not want to learn. I know, for I have gone through the very same thing."

Although I was not happy with his words, I said, "My friend, I will do this. A higher force than mere man calls me. If I gave up now, my life would be a failure, for I have been propelled forward, toward this, my whole life. When God is ready to release me, if it is my fate, only then will I be released. As for marriage, I do not have the time. In the year left to me to live, I will give gladly to my creator."

He got up and walked over to the windows. I knew he was disturbed by what I had said. "Why do you say such a silly thing?" He asked, still gazing out of the window.

I told him the story I had told Dr. Holloway, of the brother who had passed on years ago, and returned to me in a dream. The dear brother who had told me that I would be with him in 1956.

"This is the reason I have prayed to be allowed to do the Lord's work. Even if it is only to give messages of love and comfort to His children."

Coming back to his chair, he held my hand in his and said, "Maya, don't you know that you can change the course of things by prayer for yourself as well as others. Pray, my dear, to live a long, long time. Shall we pray together?"

Long after the good Professor had departed, I sat in the dimming light and thought of what he had said. This is what Dr. Holloway had told me. These two men definitely knew what they were talking about. "Could it be that God would grant me more time?"

THIRTEEN
My Arrest

In the middle of the month of May, 1955, I was working with the help of a young singer, Tony. He did not have any money, so in exchange for spiritual help he had agreed to type for me. We were in the midst of typing a lecture when the telephone rang.

The woman on the other end of the line wanted an appointment to come in right away to see me. I did not care for the vibrations I was receiving, so I told her I was very busy at the moment, and to call me sometime in the future. She was very insistent saying she was from out of town and this was the only opportunity she had and she was desperate. I did not wait to ask the inner Spirit. Her appeal clouded my psychic judgment. Definitely the impressions I was receiving were not good. The web was weaving around me. I agreed to see this strange woman.

I asked Tony to wait outside until I was through with the consultation.

First I prayed and gave her a message and we talked of her family. I did not feel right. I prepared to dismiss her, for I was feeling very uncomfortable with her. She was not sincere with me and I began to doubt her motives for consulting me. As far as I could determine there had been no emergency that had warranted the insistence that she had given.

She was not ready to be dismissed and insisted that I give her further information. "Will this government job that is coming up prove to be good for me?" she asked. I looked her full in the eyes and answered, "If I answer this for you I will have to call up the Spirit guide to help."

"Please do this for me," she persisted, "I am very interested in knowing."

I intoned myself and called out to the Spirits. The woman's grandfather appeared. He was short and stocky and he was dressed in tan shirt and pants. I described him to the young woman. Yes, she recognized him. I then asked the grandfather the answer to her question.

"My granddaughter is working with the government now, but she will leave to marry the young man she is now going with. After five years she will return to work," the grandfather answered and then faded away. I repeated the message to the woman. Apparently not satisfied, she handed me a dollar bill, then asked, "What do you see in my palm?" I did not answer her, as it was legal to give a palm reading in a club, but not in a place like Carnegie Hall.

I did not accept the dollar, so she put it down on my desk. "I do not charge for my consultations," I told her. "A dollar donation is given for open lectures." The woman then put down another dollar and hastily left the studio without saying good-bye.

Ten minutes later I was instructing Tony as to how I wanted this lecture typed up when the doorbell rang. It was the same young woman accompanied by a dark young lady shorter than she.

"Miss Perez,"' said the tall woman, "I am with the police department. You will have to come with me."

"I do not understand," I said, "what is the charge? I have done nothing wrong. I did not even charge you." With an unrelenting look on her face she sternly sneered, "The charge is palmistry."

At this point I smiled for I did not read the woman's palm. Even if I had, I was one of the five people on the police annals who had made palmistry a scientific method of analyzing people's characters.

Informing Tony that some difficulty had arisen, I went into my room, changed my dress, took out my church Charter and twenty-five dollars. I was ready.

At the station house there were many officers who requested messages, but the tall girl would not permit it. One officer scornfully asked me, "If you are so psychic, why were you arrested?"

"Was not Jesus arrested also?" I asked.

After my reply the officer who was of the Catholic faith, turned away and made no further comment. The van had arrived to take me to the Tombs.

I sat in meditation and prayer as I rode in the van. I was puzzled as to why I must have this experience. The short police woman sat opposite me. She was studying me. I felt her probing eyes. Looking up from my meditation I found her eyes searching me and it seemed they had softened, for she had been quite rough back at the studio, when she thought I was taking too long to ready myself for the trip.

Now I felt my calmness was disturbing her. I did not know why but I felt sorry for her. I felt compassion well up within me. "You are not very happy," I stated.

"Who is?" she asked curtly, not wanting to be friendly.

"I am," I said, "and you will be also when you learn to pray." At this statement, the young woman looked at me in surprise. "How do you know that I don't pray?" she asked. She was now interested to hear what I had to say.

"Your aura is quite dark. You will not be happy until you accept the teaching of the Christ dwelling within. At this very moment your life is in great turmoil. This work you are doing is not your true destiny. You are not in harmony with this work."

Even though she had been rough and fresh with me I was truly sorry for her. She had only been doing her work, which I realized she did not enjoy. "Would you like me to go into prayer with you?"

Looking at me with tears in her eyes the girl said, "Could you pray for me? You see, I do not know how to pray."

We bowed our heads and prayed for the illumination and light to seep into her soul. I asked God to give her the work that would make her happy.

We had to wait for night court so I was left with the matron. She, too, informed me of her many problems and I prayed for her also.

The Judge was a woman. I told her, "I did work in the nightclubs, as a licensed palmist, until recently. Through a vision I left the clubs and went into Carnegie Hall. I give lectures and counsel people who are in need of spiritual help. I am a spiritual minister. I had gone into a semi-trance to give this woman, who turned out to be a policewoman, a message. When I had finished she thrust her hand in my face and said, "Tell me about my heart line." I did not read her palm neither did I charge her for the reading."

The Judge listened carefully to my story. "I feel you are telling the truth but I also feel this case warrants further investigation. Bail is set at twenty-five dollars."

Just the amount the spirit told me to bring.

The clerk further explained to me that my Charter was not legal, as it had not been signed in Albany and that, too, would have to be looked into more closely.

As I went down the steps of the court to go home, I met the short dark policewoman coming up the stairs.

"Mrs. Perez," she commented, "the Judge was very nice. That was a very small bail. I am happy for you."

I felt kindly toward this new friend of mine and answered, "My dear, I prayed. It is through prayer that we are lifted up and our problems solved. I am not guilty, just being tested by the higher forces. I shall pray for you also."

"I know that you will, thank you and bless you," answered the policewoman.

In my heart I thanked God for bringing this girl out of darkness. I never saw her again, for when my case came up in July, only the tall woman appeared against me.

I returned home around eleven o'clock in the evening. This had been quite a shattering day; shattering to one's peace of mind and morale.

To relax I took a hot bath and as the tensions eased, I began to talk to my divine Father. "Father, what am I going to do now? You gave me this studio. Now you have to help me. You guided me here with the vision and directed me to the source of financial assistance, now what is this new situation? I am sorry, Father, but I do not understand why I am being knocked down. Oh, dear God, what is the reason for this? Please, I must have an answer."

Suddenly a beautiful feeling of peace and quiet came over me. It was as if God put his hand on me and quieted my whole being.

The next morning I thought, "Now I am going to lie here and meditate and wait until I get the answer to my question of last night, even if I have to lie here in bed all day."

It might have been one or two hours, but suddenly I heard a voice coming from the top of my head as if coming through a funnel, "I can do nothing. It is you the mortal, with your faith, that opens up the way for Me to do things for you. You are the key, I am the door." Then I felt something happening, as though I were being lifted up out of the body. All my cares were dissolved into nothing and an overwhelming sense of peace overcame me as my spirit floated above my body. A feeling of ecstasy coursed through me. I looked at the sun shining into the studio, indeed it was bright and luminous. Was this a vision? But no, for now I felt myself going back into the body and I knew that this was real.

I quickly jumped out of bed and hurried to the telephone. I called my friend Alvina. "I have something to tell you, Alvina, so please meet me in Central Park at noon."

I had to tell someone of my experience and Alvina was an interested listener.

"Maya, these things are happening for a purpose. This new experience following the arrest means you are going through a crisis, but God wants you to know that you you are not alone and that you must continue to pray, for our prayers give power to the Father to express through us. You must be more patient, Maya, for you and I both know that all will be well. What more assurance do you need than to hear the voice of God?"

I left Alvina feeling as though I were walking on air. Arriving back at the studio, I found it had suddenly become diffused with a beautiful unusual light. I sat down to enjoy the feeling of peace and serenity that was slowly seeping into my being. Again words started to flow to me, "Mortal man is really the power behind the God-self. It is through the mortal that the foundation and path of life are chosen. It matters not how high he chooses to go, if he has the faith and stamina to go through the many tests necessary, then God will help him to obtain it. Yes, it is man himself who must determine how great his work must be, for mortal man is truly the master of his destiny by using the gift of free will given to all men by the Heavenly Father."

As this message was revealed to me through my conscious mind I answered, "Father, help me to do the work. I need strength to rise above the many blocks that I will encounter on the way up." Instinctively I knew that certain events were to follow that would not be to my liking. No man rises without crosses to bear and these crosses he must carry willingly. For this moment I was fortified, knowing I walked closely with God. This new cross, too, would soon pass away.

That afternoon I called Jess, telling him of my new experiences and of my arrest. He listened carefully then he advised me not to tell anyone of the events. The arrest was not good publicity and the revelations from God was indeed wonderful, but people were too skeptical and would not understand. "Maya, people will think you have gone off your rocker!"

At this last statement I inquired, "Jess, do you think that I have gone off my rocker?"

He slowly answered, "No, Hon, I happen to believe these things, but others won't. About the arrest, I would get a good lawyer if I were you. Otherwise, how are things going with the studio?"

"Fairly well, Jess. You remember my mentioning Loretta Duncan? Well, she is helping me with the classes and lectures. Also a Dr. Meyers is doing some healings here, but only Andrew, the Trinidadian mystic, is paying me for the use of the studio. Up to now there has not been much money coming in."

"Maya, do you have any idea who your enemies are?" Jess asked, concern reflected in his voice.

"I certainly know of one," I replied. "My neighbor, Reverend Almo, is the one who informed the police department about me."

"Maya, I have an idea. Bob Sylvester might be able to give you some good publicity. I'll speak to him about you and maybe he'll go for it. I still don't approve of your advertising and pulling people in off the streets. You just don't handle your business affairs properly."

"I am sorry, Jess, that you do not approve, but I feel that if I am to do God's work, I must do it openly and without fear. That is what the Master would want. If it were money and protection that I really wanted, I could return to the nightclubs and earn a good living. At least I had police protection in the clubs as a licensed palmist. Now I am doing the work that the Higher Forces directed me to do, therefore I must not be concerned with my personal welfare. God has put me here in Carnegie

Hall. I had only ten dollars and he helped me. No matter what happens, I know the angels will guide me to the light. God the sun is light. I am His child walking from darkness to light. Soon, very soon, I will be free.

As these words seeped into my consciousness, I felt perfect peace in my soul and I knelt down and thanked God for His merciful help.

Around the middle of May, Bob Sylvester brought out a story of my work in Carnegie Hall in New York's large newspaper, the New York *News*. Reverend Almo, my neighbor, was included. The publicity was great but the Reverend was furious and all Hell broke loose. For several days I felt wonderful and all my friends were happy. Then came the problems.

FOURTEEN
Tragic Souls

Several days after the excitement of the publicity had subsided, Julie came to my door with her arms laden with packages. In the past few months I had seen her several times at the lectures. Julie was the only child of wealthy parents and had become involved with a married man, whom she had lived with for almost two years. Shortly after her family had pressured her to leave him, she had a nervous breakdown, and was presently receiving psychiatric care. Her aura was wide open and she had picked up a very religious entity.

"Oh, Reverend Perez," she excitedly exclaimed, "I want to study mysticism with you, but I do not have any money, so I have brought you some gifts." As she spoke she opened her packages, revealing sheets, dishes, silver and miscellaneous items, which she arranged on the table. I smiled at her enthusiasm, and gifts.

"Julie, I think it best you keep your things for when you set up housekeeping again."

Julie started crying. "Reverend Perez, I wasn't really married," she whispered, "that is why my parents made me leave him."

I had been aware of this, but I had not mentioned it to Julie, for I did not want to hurt her unduly, and I knew that in her own good time she would tell me.

"Now Julie, don't cry, just remember you cannot live in the past. Forgive yourself child, and plan for a wonderful future with constructive thoughts. Start over again. In time a good man will appear and love and appreciate you, as you deserve. Lift up your consciousness by thinking big and positive. With prayer we can change anything."

"But Reverend Perez, I pray all the time. A few weeks ago another medium told me to go into my closet and pray. I took her literally, don't laugh at me please. I went into my closet and stayed there praying. I almost suffocated."

She was so emotionally intense that she was reliving the experience, and for a moment I thought that she would really suffocate. How could anyone laugh at this poor misguided soul.

"Julie, I am sorry, but don't feel bad. Many people do not understand the instructions to go into your closet and pray.

"The Bible is difficult to understand, but start reading it, and read it through with prayer and meditation there will come understanding. The closet is your heart, located in the house of your body, the temple of the living God. It is there that we commune with the Father. In the Book of James, it says, 'Faith without works is dead,' so one must start to do good works. We must help one another, then we will start to evolve. But first you must start by helping yourself. Take pride in yourself again, by dressing neatly. As your body is the 'Holy Temple,' take care of it; treat it holy. See yourself dressed in beautiful clothes and yourself living in a lovely home where you are the hostess. Visualize the right husband in your life. As life is an illusion, therefore what-so-ever a man thinketh and desireth in his heart it will surely manifest. As you are a spiritual image of the Divine Creator, you are a co-creator. Remember this, whatever your thoughts continually dwell on, it will come to pass."

Loretta came in at that moment, and after introducing them I left Loretta in prayer with Julie, while I ran some errands. When I returned in an hour, I overheard Loretta saying, "Yes, marriage would indeed solve your problem."

Calling Loretta into the other room I whispered to her, "Please don't put such a burden on any man, Julie needs psychiatric help. At this moment she is in the care of a psychiatrist."

Looking up, I saw Julie standing in the door, she had heard every word.

"Look here," she shouted, "you needn't whisper about me, that I am crazy. Just tell me, tell me! If you really think so, do you think so, do you believe I am crazy? If so I will leave, I don't intend to stay here and be insulted!"

She was verging on the border of hysteria and I tried desperately to calm her.

"Julie, my dear, I did not mean that you are insane, but you do need medical and spiritual help. You have had several nervous breakdowns, but you are not crazy—just emotionally insecure. There is a physical body that needs care and a spiritual body that needs prayer. Please, don't be offended, I do want to help you. You are not ready yet emotionally, to accept a marriage, but with a little help, in a short time you will be able to cope with your problems all by yourself."

My attempt to placate Julie had been a failure, or so I thought as she turned from me and left without any comment, but early the next morning she called, wanting to come up for a consultation.

"No," I answered firmly, "I am sorry Julie, I don't feel that I am the one to help you. I am not a physician and that is what you need. I can help you with your spiritual needs but first you should seek help from a medical doctor."

"I know why you don't want me to come up to see you," she shouted into the telephone, "you are going with my boyfriend, I know you are."

"Why Julie, I don't even know your boyfriend," I said in amazement. I wondered what in the world was wrong with the girl. I suspected she was heading for another breakdown.

"Julie dear, I am very busy at the moment, please try to calm yourself. The only way I can help you at the moment is to pray for you, which I will do. I will pray and send you the healing light of Christ."

"Oh, no, you don't," she screamed, "I want to see you now! DO YOU HEAR ME?"

Trying to stay calm I put down the receiver and thanked God that Loretta was due to arrive soon. An hour later the door bell rang and I cautiously opened the door. I was not cautious enough, for a big foot pushed its way through the open door and wedged it open wide. There stood Julie with a big, tall man with an angry face. They both entered immediately, pushing me aside. I was so surprised that I just stood there, unable to speak.

"Reverend Perez," said Julie haughtily, "this is my doctor, my psychiatrist. I brought him here to meet you."

Without being asked, they both took seats while I remained standing.

"So you are Reverend Perez," the big man said with a sneer on his face. "You are the woman that is going around telling young girls they are crazy. I can report you to the Medical Association for diagnosing cases. What makes you think that you are qualified to diagnose?'

I stared at him praying inwardly, for I now realized that Julie was not the only one ill. Silently I said, "Oh, God, please give me the right words. Please, dear God."

"Julie shouted, "She is going with my boyfriend, I tell you she is. That is the reason that she doesn't want me to come up here and she says that I am crazy—look at her."

The doctor looked at Julie in amazement, finally realizing that he himself might be in a questionable position. With dismay in his voice he asked, "Reverend, do you know her boyfriend?"

I am usually never at a loss for words, but now if my life depended on it I could not answer.

It was Julie that again shouted, "Of course she does, that is why she does not want to see me here anymore."

"Julie, I asked Reverend Perez the question, not you," the doctor replied with authority in his voice. He was becoming annoyed with the girl.

"Reverend Perez," he said turning back to me, "I asked you a question?"

"I do not know the man you are referring to," I replied, with what I hoped would be calm dignity, "and it is obvious that neither do I know you. I would like you both to leave my studio immediately."

Just then Loretta walked in the open door, "What is going on here?" she inquired.

"This woman has been bleeding my patient for money and whatever she could get out of her," said the doctor in reply.

Both Loretta and I burst into loud laughter.

A look of astonishment came over his face as he turned to Julie and asked, "You did pay her money, didn't you?"

"I did not have any money," Julie answered truthfully, "you knew that."

I think then the doctor fully realized that he had made himself look quite ridiculous, if the dismayed look on his face revealed anything.

"Julie, haven't I been nice to you, every time you came to me I tried to help you. Why did you bring this man here to disturb me?"

Julie started to cry and the doctor taking her by the hand led her out the still open door.

Through the year, I have seen Julie, at the lectures. She is a little neater in her dress and appears more at peace with herself, but her eyes tell me that she has not found her God. I pray for her and all those "Julies" who are sincerely trying to find the inner God self.

My door was open, to let the air in that warm summer day. Sometime later, a tall, pretty girl with the big brown eyes, and dark brown hair in ringlets around her face walked in. She appeared to be twenty-three or twenty-four years old.

"Do you have a piano that I can use?" she inquired.

"No, I am sorry, but I do not, but there is a professor down the hall that rents his by the hour. Perhaps you can make arrangements with him."

"My name is Marianne and I am a singer, what do you do?"

"How do you do, I am Reverend Perez, a metaphysical teacher. I try to help souls that have lost their way in life."

"Oh, how wonderful, please, help me, I need lots of help. Could you give me an appointment? Today I have to go to work, I am a waitress, but tomorrow I get off work early."

Studying her aura and feeling her vibrations I answered, "Yes, Come in tomorrow after work."

Promptly at five the next afternoon, Marianne came in for her consultation. We were relaxing after our discussion, when I casually asked her to sing for me.

"I would be happy to, Reverend Perez, for I enjoy singing so much."

Her voice was tremendous. I was amazed at the tonal quality and her control. The telephone rang, and when I answered and learned that it was Jess, I enthusiastically told him of this beautiful young German singer. He said immediately that he would like to meet her.

In a very short time he arrived. He too, was intrigued with the beautiful Marianne and her lovely voice. Yes, Jess thought that he could help her.

The next morning Jess called. He had spoken to his friend Jaffe, who was connected with the world of television and music. Jaffe was going to introduce Marianne to some friends in this world that could help her.

The first time I had spoken to Marianne, I had sensed her great emotional fears. She later confided in me. She had been on the edge of success in the opera two years ago, in Germany. She had tried to take her own life when a love affair ended. After this tragic event, she was avoided by friends and family and the door to her beloved world of opera was completely closed to her. She suffered a complete nervous breakdown. When she recovered her family sent her to America. She spoke often of the war, the theater, and the hospital for the insane. Her description of the life in the hospital was tragic. One man, a former violinist, would go around playing an imaginary violin. Another, the young man who had been in politics, thought he was Hitler. The young actress would impersonate the leading stars. So sad.

The next week, through the influence of Jess, the arrangements were completed by Jaffe, for Marianne to make an appearance during the cocktail hour, at one of the leading East Side night spot restaurants.

Around four o'clock, Marianne called me, asking me to go with her. I felt that she was nervous and I told her that I would go, but I could only stay an hour as I had an appointment at seven. Marianne was delighted.

We arrived at the club and the owner introduced us to several of the guests. Marianne sang three songs and received tremendous applause. I left Marianne with her new friends.

I was just getting into a taxi when I saw Marianne leaving the club in a hurry. I waited for her.

"Why didn't you remain and enjoy your triumph?" I asked as I moved over to make room for her in the taxi.

"Oh, Maya," she exclaimed impetuously, "these people bore me. I just had to leave."

I was shocked at her statement. Didn't she realize that a singer had to entertain her customers. That was the biggest part of her job.

Dropping her off at her hotel, I went on to my appointment, but I was very disturbed at Mariane's childish behavior.

Noon, the next day, she came in unexpectedly.

"Let's sit and have a good talk, Marianne. You know Jess went to a lot of trouble to get you this appearance. You fluffed it. I am sure that Jaffe will not give you another chance." I looked at Marianne. Her eyes were filling with tears.

"Come, let us do something about this situation. I feel that you have a condition from the past that will have to be removed. Do you believe in prayer?"

"Of course I do Maya. You know that."

"Marianne, I will help you but only on one condition that you do not inform people of my work. They will not understand and will just laugh. I know I can make anything happen, but you must believe in the power of prayer."

"Please believe me Maya, I won't say a word about what you are doing. Believe me I will not."

With her promise we went into deep meditation and prayer, asking the Dynamic Masters of the Universe to come in and open up the doors for her.

Loretta and I were surprised to see the studio full of people, the night of our lecture. The publicity had really filled our house. I gazed at a woman and found a pair of big, dark eyes, staring back at me. I sensed a kindred spirit flowing from her to me and knew that she was in great need of spiritual help. When the message session began I told her that she was surrounded by doctors and that she was in great need of spiritual healing. I felt a strange urge to put the healing light around her and did so. Loretta and I held out our hands toward her and sent out divine sparks of love and light. I then told the woman with the tragic eyes that the spirit of a woman, who had just passed over, was haunting her. She put her hands to her face and broke down with a torrent of tears. After the meeting, she asked for an appointment, for private counseling.

At 2 p.m. Saturday, Betty kept her appointment. We were discussing her strange life, when suddenly I felt the presence of a spirit. It was a woman, that had gone out of the body hating Betty. I felt though waves were coming to me, as the woman spoke through the power of the mind. "Betty is guilty of killing my body. She and that man that I was married to. They both sent me evil thoughts. I know that I must forgive them, before I rest, but oh dear God, how can I?"

I felt her distraught presence, and in my inner mind I could see her wringing her hands in sheer agony. Coming out of my trance, I said in a soft tone of voice, "Betty, a woman is here. She is tall and on the blonde side, but very thin. This woman feels that you and her husband sent her thoughts that destroyed her body." Holding Betty's hand, I asked, "How did this woman come to believe such a terrible thing?"

For a moment, Betty could not speak. She was amazed at this strange message.

Slowly she answered me, "Maya, I need your help. I will confess to you all that I can remember. Dr. Al is my boss. Shortly before the late Mrs. Al committed suicide, I sensed that he was becoming indifferent, and very distant to me. You see Dr. Al and I have been lovers for a good many years. I created and ran his business, pyramiding it from twenty thousand to well over two hundred thousand dollars. I could see that he only had a deep feeling of gratitude for me. He did not really want to be with me.

"One evening, I asked him for a little hope, just a straw. A few days later he gave me a whisk broom. Becoming provoked at his nonchalant attitude, I put two of the straws from the broom in a letter and addressed it to him. Mrs. Al opened the letter and recognizing my handwriting she put the envelope containing the straws into her vault. During the investigation after her death, the FBI opened the vault. They suspected that it might be murder and they hoped to find clues there. Finding the letter with the straws they naturally called me in for questioning. It seems that in New Jersey there is a religious significance of someone sending straws to another. Do you know anything of this particular religious ritual?"

"Yes, I have heard of a similar case but they used wood instead of straws. Remind me to tell you the story later." I went into the meditating silence, trying to absorb the meaning of what I had been told.

"Anything is possible with the mind," I informed her. "If someone gives you a straw, or a piece of wood, telling them what these items will do, that thought will go to the subconscious mind, and these patterns will be manifested.

"If you have a stronger will than the person that gave you the item, then the thoughts that were associated with the wood or straw sent to you, will be deflected, and returned to the sender. If the thoughts were of illness, or even death, then these things will be manifested, to the sender. It is our own negative thought forms, that knock us down and try to destroy us. This is the Universal Law; the 'Law of Abundance.' Whatever is cast out will return ten-fold; whether it be positive or negative, for the law of the subconscious cannot reason.

"Now, in truth, Mrs. Al attracted the straws to her, that you had sent to her husband, by her own psychic thinking. She felt the destructive thoughts associated with the straws, and assumed they were directed toward her, consequently making them her own. She thought she knew who the persons were, that were sending out these negative waves. You were innocently returning to Dr. Al, what he had given you, but his wife picked up, not only the thoughts, but also the gift."

Betty began crying, "I did not really want to hurt her, please, tell her this for me. I cannot stand the pressures of these haunting vibrations. Dear God, if I have harmed her, please forgive me. You know, Maya, she made three attempts on her life, before she was successful. Months ago, she had gotten up out of bed after hearing a voice and turned on the gas. Fortunately, the house-man smelt the gas escaping, and came in time to save her. The next time, she again heard a voice telling her to kill herself. She had been driving down a highway and the voice told her to run the car off the road. Only that time, she resisted and prayed and the thoughts went away. Three weeks ago, she again turned on the gas, but this time no one was at home to save her."

Then in despair, Betty looked at me through her tears and asked, "Surely, Maya, these were not my thoughts, for I did not knowingly think of these things?"

"No, Betty, they were not your thoughts, but the thoughts of someone that deliberately wanted to get her out of the way. I am sure we do not have to look very far for the guilty party."

Holding her hand, I prayed for the soul of the poor departed woman, and also for her husband, who was planning to be married, to a much younger woman. Apparently, it was this woman who had willed the death of Mrs. Al.

Much relieved, Betty said, "Maya, please tell me the story of the piece of wood."

I smiled as I thought of this particular story. "A friend, who was a practitioner of both good and evil came to me a few years back with a problem. She had to leave town and did not know where she should go. I looked into her consciousness, and saw great confusion. I saw a woman in a hospital bed, and I received the message that it was my friend who was responsible.

"Who is this woman I see in the hospital bed," I asked my friend, "and in what way are you responsible?"

"She then told me this story: The ill woman in the hospital had come to her for help. She had a lover and every time she saw the lover her husband would give her a sound whipping, when she returned home. She said, her husband told her his ESP told him that she had been unfaithful. Well, it seems that she did not want to give up her lover, and she did not want to suffer any more beatings.

"The practitioner prayed over a small piece of wood, and told the woman that now she was protected and she could go and see her lover. She instructed her to put the wood in her mouth when she returned home and her husband would be powerless to harm her. The wood had the power to save her from all evil. She was not to speak to her husband, just listen to what he had to say.

"The woman was delighted with the practitioner's advice and immediately went to visit her lover. When she went home, the husband asked where she had.been. When she did not answer he began calling her all sorts of vile names. The poor wretch forgot that she was not supposed to speak, and opened her mouth to say something and the piece of wood went down and lodged in her throat.

"The husband had to rush her to the hospital, for emergency surgery. The woman told her brother, when he came in to see her, what had happened and immediately he stormed out and went looking for my friend. Fortunately, she was not at home, but he left a message with her sister, that he was going to come back and kill her for damaging his sister's health.

"When my friend returned home and received the message she came rushing over to see me, seeking advice. We prayed together, and she made a decision to move to a nearby town."

Mrs. White, Betty's sister, called the next week. "Please, could I have an appointment to see you right away? I am visiting from out of town, and cannot stay over. It is quite important that I see you."

"Why, yes, I am free for the moment, come right over."

After consoling Mrs. White, regarding some of her own personal problems, she immediately mentioned the real reason for her visit. "Reverend Perez, I want to use our combined powers to persuade Betty to quit her job."

I knew that Dr. Al was paying Betty a fabulous salary, but I was not sure that she could find another job. I began receiving messages, which I relayed to Mrs. White, "I do not see Betty leaving her job, as she desires to marry this man. But he has a young sweetheart that he is in love with. I also see Betty has an emotional disturbance, which will bring on a nervous breakdown."

"Mrs. Perez, I feel that this man has a power of control over many people. He has studied psychology and also hypnosis. He had a hex over his late wife, and I am afraid that he will try to put a hex on Betty, who may also try to commit suicide ."

I listened patiently, then I replied, "Mrs. White, I feel that it is the will of God that your sister remain with the doctor until she learns the lesson that she must learn from this particular experience."

Sounding very much annoyed, Mrs. White exclaimed, "My God, Mrs. Perez, how much more must my poor sister suffer? She is a nervous wreck now. This man has caused his poor wife to commit suicide, and I just know that he will make Betty do the same thing."

Answering the angry woman I said quietly, "I will pray for your sister. I cannot persuade her to leave a job paying her a tremendous salary, unless I could promise that she will get another that is just as good, and that I cannot do. You must admit that she has helped you and others in the family. We must be very careful, if we are to help your sister. She has a very strong will of her own, and can control anything and everything, except this relationship with the Doctor. There have been many instances that your sister has used her mind destructively. No, I am not judging her, for I know that everyone has at some time or other used their minds to create evil. We are here on this plane to learn our lessons, both good and evil. We must endeavor to help each other, only if it is the best for them."

Mrs. White said haltingly, "I realize that my sister has her faults, but yes, yes, she has been very good to the family. Please, see what you can do to help her. Don't mention to Betty that I came to see you. I'll come and see you another time, good-bye."

FIFTEEN

My Case

The case had come up twice before, but was postponed both times, because I did not have a lawyer. Then the second time when I did find a lawyer, Mr. Roy Spraggins, he wanted more time. Dr. B. J. Fitzgerald had written to say that he was expecting to hear from Albany and that soon everything would be in order with his charters in the East.

It was in the middle of July when the case was called, for the third time. However, my lawyer still wanted further extension, but the judge said,"no."

Only the tall blonde detective called Dorothy had appeared against me; the other dark girl stayed away purposely as she did not want to appear against me. Mr. Spraggins informed the judge that I was an old friend of many years and that he had always found me to be an honest and sincere person, also I was a bona fide minister who was trying to help mankind.

The judge said that he did not believe that I was running an honest organization to help people and that I was using the money I took in for my own purposes. I smiled at that statement, recalling the times I paid Carnegie Hall two hundred dollars, then the newspaper ads and the light bills. Many times I was left with just three dollars in the bank and did not have money to buy food and other necessities. But, thanks to the good Lord, who always provided that my needs would be met, help came through kind and thoughtful friends. It was noon when the judge found me guilty and adjourned the court, saying that I would be sentenced later. My lawyer looked over at me with a scared look, then said he was going out to lunch. He never came back.

I was then taken to the back of the courtroom and given into the custody of a matron, who was a kind and sympathetic woman. She asked if I would care to have a sandwich and hot coffee. I thanked her and said that I would. She put me in a cell, locked it and went off to get my food.

I was happy for the few minutes alone, so immediately went into deep meditation, asking God to help vindicate me. I was not angry because even though I realized that I was innocent of any wrongdoing, yet I felt that this was a karmic pattern which had to be fulfilled and that in due time God would open all doors and I would see the rainbow over my head.

The matron returned shortly, unlocked the cell and told me to sit beside her in the small alcove. She asked me what the charge against me was, so I told her it was palmistry, but that I was a licensed palmist, and before going into Carnegie Hall, worked in many famous night clubs and restaurants.

"Miss Perez," she asked with a serious look, "Could you read my palm?" I have had a lot of trouble in the family recently and am at my wits' end to know what to do about the problems that I am facing."

Putting the sandwich down, I sipped the coffee and then glanced at her palms. "I see two marriages here, one is rather late in life, but the first will not be ended for a while yet, and it will be through God. You can't leave this man because there is a karmic tie. He is very ill and if you leave him, he may die. You will never forgive yourself, and neither will your children. Try to pray for his release and in time God will see fit to take him out of your vibration."

She clasped my hand and said, "Thank you and God bless you for your message. I will try to hold out. Yes, I have thought of leaving him." Then she looked at me thoughtfully and asked, "When will the karmic pattern be broken?"

"This tie will be completely broken when you have learned the lessons of patience and giving of yourself. You do not have patience with those who are ill. This is because you are so healthy and can't conceive of anyone being constantly ill."

"So true. Can you give me a message about my daughter? She has been going with someone whom I don't approve."

We were discussing the problem around her daughter, when a court attendant came to say that the judge was back and my case was about to be called. I looked around the courtroom trying to find my lawyer, but he was not in court. The judge also gave me a strange look. I imagine he, too, was wondering where my lawyer had gone. Anyway, he fined me fifteen dollars. I had thought that the case would be thrown out of court, so did not bring any money with me and when I asked the clerk if I could pay the fine with my bail money, he answered no. I then asked if I would be able to give him a check for the fifteen dollars. The clerk spoke with Mr. Conroy, the head clerk and then spoke with the judge, telling him my problem and asking if I could go home and bring the money in the next day. When the judge consented, I left the court.

The clerk who had fingerprinted me followed me down the stairs and whispered, "Miss Perez, our records prove that you have never been in trouble before, and if I were you, I would not let this case go at that. It is a shame you had to join a religious order and then get arrested. I can't say too much for I work here in court, but I would clear my name, if at all possible."

He was so sincere and kind. I was thinking, maybe it is because he is South American that he is trying to help me.

Looking at him with a smile, I answered softly, "I can't do anything because I don't have money and my enemies are very powerful. They are all in the religious work, but God will take care of it for me. This I am certain of."

He smiled as he answered, "God takes care of those who help themselves."

At the foot of the stairway I saw the chief head clerk. He was standing as if waiting for someone. He introduced himself saying, "I am Ed Conroy. I am sorry about the way your case has gone."

I did not answer. Just stood there wondering why he was so concerned about my welfare. It was he who had asked the judge to give me permission to go home. I had spoken to him a few times in the past few weeks.

He pulled me out to a shady corner of the doorway, out of the hot July sun, and asked, "What are you going to do about your work now, Miss Perez?"

"I don't know," I answered impassively. "God will take care of me. He put me in Carnegie Hall. I am sure that He will open the way for me to stay there."

"Why not go to California?" he suggested kindly. "Your chapter seems to be legal in that state."

"Mr. Conroy," I answered with spunk, "God put me here in New York and He will protect me. When He tells me to go to California, then I will go—not before."

Just then, the detective called Dorothy came down the stairway and Mr. Conroy said out loud, "Miss Perez, do your work, but don't read girls like Dorothy."

In an angry tone of voice, Dorothy answered, "Miss Perez, do your work but don't give people false hopes and upset them by predicting."

As she went down the street, Mr. Conroy turned to me and asked in a pensive tone of voice, "How did you ever come to leave the night clubs and go into Carnegie Hall when you had a license for palmistry?"

I told him of my brother who had passed over and his message to me, that in 1956 I would be with him. I also told him of the vision of giving lectures on the platform. Then I said, "I am tired of the world because of the unreality and insincerity of those who called themselves Christians and who were supposed to be working with the Lord."

He listened very intently to all that I said, but did not try to advise me about my life. Suddenly he said, "Do you know who caused you all this trouble?"

"Yes, I know, it is a woman who is my neighbor. She is a spiritualist teacher. The Rev. Almo feels that she is the one to keep the religious order clean. Many people have said that she should first clean out her own house and by that time she may be clean."

"Yes, that person wrote a letter and called up twice. We had to call you in, whether we wanted to or not. You are not a bad person. As a matter of fact, you are rather nice."

I smiled at him and thought, "Yes, this man and I could have been good friends, if he were not working here in the police department where I had been arrested."

I told him that Jess Stearn and Robert Sylvester had given me some publicity because of this trouble and they had put in my neighbor for good measure. He asked what day the publicity had come out, and in which paper. I told him it was the *New York News* on the 7th of June, 1955.

"What are you going to do about this neighbor?" he asked, rubbing his chin.

"Nothing," I answered complacently. "I feel sorry for her."

A little annoyed at my indifference he asked again, "Why aren't you angry with this woman who has caused you so much trouble?"

Smiling at his burst of temper, I answered quietly, "Because she is a very sick woman. Only sick people try to get others in trouble. I can't go to her and say, Now look, Reverend, you are sick. Stop annoying me. I can only pray and send light to her dark world."

"How do you know that she is ill?" he asked, looking at me with a piercing look that seemed to penetrate into my soul.

"A friend told me. They both go to the same doctor, she is concerned about the Reverend."

There was a moment of silence, then I asked Mr. Conroy, "Will this case harm me, if at some time in the future I should decide to go back into the nightclubs?"

"Yes, it will," he answered seriously, "because you will have to say that you have been arrested and state the charge. Don't worry about that now. The main thing is that you will be all right." I knew that he was my true friend and asked, "Will you come to see me in Carnegie Hall?"

"I would like to. Yes, I would like to very much," he answered smiling down at me.

I bade him good-bye and thanked him for everything. In my heart I blessed him for being truly a good man and a man of God.

SIXTEEN

Spirit Conditions and Miracles

It was now the third week of July and very hot. Loretta and I had decided to stop the lectures. Just a few people had been coming to the sessions.

Andrew Choike had stopped his developing class and Dr. Kaplan had left town. It was very quiet in the studio, Sometimes Betty, who was still being haunted by the spirits, would come in to see me and several times we had gone out to dinner.

July 28th, Ruth Conte called me on the telephone. She wanted to bring her mother, who was visiting her, over to see me.

About 4 p.m. Ruth, her mother and John came into the studio. Looking at her mother I thought, they could be sisters instead of mother and daughter. Ruth was very beautiful but her mother had grace along with her beauty.

After the introductions and the usual small talk, I went into a semi-trance. I saw a big house in the country surrounded with trees and a lovely flower garden to one side. It was a house that anyone would desire, yet I felt an aura of sadness and death. Looking further, I saw an elderly gentleman appear. He was tall and thin and his hair was very white. I described him and Ruth's mother said that the description fit her husband. She asked what I saw for him and I said, "You will outlive him and later think of remarrying." I did not see this for a long, long time. I saw papers and knew that a large legacy would be left.

After I was through speaking to Ruth's mother, John said that everything was going very well but nothing fantastic had occurred. I had told them in my cosmic chart that something very amazing would happen in July pertaining to a large contract in Hollywood and a big house and swimming pool would be manifested.

John kidded me about this miracle and I answered, "John, July is not over. Have faith and believe that a miracle will happen." Everyone laughed and then they left.

It was 7 p.m. when Ruth called. "Maya, John just got the call from California," she exclaimed excitedly. "We are leaving for Los Angeles next week, just as soon as John can make arrangements to get away from the studio. Oh, Maya, miracles do happen, don't they? But most of us don't have the faith to make them happen."

Putting the receiver down, I thanked God for manifesting this wonderful blessing for my good friends. Later John got a five-year contract. The big house and the swimming pool were also manifested.

The next day, Jess Stearn called around 11 a.m. He was excited about the good news. Ruth had contacted him the night before. "May," he exclaimed, "I heard the news, it's fantastic! John and Ruth are going to Hollywood. He got the big contract. It's for five years. A million dollars a year. You visualized it."

"No, Jess. It was God who made it happen. I asked him to help John." At my words Jess laughed and said, "Well, thanks to you and God it happened. Please make something happen for me!" Jess spoke those words with a tone of humor, but I felt the urgent feeling and knew he really meant what he had said.

"I will Jess. I will."

"May, how much longer must I wait? Every time you look into the Akashic record you see such wonderful things for me. Just when are they going to happen?"

"Now, now, Jess. Just be patient and in time good things will come!"

"I hope so," he said and hung up the receiver.

That same night, Jess called again. He sounded angry. "May, what is wrong with Marianne? She came into the office today and complained about you burning candles and incense. She does not believe in your prayers nor the burning of candles to spirits. She thinks your spiritual rites and prayers are the evil Gods. You can go right ahead and help her but I want no part of her. I can't manage myself at the present time, so why should I take on somebody else. We need help so let us work on ourselves."

"Oh, Jess. This is terrible. Was Robert Sylvester there?"

"No, thank God. I was fortunately alone in the office. Believe me, I was happy for both of us that she did not say this before Bob."

"Jess, I am sorry about this. I was trying to remove fears from her subconscious realm. She asked me to help her and the only way I knew was to ask God." I was quiet for a moment, then continued, "Some years ago while Marianne was living in Germany, she had a nervous breakdown that caused her to lose her chance for a fantastic career as an opera singer. Now I will put up these lights and prayers for both of us."

"That's the best idea yet. Thank you for helping me. Bob can stay here for the rest of his life, but I want bigger things to happen for me."

"Jess, you will have big things happen," I answered seriously. One day you will be a great writer of many many books and remember my words. Your third book will be a best seller." I stopped for a moment while Jess waited patiently for me to continue. He knew that it was the inner man who was speaking and felt this was a true message that was coming through me.

"Yes, Jess, after that you will be on the road to great success."

Jess replied in a grave tone of voice, "I believe every word of it. I can't wait for it to happen."

The next day, Marianne arrived very early. I was still busy typing out some charts. I heard her walk in the door, but did not turn around to welcome her.

I felt her nervousness, but continued on with my typing. I knew that she was aware that Jess had contacted me and explained what had transpired in the News Building the day before and naturally expected me to be angry about the matter.

Fifteen or more minutes passed before I finally got up and said calmly, "Marianne, come with me."

Taking her hand I led her into my small back room where the lights were burning on a small altar, then spoke. "You came and asked me to help you. I took you into my studio and introduced you to several friends. I made it possible for you to take singing and dramatic lessons with my friend Betty Cashman. Marianne, why did you tell Jess those awful things about my work? If you did not understand these mystical rituals, then the proper thing to do would have been to ask me. Jess thinks that I am a fool to take you in and spend time and money trying to help you. Why did you do this dreadful thing to me?"

At this point Marianne pulled away and ran back into the large room where she threw herself onto the sofa and cried as if her heart was breaking. I followed her and said, "Crying will not help you this time. I have decided to use the lights for myself. I could use a few T.V. appearances and certainly need help. Charity should begin with me."

Marianne got up and wiped her tears away and then said in a quiet tone of voice, "Please forgive me, Maya. I know I did wrong to tell Jess those awful things about you. I don't know why I did it. Maybe you are right. I am not well. Who knows, I may still be mentally ill."

There was complete silence for a few moments, then she continued. "Maya, you have to help me. I lost my job. I was so upset about the nasty things I said about you to Jess, I did everything wrong this morning and the boss fired me."

I did not answer her, instead, I went over to my desk and sat down to meditate and pray for a few minutes. After I was through, I glanced over at Marianne who was still crying softly and spoke in a trance-like tone, "Marianne, you will get help. First you must pray sincerely about this problem between us. Do this for a few mornings. Someone will offer you a job. It will not be the type of work that you have been doing, but it will be what God wants you to do. You must take it."

Marianne nodded silently. She was too emotional to answer. I went over and put my arms around her and gave her a friendship kiss on the cheek. With gratitude and love in her voice she said between sobs, "Oh, Maya, I am so happy. This morning I felt as if the world had suddenly become dark and lonely. For me it was the end."

"Pray, Marianne and God will guide you always in the right direction. He will hold your hand at all time. Remember this."

"I will, Maya, I will. Thank you for everything," she answered smiling through her tears of joy.

SEVENTEEN

Betty and Marianne

In August of 1955, Betty hired Marianne to stay with her and also to help with some light housework. Her maid came in twice a week. Marianne was told she could take a part-time job, but she felt she should pursue her singing lessons.

I was very happy for both of them, because I was afraid Betty would try to commit suicide, and if no one was around it might be fatal.

Around the last week of August, I was awakened by the continual ringing of my telephone. Looking at the clock, I saw it was almost midnight. It was Marianne. She sounded frantic.

"Maya!" By now almost everyone was calling me Maya. "It's Marianne, I have just come back from Bellevue Hospital. Betty tried to commit suicide. I went out for an hour and came back just in time. The gas was turned on full! Oh, Maya, please come over. I am afraid to stay here all alone."

I dressed quickly and hurried over to 59th Street, where Betty had a luxurious apartment. I found Marianne in tears and shaking like a leaf.

"Oh, Maya, dear, what am I going to do? This brings back the memory of the time I, too, tried to commit suicide."

I made a cup of tea for her and made her drink it. After that, she calmed down, while I prayed for both Betty and Marianne; who now felt she was incapable of protecting Betty.

Around 1 a.m., I decided to leave, but Marianne insisted that I spend the night with her. Going into one of Betty's drawers, she brought out a beautiful satin negligee and insisted that I put it on. I did so, very much against my will.

The next morning, I woke up to find Marianne shaking me. It was very early around eight o'clock and the first thought that came to my mind was wondering why she was waking me up.

"Maya! Get up! Betty's sister is here. She wants to know what has happened to Betty. They called her from the hospital."

Rubbing my eyes, I quickly put on a gown and followed Marianne out to the living room. Betty's sister stood there looking as if she had been crying.

"Reverend Perez! What has happened to my sister?" she asked. Then looking at me closely, she shouted, "You are wearing my sister's best negligee. You and this young woman have taken over my sister's apartment and are wearing her clothes!"

I stared at Mrs. White. I could not believe my ears. Surely, I must be in some sort of nightmare. This could not be the same woman who came to me in July, asking me to pray for her sister. Suddenly, I knew, this apartment was haunted. This is the reason Betty was so afraid and was always thinking that she was being attacked by evil spirits. For the life of me, I could not speak. It was as if I, too, was possessed. I remembered Betty saying, "I was driving over the bridge from New Jersey to New York and a voice was telling me to kill myself." Yes, I had to get out of this apartment or I, too, would be destroyed. Coming back to reality, I heard Mrs. White say, "Take off my sister's clothes and leave this apartment."

I don't remember what I said, it may have been, "I am sorry you do not understand."

Marianne had run into the back room like a scared rabbit. Later she came in and helped me dress.

That afternoon, around 3 p.m., Marianne phoned. "Maya, I am very sorry that Mrs. White spoke so unkindly to you. Please forgive her."

"Marianne, not only Betty needs spiritual help, I am afraid Mrs. White is also in need of help."

"Why did this have to happen, Maya? It's all so very strange."

"Marianne, I believe there is an evil spirit in that apartment. It's like a curse. I have been there twice and each time I felt as if the walls were closing in on me."

"Maya, you are right. I am not happy here. I do admit the apartment is beautiful but it's not a happy place."

There were a few moments of silence then Marianne asked, "Maya, will you be able to go with me to see Betty?"

At first, I hesitated but as she pleaded again, I said, "Sure. Meet me at 4 p.m."

I had never been to a mental hospital, so I was shocked when I saw Betty. She was dressed in an old gown of grey stripes. Her hair was dishevelled and her hands were shaking. We could not go in to kiss her as there was a wired gate that enclosed her. There were many people in that room and it was very noisy. I could not believe that this dishevelled, unkempt woman was my friend Betty. I asked her when she expected to leave this place and she seemed confused.

"Maya, I called my psychiatrist, but he thinks I will be here for a few days. My boss is coming tonight. He may be able to help me. Oh, Maya, please pray for me." Marianne handed her a few dollars and we left.

"Maya," she whispered as we got into a cab. "Betty knows her sister was rude to you. I told her, but I did not tell her about the negligee or that her sister had asked you to leave."

"Marianne, that apartment has to be cleaned out. I will give you a mixture of ammonia and salt. You add a glass of water in the mixture then bless the apartment with it."

"Oh, Maya, I can't do that. Please don't ask me. I don't believe in these mystical rites."

"Marianne, if you don't do what I tell you, then I will have to stop working with you." I was angry and for a moment I felt this girl was impossible and was not ready to learn these mystical works.

We arrived at Carnegie Hall. With a hasty good-bye, I jumped out of the cab and went up to my studio. I felt I had arrived at a door of no return.

The next morning, I got a phone call from Marianne saying that Betty asked if I would bless the apartment. I agreed to come, but with a heavy heart. Marianne was in tears asking me to forgive her.

"Maya," she said tearfully, "Please try to understand. I came from a family who believed in God but never prayed nor did they burn candles or ask forgiveness. This is all new to me. Please Maya, try to understand."

For a moment, my heart went out to this girl, and I said, "Marianne, God is you. When we pray we are really praying to our own God Force. These prayers feed all thought forms and in turn they manifest our desires."

"Oh, Maya, this is all so new. I have never heard any priest or minister say these things. Please be patient with me. I will try to pray," I held her in my arms and patted her. Shortly after, I left.

On the way back to the Hall, I met Mara. She was a young dancer who had come to me for readings while I worked in the nightclubs. She had also visited me in Carnegie Hall and knew I had been arrested for palmistry.

"Hello, Maya," she called out. Then coming up to me, she held out her hand and said, "It's so good to see you. How are you?" In a soft whisper she asked, "How did the case come out?"

"Oh, Mara, I was just fined $15. Everything is fine now."

"Maya, you should never have been arrested. I think you should try to clear your name; especially as you are a minister now."

I smiled at her concern saying, "Mara, I don't have time to do that. Right now I go from one problem to another and they seem to get worse each time."

"Maya, you left the nightclubs. Those people came in to drink and have a good time. Now that you are giving private readings you get sick people. Those who are mentally and spiritually disturbed."

With a sad smile I said, "I know Mara, but it seemed as if it was God who directed me to Carnegie Hall."

"Yes, I know. But how are you doing? Is everything O.K. with you and the Hall? What did they say when you were arrested, or don't they know?"

"Yes, they know." I answered. "My neighbor, Reverend Almo, who had me arrested told them, but so far, I have not heard anything."

"Come, Maya," Mara said, taking my hand, "Let's have a cup of coffee. I have some things to tell you." We took a seat in the back of the coffee shop where it was quiet.

"Maya, I am concerned about you in Carnegie Hall. First, how are you doing financially?"

"Mara, I have almost used up my security deposit and now I have asked my friend Lola to help me again. She has said it will be O. K. but I, too, am worried. I called Miss Sheers and told her next month I will bring in the rent and she told me not to worry. Yet, I do feel as if they are just waiting to see if I will bring it in and also replace what I've used from the security deposit."

Patting my hand Mara said, "Sometime back a friend of mine, Tony, had a studio in Carnegie Hall. He was gay and gave astrology readings. Tony, too, was arrested. Not for readings. It appeared he tried to pick up an undercover cop. Maya, he was such a good person. I always felt so wonderful after I had a reading. Well, he was not able to pay his rent and the Hall told him to leave. This was too much for him to overcome. He committed suicide."

She was quiet for a few moments and I, too, felt sad for this poor young man. I felt as if I had known Tony and it was also my friend who had died.

"Maya, what do you think of gays?" Mara asked still holding my hand.

"They are very high souls who have come down to earth in trapped bodies. Some of them are able to overcome their sex urges and in time these souls usually become priests, ministers or in their next lives, they are given bodies of Light."

"Maya, I have dreamed of Tony and he has told me he is doing the work of the Inner Masters. He is now helping gays to be celibates. Is this possible?"

"Yes," I answered, "it is possible that Tony is doing this work. We must pray for him."

Two nights later, I had a vision of Tony. I had never met him, yet I knew this handsome young man, that I met in the garden, was Tony. He thanked me for the prayers and said, "Maya, I am working to help

God. It is very important that I do this work, so when I come back to life, I will be a much higher soul. I have a center and many souls who are blocked with sexual desires come to me for healings."

We walked around the garden which was filled with beautiful flowers and also fruit trees.

The next morning as I woke up, I felt as if I had had a spiritual cleansing. For a long time I lay in bed and felt the healing waters of life flowing through my whole being.

Around the late part of September, I woke up with a voice saying, "Go and talk to the administration department of Carnegie Hall." I got up, prayed, then dressed and went up to the office. It was just after 10 a.m. when I arrived. First, I visited Miss Sheers who was happy to see me. After a short conversation, she advised me to speak to the head of the office; a medium size man with a round face and short blond hair. I was just about to give a young girl, in the office, my check for the month of October, when Mr. Benson came up and said, "Miss Perez, we can't accept your check. You have been arrested and it's against the policy of Carnegie Hall to accept your check and let you stay."

I stood in front of the man in a state of shock. I tried to say something but no sound or words came out. Suddenly, as if I was possessed, I knelt down and in a very loud tone of voice shouted, "Father, forgive him. Forgive him, God." He turned to run but I held on to his coat and I heard him say, "Oh, my God, she is crazy." I don't know how long I held on to him but after awhile he pulled himself away and ran to his room at the back of the office. As if in a deep trance, I followed him. He saw me coming down the hall but he was unable to close the door fast enough. I walked in his part of the office saying in a soft tone of voice, "Father he does not understand. Please forgive him."

I looked at the man who seemed as if he were about to have a stroke, but yet, I could not stop. I felt I was in a trance-like state. After walking around his chair and desk, I again went back to the entrance of the office and sat in a chair where I could still see Mr. Benson. He was sitting there as if in shock and I continued to pray. About half an hour later, I heard the girl in the front office saying, "Miss Perez, please go home. Please go home."

It may have been the young girl's soothing voice or it may have been that the spirit of the gay young man, who had committed suicide, had left me. Quietly I got up and left.

EIGHTEEN

Vindicated and Re-established

On the 21st of October, my stay at Carnegie Hall came to an end. The experiences there were tremendous, traumatic, and at times cruel. Now I am happy that God gave me these difficult problems in order for me to bloom forth as a whole individual.

After leaving Carnegie Hall I went to stay with Reverend Eunice Parker, and it was she who, with the mutual help of Jess Stearn, helped me fine renewed energy so that I could cope with the material world.

One day Jess called to ask if I could come over with a couple of friends. I agreed and he later came in with two beautiful girls. One of the girls worked in an East Side club. She was a singer and was interested in the club because a friend owned it. She asked if I would care to go back in the nightclubs and I answered vehemently, "No, no, I am definitely through with that side of life."

Jess smiled at me and asked jokingly, "Are you quite sure?" In a serious tone I answered, "Only if God wishes me to go back, and if so, he will open the way for me."

Strangely enough, one month later I met a theatrical agent on the street, who was happy to see me and asked if I was doing anything in particular.

Upon receiving my negative reply he asked for my phone number saying, "I have a client who is searching for a palmist and who has exactly the type of place where you would enjoy working. Take my card and call me soon."

With a faraway look, I said, "Ernie, I am not interested in working in the nightclubs. I have gone into the religious fields."

My friend looked at me as if trying to find out if I were all there, then tipped his hat and went off saying, "Call me if you change your mind."

Over the telephone that evening I told Jess about the offer. Without hesitation he said quickly, "What are you waiting for? You told me if God wanted you to go back into the nightclubs, he would open up the way."

The next morning I called Ernie, who was delighted to hear my voice and asked if I had changed my mind. When I told him, "Yes," he asked if I still had my club license, and if not, I should obtain it immediately, as the job was mine. He had spoken to the owner and it was settled.

The next Monday I went down to the license bureau. It was a dreary November day and in my heart I felt blue and heavy. I was concerned about what I should say on the report. I knew that it was important for me to tell the truth about my arrest. If I told an untruth, it would be found out, so it had to be the truth and nothing else.

The clerk remembered me and smiled, but I just said, "Hello," and did not smile back. He said nothing as I took the paper from him. When I returned the report, which he hastily examined, I saw a worried expression on his face as he asked in a shocked tone of voice, "Miss Perez, how did you come to be arrested? You are a licensed palmist. What happened?"

With tears in my eyes I explained about the vision which inspired me to take a studio in Carnegie Hall, then of the policewoman and my subsequent arrest.

Still very puzzled he said softly, "Yes, but this is serious. Let me call the Captain. He is new here and a very nice man."

A few minutes passed while I impatiently waited outside. The clerk came back with a tall man whom he introduced to me as the new Captain. The Captain greeted me with a kind shy smile. After the clerk left he looked at me seriously and asked, "Miss Perez, I understand that you have been a licensed palmist for many years. How did you get arrested?"

I knew it would be rather difficult to tell my story with all the people milling around, so I motioned for him to come over to the far corner before explaining the situation. With tears streaming down my face I said, "I had a vision which inspired me to take a studio in Carnegie Hall in order to give lectures and help people. That was my sole purpose. A policewoman came into my studio and asked for a consultation. After I was through she put up her hand and asked me to tell her about her life line. I did not even look at her hand, but nevertheless she came back with another woman and informed me that she was arresting me on the charge of palmistry."

The Captain listened intently to my story then excused himself and went back into his office. A few minutes passed while I composed myself and waited for him to come back with the verdict.

Coming back, he looked at me and smiled, saying, "Miss Perez, I called the precinct and spoke to one of the clerks who said that it was a minor charge with a very small fine of fifteen dollars. The clerk spoke highly of you and said that you were a very fine person."

At those words the tears flowed and I wept as if my heart was breaking. The Captain looked at me in astonishment and asked, "Why are you crying? We are going to make an exception with your case because the nightclubs need more people like you."

At his kind words again I wept and just could not stop. By now the Captain was very puzzled about my condition, especially as several persons were looking skeptically at him and wondering what he was doing to make me cry so hard.

"Miss Perez," he said in a soothing tone of voice, "I told you that we were going to give you your license, why are you still crying?"

I knew that he was embarrassed, but I could not help myself. Finally, through the tears I blurted out, "I am crying because I am so happy. I thought the world was so evil and that was the reason I left the nightclubs to get away from the material life. Now, I realize that the religious people are not sincere or truly good as they profess to be. It was in the religious field that I was crucified and pushed down into the pit of despair."

The Captain patted my arm saying, "I understand. Go over to that policeman who is not busy and he will give you the license."

"Thank you, oh, thank you very much," I exclaimed, trying to smile through my tears.

When I sat down in the empty seat next to the policeman who remembered me, he asked, "What is wrong?"

I told him what had transpired since he saw me, and he said kindly, "Look, Miss Perez, if anyone bothers you, just come here, we will take care of them for you. Remember, we are your friends."

I nodded, for one moment I could not speak. My heart was filled with an indescribable joy that was beyond words.

Around the Christmas season, I was standing on the subway platform when I saw the good Captain with a lady whom I immediately knew was his wife. He came over and shook my hand, then guided me back to the lady saying, "Dear, this is Miss Perez, the lady I told you about who had a studio in Carnegie Hall."

His wife smiled and greeted me saying, "Oh, Miss Perez, my husband has spoken of you many times. I am happy we finally met. Where are you working?"

I gave her the name of the club and the address. I felt she wanted to prolong the conversation in order to get an invitation to come in and visit with me, but just then the train pulled into the station and the Captain diplomatically turned his wife away. They waved good-bye, leaving me with a warm and happy glow. January 15th, I started to work at Cole's restaurant and club on Lexington Avenue and 61st Street, in New York.

NINETEEN

Accident on a City Bus

On March 11, 1956, I went to a lecture with Nellie, a new friend. The lecturer was Reverend Eunice Parker. A little after 10 p.m., we left the lecture hall and strolled along 50th Street.

"Nellie, I feel wonderful," I said as we crossed over to take the bus on Lexington Avenue. "Do you think that God has given me a new body to take with me when I go over?"

Nellie did not answer for a few moments. Now I know that she was trying to find the right words in order to change my thinking.

"Why do you persist in taking a vision so seriously, Maya?" she asked quietly. "God is not going to take you away from us, not for a long time. You, of all people, should be the last to think of going over. The world is so very confused and it's going to get worse. We need you here."

"Nellie, dear," I answered in a positive tone, "it is all settled. My brother told me that this is the year. Last year I left the nightclubs so that I could help people. Now, I am ready to go over."

Just then a bus came along. We got on and Nellie said, "Go sit down and I will pay the fares."

Suddenly, the bus lurched forward. I clutched for the bar but it gave way. I fell and struck my back on the edge of the seat.

Everything became confused and blurred. I heard Nellie asking me if I was hurt. I tried to speak, but no sound came out as I lay there in shock. Someone assisted Nellie to help me onto a seat.

The driver asked Nellie if she wanted to call an ambulance. I heard Nellie's voice from far away. She asked me if I wanted to go to a hospital. I felt as if the woman on the seat was not me. No, that couldn't be me for I was vital and full of life. Finally, I answered Nellie saying, "No, please, don't call an ambulance. I don't want to go to a hospital." I stopped to get my breath then continued, "Let me try to walk home."

Nellie went back and forth giving the driver information and writing on a card that the driver had given to her. A woman came and sat next to me. She told me that the bar was loose. Nellie came back and they both examined the bar, then went to the driver and told him of the defect.

I lived about half a block from the bus stop. When we arrived at my apartment, Nellie helped me to undress. There were black and blue marks on my back, and on my lower spine there was a large lump.

In pain and fear, I started to cry saying, "Oh, Nellie, I had another injury to my spine a few years ago. It was a broken coccyx caused by an automobile accident and at the time the doctors did not think that I would ever walk again.

"Don't worry, Maya dear," Nellie said consolingly, "I will call you in the morning. I am sure that you will be all right." Putting on her wrap, she kissed me and left.

The following morning, I could not get out of bed. I was stiff and full of pain. Nellie tried to contact me by phone but getting no response she took a taxi and came over. When she got there, the landlady was giving me a cup of broth. After a short conversation with Nellie about my accident, Mrs. Myers left the apartment to attend to some neglected business matters.

Nellie sat on the side of my bed, which I used as a couch during the day.

"Maya dear," she asked gently combing back my hair "Wouldn't you like to see a doctor? Please tell me what I can do for you. I feel that we should inform the bus company of your illness, then get you to a hospital."

"No, Nellie," I answered trying to get up to sip the broth. "I do not want a doctor. I need prayer to make my body strong and well. I have tried to pray, but I am so weak, and my mind cannot seem to focus. I lie here so helpless, wondering, is this me? How did it happen so quickly? Yesterday, I was well and happy. Nellie, I don't mind dying, but God knows, I don't want to be an invalid. I feel powerless. Oh, my God, why?"

Nellie looked at me, she was shocked and angry at my senseless ravings. "Maya, why do you ask God? For years you have been creating this accident in your mind. You created this accident. You asked for it. Now, that God has given it to you, you lie there and ask why?"

I stared at Nellie not believing my ears. She was always so kind and loving to me.

"I am not scolding you, Maya, all I ask is for you to stop believing this silly vision and I'm sure that all will be well. I can't understand you, or for that matter, all the teachers. They say everything is created by thought, and they tell you not to think negative, but when trouble comes to them, it is the worst. Why don't you people practice what you preach?'

I looked at Nellie feeling a deep compassion for her. I then asked, "How do you know that the vision was silly? Everything is ordained by a big hand or by a host of great minds. This accident was planned long ago and for this reason Cecil came through and implanted the vision in my mind. I still believe I am going to die."

She looked down at me sympathetically and continued in a softer voice, "Maybe you will die, Maya, but not physically. There are many types of death. We can die mentally and yet live in the body. There are many people who are spiritually dead. They walk, they talk, but the divine spirit within is actually dead."

Suddenly, Nellie thought that it was a waste of time to try to change my mind, so she got up and straightened out the apartment. When she was through, she asked if there was anything else that she could do.

"No, dear," I answered listlessly, then remembered that I had not yet called the restaurant to tell them of my accident. I asked Nellie to go in and tell Mrs. Cole what had happened.

Two days passed and I still did not feel any better. I took a cab over to Metropolitan Hospital. After a thorough examination and X-ray, Dr. Larry called me into his private office. Giving me a chair he said gently, " Miss Perez, we find no break in your back, but don't feel happy, for you have contusions to the lower lumbar vertebras. You will have trouble for a long time, as a matter of fact, it will get worse before it gets better.".

I sat there with tears streaming down my face. How could I get worse when already I felt as if my back was being torn in two?

"Now, my advice to you would be to get a good lawyer and sue the bus company. Don't quote me, please. I am just telling you this out of kindness. Remember, get a private doctor."

"I don't have money, doctor," I said still crying. "I work in a restaurant reading palms, but I don't think that I will be able to work for a long time."

The doctor looked at me with new interest. "You tell fortunes, read palms?" I nodded, and he continued quietly, "I would like to help you, but in this case, you will be better off with a private doctor. Get a doctor with the understanding that the bus company will pay you. You have a witness, so what are you waiting for?"

"Doctor, it's not just a case of suing the bus company." I stopped to catch my breath as the pain moved up my neck. I held my hands before my face. After it had passed I continued, "Many years ago I lost a dear brother who returned to me in a vision. He looked very ill and I felt that I could help him if I were there. He read my thoughts and said to me, "No, don't come now, but in 1956 you will be with me." I believed this and lived thinking that I would pass out of the body this year. I did not think that I would become an invalid. Don't you see? There is more to this than meets the eye!"

The doctor looked at me and a deep feeling of understanding passed between us as he said, "I, too, have had visions. Once with my mother, who had just passed over. The other time, it was of a sister who was very ill; we all thought that she was going to die, but I had a vision that she was going to get better. These visions were very real. They made a deep impression on me. I shall never forget them. I believe that our loved ones go to a place of rest and peace, according to what they have done here, but my advice to you is to start believing that you are going to get well."

"Yes, doctor," I said philosophically, "such advice is very sound and good, but how can I follow it? Did you not say that I would get worse before I got better, and that my injury was very serious?"

"Now, now," answered the doctor in a pacifying voice, "you go home and get a private doctor soon. There are other patients waiting for me."

I left the hospital with a feeling of guilt for having talked so much. I was disturbed about telling him about my visions. I knew that everything I said would be put on my record.

The next day Betty Campbell, a close friend of mine, spoke to her private physician, Dr. Nonas, who agreed to accept my case providing the bus company paid him for his services. After Nellie called the bus company and got their permission, I went to see Dr. Nonas and remained his patient for a long time.

In May, someone told me of the Diplomat Hotel on the West Side, where I could get room service. At this point I could not bend over without going through excruciating pain. Shortly after moving to this hotel, I went to the Polyclinic Hospital for a check-up, and was told just as Dr. Larry had said, that I was steadily becoming worse. Each time after eating, my heart would start to pound. At times it felt like hammers beating against my body. I spoke to my physician Dr. Nonas and he advised me to try eating everything and then discarding the foods that disagreed with me. Everything was disagreeing with my system, so I finally stopped eating solid foods and instead I resorted to a little soup or drank juices.

In June there was a series of write-ups about mystics and palm readers working in the various clubs around New York City. It was in the New York *News*. I was the last subject in the series and that article was considered the best of all by those who had read it.

I was later chided by Zaza, who worked at Armando's across the street from Cole's restaurant. She said that Robert Sylvester was a close friend of Jess Stearn, who favored me. To this silly remark I only smiled. I was very fond of this amazing woman. Usually, when Zaza was finished with her clients, she would come over to Cole's and have a drink with me. I would order a lemonade and sip it while we talked. Often the topic of conversation between us was psychic phenomena, which we both loved to discuss.

TWENTY

Yuri Andropov and a Man Named Michael

One afternoon in June 1956, I was reading the palm of a lady friend. She was experiencing many problems, and the practical advice I was offering seemed to provide the solace she needed. During the reading, I noticed two men standing at the bar. We were sitting quite close to them, so it was relatively easy for our eyes to meet. The older of the two men, a tall, striking-looking man, kept glancing over at me. His apparent fascination with what I was doing struck me with a bit of humor, but I must admit I was just as curious about him. He looked familiar to me, but I just couldn't place his somewhat stern, piercing appearance. Finally, my lady friend left, and within an instant this man came to my table and asked to have his palm read. I cordially smiled, and he sat down next to me. When I looked at his palm, I immediately noticed the many strange lines that foretold his inner complex personality. I was silent for a few moments and then said, "You have a very, very complex nature." Without hesitation and with a most serious expression he replied, "What do you mean?"

I paused for a moment and said, "You have three natures in your body." I was quite certain he didn't understand what I meant, but nevertheless, he remained silent so I continued. "Your work takes you to many countries, and at times it could be very dangerous." He nodded in agreement, but continued to remain silent. The reading shifted to his family. I visualized three children, but he acknowledged two, a son and a daughter. I had a strong feeling about his extraordinary affection for his daughter and that she likewise adored him with equal fervor. In contrast, I felt his son was close to his mother, and although I had no special feelings about his relationship with his wife, I did sense a separation, but not a divorce.

Still unaware of who this intriguing man was, I asked him his birthday. He replied, "June 15, 1914." A shudder ran through my whole being. He must have sensed my fear, and although I uttered nothing, he asked, "Is this a bad birthday?"

"No," I answered in a hushed voice, "it's not bad, but you have great powers that must be used for the purpose of helping humanity."

Again silence. Neither of us spoke. My thoughts were racing, even though my actions were still. Good God, 6-6-6! His birthday is the dreaded number in the Holy Bible. It's the number of the beast! All at once, all the implications of 6-6-6 rushed in and out of my head. I thought of my sister. My poor sister. She, too, has this birth number and her life has been a living hell. She has been plagued by illness after illness, and although her fights to survive each illness have been successful, her life has been marked by dissatisfaction. Always dissatisfaction. She was forever moving and building a new home (when her health permitted!). She seemed to find little peace in whatever she did.

In a few moments, this 6-6-6 man broke the silence and asked, "How do you get your powers?"

I gave him a little smile and told him that I talk to "my spirits." With an amused grin, he thanked me for the reading and left.

A few days later, he appeared again. I was sitting in the back of the restaurant sipping some chicken broth and nibbling on a piece of dry toast. "Hello, remember me? I am Yuri," he said in a genuinely warm demeanor. *Remember him*! How could I forget the man with the dreaded number! I smiled, nodded and made room for him next to me. The waitress came over and Yuri asked for a sandwich and a cup of tea. I was just finishing my broth, and when the waitress took away my cup and I told her that was all I wanted, Yuri looked puzzled.

"Is that all you are having for lunch?" he asked with sincere concern.

"Yes, I haven't been able to eat heavy food since my accident earlier this year. Even this broth seems to bother me at times. "

He leaned over close to me and said, "I'm so sorry. How did it happen?" His interest seemed so genuine that I began to tell him the unfortunate circumstances that led to my lightweight appetite. I had been on a bus, and the bar that I was holding onto suddenly broke. Before I realized what was happening, I had fallen and struck my lower back in the fall. The injuries to my lower back caused serious problems to my digestive system, and almost anything I ate would result in gastric or stomach ailments. Initially, all I could eat was a piece of dry toast and a cup of weak tea. As time went on, I could tolerate chicken broth and a little rice fairly well. Yet, as I was telling Yuri, there were still times when even this minute meal was uncomfortable for me. Yuri listened with great intensity as I told him my tale of woe. During this brief meeting with him, I was doing most of the talking, and after he finished his sandwich, he again politely said how sorry he was to learn of my problems. At that he left the restaurant.

After Yuri was gone, I began to ask myself—why did I meet this powerful man at a time when I was so ill that doctors were giving me just a few months to live. (I hadn't disclosed this to Yuri!) What *was* the karma between us? By this time, I realized that Yuri was the head of the KGB in Russia, but my concern was OUR relationship, and that awesome 6-6-6. Was Yuri a beast, a saint or the son of the living God? As the questions kept flooding my mind, I thought back to the time when I was a little girl. I was a mere toddler, just three years old and as most little girls enjoy playing with dolls, I was no exception. I remembered, again, that morning when the whirling light formed above my head. The light came suddenly, and its memory is as clear as if I saw it yesterday. From within, I heard a Being speaking. "I do not wish to live this life, because I am going to be bad. I do not wish to be bad." As quickly as it came, the light disappeared, and thinking nothing, I went on playing with my doll. However, that vision has been significant throughout my life. Whenever I have been in great danger, I've asked God for more time. Unquestionably, I needed that time then. Instinctively, I knew there was a reason for this man coming into my life, and important reason. Unless I was given the time to understand, to see if there was a greater work that must be done by this man and by myself, I felt we couldn't fulfill whatever destinies we were meant to fulfill. I also instinctively knew that Yuri and I had lived many past lives together. But why did he seem to be running now? Who was he running from and why? I had so many questions.

"Oh, God," I thought, "give me the time to understand the answers I know you want me to have!"

Weeks went by and I saw Yuri many times. He come in almost every other night, and everyone began to think he was my boy friend

Although I had outsmarted the doctor's predictions (of course, with the grace of God!), my health was still not at a premium. It must have been the last week of July or early August, 1956, when I saw Yuri again. This time he wasn't alone. He had brought with him a tall, handsome, distinguished gentleman who was decidedly younger than Yuri and just as intriguing. They were standing at the bar, and I was talking with a friend not far from where they were. As soon as my friend left, Yuri briskly walked over toward me, followed by his companion.

"This is Michael," he blurted. "Tell him something." Yuri sat down, but Michael remained standing, authoritatively, I might add. Michael had an amused smile on his face as he said, "What do you see for me?" The sound of his voice literally propelled me up. Suddenly I was standing directly in front of him. I felt an abundance of energy and light surge from my solar plexus, and a feeling of oneness seemed to connect us. As if hypnotized, I exclaimed, "You will one day be the top power in your country."

I cannot describe the look of ecstasy that permeated Michael's face. It was absolutely sublime. Although at that time I knew him only as

Michael, we both knew that my prophecy would one day come true and indeed it did come true in 1985 when Michael, who we know as Mikhail S. Gorbachev, became General Secretary of the Soviet Union.

At that moment my mind was focused on Michael, but shouts from Yuri startled me.

"Do you *know* who he is?" Yuri exclaimed, "do you know who is he is? Don't help him. He is bad!" As Yuri continued to rant and rave, both Michael and I kept calm. Within a few moments, I felt the surge of energy between us subside, and Michael left the restaurant.

I sat down next to Yuri. I was baffled by his behavior. Why had he been so disturbed? Why didn't he want me to help Michael? Insecurity? Jealousy? True, Michael was younger than Yuri, perhaps by twelve or fifteen years or so. He was good looking and yes, he dressed impeccably. Everything suggested wealth and luxury. But Yuri was his boss! Did Michael's "king-like" attitude so unnerve him for a particular reason? Yes, I thought, Yuri—this conservatively-dressed and certainly enigmatic man—was jealous of this younger man, even though he was his superior.

Yuri was quiet, almost stoic. It would be an understatement to say that he was embarrassed by his out burst of words. In a compassionate voice I told him "You, too, will be a great power, not only in this world, but in the next." He seemed stunned by my inference of the "next world."

"Why do you say this? Do you think I am going to die?"

"No, no," I quickly assured him. "I just see special things for you. Your destiny is special."

That night I prayed about the strange phenomenon and strong energy that reverberated between Michael and myself. My life had been replete with odd incidents and happenings that were not of this world, but this was the first time I had experienced energy being manifested from the solar plexus area to another being. Many of my friends are involved in metaphysics, but in my recollection, none had ever remarked about this type of miraculous happening.

For what seemed to be a long time, I prayed and meditated for answers, the right answers. I kept recalling the ecstasy that had appeared on Michael's face, and I kept sensing the great power I knew he'd have on this planet. My prayers continued, but answers were not coming forth. Soon I drifted off to sleep, and the focus of my dreams reflected the psychic vibrations I was receiving not on Michael, but on Yuri. I dreamt there was a great uprising. Hundreds of people were angry, and I saw them running with sticks, in trucks and fighting man-to-man. Riots were breaking out all over, and heavily armed soldiers were shooting at the people. Then I saw Yuri. He was standing on a platform, confident, strong, powerful. He was addressing a large group of men and women, and he so had their attention that they appeared to be hypnotized by him. I thought, my God, Yuri is a master! He's quieting down these people and restoring order. As that thought was occurring in my mind, Yuri glanced over at me, and our eyes met. I immediately awakened and began to pray, the "ohms." Remember, the year was 1956. It was summer and Yuri Andropov was running away from his destiny. The Hungarian people took to the streets in October and November of that year in a bloody revolt, and what I came to realize was that God was allowing me to look into the Akashic record. I was seeing a view of what was to happen thousands of miles away, months before it occurred. In my mind, Yuri was the son of God in the "lower realms" and he was vibrating as a teacher of life on all planes of consciousness.

The very next afternoon, Yuri returned to the club. He was alone and I was with a friend when I saw him walk through the door. As soon as my friend left, he came to my table. His manner seemed subdued and I wondered if something had happened. He looked at me and said, "Do you know who I am?" Smiling, I replied, "Yes, I do."

For several minutes, he was silent. I patiently waited and then broke the silence with a question. I asked him if he'd had a dream the previous night. Puzzled, he said, "Yes, but it was a nightmare."

Gently I asked him if he wished to tell me about it. I felt certain his dream would mirror mine, but I wanted to hear his words telling me in his own style. In a simple sentence or two, he said, "Yes, I'll tell you. I dreamed I was fighting a battle, and in the end, I won the war."

My thoughts were confirmed. "Yuri," I said, "I had a dream, too, about you. There was an uprising and many people were enraged. In the end you spoke to a large group of men and women and were able to calm their fears."

"Maya," he said in a voice that was almost a whisper, "you are amazing. How do you know these things?"

I avoided his question and instead responded in a clear, certain tone, "You, my friend, are the one that's amazing. Yesterday, when I gave Michael his message, a strange energy emitted from my solar plexus and connected with his solar plexus. I knew it was a true message, and it was you, Yuri, that gave me the power to give Michael that message."

"But you gave him a better message than the one you gave me," Yuri insisted. Just like a jealous little boy, I thought to myself.

Smiling at Yuri, I said, "He will be the top power in his country one day. But you, Yuri, you will rise to be a power not just in this world, but in the world of spirit."

He looked at me, questioning, uncomfortable. "I do not like that message. Am I going to die?"

I knew my message disturbed him because he was again repeating his question about his own mortality.

"Eventually we all die, Yuri, but you have special work to fulfill. God will help you and I will pray for you." He softened and said, "Thank you, Maya, I need all the prayers I can get."

About a week had passed. It was in the middle of August, and the humidity of the New York sun was weighing heavily on everyone. I was again sitting in the back of the restaurant, when Yuri walked in.

As he sat down next to me, he asked, "What are you doing tomorrow?"

Since "tomorrow" was a Sunday, I told him I was planning on visiting my cousin Gladys and her daughter, Renee. They lived on Long Island near to the beach at Fire Island. Yuri seemed to like what he was hearing and in a manner of voice that was most pleasant, he said, "Maya, I have my daughter, Irina, here with me, and I'd like to take her to the beach. I have a car." His words were almost pleading. I asked him how old Irina was, and he said she was seven.

"Well, I could bring my granddaughter Lois and my grandson Richard is already there at my cousins. He is four and Lois is six. They will all be good company for each other."

"Then I can bring Irina?" Yuri asked.

"Yes, of course. I'll call my cousin and tell her you and Irina will be with me. I'm sure there won't be a problem."

After he left, I thought, "Amazing!" What a transformation from the quiet Yuri, the stern Yuri to a man who is being so outgoing and friendly. In my meditations that evening, I asked for answers to the sudden change of tone and attitude. The answers came. Now that he knows you are aware of his career and who he is, he feels more secure—he feels safe. Yes, that's it. I've gained his confidence. I felt as if a dark night had blossomed into a lovely morning.

That night I phoned my daughter, Yvonne. I told her of my plans to visit Gladys and Renee, and she had no opposition to my taking Lois with me. I told her I'd be by at about 8 a.m. to pick up my granddaughter.

The next morning, Yuri arrived at my hotel at 7:30 a.m. He was happy, cheerful, and his daughter, Irina, was as lovely as he'd described.

Sweet, pretty, and friendly, Irina was looking forward to the day with great anticipation.

Once we picked Lois up, we were on our way to my cousins. The two children sat in the back of the car, and instantaneously they were like old friends, laughing and enjoying the countryside. Yuri and I chatted about the children, and our conversation was light. This was to be a "fun" day and the chatter between us was purely social. All went well until we arrived at Mastic, Long Island, where my cousins, Gladys and Renee, lived. Yuri had a map of Long Island, but the streets of Mastic were not clearly delineated. He had expected me to direct him to my cousins' house, and as hard as I tried, I could not remember where they lived! Yuri was being as diplomatic as possible, but I sensed his agitation and impatience, and quite frankly, I couldn't blame him.

After going around in circles for a while, I suggested that we go to the railroad station and call Gladys. We did and within minutes, Renee met us at the station. We followed her to my cousins' house, just in time for lunch. By that time, we were back in good spirits again, and Gladys prepared some tea and sandwiches for us. I was still having problems with eating, so I opted for the chicken broth Gladys had made for me that morning.

Lunch went well. Yuri, Gladys, Renee and I talked about the trip to Mastic while the children played in the garden together. Seeing the children together was a joy in itself. Their rapport was incredible. It was as if they'd known each other all their lives.

We left for Fire Island about 1:30 p.m., using Yuri's car. Irina sat in front with her father, while Renee, Lois, Richard and I were in back. Gladys remained at home. Immediately I noticed how little Irina loved to touch her father's face. It was as if she were afraid he would disappear, so she kept touching his face to make certain he was still near. Both Renee and I remarked about this unusual adoration of daughter for father. I was sure it was karmic. I'd picked up this sensitivity when I'd first met with Yuri, and now seeing this attraction before my eyes, all my earlier feelings were substantiated.

When we arrived at the beach, the children headed straight for the water. Yuri, looking as though he was having the time of his life, set out to teach the girls how to swim. Irina was quite good, but it was obvious that Lois needed many more lessons. Renee and I were sitting under the shade of the umbrella, comfortable as could be. Before long, the conversation drifted to Yuri and Irina. Renee was expressing her feeling about the situation and commenting on how she felt about Irina. "She's so afraid of losing her father."

"I know," I replied, "this is the tie that will make Yuri go back to his home. He is very confused, Renee. Please pray for him."

"I will," she chuckled. Yes, she was laughing! Renee had this incredible habit of always laughing at the most serious of conversations. I really believe this has been her way of surviving several of her own grave problems. She just laughs her way through them!

I told her to hush, because I saw Yuri approaching us. "Why don't you girls come in the water?" he asked. We graciously declined, and in watching Yuri gently pat dry his precious Irina. I went within to ask my spirits, "Why such deep devotion?" I heard a voice speak to me. "Irina is the key that will open up the door for her father to face his responsibilities and go back to his home. His greater destiny will be fulfilled in his home of birth."

Late that afternoon, around 4 p.m., Renee took the children to a hot dog stand for some refreshments. They brought back food for everyone, and although I couldn't eat any of it, I wasn't the least bit jealous! Food was upsetting to me at that time, due to the fall I had taken on a bus, so I'd lost my desire for it. I was just glad to see everyone else enjoy themselves, and I sipped on some iced tea Gladys had made for me. After the children finished their hot dogs and cokes, Renee took Irina and Lois for a walk. That gave Yuri the perfect opportunity he had been waiting for.

He fixed the umbrella to give him some greater shade and sat beside me.

"Maya, I had another vision last night. I was in a large field with Michael. I was teaching him to fly, but I could not get him off the ground. Finally, I was so tired, I just gave up. Then, suddenly, he began to fly, and he was enjoying it. What do you make of this dream?"

I said, "Yuri, you have been Michael's boss a long time, so he has listened to you; but now he feels you are not in tune with your comrades, and he does not want to follow your radical ideas. Michael wants to do his own thing. When you stopped pushing him, he flew on his own power. Subconsciously, he admires you, but his conscious mind thinks you are crazy. This is why your subconscious mind gave me the power to release the vital energy from my solar plexus. It, in turn, gave me the message that will one day come true."

"But how about *me*?" Yuri demanded. "What do you see for me, except that I am blocked and stubborn." A smile came quickly to my face, for Yuri had answered his own question.

"Yes, Yuri, I agree that you are blocked and also very stubborn. I also agree with Michael. He will stay with his country and help them to purify their outer and inner faults. He is not running away like a scared rabbit."

For a few minutes, we were both silent. Then Yuri blurted out, "You are agreeing with him, Maya! He thought I was crazy to be following you for the answers to my problems!"

His anger was mounting, so I remained quiet and gently patted his hand. I thought to myself, thank God Yuri came to me! He had to speak to someone. If he'd spoken his thoughts to another, he might have received negative advice. I was so thankful he had been brought to me. Otherwise, he might have risked the death of his Higher Self.

It was now close to 6 p.m. and most people had left the beach. I saw Renee and the children approaching, so I quickly said to Yuri, "Have no fear, Yuri. I will send you light. Soon you will be guided up the spiritual path. Even as I speak I can see you walking into a golden light." Yuri bowed his head in his arms, and for a moment I felt God had reached his innermost soul.

Arriving at my cousins' home, everyone had a cocktail, except me. Even the children had pink lemonade. Renee turned on the radio and we listened to music. After that Gladys served dinner. I had chicken soup and toast.

Around 8 p.m., we left for the city. The two children sat in the back seat, and Yuri and I sat in the front. After a while, we could tell they were sleeping soundly. Yuri had wrapped a blanket around them.

We had no problem going home. Yuri had found a map of Mastic, Long Island, and had studied it. There was a long period of silence while he found his way out of Mastic and onto the Long Island highway.

As we sped along the highway, my mind reflected over the two children sleeping in the back of the car. What was the difference between these two children? Irina was seven, yet she acted like a teenager. She spoke English fluently, and was quite disciplined. Never once had she made a mistake or asked a question that was not in order. Here was my granddaughter, a normal six-year-old, but without the inner poise and awareness that Irina seemed to possess. Why was this? There must be something more to the Russians than the outer world knew. What was their secret? Thinking more deeply, the answer came. They are being trained for a challenging and more difficult way of life. Spirit God is training them for something special. They are being disciplined for a great work.

Just then, I heard Yuri's voice, "Tell me about my strange birthday and destiny. Do you really believe that I am different?"

I replied, "Yes, Yuri, you are different, like me. You have a special destiny path. Your birthday, which is 6-6-6 gives you the power to be a teacher on all the planes of consciousness. At present, you are in a 6 personal year," I continued, "and some day, you will understand your true purpose in this life."

"What does a 6 personal year mean?" he asked, as we paused in the traffic.

"It means you are learning your lessons in the inner schools as you sleep at night. Have you had dreams where you were in a school?"

With an amazed look on his face he replied, "Yes, remember the dream we both had last week of my speaking to a large group of people? I have had that dream many times. Sometimes I am speaking, other times, a man or woman is speaking and I am in the audience. Then there are times when I am relating my problems to a man who appears to be a guru, and I usually wake up with the solution to my most difficult problems. Within the last two years, I have not been able to get my problems solved. Why is this?"

I thought for a few moments then answered, "It is because you are running away from yourself. Go back home and face your problems there. When you stop resisting and return to fulfill your destiny, then and only then will the Inner Masters be able to give you the advice that you need. Peace will then manifest in your inner and outer worlds. By the end of summer you will know why you should go back home. Yuri said nothing, just shook his head slowly.

Silently, I prayed that he find peace within his innermost being.

I knew this man was a great soul and that he was born of a womb that was full of turmoil. Yuri was conceived in 1913, four years before the revolution in Russia in 1917. His father was involved in the political movement, and he was full of resentment for the rich people who had taken everything from the poor, and also for the church which had done the same thing. His mother loved the church, but was afraid to speak up, therefore her innermost thoughts were of great conflict and anguish. Thoughts become thought forms, and thought forms become spirits who can either protect or destroy us. Yuri was created with multiple personalities. Some were very powerful and negative, others were very powerful and positive. At this point he was making a transition from the negative to the positive. Therefore, in 1956, he was between planes of consciousness and did not truly know who he was. Many people at this state of life can become insane, and many of Yuri's comrades were thinking that indeed he was insane. I knew that the next year, 1957, he would become aware of his purpose in life, and in time adjust to his true self. Yuri did not like his work, nor did he like himself. Many of us go through this stage in life, but we are able to lift up our consciousness through meditation and deep sincere prayers. Unfortunately, because of his total disbelief in the God Force within, this was very difficult for him to accomplish. Yet, I was aware of this man's goodness, and that he was talking to himself. This was a form of prayer. At the present time there were two people that he believed in, a female friend and me. If we failed him, his entire soul would be lost.

Just at that moment, I was awakened from my reverie. "Maya, you said Michael will be a top power in his country one day. Please explain what you mean."

"There is nothing to explain. I mean just that. Michael has his feet placed firmly on the ground. He was once a great king. The moment I saw him, I knew he came from royalty. He dresses like a king and he thinks like one. He is very powerful, but his power is of this world. He is not mystical like you, nor does he have multiple personalities. He is Michael the Great. He will one day be a great organizer."

Yuri smiled wistfully and said, "Yes, he would like to organize me, but I seem to be too much of a problem. Since you told him of his power, he has forgotten about me." At that remark we both laughed, and I thought Michael had either left the country or was about to leave. Nothing more was said as we were entering Manhattan and Yuri had to watch the traffic.

That night I had a strange vision. I was in a large house located in New York City. I felt as if a spirit was guiding me to a bedroom at the back of the house. There, I saw Yuri kneeling down and praying; over his head was a very bright light. I looked down at the kneeling man, then quietly left.

When I woke up, I knew Yuri had started to pray to his God Force. He had arrived at a place within his soul where there was peace. I, too, felt peaceful within, and I thanked God that He had shown me this vision.

A few days after our beach experience, I saw Yuri at the bar in the restaurant. He was with a friend. They may have been speaking of me for Yuri looked over and waved, and the man nodded and smiled. The other man seemed to be about five feet ten inches, well built with brown hair and deep-set eyes that seemed to look right through you. I was very busy as there was a party of five who had come for cocktails and wished to have palm readings. When I was finished I went over to the bar, but Yuri and his friend had left.

I saw Zaza, a psychic woman whom I had known for several years, sitting at another table. We had worked together in Armando's club on

East 55th Street, and although Zaza was now semi-retired, she still worked a few hours at Armando's which was now on 61st Street. I felt very close to her as we both had heart problems, and we seemed to feel as sense of responsibility for one another. As I sat down next to her, she held my hand and asked, "How are you today Maya?"

"This is one of my good days, Zaza. I had a small piece of fish with an even smaller potato and so far I have not been bothered," I replied, sipping a glass of lemonade.

"That is good, Maya, eat small portions and eat often," she advised still holding my hand.

"How are you feeling, Zaza, are you eating?" I asked her.

"No," she answered, "I don't have an appetite, maybe after a few drinks, I will eat."

"Please, dear, try to be moderate. With a heart condition, one should not drink," I said softly. Zaza did not reply, so I continued, "We need you here."

Just then, I looked over at the end of the bar, and there was Yuri. I waved and he came over.

"Yuri, I looked for you and your friend, but you had left. Meet Zaza, she is one of the most famous psychics in America." Both Zaza and Yuri laughed at my description of her.

"Zaza," I said pleadingly, "please give Yuri my friend, a reading."

"Do you wish for a reading, Yuri?" Zaza asked skeptically.

"Yes, I would love a reading. If Maya says you are good, then I am sure you must be."

It had been raining all afternoon and the bar was almost empty, so Zaza sat in the corner with Yuri, while I disappeared to the ladies room to freshen up my make-up.

Around seven p.m. I looked over at the bar. Both Yuri and Zaza had disappeared.

The next evening Zaza came in. I was not busy and she sat down at my table saying, "Maya, that man is fantastic! He is connected with your destiny. He thinks you remind him of his mother, who was a very spiritual person."

"Yes, Zaza. I am only nine years older than Yuri, but I fell like his mother. What else did you see for him?"

Zaza was silent for a few moments then said, "He is in connection with the Russian secret service. I see grave danger, but he will be protected. I also see in him power, but with many negative people trying to oppose him. He needs you, Maya, your prayers will help him to overcome the many blocks that will be put in his path."

Just then a waitress came over and Zaza ordered a drink. I saw her hand shaking and thought of scolding her but remained silent.

After the drink arrived, she sipped it and said, "He took me to dinner and we both drank scotch. I got a little bit happy and we both had a wonderful time."

I wondered what Yuri thought of Zaza getting happy. I knew that it may have been more than that, but said nothing.

After several minutes of silence while she sipped her drink, I touched her hand and said, "Zaza, please try not to live it up. Take it easy."

She smiled sadly and then asked, "How would you like to do a seance for my niece, Alma, and me?"

"Yes, I would like that. We both need help from the Inner Masters. When shall we have it?"

"Today is Thursday, how about tomorrow night after nine p.m.? Friday is always perfect for a seance."

"Good," I exclaimed, "tomorrow night it will be."

"O.K., Maya, we will meet you here and walk over to my place."

The next night, Zaza and her niece, Alma, came in. I was busy and they had a drink while I finished with my client. Around nine-thirty p.m., we left for Zaza's place.

First, we prayed and then went into the seance. Alma gave me a message. She saw me working on a journey, looking well and happy. Zaza was unusually silent. I gave her a message to watch her diet, but she did not respond. This was very strange. She was in a state of deep trance. After about an hour, again we prayed, but Zaza still remained silent. About eleven-thirty p.m. she came back to reality, but very quiet. At midnight, we left and took a cab home.

That night i had a strange vision, Zaza had died, yet she was alive and well. I saw her in a large mansion which seemed to be a center of healing. Zaza was the high priestess, healing with the light. She looked very happy and radiantly alive and well.

One day, in September, I arrived at the restaurant about noon. Zaza was there having a drink, she called me over and said, "Maya, remember your seance? Your brother Cecil came through. He took me by the hand and showed me the future. I am going to die very soon, but you, Maya, will live to be very old. You have a great future ahead of you. In time, the wisdom from your Egyptian heritage will come through and you will have world-wide fame. You will grow more spiritual as the years go by, and late in life you will have many guides. Yuri will be one of your greatest and most useful guides. He is a great man, Maya, and one day you will remember my words, for you will both be spirit wands for worldwide peace."

I listened, enthralled by her words. It was as if she had hypnotized me. I left Zaza, but must still have been in a trance-like state because all I remembered of the rest of that day and night was going home and praying for almost two hours.

The following Monday afternoon, Yuri came in with his friend Bill. Yuri introduced us and asked if I would give Bill a reading. After Yuri left us, I looked closely at Bill's palms. In both hands the life lines were very long, but the head lines were extremely long and powerful. Bill gave me his birth date. It was in June, but I cannot remember the day or the year. He was about ten years younger than Yuri, but looked older. His face was full of lines, and he was emotionally disturbed. I also knew that he had problems in the solar plexus and spleen, and that God would call him soon. I talked of his wife and children who were living in a foreign country. I believed it was Hungary, but was not sure as we did not go into details about his personal life.

There were many things that I saw in his vibration, but I was careful about repeating them to him. We talked of music. He loved Gypsy music and it always healed him. He also told me that Yuri loved the same things he did and that they had a lot in common. He gave me his wife's birthday and year. She was a Leo. I knew that she would outlive him and in time to marry again, but did not relate this to him. How can you tell someone that their destiny is soon to be in spirit? And that there was no future in this physical plane. I spoke of his work which is very dangerous, and advised him to read the psalms of the Holy Bible. I told him of the power of the 91st Psalm and the miracles that it could manifest. He listened and I knew that he was aware that his life would soon be ended in this world.

Bill asked about his health and I advised him to see a doctor, and also to be very careful about his diet.

He asked, "Is there a problem with my heart?"

"Yes," I told him, "it is more emotional plus your constant worry about every little thing. Also, you are not praying in the right way."

"What is the right way to pray?" he asked, looking at me with deep-set eyes that seemed to penetrate into my soul.

"One must pray in a loud tone of voice, this makes an imprint on the solar plexus. It is like a message that the angels see and send up to God. Pray with faith. Have confidence that what you are praying for will be manifested in your conscious world. It is your faith that gives the angels power to open up the doors of the inner worlds for you. If you have a problem, pray and give it to the spirit within."

I stopped for a moment while Bill stared at me. I felt I was going to deep, but for the life of me, I could not stop.

I said, "If you have a problem, don't go to sleep with it. Pray and give it to the spirit of God. Your sickness is from too many negative problems that were not purified and they are all smoldering in your solar plexus and spleen. This is what is causing your heart to skip beats. Heart problems are really indigestion problems. Our food and our thoughts give us indigestion."

At these words Bill exclaimed, "Maya, you are right, it's usually after an upsetting day that I get nightmares and back problems."

"That is right," I replied softly. "Pray and cast your problems at the feet of the God Force within. Do you ever read the Bible?"

"No, I have not for a long time, but I will."

We were both silent for a few moments, then Bill said, "Maya, you are very ill. Yuri told me that doctors have given you a few months to live. How can you advise me when you cannot even help yourself?"

I smiled sadly at his question, then replied, "It's a long story, but I will try to make it short. When I was three years old one morning while playing with my dolls, I suddenly saw a bright light whirling over my head. Subconsciously, I knew it was my God Force and said, "I do not wish to live this life, because I will be bad and I do not wish to be bad. The light disappeared and I went on playing with my dolls. This light has been very important to me, every time there was danger, the light would appear and I would be told or guided into a higher plane of consciousness.

"When I was twenty my brother Cecil, who named me Maya, died. I was devastated. Even though he was two years younger, he was my guardian angel. Three days after his passing I had a vision, I was with Cecil and I was healing him. He had a fever and I was putting wet cloths on his forehead. After he was better, I told him that it was my desire to remain with him. He looked happy but shook his head saying, "No, you cannot stay here. You must go back. You have great work to do, but in 1956 you will be with me."

"January 3rd, 1955, I had a vision of being in a very large studio. I was lecturing and healing many people. I felt that this was the work God had destined for me. It was the last year of my life and I must go and fulfill his bidding.

"With ten dollars and faith and the help of a Jewish friend, I moved into Carnegie Hall. There I remained ten months and in February 1956 went back to the night clubs.

I had and accident on a city bus and yesterday, Zaza, told me that Cecil had come through to her. She would die, but I would live a long life. She also said that Yuri would be one of my greatest guides. Between us we will work for world peace."

"Maya, your story is amazing, but so you believe this psychic? Do you truly believe that God will give you more time?"

"Yes I do. I also believe that Yuri and I met for a purpose and that its God's will."

I do believe that, Maya. I have never seen Yuri so overcome by anyone. There is a friend, a woman friend in Russia, that he also believes in. He also speaks highly of you. Maya, he is a great man."

"I know, he is great not only in this world but also in the next. God has shown me many good things about Yuri."

We were both quiet. The restaurant was getting busy and I felt that I should finish this long session.

"Maya, I must leave you but can I meet your friend Zaza?"

"Yes, Yuri has met her and I'm sure he has her phone number. Ask him."

Just then a waitress came over and said, "Madame Perez, there are two ladies that wish to have consultations when you are free."

The next night around nine p.m. I was not busy and Zaza came over. After greeting me, she asked, "What have you been doing today?"

"It has been very slow, but yesterday I was busy. Yuri brought in a friend; Bill. We had a long session and I told him about you. Did Yuri call you?"

Zaza looked at me, then said, "Yes Maya, I saw Yuri and Bill. They came to Armando's and I gave Bill a reading." She was very quiet then blurted out, "Maya, this man is a double agent."

"I suspected this. I am concerned about him. I feel that he is a very unhappy man and his conscience is disturbing him. Zaza both of his lifelines are very short. I do not feel that he will live a very long time." I was quiet then whispered, "Zaza, this is why he has problems with the solar plexus and the spleen. It's all guilt feelings."

"Maya," Zaza said speaking softly, "you must never tell Yuri or anyone, if you do, it could cause a lot of trouble."

"Don't worry, Zaza, I won't say a word."

That same night, I had a vision of Bill. He was two people. One was trying to tell him not to leave the country, and the other was saying, "You have work to do, come let us go." As I woke up I thought, "I must tell Bill not to leave the country. Here he will be safe, but if he goes abroad he will die."

For several days in September, I looked for Yuri and Bill but neither of them came. It may have been around the middle of September—I'm not sure of the date—when Yuri came in. I was not busy.

He came over to my table saying, "Maya, I need another reading. There are some problems facing me." It was about 5 p.m. and the restaurant was not busy, except for a few stragglers at the bar. He ordered a drink, and I saw his hand shaking as he lifted the glass. I held his hand to look at his palm, but I already knew Yuri had received very bad news from home. His hand was cold, as if the blood was drained out of it.

"Yuri, there are great problems in Europe and it is connected with your country." I was silent for a few moments then continued, "You may have to go and work with this problem."

He was silent, but I could feel his hand shaking in mine. After a while I asked, "Is Bill going with you?"

"That is another problem. Bill is not well, but he plans to leave the country." A cold chill came over me as I thought, "Oh, Bill must not leave." But for some strange reason, I could not speak. I looked deep into the inner realms and saw a bright light. It was the light that had guided me all through my life. With a light heart I said, "Yuri, go and do what you are supposed to do. God has shown me the light. Everything will be wonderful. You have nothing to worry about."

We talked of his daughter Irina, his son Igor and his wife. We also talked about his friend. A female Jewish friend that would in time be with him, but I did not see a divorce. I cannot say how long we talked, it may have been an hour, or maybe more. During the dinner hour I was called away to give some readings and Yuri left with a smile on his face and a light heart.

This was the last time I saw him until the next year in February, 1957. He came back to New York from Hungary. It's amazing how Yuri Andropov and I understood each other. Later, I learned, in a past life, I had been his older sister and was like a mother to him.

Life is strange and mysterious, and only one who is born with a veil can read and see and understand the mysteries of the unseen world.

TWENTY-ONE

Spirit Lovers

On August 1, 1956, I happened to be standing outside my room. I had forgotten my key. Several minutes had transpired when a tall, attractive, blond woman about fifty, passed and smiled at me. I returned her smile and she went into the room opposite mine.

The next morning I saw her again. This time she was in the hall speaking to the maid. I waited, as I wanted to ask the maid for some stationery paper. The blond woman was still there, after the maid left, and she introduced herself. We immediately started talking on a first-name basis.

"Maya, what a beautiful name. I like it," she exclaimed. Looking at me more closely, she continued, "You do have extraordinary eyes. It is almost as if you were looking right through me."

"I am a mystic, Andrea," I said, smiling. "Usually, I am not aware of using this trait. To me it is second nature to glance at someone and see what they really are inside."

This answer seemed to impress her. She invited me into her room and for several minutes we sat and discussed spirit phenomena. I was pleasantly surprised to learn that she understood and loved the invisible world of spirit as much as I.

Taking another look at her, I informed her that she too had the mystic eyes, and could read the aura of a person. This delighted her and for a moment she was quiet, as if trying to define my words. Then she said slowly, "Maya, I don't understand about reading auras. How can one know if they are reading an aura?"

"One has to feel an aura before it can be seen through the inner eye," I answered, trying to speak slowly in order for her to fully understand me. "After the inner vision gets stronger, then it appears in flashes; maybe a warm or heavy feeling. At first, you may think it is a figment of your imagination, but later, you will be able to analyze those situations. Haven't you gone into a room and felt the vibrations were heavy?"

"Yes, yes," replied Andrea excitedly, "I have often felt vibrations of houses and people, but did not know that this was reading an aura. I naturally took it for granted that I was sensing the situations around them."

We were both silent for a few moments, then she went on, still excited about our discussion.

"Tell me, my dear, how do you define a Mystic by the eyes?"

"It is by the expression of the eyes. Some people have more depth than others. There is an old saying, the eyes are the windows of the soul. Give me your birthdate and year."

She gave me the dates and I added them up in my mind, then said, "Andrea, you have the ability to write and be a practitioner. Your path is a seven. This is the mystical number and you are awakened."

"Maya, I am amazed," she answered in astonishment. "This is true. I am a writer of both occult and deep mysticism. I have delved into the occult, and now I am studying spiritualism. This subject fascinates me, but it is this feeling or sensing of the aura that puzzles me. Tell me more about it."

"If the colors around the field-force are light, then you will get a relaxed feeling, but on the other hand, if they are on the dark side, invariably you will get a heavy, or sometimes in deep cases, you could get a nauseous feeling. When this happens to me, I usually send the light to them, for their channels are blocked."

"That makes sense," she said looking off into space. "Tell me more. In giving a consultation, how do you approach the subject? Is there a set rule, or do you merely use your intuition?"

"Yes, there are set rules. I use the scientific approach, except with a large audience. Then I pray and accept the thoughts that are sent to me from the inner-consciousness. With lectures, I usually give aortic impressions. That is, reading the colors from the field-force. With a private consultation, I get the birthdate and year. This gives me the path the person is to tread in this life. This method is the best, as it tells what a person has gone through in past lives, and what they are doing now. It also describes the trials that they will encounter, and how well equipped they are to face their problems here on earth. If someone gives me a wrong birthdate and year, I would still get the answers from the aura, but it would not be as good. First, I would explain that they are not telling the truth. Then, if asked to continue, I would pray for them. In some cases, I just pray and say nothing."

"So you are an astrologer and numerologist. I, too, have delved into both of these sciences."

Quickly, I answered, "I am a cosmic astrologer. I know nothing of the chart. Through the years, several of my friends have tried to teach me, but having found no need for the chart, I have never studied this very complicated science. As a cosmic astrologer, I get all the answers from within."

Looking at me closely, Andrea asked, "Maya, on the second of January of this year, I saw a woman on television. The program was the

Morning Show with Dick Van Dyke. This woman claimed to be a cosmic astrologer. Was it you?"

I smiled and nodded. "You do intrigue me," she went on. "I felt that you were so aware of what you were talking about when you said, the master within, or was it, the voice within, which gives you the answer?"

"I must have said, the voice within," I answered, thinking what a tremendous memory she has.

Suddenly, she looked at her watch and said, "This is all so very interesting, and I do not want to leave, but I am going on a boat trip to an amusement park. Please be my guest. I promise to get you back by eight or nine this evening at the latest."

"Thank you, Andrea. I will go with you, but you are visiting New York. Please by my guest." As we were talking, I had been looking at the dark circle I saw floating around her lower female organs. I knew immediately Andrea had a sex problem.

"No, positively no. You are my guest," she exclaimed firmly. "The maid informed me that today is your birthday. Also, that you had not been well and must watch your diet carefully. It would be my pleasure to take you to dinner after the boat ride. You choose the restaurant. Oh, yes, I did a little investigating to find out who you were."

I smiled at her frankness and liked her for it. As I dressed to go on the boat ride, I could not help thinking of the dark circle that had appeared around Andrea. I did not wish to intrude into her personal life. I knew that she would soon bring up the matter.

On the boat trip we talked of several phases of mysticism, when suddenly Andrea asked, "Maya, do you believe that a spirit being can come back and have an affair of passion with a living woman?"

"Yes, Andrea." I answered, wondering why she had asked such a weird question. Then the dark circle that I had seen around her, flashed back to my mind. Maybe it had something to do with her question.

"When I was a little girl about seven or eight, I remember listening to my mother and one of her close friends who had just become a widow. Now I blush at the memory of how I used to sneak behind sofas to listen to the conversation of my elders. This widow told my mother that her husband was still coming back to her in his astral body to have sex. At the time, I did not understand what they were talking about, but I did realize that the man was annoying his wife. This woman felt that my mother would have been able to help her, as my dear mother had delved deeply into spiritualistic matters. Distinctly, I heard my mother say to her, wear some black drawers. She meant black panties. At this point, I burst out laughing, much to my sorrow, for the woman got up and left in a hurry, and my mother rooted me out from behind the sofa and gave me a sound whipping.

We both laughed, as I described my youthful escapade, but in a moment, Andrea became serious and said softly, so as not to be overheard, "Maya, I have a spirit lover. I have wanted to speak to someone about this matter for a long time."

I was shocked at her words, and for a few moments sat in silence. In my work I have heard many strange problems, but none so strange as this. If I had not been in contact with the spirit world, I may have thought that she was exaggerating this particular phenomena. But strange as it sounded, I believed every word that she had said.

Andrea noticed the amazed expression on my face, for she quickly got up and said in a more natural tone of voice, "Come, we will go and have a cup of coffee. I will tell you my story later."

As we sipped our coffee, I could not keep my mind on anything but this spirit lover of hers. When we got back to our corner on the top deck, she began her story.

"I was born in Switzerland and came to this country when I was very young. When I was twenty, I married a man from my home town. We had two boys, and several years ago he passed on with a heart attack. A few years later, I went to Switzerland to visit my youngest son, Leif, who was in school there. One day, while returning from a visit with him at school, which was in the country, I stopped at a quaint little inn to have an early dinner. The table next to mine was occupied by a rather tall, dignified gentleman. He was not handsome, for he was far too rugged an individual to be called handsome. He had the strangest eyes; they seemed to look right within you. Believe me, I just could not keep my eyes away from his. Every few minutes, I would find myself looking in his direction, and he was always staring at me.

After I ordered my dinner, he came over and asked if we had met before. I heard his voice saying, "You look like someone I have known, yet I can't seem to remember where we met."

Maya, I could not for the world answer him. It was just as if someone had hypnotized me. Finally, I gathered up enough strength to nod my head, and he sat down. I remember he asked me to have dinner with him the next evening, but I can't remember what he said or anything of what I said to him. The whole time in the restaurant was a total blank. I do know that I felt as if I had suddenly been lifted up into another realm of complete bliss. There was such a feeling of serenity that swept over me, that nothing else mattered.

About midnight, I arrived home and I remembered that he handed me a card, and asked if I would care to visit him in the morning. If so, he would call the next morning to make arrangements for someone to meet me at the train.

That night I did not sleep. I remained in my heavenly trance until early the next morning, when I dozed off into a deep sleep. I woke with a start, for I heard someone call my name. The voice sounded like my friend of the night before. He repeated my name three times: "Andrea, Andrea, Andrea." I looked at the clock; it was 7 a.m. Quickly I got up and dialed him. Yes, he was expecting me, and will send his man down to meet me at the station.

At the station, an old hunchbacked man was waiting. He told me Count Faultberg had sent him to meet me. It was not very difficult for him to find me, as I was the only lady that had gotten off at that weird place. I got into a wagon drawn by a mule, and up and up we went. At the top was an enormous house, or what they call castles in that part of the country. It was surrounded by a big wall.

I won't waste time describing the castle. Suffice to say that it was immense. When the hunchback helped me out of the wagon, I had a feeling of fear that seeped through me, and I wondered why. I felt like turning back, but how could I, after coming this far. Anyway, it was too late, for in the doorway stood my friend with the strange eyes.

There were only three servants in that great big house. The hunchback, the housekeeper, and a very thin housemaid. It was the housemaid who showed me to my room on the second floor. The house was three stories high with a turret at the top.

While I took my bath, Tina, the housemaid, laid out my clothes for me. It had taken several hours for the train to get there, and I was a little bit tired, so relaxed in the bath. Later Tina helped me dress my hair and I noticed that she was an expert in such matters. I asked her where she had been trained. "Paris," she answered shortly. To anything that I asked her, she would give a short, terse answer or would say, "I do not know."

He served two different kinds of wine, with music in the background, but I do not remember what we had for dinner. Oh, Maya, it was such a delightful evening. Axel, my host, was the perfect gentleman. After dinner, he played the piano and we sang together. Later, we danced and danced. What a heavenly evening! It was like fairyland. If I had any qualms, believe me, after that first night, they disappeared into nothingness, for my Axel was the perfect lover. No, he did not come to my room. I went to his. When I arrived, the door was open and he was standing by the window waiting, just as if he had expected me to respond to his will. He received me with open arms.

At first, we just stood by the open window looking out into the night. The sky was filled with countless stars. Ah, Maya, when one is in love, suddenly the night can become enchantingly lovely and more beautiful.

Yes, with Axel's arms around me, for the first time in my life I was supremely happy. Later, he took me to his bed.

For one week I lived in a dream world. I did call my son, explaining that business had detained me, and gave him Axel's number, just in case he needed me. The last night, Axel held me in his arms and asked me to marry him, but I could not. I had important business matters pending, and had to return to the United States. Anyway, he made me promise that I would return and marry him when my business affairs were settled."

For a long time Andrea sat in silence. finally, she continued, "How can I tell you what happened? It was so dreadful! We kept in touch. Axel called every week and he wrote me almost every day. Two months later, one night past midnight, I received a call. Axel was disturbed. That morning his doctor had told him that he had a damaged heart and gave him only a few more weeks to live. He pleaded with me to return to him. His last words were, "Andrea, my love, come quickly. I need you very much."

I booked passage immediately, only to find that he had died a few days before, and had been buried the day before I arrived.

He had left the house and many of his writings to me. Yes, he wanted me to live there alone. How could I? I spent a few days there and the house felt like a tomb. Later, I sold the house but kept his writings. Every so often, I would read them and it would be like the voice of my beloved whispering sweet nothings to me.

Three months after his death, I dreamed of being in his arms. I awakened and found my beloved in bed with me. The phenomena had begun. This unusual experience lasted for two whole years, then I met my present husband. I married him, hoping that marriage to a man in the physical body would break the contact, but it grew worse.

If I did not do what Axel desired, then I would become very nervous. Sometimes I felt like jumping out of my body. Oh dear God, I wanted to get away, but where could I go? My husband knows nothing of this story. Once I told him my late husband had visited me during the night. He laughed and said, "Poor guy, he must still be in love with you."

She was silent for a moment, then she held my hand and asked, "Maya, do you feel that this is wrong? If so, please tell me what I can do to correct it. I do not want to go against the laws of God and more than ever I want to be a good wife. I love my husband in a calm, quiet way. It is a soothing type of relationship and he has been good to me and the two boys."

I closed my eyes and waited for the answer. It had to come, for Andrea seemed overwhelmed with grief.

"Andrea, who am I to say what is right or wrong? I know that God wanted you to have this experience, or you would not have been subjected to it. The only antidote I could suggest would be to pray for Axel's soul. In time he will rise to a higher plane of consciousness."

There were tears in Andrea's eyes as she spoke, "Thank you, Maya, for being so understanding. I have tried to tell my story to doctors, psychologists and even ministers. They all think that I am crazy and look at me as if I were out of my mind. One man said that the insane asylums are filled with this type of ailment." She stopped for a moment, then continued, "Some day, Maya, you will be well and strong. Here is my card. I live in California. Come and visit me."

"Thank you, Andrea, but several doctors have told me that my illness will be for a long duration. Also, I was told by my brother who passed on, that I would be with him this year. I am ready to make the transition."

Looking wide-eyed at me, Andrea exclaimed, "Oh, dear God, No! You do not really mean this, do you Maya?"

"Yes, I do", I said positively. She gave me a piercing look.

"Don't you know that you could die a mental death and yet live in the body? I mean that God could give you a new spirit to revitalize and rebuild the body. I have seen this happen."

"I wish that I had been able to go sooner to Axel. I feel that he would have been alive today. Maya, perish the thought of death. I decree that you will live to a ripe old age. I also visualize you living in a fully revitalized body."

Just then, the boat pulled in at the amusement park.

Back at the hotel we bade good night and I retired to my room, having no preconception of the events in store for me that night.

It must have been around three o'clock in the morning when I awakened with the sensation of someone gently caressing me from the back, and wondered who was in bed with me. Strangely, I felt no fear. I was only puzzled as I lay there, feeling a warmth of love permeating my entire being. Suddenly I realized someone was endeavoring to hypnotize me. Feeling the presence of the other person's body near me, I thought possibly someone had entered my room with a pass key, but as I was facing the door I could see that the chain was still on the door. I knew no one could have entered the room and again wondered who was in my bed. I was still trying to analyze the situation when a voice within me spoke.

"Do not go back to sleep. Try to see who is here in bed with you, or in the morning you will think that you are dreaming. Stay awake!

Making a great effort, I turned to see who was there. Then I saw a cloud-like form floating over the bed. The being was very tall and appeared almost to reach the ceiling. Still I felt no fear for it was like gazing at some fantasy and I wanted to see what would happen next. The thought came to me - this must be God who has come to take me. The spirit read my thoughts as his eyes penetrated mine. After staring at me momentarily and realizing his inability to hypnotize me, he spoke without sound.

"I am your soulmate. It has been a long time since we parted on Pluto. Now I have found you and we must never part again. Never! Remember, do not divulge my visit to anyone. If you do I shall lose my power."

His words put me in a light hypnotic state and I was unable to move, but knew and felt all that was transpiring. For hours he caressed me. At times I could feel the weight of his being on my body. At this point there was no conversation.

Toward morning I dozed off into a deep sleep. It was seven when I awakened, feeling woozy and found the spirit had vanished. Remembering what had happened, I jumped out of bed and called Andrea. "Something strange happened to me last night," I said. "I can hardly believe it." I quickly told her part of the episode.

"Perhaps it was your story of Axel, I don't know, but I tell you it has left me exhausted. Oh, Andrea, I must come over and tell you."

She became excited and asked me to come to her room.

I dressed quickly and rushed over to her. Andrea had a light breakfast ready, and she looked just as excited as I felt. I could hardly wait for her to sit down and listen to my strange experience.

"Now, tell me Maya, what happened last night?" she asked, as she poured me a steaming cup of coffee. She looked rested and gave me the impression that she had slept well. My thoughts were: "of course she slept well!" That was probably Axel bothering me all night. I took a sip of coffee and started my strange tale.

"I was awakened in the middle of the night, and I felt someone caressing me on my back. I thought I was dreaming, but it didn't take long for me to realize that someone was trying to hypnotize me!"

"Oh, Maya, no!"

"Yes, Andrea, someone was definitely in my room, and I forced myself to stay awake. I had to figure out what was going on. Then I saw a cloud-like form hovering over my bed. You cannot imagine how I felt. I had to use all my energy to keep calm.

Andrea thought for a few moments then said, "Sometimes we meet our soulmates in dreams, but you were fully awake. How do you explain this?"

I thought to myself, she suspects Axel.

Slowly I answered her, "At first I thought it was God, but the being told me that he was my other self. Today I feel drained. Almost lifeless. Is this how you feel when Axel visits you?"

She looked at me and did not answer. Then she said, "Maya, it has been most embarrassing for me to speak about the strange visits from Axel, but you now understand my dilemma since you, too, have had the same thing happen to you."

She sighed, as though relieved that it was not Axel.

"Yes Maya, sometimes I do wake up feeling tired, but then there are times when my body feels exhilarated and completely happy. These are the times when Axel is able to regenerate my body with ecstasy. It is the times when I do not try to resist him. Then all goes well."

We both sat silent in our thoughts, and I soon left to start my day.

There are many unexplainable things that happen in our mortal world. I have had my share of strange experiences, but this one was something else. I often think of Andrea and send her my prayers. Perhaps my advice to her to send prayers to Axel will finally give her the peace she longs for.

TWENTY-TWO
Hospital

A few nights before Thanksgiving of 1956, I was sitting in the back of the restaurant. I was thinking of Zaza, who had passed on in late October. I thought of her a lot and always felt her presence when I was alone. Bobby, a new friend came in. Almost every night she would come in to see what had transpired since the night before. Shortly after, Jess Stearn, my reporter friend came in with a young lady. I gave them readings, then left with Jess, the young lady and Bobby. As we walked along the street Bobby noticed I could hardly walk and must have mentioned it to Jess, because he called a cab, put me in and sent me back to the hotel. There was a peculiar look on Jess's face as he gave me the fare, but I was too ill to worry about what my friends were thinking. The day before Thanksgiving I was too weak to get out of bed, so called Polyclinic hospital and told the nurse, I did not feel I could go on any further.

The nurse was sorry, but explained because of Thanksgiving, there were no beds available. She advised me to call the next week.

As I hung up the telephone, I felt a strange feeling as if someone was trying to give me a message. I listened. It was Zaza.

"Maya, you will go into the hospital tomorrow night. All will be well. Do not despair." That was all, but it was enough to give me hope. When one has hope, one can accomplish miracles.

Just then Nettie called, "How are you, Maya?" She asked the question as if she knew the answer.

"Not good, Nettie," I answered slowly trying to reserve my strength. "Last night my heart was very bad. I am not going back to Cole's. I feel I should get into a hospital. Just a few minutes ago I called Polyclinic, but the nurse told me, there were no beds. I must call next week."

"Very well, dear, tell me later. I am going to Dr. Barker's lecture. I go every Wednesday night. Come go with me. After the lecture we can have a bite together."

After the lecture, Nettie and I went over to a health restaurant a few blocks away. I looked at the menu and decided on a fruit salad. Had I known then what the results would be, this would have been the last thing I would have ordered. Uncooked fruit is very difficult to digest. This should never be taken, if one suffers from gas or hypertension.

About half-way through the salad I stopped eating. My breathing was getting worse. I felt as if at any moment I would lose consciousness. Nettie stopped eating and quickly paid the bill.

"Come, Maya, let me take you to a hospital. We will call a cab." Putting her arm around me, she helped me out and called a cab. The driver looked around for directions. It was I who answered, "Metropolitan Hospital, please."

Nettie looked at me, wondering why I had not chosen Polyclinic. Seeing her look of puzzlement, I said, "Something told me to go there. They took X-rays of my accident, I remember."

With these words I fell back in silence. My heart was beating as though it would burst. Arriving at the hospital, I was taken into emergency. Two doctors examined me. One asked if I would like to remain in the hospital that night, remembering what Zaza had said, "I told him no." The doctor prescribed a sedative which he gave me. I was to take it before going to bed. I was told to come back to the hospital the next day at three p.m., and I would be admitted.

The next morning Eunice Parker called. "Maya dear, how are you?" she asked with deep concern in her voice.

"I am not well, Eunice. I am going to the hospital. Metropolitan has agreed to admit me today," I replied softly.

"Oh, Maya, I am sorry to hear this. You know, I don't care for hospitals. They will give you food that is not good for you. Please, Maya, think about this!"

"No, Eunice, I feel it is imperative for me to go. Zaza came through and told me that I will be admitted today and all will be well."

"Maya, I will send John to pick you up. Come by and I will give you some health broth to take with you to the hospital. John will take you around six p.m. to the hospital. Please come."

Thinking about what Zaza had said ,that I would be admitted that night, I consented and this was how Zaza's prediction came true.

Thanksgiving Day I was admitted into the hospital. I arrived at seven p.m. and was told the doctor would not be back until ten p. m. I was told to wait. Finally, shortly after ten, the doctor came in and I was taken into the back room.

After an endless series of examinations from several doctors, a wheelchair was brought in and I was taken out to the ward on the main floor. The night nurse gently undressed me, after I was given some hot tea and a sedative.

Early the next morning I woke up and looked out at an endless stream of drunks that were leaving from the night before. One blond man looked in at me and smiled. He was all bruised with a black eye.

"Hello there. What is wrong with you?" he asked as he came in through the glass door.

"I have hypertension from an accident a few months back; and you?"

"Oh, I was just a bad boy. I had words with another man in a bar and I got the worst of it. It could have been worse—life is like that."

"Yes," I said looking at him searchingly, "life is what you make it. You get back what you put into it. Why does a nice man like you get drunk and fight? Why don't you try to make something of yourself?"

He smiled then answered quietly, a little ashamed, "I am very bored with life, but why am I telling you all this? Who are you anyway?"

I smiled. He reminded me of a very inquisitive child. I remained quiet and he continued, "You seem different. That is why I stopped to chat with you. Who are you?"

"I am a mystic. Many people bring their problems to me. Now I am ill. You have heard the saying, physician heal thyself? I cannot. Only God can heal me. If it is His will I shall be healed."

"You believe in God? Wish I could."

His blue eyes seemed so sad as he said these words and I held out my hand to clasp his saying, "I will pray for you. Please believe me."

He bent over and kissed my hand as tears streamed down his face and he left quietly, closing the glass door behind him.

Such an incident happening to another soul would have been unusual, but to me it was like drinking a glass of cold water, so I just turned over and went to sleep until the day nurse awakened me for breakfast, and then took me to the upper ward.

The first day nothing unusual happened. I shared a room with two ladies. The older woman was in for an operation which she already had. She left a few days later. The other was Maria, a girl in her twenties, who was expecting a baby and could not keep her food down, or if she did had great discomfort.

Around ten a. m. a visiting specialist came by with Dr. Bruno, the head of the ward. After examining and asking many questions of my past illnesses and religious beliefs, he said decisively, "It was the accident that caused the hypertension, owing to a peculiar fear within the patient."

I told him I was a spiritualist and was listed as such.

At eleven a. m., the welfare agent came. He asked many questions. To all I answered frankly. He was very patient and considerate of my discomfort in speaking. He also asked if I were suing the bus company. I told him a friend had gotten a lawyer for me a week prior to my entering the hospital. After that he seemed more at ease.

At two p.m. I was taken down and X-rayed from head to foot. The same man had X-rayed me in March. He informed the doctor of the other X-ray and they brought these out and checked to see what had developed since then. Now there was a great deal of arthritis in the lower spine.

That night a black nurse came in. She told me she was Miss Watts. Looking at the chart she saw spiritualist listed, and asked if I were the one that had a studio in Carnegie Hall. I nodded. I did not care to speak as my back was aching and I was very tired. The nurse did not wish to leave, instead she kept lingering, putting the covers straight and fixing the roses that a friend had brought that afternoon.

Finally she leaned over and whispered, "Could you give me a reading?"

To this I complied, thinking, there is no rest for the weary at heart and body. After I was finished, Miss Watts went out and told two other nurses who came in but I pretended I was sleeping.

Saturday, the nurses tried to encourage me to eat, but I refused all food they brought. My friend Eunice Parker had brought a bottle of health food. To this I added hot broth which was quite palatable. Later that night, Miss Watts brought some hot tea and Jell-o.

Shortly after nine p.m. Miss Johnson, the night nurse, brought in my medication, consisting of two little white pills. Immediately after taking them, my heart started to beat very fast. Maria heard me crying and called the nurse. Miss Johnson came back and immediately went out to call Dr. Bruno, who came in with two other doctors. One doctor held my right pulse and Dr. Bruno the left. The third doctor stood at the foot of the bed looking on at the proceedings.

The doctor on my right said, "I think she is all right. It's just a little more than usual."

Between gasps, I exclaimed, "I don't feel right, Doctor."

The doctor picked me up and swung me backwards and forwards. Dr. Bruno was trying to get the circulation started and relax me, but this method made me gasp more as the blood rushed up my spine. He laid me back on the bed when he noticed the effect of the treatment was too harsh.

Catching my breath, I said, "I think I am dying, Doctor. Feel my feet. I can't move them and my fingers."

Dr. Bruno tried to pick up my foot but it was as if it were dead. Then he tried to uncurl my fingers but they were in a death grip.

It was then I looked at the three doctors around my bed and thought, "These are not wise men, they know nothing of what is happening to me. Why do I waste my time. Why don't I get in touch with my heavenly Father?"

Suddenly I felt my body floating up. It was going faster and faster. I could see a very bright light. I was floating towards the light and then I was in a large hall.

I said, "Father, into Thy hands, I commit my soul."

A beautiful melodious voice answered, "If you are part of this vast intuned Mind you do not have to die." And I answered, "Father, if I am part of this vast intuned Mind and do not have to die, then give me back my health and I promise to help heal your children."

Again I was floating down, down, and found myself in the corner of the hospital room. The doctors had left. Maria was praying and her voice sounded as if she was trembling. My body was jumping up, and the bed was shaking as if from an earthquake. A fat black nurse was trying to hold my body down on the bed saying, "Don't do that. Stop it, Miss Perez!" A very skinny nurse, also black, was standing at the foot of the bed watching. Her eyes were bulging and her mouth was open. After a few moments I jumped back into my body and the nurse turned me over as I stopped jumping up and down.

As soon as I became calm, the fat nurse put two pills down my throat. After a few moments the fat nurse turned to the skinny one and helped her out of the room. She could not walk by herself. Fear had stopped her sense of movement. She had lost all control.

Maria was still praying softly, as if chanting. I was breathing more regularly. On my face was a slight smile of peace and happiness. I was still in the world of the living.

Now I know you can die in the spirit and still be renewed and live in the body.

The next morning, Sunday, Maria was sitting up and smiled as I said, "Hello." The other patient was gone. She may have left the night before or early that morning. I was very weak. I drank some juice and hot tea that was on my tray. For lunch, some health broth and Jell-o was on that tray.

That night, Miss Watts brought in my medication. I looked at the little white pills that had caused me to become so ill and cried out, "Nurse, I can't take these pills. They made me very ill last night. Don't you remember?"

"Miss Maya," said the nurse, persisting to give me the pills, "these are what the doctor prescribed for you. It's not the same pills that made you ill. You became ill because you are not eating. Why don't you be good and eat your food?"

I looked at the nurse in amazement, and replied, "Nurse, I want to eat. I want to eat very much, but the food does not agree with me and these pills are too drastic on an empty stomach."

The nurse shrugged her shoulder and left, taking the medication with her. I knew I was now in disfavor with the doctors. Inwardly I was shaking, as I chastised myself for allowing an outside force to annoy me. Why could I not control my world. Why, oh why? Turning to Maria, who was sitting up in bed, I asked, "Maria, please pray for me. I am so tired, so very tired of it all. Life seems to be just one endless dream of errors and tests."

"I will pray for you, Maya," answered Maria pensively, "but you seem to have more power than I. At least you can talk back. My food does not agree with me, but I eat it and make myself sick every day."

I looked at Maria for the first time. I was seeing this girl in her true light as I penetrated my consciousness deep into her soul.

"Maria," I said in a far-off tone of voice, "I shall pray for you. It is will power that you are lacking. Soon you will have it."

The next day, Monday, Dr. Bruno and the specialist came into the room. They went to Maria's bed, but overlooked me. Tuesday the same thing happened and also Wednesday. Now I was sure that Dr. Bruno was trying to keep the nice doctor away, for fear I would tell of the events on the previous Saturday night. I tried calling the specialist, but he just said, "Hello" and left. Why, oh why, didn't he come and talk to me? Just a few words of consolation. How could Dr. Bruno think that I would hold malice against him? What was happening in my world? Nothing was coming out right. It was as if a great big hand was making me do all these wrong things. All I could do was to sit and just suffer. Just then, a nice-looking young priest came to speak to Maria. He had been in before and had spoken to me. I had recognized the spiritual qualities within him. I knew he was my friend.

He was of medium build with brown hair and brown eyes that seemed to look within the soul. I called to him.

"Father Ryan, please pray for me."

He came over to my bed and asked, "What is wrong? You are quite disturbed."

"Yes, Father," I replied with a gloomy smile, "I seem to be in disfavor with the doctors."

Sitting down by my bed he asked, "How did this happen to you?"

"Through an accident to my back. I have not been able to eat for several months. Now they give me food I can't digest, consequently I don't eat. Last Saturday night the medication they gave me was too strong on an empty stomach. It made me very ill. Now, I either refuse the medication or pretend to take it. Lately I have been taking half to see if it still disagrees."

The priest had a faint smile on his face, as he listened to my tale of woe. Getting up to leave he said, "I will pray for you, but I want you to do something for me also. Please pray for me."

Tuesday Nettie came by. I told her about what had happened that Saturday night and the coolness of all the doctors, even Dr. Mack, the nice young ward doctor. He, too, had suddenly become cool; possibly this was because I had refused to take the medication. Maybe Dr. Bruno had put the blame on him and he was angry.

Nettie listened to me and summed up the situation. She had studied law and for a time had worked with the FBI, so her deductions were always to be relied on.

"Yes, Maya, I am afraid you are in bad with Dr. Bruno. He is naturally trying to save his face, and Dr. Mack, too, must have been called on the carpet, concerning the medication which was too strong on an empty stomach. In some cases of heart, that method of swinging the patient back and forth is all right, but in your case it was definitely wrong and the other doctors knew that. Don't forget these doctors do not always agree with the methods of their colleagues. Have they given you any medication since Saturday night?"

"Yes," I replied with a grave look, "the nurse gave me the same white pills on Sunday night. I refused to take them. Monday they brought me some pink ones. I only took one of those. So far, there have been no after-effects. Maybe from now on, I will take two. Eunice Parker brought me some powder to make broth, that keeps me going, with the grapes as well.

Kissing me, Nettie left and I immediately went to sleep.

Friday morning a tall handsome priest came to see Maria. He ignored me. Someone must have told him I was a spiritualist. I wished to speak to him, and as he started to leave, I said, "Father, I would like you to burn a nine-day candle for me and put up a novena for me, please."

He did not come over to me but said, "I will burn the candle, but you will have to do your own prayers."

Maria looked at me to see my reaction to this cool statement. She realized I was in hot water with everyone. I ignored his coolness. I knew he was aware of my form of religion and did not care to make an issue of it.

"Thank you, Father, here is some money for the candle," I said getting my purse for the bills.

"I would rather not take the money," said the priest curtly, but seeing the sad look on my face he said in a more gentle tone, "Don't you know the Roman Catholic church was built on a rock? It is the only Church left here on earth, for He said, "On this rock I will build a church and nothing on earth or in heaven shall put it asunder."

He stopped to see the effect of his dynamic words on me. But I looked him calmly in the eye and replied quietly, "Yes, Father. I realize all that you say is very true. I like the Roman Catholic Church. Many times I have gone in to pray and burn a candle. It always soothes me. Thank you very much for the candle and I will pray for both of us." I handed him some bills which he took and left.

He never came in again. I knew he was embarrassed by my words, yet I was sure that he kept his word and burnt the novena. Even now I often think of him and send him light.

Nothing was being done for me. The doctors were nice, the nurses were angels, but I felt there was a great big block.

One day for lunch the nurse brought me ham and spaghetti. I told the nurse, "You have the wrong tray. I am on a fat-free diet."

The nurse shook her head and said, "This is the tray assigned for you."

Later the head nurse came in to see why the tray had not been touched.

"Nurse," I said resignedly, "I am here in this hospital because I cannot eat. I am positive if I eat that food, I would have another heart attack."

The nurse looked at the ham and spaghetti, then bent over to read the chart. She said nothing but I was sure there was some mistake. After she left, I looked over at Maria to see how she was. She was sitting on the bed crying. Maria had been in the hospital ten days, and the food was still disagreeing with her.

I thought for a moment then said, "Maria, you don't have to take my advice, but there is nothing wrong with you except your baby is very sensitive and has picked up your nervous tension. This is why the food is disagreeing with both of you. Stop eating for a few days. Take liquids and see how you feel."

Just then the nurse came from the bathroom. She had overheard the conversation.

"Miss Maya," she said angrily, "stop giving advice to the patients. We have doctors to do that in the hospital."

Both Maria and I remained silent until she left, then Maria plied me with questions about how to overcome this sensitivity.

I thought for a moment then said, "Your trouble is emotional. There is someone in your home that is jealous of you. It's a woman."

Looking at me in amazement Maria said, "Yes, it's my mother-in-law. She lives with us."

Maria wept for a moment then continued. "I have never told this to anyone. I was too ashamed of myself for thinking such evil thoughts. I also have been afraid of losing my husband to a former girl friend that his mother liked.

"Did you tell this to the doctors?" I asked quietly.

"No, Maya, they would not understand. I have told them nothing."

The next day Maria was careful of her diet. She threw away her food, as she did not wish the doctors to get angry with her. Some soup strained of all fat was brought in by her husband. This she ate with some grapes that I had given to her.

TWENTY-THREE
Diet

One night, around seven-thirty, I went to the phone booth to call Lola. I wanted some grapes. Looking into the little office I saw Dr. Mack. He was the ward doctor who was prescribing my medication and diet. He was talking to a tall blond man who was not as good-looking as Dr. Mack, but he had a very interesting face.

"Dr. Mack," I said going up to the two men, "I can't eat the food that is given to me. I can only eat chicken or very lean meat, and on my chart my diet says fat-free. I have not been eating for many months.

"Miss Maya," Dr. Mack said coolly, "I am sorry if you can't eat the hospital food, but we can't pamper our patients. After all, we are not here to pamper you." The blond doctor and I looked in amazement at Dr. Mack. I started to speak, then thought it best not to say anything to him and silently I walked away, but not before the blond doctor had seen the tears of frustration in my eyes.

Two nights later I was in great pain. It was around 9 p.m. The nurse had given me some medication but it had not stopped the pain. I was quietly sobbing in my bed so as not to disturb Maria who was sleeping.

Hearing some noise at the foot of the bed I looked up to see the doctor who had been talking to Dr. Mack. He leaned over and asked if I were in pain. "Yes, Doctor," I answered noticing the doctor's insignia on his coat. "Who sent you?"

"No one sent me," he answered quietly sitting in the chair beside my bed.

"Oh, yes," I insisted, "God sent you. I have been asking him to send someone to ease my pain."

"No, God did not send me. I saw you outside in the office. You looked so miserable. I just could not forget the look in your eyes, they have haunted me ever since. Yes, for the past two days, I just had to come."

"Then God sent you," I went on with an air of determination. "I have been praying for two days. God is very good to me." He looked at me with all my pain and grief, wondering if God was good to me, then why all this suffering. He was unaware that I could read his thoughts, but I said nothing about it to him.

"I do not believe in God," said the doctor solemnly. "I am from the Balkans and have suffered a great deal from people who called themselves Christians. I have seen too much, so consequently do not believe there is a God."

I looked into his eyes. There I saw the suffering from the past and many other things, that I did not care to reveal to him.

Softly I said, "I understand, do not say any more."

For a few minutes we were both silent. Then he asked, "How would you like to try out a new medicine? I am now working on it. So far we have had some success, but the hospital would not allow me to use it without your permission. Is it all right?"

Looking at this strange man, I asked, "What is your new medicine, and what do you call it?"

"Number Nine so far. It is just an experiment, so you will have to give me your word, just in case it has repercussions."

I thought for a few moments, what have I to lose? They are not helping me, so anything is better than nothing, even if it is an experiment. God sent him. I will be protected, so why not?

"Yes, Doctor, you may try your experiment. I promise not to say anything if there are any repercussions. I have faith in God. It was He who sent you, even thought you may not know it now, but truly you are a man of God."

He was Dr. Vassilli, one of the many scientific doctors of the hospital. He returned with medicine that looked like mercury, but lighter in color. He filled a needle, then, turning me over, asked where the pain was. He shot the needle directly in the spot. I held my breath and it did not hurt. After that he left, saying he would return the next night to see how I was feeling.

Two days later, Maria left the hospital. She thanked me for my prayers and other advice. She was now free emotionally and left the hospital with her husband, who was happy to see her quick recovery.

Her bed was taken by an older woman who was full of water. She weighed about three hundred pounds and could not walk, so they brought her in a special wheelchair. I looked on at the many relatives and doctors who were coming and going for about two hours. At last all was quiet. The patient was resting and I was trying to relax in order to meditate. But I was not doing a very good job of it.

Suddenly, in the doorway, stood a dark man. He was of medium build. There was deep spirituality in his face. Glancing at his dark clothing, I saw that he wore a clerical collar and knew he belonged to a religious order.

"May I come in?" he asked quietly, not wanting to awaken the other patient.

I nodded. These days I refrained from speaking even a single word. It took too much effort.

Coming to the foot of my bed he continued, "I did not want to intrude on your privacy. Are you Catholic or Protestant?"

I waited for a few moments before answering, all the while studying his countenance and quiet dignity.

"I am of God," I answered softly, "you, too, are a man of God. Come, hold my hand and pray with me."

The minister held my hand, in silence he bowed his head. For a few minutes he remained so, then as if inspired by another being he spoke, "May the living God, who has promised that wherever two or more are gathered, there will I be, and whatever is agreed upon I shall manifest in the world of man. Now we are gathered here to ask for a healing for this beloved sister, who in spirit is perfect, so, oh Father, lift up her consciousness so that she may see herself perfect as you made her, put light into her mind, release all negations from her consciousness and free her forever and ever."

At the end of his prayer I was crying. The tears were streaming down my face. The clock struck nine thirty.

"Are you in pain?" asked the minister. "Tell me about it."

"There is not much to tell, I fell on a bus and struck my spine. It has disturbed my whole nervous system. Even speaking is difficult for me," I answered between gasps. "Tell me who you are. I am interested. while you stood in the doorway I saw your aura. It was gold and very clear."

The minister glanced at me, for he was still praying and listening at the same time.

"Are you a mystic?" he asked, looking more closely into my eyes.

"Yes, I am a spiritual mystic. I believe in all denominations, for all truths lead up the path to the Father of light. We are his children who ages ago lost our way."

He thought over my statements for a moment then added, "You said spiritual mystic. Is there a difference between a mystic and a spiritual mystic?"

"Yes," I said, "there is a difference. A mystic is one who has second sight, but has been sent here to earth for a particular purpose. But a spiritual mystic is one that was born with a veil and is guided by the hand of God, but please tell me about yourself."

"You are a very interesting person. I would like to continue our discussion some other time. I realize it is difficult for you to speak so I shall tell you of myself. I am Rev. Thorne from Trinidad, B.W.I. Of course, you know there are three churches here in the hospital. Catholic, Protestant and Jewish."

I nodded and he continued. "I am one of two ministers in the Presbyterian Church. The other is Rev. Williams, and now that we know each other I will leave. Good night. God bless you."

I smiled faintly saying, "Thank you, Reverend Thorne. Please pray for me. May God hold your hand guiding you at all times. Good night."

TWENTY-FOUR

Problems

One afternoon, Jess, my reporter friend, came by. He told me that he had called my private doctor, but he was on his way to Europe. There was no hope of my changing hospitals. It just was not done. Seeing the forlorn look on my face, Jess changed the subject.

"Bob Sylvester is coming to see you, possibly tomorrow. We are all disturbed about you. I saw Walter last night, he feels that you will lick this thing."

I smiled weakly. "I really don't know if I want to lick it, Jess, I am so very tired, I just want to go to sleep forever."

Jess looked serious, as he said quietly, "Now, Maya, you have to make up your mind you can. If you really want to, you can."

"Who will I get to advise me?"

"Oh, come now, Maya, we really need you."

Slowly I said with difficulty, "Well, Jess, this is the year and it really looks as if I will go out, but I will always be with you in spirit. Where I go all my friends will follow sometime." I stopped talking as a pain shot across my back.

Jess sat in deep silence for a few moments. He knew that I still believed in that vision of mine. Suddenly, getting up to leave, he said, "Maya, I will pray for you, I will."

"Thank you, Jess. We will need lots of prayers and strong ones if we are going to lick this thing. Good-bye, Jess, God bless you."

A few minutes after Jess left, Lola, a friend of many years came in. She told me that Bev had brought some chicken soup. She stopped to show it to the nurse. Bev was the wife of my lawyer. Lola and I waited for Bev to bring in the soup, but she came in without it, saying it had been taken away from her. I was not allowed to have any food brought into the hospital. At this information, Lola went out to speak to the doctor in charge, but he was adamant.

"No food will be allowed to come into the ward. No, Miss Maya will have to eat the hospital food."

When Lola told me this, a frustrated look came over my face. I knew the doctor had a personal bone to pick with me. Lola promised that she would sneak in a piece of broiled chicken the next day, which she did.

That evening Dr. Mack, the ward doctor came in. He sat down with a sheepish look on his handsome big face, waiting for me to ask about the food but I said nothing.

"Miss Maya, I am sorry about the soup but it was not up to me. I am leaving the ward and going up to another floor. Please try to understand, we have to work under orders. I do hope that you will get completely well. May I come down to see you sometime?"

I felt sorry for him and held out my hand to show him my sincerity.

"Yes, Doctor, please do come down any time. I am not angry with you or anyone else for that matter. " I stopped, in pain, then continued more slowly, "All I want is to eat just a slice of bread and butter without any bad effects. That would mean a lot to me."

Dr. Mack got up to leave, "I am truly sorry about the whole matter. I want you to know that it was not up to me. I'll drop down to see you sometime."

After he had left I looked out into the night, asking myself what was it all about. Why were the doctors fighting about me? Why did this young doctor come in to tell me that he was not to be blamed for not giving me the soup? Could it be that Doctor Bruno was still holding the unfortunate incident of the stroke, two nights after I was admitted into the hospital? Was he afraid of losing face? Oh, dear God, what is it all about?

The next day I waited patiently for Bob Sylvester to come by, but feeling sleepy, I dozed off, only to awaken and find Miss White waiting for me to wake up.

"Miss Maya, a gentleman was here to see you. A Mr. Bob Sylvester. He left this note for you."

I hurriedly read the note. "Maya, dear, you sleep just like a baby," signed Bob. The fat patient in the next bed asked if this was the famous Bob Sylvester and I nodded. I felt disappointed not to have seen Bob. I wanted to tell him of the many incidents that had happened to me in the hospital.

That night while I was eating dinner, which was lean meat and Jello for desert, Lillian, a patient from the next room came in. She looked like a ghost. Coming over to my bed she asked, "Maya, can I have your bread and butter?"

I looked at her for a moment, then answered slowly, "I am sorry, Lillian, but you are not supposed to have bread and butter, you are on a strict diet for your heart."

"All I get is rice, rice," she answered, "I am starving slowly. Look here, Maya, they give you bread and butter, but you can't eat it. They give you all sorts of food that you can't eat. I can eat it, so why not give it to me?"

I looked at this poor woman begging for bread. I felt sorry for her. "Lillian, I won't give you the bread but you can help yourself."

Lillian snatched the bread from the plate and left.

This was the beginning of a peculiar friendship. Whenever I needed anything Lillian was there to help. Two days later, I was not feeling well and I was telling the nurse not to bring my lunch when suddenly I looked out the door and saw Lillian making frantic signals, telling me to take the lunch.

"Very well, Nurse, bring me some lunch."

"Make up your mind, Miss Maya," the nurse said leaving the room not knowing what to think of me.

Several of the nurses were coming to me for spiritual advice. Now it was known all over the hospital that there was a mystic reader on that floor. Some of the patients were asking advice of me as I went to the phone booth, and sometimes they would come back to my bed.

One morning a cleaning man came in. He cleaned the room and brushed off the windows. After a long while he said to me, "Miss Maya, do you remember me? I used to go to your lectures in Carnegie Hall."

I looked at him but could not remember who he was. After a few other remarks, he told me of a patient who would like to talk to me. It was his cousin. She was under a spell, or so she thought. No one could change her mind.

"Can you see her?"

That afternoon I went out into the waiting room and Neal, the cleaning man, introduced Lucille to me. For one hour I listened to Lucille, who definitely felt that something had been done to her by a former boyfriend. I did not say too much the first day, but a couple of days later she came back and I won her confidence. She agreed that destructive thoughts had been sent to her subconscious mind. These thoughts were being attracted by the malice and hate within her conscious mind.

I said, "Remove that malice and hate by praying for this man who is trying to destroy your being. Send love and prosperity to him, thereby dissolving the destructive forces that are around him and in time these same blessings would return to you, the sender, ten hundred fold."

Lucille was too angry with this man who was slowly trying to destroy her. "No, I cannot pray for him; ask anything else, but not this, Miss Maya. You don't understand. He even tried to murder me."

On and on she raved, telling me all the terrible things that this old lover had done to her. Even to me it was inconceivable that a human being would go to such lengths to destroy another. Again I insisted that to pray for him was the only way for her to break the spell of evil thoughts that were seeping through to her subconscious. Yes, this was the way to bring back the health and strength to her physical body.

A week later, Lucille left the hospital. Her strength had miraculously returned. When I heard the good news from Neal, I was happy for Lucille but puzzled. Why was it that I could find the key for all who came to me for help, but could not find it for myself?

"Oh, God," I cried, "Give me back my health and vital strength. Give me a new spirit and a new body."

One night Dr. Vassilli came to give me my usual injection. Shortly after, Dr. Bruno came in and asked if Dr. Vassilli was going to have his palm read. Dr. Vassilli turned around saying curtly, "No, I am going to give her an injection."

Dr. Bruno left. There was a look of disappointment on his face. There would be no palm readings for him that night. We both knew of his disappointment, but did not care to pamper his whims.

After the injection Dr. Vassilli asked me if I would like to meet a psychologist. His work was similar to mine and he was sure I would find this man very interesting. I agreed and next morning at ten-thirty, Dr. Hartly appeared. He was a stockily-built man of medium height, with bushy eyebrows and lots of bushy hair, which he combed straight up on his head giving him a very fierce look.

He said good morning and sat down with a definite air. One who has come to conquer. I gave him the once-over and knew that he was a psychiatrist even before he introduced himself.

He asked many questions of me. I replied frankly to all. Some of the answers he did not expect and I was aware of this.

First question: "Are you a mystic, and how do you define mysticism?"

Answer: "Yes, doctor, I am a mystic. I was born with a veil. A mystic is one who can read the thoughts of others." At this unexpected answer, he scrutinized me more closely from under his bushy eyebrows.

Q: "Do you have visions?"

A. "Yes, doctor, I have had many visions. Some have been very constructive in my life."

Q: "Do you have boyfriends?"

A: "No, doctor, I do not."

Q: "Don't you ever have the urge?"

A: "Yes, doctor, I do, but I pray myself out of it."

Again he looked more closely and asked, "Could this be part of your illness?"

I stared at him for a moment, wondering what force within my being had manifested this visit which resulted in such silly questions and answers.

Quietly I said, "Doctor, my sickness was caused by an accident to my spine." He chose to overlook this statement and went on with his next question.

Q: "Did your mother or anyone else in your family also have visions?'

A: "No, doctor, there is never more than one mystic born in any family. As a matter of fact, my mother was always afraid of what I would do or say, also what people would think of me, but since she has passed on, I have met her on the other side and she admitted that she wished she had understood me in life as she does now."

Q: "What do you mean by seeing her on the other side?"

A: Doctor, I leave my body and go over into the spirit world. I can go anywhere in this world, I just think myself there and soon I am there." I stopped. By now the doctor's eyes were bulging. I thought, "If he has thought of scaring me, he cannot, for now I have turned the tables on him."

The doctor seemed to be in deep thought. I kept asking myself, why did he not leave, why was he staying so long? What was he trying to accomplish? I glanced at the clock, it was way after eleven. Suddenly he came to life.

"Miss Maya, my summation of you is that you are a neurotic and highly nervous person."

I glared at him, wondering how he had arrived at such a fantastic statement. Then, as if a movie camera had flashed across my mental mind, I saw this man, sick and depressed by an inferiority complex. Now he was the patient and I the psychiatrist.

"Doctor, do you pray?"

Glaring back at me, briskly he replied, "No, I don't believe in prayer."

"Then," I said calmly as if speaking to a little child, "I will pray for you."

"I don't care what you do," he answered like a naughty boy.

"Doctor," I said, wondering what bomb could I use in order to remove him from my presence, "I am a writer." At this statement he again came back to the world of consciousness.

"A writer?" he questioned, not believing he had heard the right words.

"What do you write about?"

"Oh, everything that happens in my life. I memorize and put it down for later," I said with the assured air of one who has found a soft spot and knew it.

"Have you published anything?" asked the perplexed doctor.

"No, so far I have only given out one story to my friend Jess who is a very famous reporter. He thinks that the world is not ready to believe my stories, so he will hold it until the proper time."

"Well, well, that is very interesting. I must go now." Without saying good-bye, he left and I closed my eyes trying to forget his summation of me.

Suddenly I felt all alone in a world of many minds, all in conflict with mine. I looked around for someone to talk to, but only the fat patient was there and she did not speak English except for a few words. I thought of Father Ryan.

"Oh, God, please send the kind father to me, Please send him. I need someone to talk with."

Getting out of bed, I thought I must call Jess. He would understand. Passing the little office on my way to the phone, I saw both Dr. Vassilli and Dr. Hartly in deep conversation and knew that the topic was about my writing. I was sure that Dr. Vassilli had informed the psychiatrist of the reporters who had come to see me and that they were very well known.

After contacting Jess on the phone, he listened to my story patiently and sensed that I was crying. "Now, now, Maya, don't get upset," he said, trying to calm me, "or you really will need psychiatric care. Go back and quiet yourself. I will see if I can arrange to get you out of there. In one way or another I will help you, keep your chin up."

Walking back to my room I saw that the doctors were still in conference. This time they both looked up and saw me as if sensing where I had been and what I was up to. They glared at me but did not speak.

Down the ward I saw Father Ryan. He was in front of my door, turning all around looking for me. He had received my mental call.

"Oh, Father," I said excitedly, "I want to see you. Something terrible has happened."

Taking my hand he led me back to bed and asked what happened. I told him what the psychiatrist had said to me.

"I would not worry about that. They have said worse things about very intelligent people. After all his opinion is not to be taken seriously; he just did not understand you. I think your ego is hurt. You are usually the one to make summations of others, and now for the first time someone is summing you up. Come now, cheer up, all will be well. Soon you will be out of here living a healthy and wonderful life. By the way, how did you call me."

"I prayed and asked God to send you to me," I said.

For a moment he looked at me, not wanting to believe what I had just said, but something in my eyes seemed to convince him of the truth. Bowing his head he prayed fervently.

At three p. m. that same day, I was surprised to see six doctors walk into my room and come directly to my bed. Leading the way was a small dark man with penetrating eyes that seemed to look right through you. This was Dr. Orzo. He was Greek and one of the leading physicians in the hospital. I learned later, but didn't realize then, that to get this Greek doctor to pay a visit to anyone was a great honor.

Dr. Orzo leaned over and patted me. On his face there was a charming smile as he said, "Miss Maya, nice hospital, nice doctors."

I looked at his benign face and answered slowly, "Yes, Doctor, you are very nice." I emphasized "you" making him aware that the compliment was meant for him alone.

Dr. Vassilli, the scientist, who stood on the opposite side of the bed from Dr. Orzo, said, as if trying to warn the doctor, "She has a very awakened mind. She can actually tell things about you."

I remembered the time when I had told Dr. Vassilli that he was a philosopher. I had not thought much of it at the time but it must have made a deep impression on him.

Learning of my psychic powers, Dr. Orzo asked, "Am I married?"

I looked at him with an amused smile, but did not care to answer such an obvious question. He tried again.

"Have I any children?"

"Yes, doctor," I said looking off into space, as if reading the answers on a blank wall, "You have three children. You are very disturbed about one tall boy."

At my amazing statement, he looked around to see who had given this information to me, but seeing no one who could possibly have known about it, he stood there too shocked to ask any more questions.

Dr. Bruno spoke up, his curiosity overcoming his sense of good judgement. "Am I married?" he asked, putting out his hand for a complete reading.

Looking at him disdainfully, I answered, "No, Doctor, and you will not marry your present romance because your independent and forceful nature clashes with hers."

After these deductions about their private lives, the other doctors refrained from asking me any other questions. Silently they walked out of the room with puzzled looks on their faces.

That night I had two dreams. One with Zaza and the other with Yuri Andropov. I woke up about midnight and felt Zaza still in the room. In the dream she was standing at the foot of the bed smiling as she said, "Don't worry Maya, soon you will be out of this hospital and you will be well and happy." I went back to sleep and saw Yuri and Bill who seemed to be in a hospital, he was lying on a bed and Yuri was speaking to him. I could not hear what was being said but I gathered Yuri was trying to lift up his consciousness. After I awakened from that dream I felt it was a warning for me to pray for Bill. This I did and felt better. The next morning I woke up.

TWENTY-FIVE

The Hand of God

The next day, after the visit of the six doctors, I was taken down to the X-ray department where I was X-rayed from head to toe. Neil, the X-ray technician, a very intelligent black man, seemed interested in taking an X-ray of my head. As he and the doctor examined it, I wondered why they were so interested in my head. It was not hurting, why didn't they examine the X-ray of my back instead?

Later I asked Neil, the technician, and he answered saying, "The doctors think that you may have struck your head when you fell."

As an afterthought, he asked, "Say, Miss Maya, have you always been psychic?"

I looked quizzically at Neil and asked, "Is that why they are X-raying my brain?"

The technician laughed as if he remembered something funny.

"Oh, boy, you have the old boy himself going around in a tailspin. They have had more conferences since yesterday. What did you tell them?"

I smiled, but did not answer. Instead I asked, "Who is the old boy?"

"Don't you know who the short doctor is? He is Dr. Orzo, the head of the hospital. I heard he left your room as if he had been shot, and the other doctors looked as if they were sleepwalking. Well, all I can say is, they need a few more mystics around here. You should take a job here."

There was a tired look on my face as I said, "All I want is to get well and I hope they don't send me any more psychiatrists." The technician looked interested as he asked, "Who was the psychiatrist that they sent you?"

"Dr. Hartly," I answered.

"Oh, no, they didn't send you that bird! He is one for the books."

I smiled and just then I saw the nurse coming to wheel me back to the room. Softly, so that the nurse would not hear, I answered, "That is the understatement of the century. He really is one for the books."

That night Dr. Vassilli came in. He was still giving me the injections of Number Nine about three times a week. After the injection he sat down. For a few moments he was quiet, then in a very soft voice he said, "Miss Maya, we cannot help you."

Looking at him in surprise, I asked, "Why, doctor, are there any more complications?"

"No, but we have come to the conclusion that your mind is sick," he answered as if not wanting to hurt me.

"Doctor, my body is ill. Relieve the pain from my back and my mind will be well. This tormenting pain is driving me mad," I said in a very determined voice.

"No, Miss Maya, heal your mind and your body will become well." The doctor spoke with an air of determination that I knew there was no need to argue the matter any further so I kept quiet. Just then Reverend Thorne came to the door. He turned to go when he saw the doctor, but Dr. Vasselli said, "Please stay Reverend, I am leaving now."

The doctor left and Reverend Thorne sat down. For a few moments he remained quiet. There was an air of excitement about him and I waited to hear what it was all about.

Finally he said in hushed tones, "I have a message for you." Again he was silent and I wondered what the message was about.

"This morning while I was in deep meditation, a voice came through. It was very plain, it said, "Tell Maya that she will leave the hospital one week from today."

I looked at the man of God, not knowing how to believe his words. "I don't know how. How can I leave? I still cannot eat and the pain has not left me. Next Wednesday is a week from today, Reverend, are you sure? I don't know how to believe you."

I lay there pondering over his words, then asked, "Did the spirit say I would go to another hospital?"

The minister remained quiet. He was wondering if he had not implicated himself in a matter that would appear like fortune telling. I sensed this, but was curious abut the matter and wanted him to explain more clearly.

As if hesitant to say any more, he replied slowly, "No, Miss Maya, that was all that I got on the matter. Please believe me, it is only because of my sympathy for you that I have given you this message anyway. I am afraid I have to leave now."

The next day, Thursday, there was great excitement around the fat patient. Her family had come in that afternoon. The doctors had informed them that she was to be removed to another hospital, on the Island. The fat patient was crying as if her heart would break. In halting English she had confided in me, asking if I would pray for her. To this I consented, but I had an inner feeling that this patient would not get better and the feeling was clarified later by one of the nurses who told me that the fat patient had passed.

That night the fat patient's bed was taken by a Spanish lady. She was brought in by a friend who undressed her and left. The new patient sat on the bed with the air of one who belongs and knows that she is welcome. Several of the nurses came to greet her, even the aides knew her. One asked how long she intended staying. To these many greetings and friendly queries, the new patient just beamed in a happy mood. I thought, how odd, this woman was really happy to be in a hospital; only that afternoon another had cried her eyes out not wanting to leave.

After the patient was made comfortable and the nurses had left, she looked around to see who was sharing her domicile. Seeing my peaked look, she asked what ailed me. I informed her of the accident in a few words for this was one of my bad nights.

Rosita was very friendly. She introduced herself and asked my name. After that she confidentially told me she had diabetes and waited a few moments to see the effect her words would have on me. I waited patiently, knowing that Rosita loved to tell about her ailments to others.

After a while she went on, explaining that the welfare agency was taking care of her. No, she had no relatives, none that she cared to see. Anyway, most relatives just came around for hand-outs, so she didn't bother too much with them. The welfare agent was very nice to her. Oh, yes, she had been in the hospital several times. She liked it here. The nurses were kind to her and they all treated her as if she were one of them. They laughingly told her this was her country home. Her house was not nice, it had big rats. Oh, it had cockroaches, too, but that she did not mind so much; it was the rats that bothered her. One little mouse thought it was his house. When she played the radio he would come out to listen. Sometimes he would turn his head from one side to the other, in order to hear the music better. Oh, he was so cute. Several times she had the chance to kill him, but he was so friendly, she did not have the heart to hurt the poor little fellow.

The city had told the landlord to clean out the house, but he was waiting for his tenants to move, then he would tear the whole building down. It was too old. Whenever things got too bad, she would tell the welfare agent and she would arrange for her to come to the hospital. "Oh, God is good to me. God is so very good, he will give me a better home, I just know it."

She looked over to see what I thought of this prediction. I nodded. With such faith that Rosita had, even in the presence of big rats, I was sure that she would get her wish. There was no doubt about that matter.

The next morning about 10 a.m., Dr. Bruno and Dr. Green, his assistant, came into the room. They greeted Rosita and asked a few questions about her health. Then they came to me and after greeting me, they went directly to my cupboard where I kept fruit and other health foods. Looking through it thoroughly, they both admitted there was nothing there that I could not eat. They went out, speaking in undertones so that no one could hear what was being said.

I was just wondering why they were so interested in my health foods, when Nurse White came in. Sensing the curiosity in my face, she said, "Miss Maya, the doctors have decided that you are not co-operating with them. You should try to eat solid foods, then they will know how they react to you."

I smiled for I knew how they reacted and did not want to experiment any further. I was just going to admit this to the nurse, when from down the hall came piercing screams.

"Oh, don't worry about her," said the nurse placidly, "that's a Puerto Rican girl. She thinks that devils are after her. She said that someone put a spell on her. We are sending her downtown."

"Downtown?" I asked in a perplexed voice.

"That is Bellevue, we call it downtown. Here she is now."

Both Rosita and I followed the nurse to the door. Being wheeled down the hall by Neal was a young girl with long black hair that hung unruly down her back. One skinny forefinger was pointing at some unknown terror as she spat out curse words. Seeing the three of us in the doorway, Neal stopped to get our reaction to the screaming girl. Turning to me he asked, "Are there really devils around her?"

I did not answer and Rosita made the sign of the cross. It was then I knew that Rosita had the seeing eye.

Twenty-six days had now passed. It was Monday and I thought of Reverend Thorne's prediction and wondered if I were going to leave the hospital in two days. If I did, I would need strength, so getting out of bed, I tried to find the shower. I was tired of taking baths in bed, tired of eating in bed, tired of bed, period.

Going to the shower, I found another patient who helped me get in and then held me while I put my gown and robe back on. After that, a nurse helped me back to bed.

For two hours I prayed for strength and power, then I got up and again went down the hall, this time to visit a friend who was interested in mysticism.

Coming out of the ward was Dr. Bruno, followed by Dr. Green.

"Ah, Miss Maya," shouted Dr. Bruno, "we were just coming to see you."

"How are you feeling?" asked Dr. Green, "we hope better because we need the bed."

I looked surprised at the doctor's statement and asked, "Why, doctor, are you sending me to another hospital?"

Dr. Bruno had stepped into the background, allowing the younger doctor to handle the situation, which he felt was rather peculiar.

"No, dear," answered Dr. Green, "we feel that there is nothing more we can do for you. We have tried all our methods and they have all failed, dear."

I looked at the young doctor. In other circumstances I would have enjoyed talking to him, for he was the soul of sincerity. Clean and unworldly. There was no deceit in his make-up, which could not be said for Dr. Bruno, who was forever trying to do something in secret. Even now he was throwing the dirty work over to his assistant, who was too young to know what he was doing.

Some power other than mine spoke up, "Doctor, please do not call me dear."

"O.K., Madame," answered the young doctor unperturbed, "We have tried everything, now we need the bed, dear."

Overlooking this last endearing term, I spoke to the young doctor, but in my mind I was addressing the older one.

"Doctor, it is not my fault that you have the brain of a monkey and cannot diagnose my particular ailment."

At this unkind remark Dr. Bruno smiled. He seemed pleased that I had insulted the young doctor, who looked at me in amazement. Noting something different about me which seemed to hold him at bay, he kept quiet. Dr. Bruno took over the situation, which had definitely gotten out of hand.

"Miss Maya, we are sorry we need the bed for another patient."

"Very well, doctor, you can have the bed, I will leave the hospital, but you can be sure that I won't sign myself out."

At this attack, both doctors looked at each other, then abruptly left in order to get legal advice and find out what could be done with a patient who knew that she could stay indefinitely at the hospital, so long as the ailment continued.

I turned to go back to bed. My feet were buckling under when a nurse came to my assistance. Several of the patients had overheard the conversation and were amazed at the tenacity of this woman who could barely get around on her own power.

After the nurse had helped me into bed, she leaned over and patted my cheek. "Miss Maya," she said, with great feeling, "I admire your courage. If more patients spoke up, we could get more done. You just stick to your guns."

I looked at her and wondered how I was going to stick to my guns, when I could barely make it back to bed.

That afternoon I looked in vain for someone in my family to come, but at the end of the visiting hour only an old friend of many years came hurrying in.

"Bell, you angel, how did you know that I needed you? I need help very much. How did you know?"

By now I was crying. Bell was telling me that something just seemed to pull her there at the last minute. Between sobs, I told Bell of my predicament.

"I just don't know what I will do, Bell. My sisters are away and my niece is having a baby. I just don't know who to call."

Bell looked at me as if not believing her eyes. This was not Maya, the bright, cheery, wonderful person. No, this woman was a desperate, sick woman who needed food for the body as well as the mind.

"Maya, dear," Bell said coming out of her shock, "calm yourself and tell me, do you have to leave the hospital? If so, think of someone that we can call, not only to take you out but to care for you."

Haltingly, I explained the situation to Bell. Getting the truth of the matter, Bell advised me to leave the hospital.

"Come, Maya, try to get up. We will go and phone a relative or friend."

Helping me put my robe on, Bell took me out to the lounge, where I gave her two numbers to call; one friend, Joann, was sure to be in. She would come for me.

Contacting Joann, Bell told her of my predicament. It was imperative that I leave the hospital. Coming back, Bell found me speaking with the head nurse, who asked what Bell was doing there after visiting hours. Taking the situation in hand, Bell explained that I was leaving the hospital and that she had remained in order to get someone to come and take me home.

The nurse looked at me, who by now looked anything but well, and went on to other duties, wondering why the doctor had told me to leave.

Taking me back to bed, Bell assured me that I would be well. Joann would be there around 7 p.m.

A few minutes later, Dr. Bruno came in. Bell excused herself saying she would wait outside.

"Miss Maya" Dr. Bruno said quietly, "Dr. Orzo, the head doctor, has decided to keep you another week in order to take some more tests."

I looked at the doctor with confusion written all over my face. One minute they wanted me to leave and the next to stay. This was not real, it was all a nightmare.

"Doctor, I just do not know what to say, my friend is coming to take me home. All at once I am so very confused." Putting my hand before my face, I started to cry.

"Now, now, Miss Maya," the doctor exclaimed, feeling my pulse, "I think it's best you stay here. You are in a highly nervous state of tension. Oh, no, we just could not allow you to leave the hospital. I will have the nurse bring in a sedative. You will be all right."

When Bell returned, I informed her of the change of plans.

"Thank God," cried Bell, fervently. "I have been praying for you to stay here. You are in no condition to leave the hospital.

"Thank God."

Going out, she called Joann, and told her of the change of plans.

It was now Tuesday morning, December 11th. I woke up feeling alive, and instinctively I knew that the forces of the doctors and the spirit of the hospital were in accordance with me. When breakfast came I took some juice, then with relish ate a piece of toast with butter and a cup of coffee. The nurse smiled as she took the tray away, thinking that at last I was myself.

A few minutes later Lillian came in for her toast and not seeing it in the usual place in the cupboard, she asked, "Where is my toast?"

By now I was feeling the effects of the butter and did not answer. Rudely shaking me, Lillian asked again, "Maya, where is my toast?"

"I ate it, Lillian, and now I am sick. Go call the nurse."

Lillian ran out to call the nurse, Miss Kelly, who was blonde and very pretty. There was a rumor around the hospital that Dr. Bruno was in love with her, but she had a will of her own and did not comply with his demands.

"Miss Maya, what is wrong?"

Before I could reply, she went on, "You are a problem. You are forever running all over the hospital prescribing and giving advice to all the patients. The doctors don't know what to think of you. If you are sick, why don't you stay in bed? That is where a sick patient belongs."

I peered at her through my tears, but I was too sick to worry about what the doctors thought.

"Nurse, it was the bread and butter. I felt better so I ate my breakfast."

"Miss Maya, you are a very intelligent woman, why do you eat bread and butter if you know that it does not agree with you?"

I stared at her for a moment, then bluntly asked, "Nurse, why is it put on my plate if I am not supposed to eat it?"

The nurse shrugged her shoulders and walked out of the room. She was caught napping and knew there was no answer.

A few minutes later, a black nurse came into the room. A few days prior to this I had given her a reading, and felt that she was a friend I could confide in. Hearing the sobs, she asked Rosita what was wrong with me, but Rosita was not one for speaking her mind. She just shrugged her shoulders. The nurse leaned over and asked me what ailed me, but I was too sick to answer and kept quiet.

Impatiently shaking me, the nurse said, "Miss Maya, if you keep on crying like this they will send you downtown."

Glaring at her I got up on my elbows and asked, "They and whose army?"

The nurse stared for a moment, then ran out of the room in a hurry. Shortly after, she came back with some medication for me. Getting some relief, I lay in bed reminiscing over the events of the morning, recalling the surprised look on the nurse's face. It reminded me of my childhood days, walking down the country road with Cecil, my brother. Spying a tiny bird lying by the side of the road as if dead, Cecil went over to examine it. Finding very little life in the bird, he got a stone, preparing to finish him off, when the beady eyes opened. Flying directly into Cecil's face, the bird scratched him and flew into the woods. I recalled the same look on Cecil's face that I had seen that morning on the nurse's and smiled as I remembered my brother's question, "Where did the strength come from?"

Yes, where do we get the strength in order for us to overcome the many trials and pitfalls that we meet on our way through life? Only God knows for He is the giver of all things.

On Tuesday afternoon, I felt a desperate urge to leave the hospital. I felt that if I were on the outside, where I could get the right food, all would be well. Going to the phone, I thought of my niece who was expecting a baby. Under ordinary circumstances, I would not have bothered her but I was desperate.

Getting Phil on the phone, I said with tears in my voice, "Phil, if you love me, get me out of here. I just can't go on any longer. I just—," stopping to catch my breath, I broke down.

"Now, now, Honey, just hold on. I will send Allie. He will come tomorrow night for you. Today is too late for me to contact him. Promise me that you will control yourself."

Phil's voice had a tremor, but behind it there was determination, and I knew that she would keep her word and send Allie, my nephew. Everyone in the family relied on him whenever there was work. It was always Allie who was called.

Feeling better, that night around eight I visited Lillian, who was complaining about the ingratitude of her roommate, a black girl who worked in the hospital as an aide.

"Maya, you would not believe it but that girl complains about everything. She has the doctors running. Today she complained about the food being cold. Oh, yes, she gets chicken and custard."

Just then the head nurse came in and Lillian changed the subject to metaphysics. Mrs. Johnson listened to the discussion for a few moments then said to me, "Miss Maya, it seems strange that you can advise everyone except yourself. Why don't you apply these same theories to your life. What is really wrong with you?"

I did not answer for a few minutes, then asked quietly, "Nurse, don't you know that I had a spinal injury?"

"Heavens, no," replied the surprised nurse, "no one told me of it. I can readily understand why you have pains in your back. I, too, had an injury and it bothered me all these many years. What with a sick husband to look after, I have my hands full. I wonder if he will ever come out of it?"

I did not answer. I sensed that the nurse knew the answer; why give her more bad news. By the time her husband passed into spirit, she would be conditioned to bear the burden of living a lonely life.

Going back to my room around 9 p.m., I found Reverend Thorne waiting by the bed.

"I see you are better. I am so happy for you," he exclaimed shaking my hand.

I got into bed and told him of the effects the breakfast had on me. He admonished me to be more careful of my diet in the future.

From outside, in the hall, came voices. Some young students were parading down the hall with torches. They were dressed in white robes, both men and women and a few children; all had lovely voices. They were singing Christmas carols. It was a very beautiful sight as they all passed singing, "Holy, Holy, all is well, all is well."

Suddenly the vibration of the hospital was lifted up and I felt as if an aura of heaven had descended on the young singers who looked like angels. Glancing at Reverend Thorne, I saw that his face was full of joy. We both revelled in the spiritual harmony that had suddenly surrounded the hospital. We were transported into a higher consciousness.

Wednesday morning I woke around six. I was sure someone had spoken to me. Looking around I saw Rosita sleeping soundly so it could not have been her. All through the hospital it was quiet, yet I was sure someone had said, "Get up, Maya, tonight you will leave the hospital."

Getting up I brushed my hair, threw on a robe and then went down the hall to the visiting lounge which overlooked the East River. There, coming up, was the most beautiful sunrise I had every witnessed. The young Spanish nurse was looking at it.

"Hello, Nurse," I said going up beside her, "I feel that I am being released from something. This sunrise is telling me there is yet life and happiness somewhere in this world."

The young nurse smiled as she replied, "I hope so, I hope it means that you will go home for Christmas. You have been here a long time."

"Yes," I answered softly as if in a trance, "twenty-eight days, but this sunrise is symbolic of something good. It has to be."

Six-thirty that evening I went into the office. Dr. Vassilli was there. He looked up as I entered and said, "I hear you are leaving the hospital. I had hoped that you would remain a while longer."

I knew that he was sincere. He was my friend.

"Doctor, I feel that it is important for me to go somewhere else," holding my hand out and continued, "I shall never forget your kindness to me in my hour of need. Doctor, if it had not been for you, I don't think I could have carried on."

He remained silent for a few moments, then asked, "Why are you leaving, does your family have money to put you into another hospital?"

"No, doctor, neither I nor my family have any money, but wherever there is a will, the way will be made clear."

"Come here," said the doctor tenderly, "let's see what is happening to you."

Looking at my forehead, he examined a boil that had broken out in the last few days. Putting some medication on it, he continued. "You know, I am going to miss you. I felt certain that the injections of Number Nine would have cured your back."

With a look of complete understanding, I said in a far away voice, "I shall always pray for you. Yes, I will ask God to make you a great philosopher and scientist. Truly, you have the makings of a great man within your soul."

Dr. Vassilli had not answered me, but I knew that something within the man had been touched. Just then Dr. Bruno and Dr. Green came in.

"Miss Maya," said Dr. Bruno, holding out his hand, "I sincerely hope that you get better."

Looking at the two doctors I knew that they were sincere in hoping for the best for me.

"Doctors," I said holding out both my hands to them, "Please forgive me for those unkind words. Truly I will pray that the dear Lord make you good doctors, not only good doctors but specialists in your line. I hope I am forgiven."

"We forgive you." It was Dr. Green who spoke. They both laughed, remembering the occasion of the forgiveness. A nurse, who was standing by, winked at me.

Allie came in shortly after.

Down on the main floor, Allie and I stopped to get my admitting card. As we waited, Allie noticed that my legs were buckling under. Calling to the attendant he asked for help. The man came with a wheelchair.

Helping me, he said, "You should not leave the hospital in this condition. The doctors want you to stay. Here is your card. If at any time you want to come back, please feel welcome to do so."

I smiled faintly, but did not answer. I felt one of the attacks coming on and did not want it to happen while I was in the hospital.

On our way over to Brooklyn, where I was going to stay with one of my sisters who had come back from a journey especially for the purpose of helping me, Allie did not speak. He felt that I would need all my strength, but his thoughts were confused. Why did I want to leave the hospital? Why was I so perturbed about the doctors? What was it all about? The doctors were all so nice to me, they had treated me as if I were a celebrity. Usually when he had gone to take anyone home, always there would be lots of red tape, now the red carpet had been put out for me. They even invited me to come back. He just did not understand.

Arriving at the house, I could not walk, so Allie lifted me out of the wheelchair. Silently I asked God to give him strength to carry my dead weight up the flight of stairs.

Saturday was the morning before Christmas. I woke up with a start. Looking around I saw Ruby Ann, my sister, sleeping peacefully in the next bed.

"Sis, wake up," I cried excitedly, "I have just seen the young Master."

Ruby Ann sat up in bed wondering who the Master was. I went on. "I had a vision. I saw myself standing in an immense hall. At the foot of a marble stairway was a large painting of a handsome man. While gazing at it, I saw the man come to life and step out of the painting. I knew it was the Master. Oh, the feeling of ecstasy that came over me. Words could never express it."

I stopped to recall the feeling that had suffused my being, and then went on. I asked him how the kingdom was coming. With a beautiful smile he answered, 'The unipegs and the water are already there.'

"I asked him if I will be accepted, and with a serious smile he answered, 'Yes. But three years ago you would not have been.'

"Then again I asked, 'Can I bring some friends?' 'Yes,' he answered, giving me a piece of parchment paper. 'Oh, dear, isn't this wonderful. I can take my family and friends into the new kingdom.'" Enthusiastically I looked over at my sister to see how she felt about this miracle of meeting the young Master.

"Please do me the favour of leaving my name out," said Ruby Ann pulling the covers over her head.

Later that day, curiosity overcame her and she asked, "Maya, what did the unipegs and the water mean."

"The unipegs are the foundation of one's innermost consciousness, and the water is the cleansing of the spirit." Ruby Ann did not say a word, but as usual, my answer confounded her.

Around 2 p.m. the same day, I got out of bed feeling that God had given me new strength and hope. Asking for some hot soup I sat in the living room sipping it. The family were all preparing for the holidays. Not knowing what to do with myself, I put the T.V. plug in the wall, suddenly realizing that I had forgotten to put it into the convertor. The current was D.C. and the T.V. was A.C. I pulled the plug out, but by then it was too late. The T.V. was smoking.

My sister, Clair, smelled the smoke and came in to find her T.V. on fire.

"My God, look what you have done. Surely you must be crazy," she said excitedly.

Instinctively I realized that it was either the T.V. or my heart. If I listened and argued with Clair, I would have another attack. Automatically pulling a veil over my being, I sat there as if dead. All outside contacts were shut off. I could see my sister but I could not hear what she was saying. Yes, Clair was raving but no sound reached my consciousness. After a while Clair stopped. She sensed that I was not there. A few minutes later I heard her say to Ruby Ann, "I don't believe she is all right. I have been speaking but I am positive she did not hear me. It is as if she is not here."

The first day of 1957 found me in Connecticut by the sea and I welcomed it with real zest. Now I knew God had given me more time to finish my work here. A friend had written that he wanted me to visit him and spend a few days in Greenwich Village, where a mutual friend,

Joann, would come and cook for me. I was to come soon and call the day before so that they would be prepared.

It was here in the Village that Jess phoned to see how I was doing now that 1957 had arrived and I was still in the land of the living. Now I must surely know that visions don't always come true.

"By the way, how do you feel now?" Jess asked sensing an unusual silence with his mystic friend.

"Jess," I answered with a slight tremor in my voice, "I'm out of the hospital but I don't feel well."

"Come now, Maya, 1957 is here. You're alive. You thought you were going to die in 1956."

I smiled to myself, for I did die. I did come back. I died a mental death, but I did not tell this to Jess. He would not understand."

There was impatience in his tone as he asked the question. For a few moments I did not answer, then as if inspired I said, "I am still not well, Jess. How about Reilly, maybe he could help me."

"You know something," Jess answered quickly, "Reilly just came back in town last night. I will call him. Wait for the answer."

In a few moments, Jess called back. Yes, Reilly was there and he wanted me to come to the health club in the RCA building, the next week. He was just the man to help me. Why, he had helped thousands. I knew he would do the trick.

As Jess hung up, I felt happy. It was as if for the first time I had been shown the light. Yes, I thought, I will move back to my former hotel. It is close to Reilly's. Yes, H.J. will help me. The next week I moved back to my old hotel where I had stayed after the accident. It was on 43rd Street in New York City.

Shortly after moving, I walked into Reilly's health center in the RCA building on 50th Street. This was very close to the hotel. Dr. Reilly's two sisters, Dot and Vi, greeted me and I was led into his office.

"Hello, Maya. I am very sorry to hear that you have been in the hospital and are still very ill. One has to expect destructive effects from a spinal injury. Yes, it is always rough. Jess told me that you had some sort of vision years ago which you have cherished in your subconscious. Now, first thing, we will have to do is remove that thought. I feel that you are secretly welcoming the thought of death. It is very easy to die, Maya, the real problem is to live and face life. Weak people take the easy way out. Are you weak? If so, I cannot help you, but if on the other hand you will work with me, to call in all your forces to help us whip this thing, I can!"

He stopped to see what effect his words had on me. I felt his penetrating eyes looking right through me, as if putting his great will to dominate mine.

"Do you wish to live?" he asked, with authority in his voice.

"No. The world is too evil."

"Is that your only excuse?"

"No." I replied, "I do not wish to live if I am going to be a cripple."

"If I promise you your health, would you wish to live?"

"Yes, H.J.," I answered, just above a whisper.

The first day I felt as if every bone in my body was breaking, as this great doctor worked to remove the tied-up nerves. Sometimes I would cry out when the pain got unbearable, then again I would just sob softly. When he was through, he told me what the trouble was. Nerves had crossed preventing the blood from circulating up my spine. Yes, I would have to watch my diet. He put me on a ten-day diet of just grapes to remove the toxins from my system.

After a month of treatment, the good doctor told me he had done all that was in his power. Now it was up to God and Mother Nature. He advised me to go to the desert where I would draw strength from the outdoors. I thanked him and went out feeling that Las Vegas would do me some good.

One snowy day, I left for Las Vegas where I had friends of long standing; however, the first thing I had to do was find a job.

Sunday afternoon, I went to visit my friend Muriel to give messages to a group of ladies. After I was through, they all advised me to stay in Las Vegas.

"Why not get a job as entertainer, reading palms, in one of the big hotels, Maya?" Muriel asked. Before I could answer another girl, Ann, shouted, "Oh, no. She has the most wonderful hands. She should go back to therapy. That is what she did years ago."

"Oh, heavens, no," said another girl, "Why waste her time giving massages when so many people need advice."

"But she is terrific," insisted Ann, "the hotels need gifted people in the health clubs. I just know that she could get into one of the big hotels."

"I will call a friend of mine," said Muriel, getting up and picking up the phone. After a few minutes conversation, she said, "You are right, Ann. Mr. Neal of the Sands Hotel needs someone. Maya is to call him tomorrow morning."

The next morning I called the Sands Hotel and spoke to Mr. Neal. "Yes," he said, "I need someone immediately. Could you come over tomorrow morning?"

That afternoon, I paid a visit to one of the leading physicians in Las Vegas. I told the doctor I wanted a check-up in order to work in one of the health clubs.

After the examination Dr. Saul looked very serious as he asked, "Miss Maya, do you know what is wrong with you?"

Seeing his puzzled look, I answered lightly, "Yes, Doctor, I am living on borrowed time."

His look changed, "Well your heart is not acting right. I don't feel you should work in a health club. It is too strenuous."

"Yes Doctor, I admit that you are right." I answered calmly, "but I would like to try it for one or two weeks. If at the end of that time I have any bad effects, I will give up the position. It is very important that I take this job. I need the money."

The doctor nodded, "Very well, come back in two weeks. If you have any bad effects, come back sooner."

Tuesday morning promptly at nine, I arrived at the Sands Health Club. The manager, Mr. Neal, was very busy. There were five women waiting to be treated. He was in one of the booths with another. Coming out, he greeted me effusively, then asked if I had my work clothes. I told him I had come prepared to work. With a look of relief, he went back to his patient and I started in on my new job.

Reviewing the situation later, I realized it was the Hand of God that guided me to that position just at that particular time.

I learned later that many excellently-trained women were waiting for that job, but when the high Masters wish you to get something, they make it very possible for you to be there just at the right time. Can it all be coincidence?

That afternoon, Mr. Neal looked up my references and told me that he was not only pleased with my work, but the wife of one of the owners had been in and had a treatment from me, and was also very pleased. The hours were to be from 9 a.m. to 1 p.m. I liked the job, especially as I was to be there alone.

The very next morning, Wednesday, a lady called for an appointment and came in for a treatment. She was Mrs. Maria Strange from Hollywood. Immediately I felt a mystic tie with this woman. She had deep penetrating eyes that seemed to peer right through me. I recognized them to have mystic perception (later Maria told me she saw the same quality in me).

"Yes," she said, "there is a feeling of complete understanding between us." Before she left she invited me to have lunch in the garden room of the Sands Hotel.

About two o'clock I met her in the Garden Room, and while we were eating lunch, Maria told me that she was there in the hotel for two weeks. One of which she had already spent. She was there to build up her health for an operation The doctor thought she had tumors. Bill, her husband, was taking care of her agency while she was away.

The next morning Maria came in, looking very pale. She had had a bad night and had not slept—thinking of the operation that she had to undergo. Taking her hand I led her to a comfortable seat.

"Now, now dear, you are building up this situation in your mind and it is getting the best of you. Look at me, the doctor told me that I have heart trouble, but I won't accept the thought. If I did, I could not work as I do."

Maria looked at me, amazed, not believing what she had heard.

"Oh, no, Maya, you don't have heart trouble. Why you look so healthy. I simply can't believe it. I won't believe it."

In an odd voice, as if not my own, I said softly, "Let's make a pact. You won't believe that I have heart trouble and I won't believe that you have tumors."

Shaking hands on the pact, Maria answered with a tremor in her voice, "Oh, God, I will not believe that Maya has heart trouble. I will not, God."

Every day as Maria came into the club for treatments, we would both repeat the pact and every day she looked better. Finally she left Las Vegas, but she did not forget to write. She told me that the doctor did not feel that she needed an operation.

In two weeks I went back to the doctor. He examined me and said softly, "I can't believe it, I can't believe it. Your heart is better."

Yes, today, there is still a problem with the digestive organs, but through prayers, diet and therapy, I have kept it under control.

TWENTY-SIX

Reincarnation, Visions & Prophecies

There have been several occasions when phenomena appeared in my life, but the strangest and most fantastic incident happened in 1961, when my good friend Emagene, who was at that time investigating E.S.P., asked me to preside at one of her meditation groups. The session was held in her home on Riverside Drive in New York City, and about fifteen people attended.

Just before the guests arrived, Ben, a mutual friend of Emagene and mine, asked if we would pray for him. Ben had just recently joined the group and was unable to pray for assistance. In this lifetime, Ben was born Jewish with round shoulders, which is a sign of bringing great burdens from the past. Ben was thinking of making a change in his business, which he hoped would be for the better.

After our prayers, we sat in the silence. Both Emagene and I had almost identical visions. Emagene spoke first, saying, "I see Ben seated in a large boat with many people. They are dressed in long robes and speak in a strange tongue, which could be Egyptian."

Listening breathlessly, for I too had looked at a strange gathering of people who appeared to be Egyptians, excitedly I exclaimed, "Yes, I can see Ben as a Pharaoh. A great crowd is assembled on the shore of the Nile. I see Ben sitting majestically aboard a large boat. There is a Queen sitting beside him. I can not see her face but she appears to be very beautiful."

By now, several friends of the meditation group had quietly walked in the open door and were listening to the conversation with bated breaths. Everyone sat in silence while the amazing phenomenon was discussed. After that we prayed and again went into the silence.

A few minutes passed and then a message came through for Ben. Touching him on the shoulder I said, "Ben, you came to this life as an eight path, which means you are a master in a double prison; both a mental and physical block. These blocks must be transmuted or you will carry it over to your next incarnation. You have been a Pharaoh in many lifetimes and you misused your powers. This is why your life has been so difficult. When we met, you could not pray, and you still can't. Someone in the past has put stumbling blocks in your will-path."

"You are right, Maya," Ben replied forlornly. "How can I change my destiny?"

"You are changing it," I assured him in a positive tone of voice. "Now you are seeking help, I am sure you will see great changes, not only in your home environment but also in your business."

"Thank you, Maya," Ben answered gratefully, "but can you also tell me in which dynasty I was a Pharaoh?"

"I believe it was in the time of Nefertiti," I answered, touching his hand to get a stronger vibration. "You may have been Akhenaton and the woman sitting beside you may have been Queen Nefertiti. She was very beautiful."

Attempting to penetrate deeper into Ben's past, I was interrupted by the rest of the group arriving.

It was at the end of the meditation session, while we were all standing in a circle holding hands and praising the Lord, that another phenomenon occurred. A strange odor pervaded the room. Ben was the first to speak. "I smell incense," he remarked looking around the room to see if we were burning some. Then others became aware of the scent, and Emagene asked, "Are you burning incense, Maya?" Joe, one of the men in the group said, "It smells like attar of roses with frankincense and myrrh."

I did not comment, for at that moment I was in a trance-like state and a strange high voice spoke to me mentally and said, "Help me, help me. I need help. My body is bound and I cannot move."

Tears were flowing down my cheeks. Someone asked, "What is wrong, Maya dear?" But I could not answer. All I could think of was that the woman who was possessing my being was in great turmoil. I knew I must help her. Mentally, I asked, "Who are you and what do you wish me to do?"

"I am Nefertiti, Queen of Egypt, I need your help. My body has been tied up for centuries. Please ask your friends to silently pray for me while you unloose my bonds."

I related the Queen's desire to the group, and as the moments passed, I saw myself being transported to ancient Egypt where I was the trusted and beloved sister of Nefertiti. We were dressed in flowing robes of white, trimmed with gold. On our feet were golden sandals.

The queen was lying on a jewelled bed. Her feet and hands were bound with cords. Quickly, I untied them, and as she rose she reached out her arms to clasp me in a tender embrace. She then approached a casement which she opened toward the bright sunshine saying, "Beloved Father, God of the Sun, I thank you."

With these words a blazing sunlight appeared in the room. It was as if a thousand suns were beaming their lights on us. I felt as if I was suddenly lifted up to another dimension, and I saw us kneeling down and worshipping the Sun-God.

It may have been moments or even hours that we knelt there together. I do not know, for when one is immersed in great bliss, time is of no importance.

As I bade her good-bye, I asked, "Shall I write this story?"

"No," she replied, "but one day you will go to Egypt, and when you return home, you will have the power to write and tell your story to the world. Before you do, I shall impart many strange and wonderful secrets to you. Thank you, my sister. Good-bye for now."

Coming out of the trance, I heard everyone speaking of the strange phenomenon of the odor of incense, and also several people in the group had had visions. I said very little, for my beloved Nefertiti had told me not to speak of what had transpired. I knew it was imperative for me to obey.

In February, 1962, Jess Stearn's book *The Door To The Future* was published. Jeanne Dixon, several mystics, and I were mentioned in it.

I was in New York at the time and Jess asked me to go on the Long John Nebel's all-night WOR radio program with him. Jeanne Dixon was scheduled to be on the same program and would arrive two hours before I did.

I was happy to be on the program, until I told a friend, who was a practitioner. She raised her brows at my words and exclaimed, "My heavens, not Long John. Why he will destroy you."

I smiled confidently and replied, "I am not worried about Long John or anyone else trying to destroy me. God will protect me."

Holding our her hand, she clasped mine crying, "Maya, let us do some treatment work for protection. I will surround you with the cosmic rays and keep up the prayers until after the program."

I agreed and we prayed about the matter. After the prayers were over, she left.

That night, which happened to be Friday, I lit a candle and filled my Buddha with incense and burned it until I went to bed.

During the night, I had a vision. I saw myself in a large room with several people. One man stood out, he was tall and had a big nose. I remember that he kept smiling at me and I felt that there was a feeling of kinship. Subconsciously, I knew he was my friend.

The next morning, I called Jess, who had to make definite plans about the time I was to arrive at the studio. During our conversation, I told Jess about my friend, the practitioner, and of her fears about me going on the program. Also, about the vision of me going into the large room and the man with the big nose. Jess did not pay much attention to the vision, but was concerned about the practitioner being afraid of me going on the program.

"Oh, don't worry about Long John. I'll fix that. I am certain he will not bother you," Jess assured me.

That afternoon, around five or a few minutes after, a gentleman called. It was Mr. Klidhi. He was an actor and close friend of Long John.

"Madame Perez," he said, "I am Mr. Klidhi. I am a friend of Long John and will be with him on the program tonight."

"Yes, Mr. Klidhi. I have heard of you through mutual friends."

"Madame Perez, Mr. Long John asked me to call and assure you that you have nothing to fear. We are looking forward to meeting you."

I held my breath while I pondered this strange turn of events. I was positive Jess had told Long John of my concern about being on his program.

"Mr. Klidhi, does Long John have a big nose?" I asked, thinking it best to come right to the point.

"No, on the contrary, his nose is just normal. Why do you ask?"

I hesitated for a moment then continued, "I did some meditation on this matter, and last night I had a vision of going to Long John's studio. There were several people there, but one tall big man with a large nose stood out and smiled at me. I thought that this man was Long John."

"This is very strange, Madame Perez," he remarked, then added, "but we are all friends and you can believe me that Mr. Long John will be most happy to have you on as a guest. God bless you. I will see you later."

I arrived at the Long John's studio around one a.m. in the morning. They were having a coffee break. A friend of Long Johns', a caterer, had sent over sandwiches, coffee and cakes. It looked like a feast.

Jess greeted me and then introduced me to Long John. He was tall and big, but did not have a big nose. Definitely he was not the man in my vision.

Next, I met Jeanne Dixon and several others, including Mr. Klidhi, who came over and greeted me as if we were old friends.

While having a cup of coffee and nibbling on a chicken sandwich, Jeanne came over and said, "Tell my fortune, Madame Perez."

I turned to the woman who had spoken and recalling the incident now, my smile was purely quizzical.

"I would read your palm even if Jess Stearn were not our mutual friend," I exclaimed, "but I beg you not to forget that my purpose in life is not the mere telling of fortunes, but rather giving instruction in the evolution of the consciousness and the creation of new life forms. Revealing the future must be simply one of the tools with which we work."

There was good reason for the "we," because Jeanne, herself, is a most popular seer.

I then asked her birth date and year. Casually, I glanced at her left hand. Immediately, I put down the sandwich and looked closer at her hand. I was astonished. It was lined with thousands of lines, crosses, stars and other significant lines.

"Jeanne, you have an amazing hand." Privately, I thought to myself, in my whole career, only two others have had such unusual palms, and they were father and son.

After a few seconds of analyzing her entire palm, I began to tell her what were my impressions.

"You have lived two lives and in ancient Egypt —" But she held up her hand to stop me and asked, "What do you see of my newest venture. Will it be successful?"

I was just about to answer when we were both interrupted by the studio page who came to announce that we were going on the air in five minutes. Looking around, I realized that we were alone. Everyone had already gone into the large room. I could have written a book or spoken for hours on that wonderful hand, but now I had no more than seconds. Her palm bore the unmistakable marking of one who had lived many past and dynamic lives. She could have been a Priestess in the temples of Atlantis and also a healer in old Egypt. Her hand showed wisdom that had been locked up for centuries.

Quickly I ventured to remark, "You will be successful in anything on which you concentrate." She smiled and we entered the broadcasting room.

The room had a large table, and several of the group, who had been standing outside, were now seated around it. Jeanne and I were seated and I glanced across the table and there was my friend, from my vision, with the big nose.

We smiled at each other and I said, "Do I look familiar to you?"

He stared at me for a moment, then answered slowly, "Yes, I do believe that we have met before."

"Yes, we did. I saw you in a vision last night," I remarked smiling, "I thought you were Long John. I asked Mr. Klidhi, this afternoon if Long John had a big nose and he said, definitely no."

At that remark, we all laughed and the tension in the room was immediately cleared.

We went on the air with a lot of small talk about E.S.P. Everybody knew a lot about it and yet nobody believed in their intuition or where the answers came from.

Someone asked Jeanne a question and she looked over at me. I knew that I should answer. After that, Long John asked if I would read his palm. I looked first at his left hand and then his right. I wanted to be sure of my impressions before I spoke. A palm has to be read from the "without" as well as from the "within" of a person. I went into a state of light trance. It's the same as when one hypnotizes himself. Then I spoke.

"I see a very independent nature here. This has caused you to have to fight for everything. In early childhood, there was a lot of confusion in the family and you got out rather early. There was a lot of traveling and adventure, as you went from one town to the other. Sometimes you had to steal a ride, but you always got out all right. You have a good strong body, but there were times when you could have been killed." I stopped as I saw where he could have fallen under a train or car, but did not mention this to him. I sensed that Long John had psychic powers which he used unconsciously, as most men do. This man had a long head line and his line of destiny was long and clear, so instinctively, I knew that he would have greater success in the very near future. I mentioned this to him. I told him it would come suddenly and unexpectedly. I saw him leaving WOR. "I see a big door opening and it will be soon." I said, "this change is liable to completely change the whole trend in your life. I also see someone closely connected to you with a heart condition. This, also, will affect your personal life."

I was then quiet. Someone spoke, but I was still in a light trance. I thought of him writing a book and knew that he would do that in a few years. I do not remember if I mentioned this out loud. After that, Long John left the table and was gone for a long time, possibly forty or forty-five minutes.

There was much talk about other matters and later, I was told that it was unusual for Long John to leave in the midst of the session. Of course, I smiled at this statement. I felt that the practitioner had come on too strong. Someone told me later that they had never seen or heard Long John being so demure.

It was Jess who informed me that Long John's wife had gone for a heart check up and was to have surgery on her heart the next day. It wasn't long until Long John left WOR for the National Broadcasting

Company in New York at triple his salary. The man with the big nose turned out to be a real estate agent from Long Island.

In the fall of 1962, another very unusual incident occurred while I was spending my winter in Balboa, California. My good friend Kathleen, who is a very clever business woman in Balboa, asked if I would care to meet her teacher in mysticism. This person had many gifts and was very knowledgeable in the deep mysteries of life.

"No, Kathleen," I answered emphatically, "I do not wish to meet this person." Kathleen did not ask why. She accepted my decision as final and changed the subject. About ten days later she invited me to her home. When I arrived about two hours later, I found a lady with piercing eyes that seemed to look right through me, sitting on the sofa. As I came in, she got up and stood before me. Suddenly I felt a blow to my solar plexus. It was a stabbing blow and I stood frozen before this strange individual. I just stood there. I could not move. Even my breathing seemed to have stopped.

It may have been a moment, or a thousand years, I cannot say. I only knew that I seemed to have lost consciousness. Nothing was registering.

A long time passed, and I heard Kathleen's voice as if it were coming from a long distance saying, "Maya, this is the lady that has been my teacher for many years. She is Master Annette from the inner planes and is connected with the Masters of Light."

At the moment, I could hear what Kathleen was saying, but could not understand what was happening, for I was under a strange power that was emanating from this most unusual being.

Touching me on the shoulder, she said softly, "It has been a long time, Maya. Blessings and light to you, my sister." Gently she guided me towards a seat on the sofa and sat down next to me.

Annette later was to become a most trusted and beloved friend, yet that day when we first met, I felt a great fear in my heart and wondered about her strange powers. Powers that gave me such a dreadful blow in my solar plexus.

Never had I ever experienced anything like that, and it was difficult for me to join in the conversation. I heard Kathleen speaking but it sounded as if they were in another dimension.

Kathleen may have sensed what had occurred to me, for she tried to be solicitous by bringing me a cup of hot tea and some cookies. The hot tea warmed my inner being which was still very cold. The cookies, however, I could not take. I doubt very much if I could have swallowed any solid food at that time.

Shortly after drinking the tea, I left and went home to sit and ponder what had caused me to freeze in such an unusual manner.

Without planning to see Kathleen, I suddenly found myself sitting in her dining room the following Tuesday. This time Annette was not there, but shortly after she arrived, we sat and chatted like old friends while Kathleen prepared some lunch which we all enjoyed.

As the weeks and months flew by, it became routine for Annette to visit Kathleen on Tuesday morning, and of course I would meet them and meditate. Many times when Kathleen was busy, Annette would come to my apartment on the Bay and we would meditate and pray together. Frequently she would bring a gift of fruit or flowers from her beautiful garden.

One morning after I had put the flowers in a vase, we sat in the dining room enjoying some cinnamon buns and coffee when we both became very quiet. This was most unusual because we always had so much to talk about.

Trying to unravel the mysteries of the past, I thought, "Why is Annette doing all these things for me? What is the karmic tie between us?"

With her quaint smile Annette said, "Maya, I realize you are wondering why I do these things for you and also you would like to know the karmic tie that has bound us from the past and even in this life."

Amazed to learn she could read my thoughts so accurately, I recovered enough to ask, "Why are you doing these things for me?"

For a split second, she looked deep into my soul, and then answered calmly, "We have been together in several lifetimes. During the time of Christ you were my little sister. I was eighteen and you, fifteen. We were Jews of the early Christian sect. Shortly after the death of Jesus, many were acknowledging the teachings of Christ. We went to Rome to tell of the wonders of Jesus. We were caught and thrown into the arena. As the horrifying animals bolted towards us, you threw yourself before me in a vain attempt to shield me from death. You took the first blow and for that I owe you my blessings. I shall never forget, nor be able to repay you with enough love and kindness."

Staring at her in utter amazement, I thought, "This explains the reason for the blow in my solar plexus and why I was unable to move when we first met. Having died in that life in great pain and fear, and then meeting again, the subconscious re-lived the horrible experience. Yes, this was the answer, even if I did not believe, at that time, in reincarnation, which is going from one stage of life's play to another in order to learn the many lessons. This one experience made me a believer. How could I not believe when I had lived it?

"Maya," she continued, "when Kathleen asked me if I wished to meet you, I immediately said, no! I wanted no part of you; yet, the moment we met, I knew you had been my little sister."

Smiling at her blunt confession, I replied, "I, too, told Kathleen no, when she asked me to meet you."

"Maya, we were destined to meet," Annette answered gently, patting my hand, "and Kathleen was the channel God used to bring us together. Maya, you are from old Egypt. I can see the sign of the priestess on your brow."

It was then I related my experience concerning Queen Nefertiti's spirit coming through to me the year before. Annette was not surprised at my story and nodded her head knowingly, then added, "One day you will go back to Egypt, for there is something in old Egypt that must be completed. I feel it is in Alexandria. Nefertiti will be the channel to guide you there."

Through the years, Annette and I have had our differences, yet there was always the unbreakable tie that bound us together. Many times when I felt her sister-love smothering and holding me back, or so I thought, then I would fight with all my strength to escape from the web that she was unconsciously weaving around me. Nevertheless, whenever I needed her great mystical powers of healing, she was always there to guide me into the inner realms for greater insight.

One time I recall, it was 1965, when trying to help Robert, who had been my husband in one of my previous incarnations. There must have been great resentment, anguish, confusion and even hate in that association, because when we were in deep meditation, I was taken out of my body by a powerful Thought Form, which tried to possess my soul.

It was impossible for me to remember anything that transpired while I was in the trance state, I only know that I stopped breathing. After about twenty or more minutes I started to breathe and I heard Robert say, "Thank God, you are back again. You were not breathing and I thought I had lost you."

The next morning, I still did not feel well. It was as if I were floating in limbo or not completely conscious. Later in the day, I called Annette and related my experience of the night before. I also informed her of the strange feeling of lightness in my body. She was silent for a few minutes then said, "Maya, you are still out of your body. Go back to bed and get some rest. At the moment, I'm very busy but as soon as I am free, I will be over."

In about one hour, Annette arrived. It was strange because when she came in, I felt another presence with her, yet, there was no one visible in the room.

What really happened that day, I could never truly explain for there were times when I felt that I was not on the bed, but in another dimension somewhere in space. Vaguely I recalled Annette working in silence with my body. Touching certain areas and then closing her eyes and waiting for direction of what to do next.

It may have been forty-five minutes or even an hour that she worked, and just touching the top of my head. At that point I was fully awake. I watched her, for I felt a direct current of energy flowing into my whole being. It was like a stream and yet it was so illusive that it was difficult for me to say where the energy was coming from. I thought it was possibly coming from her fingers. After a while, I felt as if I had come back from a long, long journey.

Pulling the covers over me, she left and I slept for two or more hours, then woke up feeling better than I had felt in quite some time.

It was because of Annette's advice that I left Balboa and went to live in West Hollywood. I have always yearned for the beach areas and knew that I would miss the ocean, yet I felt that I should listen to Annette.

Many psychics have reported that water is healing; especially if the water is salty. They also say that all sensitive people should live close to the ocean or any body of water, as they are apt to vibrate and think better.

It has also been said by mystics that the power to open the inner doors where the Masters of Light dwell can be done when we are close to salt water or in a mountainous area. I feel that this is true because I'm much lighter either near the ocean or in the mountains.

The third incident involving strange phenomena was very weird. In 1969, I received a telephone call from Dr. Earl, an oral surgeon. After introducing himself, he exclaimed, "Maya, I must see you. Our mutual friend Dr. Kathy, who as you know is a minister of Religious Science, insists that I must see you and that our meeting will be most revealing. How about seeing me tomorrow in the late afternoon?"

After checking my appointment book, we arranged to meet the next afternoon at 4:30 p.m.

I had met Dr. Kathy shortly before this telephone conversation and was deeply impressed with her mystical powers, and therefore I was looking forward to meeting the good doctor.

The next afternoon exactly at the appointed time, Dr. Earl arrived. At first glance, I had the impression that we had met before, but it was not until after we had sat down and had gone into deep meditation that I opened my eyes to find him staring at me in utter astonishment as he whispered softly, "Maya, don't you know who I am?"

I could not speak for several moments. Tears were rolling down my cheeks. The doctor held my hand and he, too, was filled with great emotion. In a hushed tone of voice I answered, "Yes, you were my father in ancient Egypt."

"Yes, Maya dear, I was," he agreed, "and this must be the reason Dr. Kathy told me I had to meet you."

After those words, we just sat and gazed at each other for quite some time. Then he spoke. "Perhaps you will be able to tell me the reason for various tragic experiences in my life?"

Again we prayed, asking for inner guidance and also the answer to his question. After several minutes of silence, I spoke, "I see you as a priest looking at the blazing sunlight. You look very solemn."

"Yes, I considered joining the order," he said softly, "but became a doctor instead. Later I studied with the Mormons and much later, with the church of Religious Science to become a minister. It is one of my great desires to be able to heal people."

"Yes, I feel this is true," I remarked sadly, "but before you can help the masses, you must first help yourself. There is an aura of blue mixed with grey over your head, and at times it is very dark. You have been a healer in several lifetimes, but I sense that you misused your powers and the Masters on the inner realms have blocked you. Your karmic patterns need to be purified."

Dr. Earl looked at me thoughtfully for a moment and then asked, "How does one do that?"

"There are many ways of purifying these karmic patterns," I answered, "but the one I use is reading certain Psalms the first thing upon awakening in the morning and also before going to sleep at night." I thought for a moment, then continued. "Certain Psalms have a particular power to relax the physical body. After that is done, you can send the Light to the soul areas in your solar plexus. In this way not only can you purify the inner levels but also protect yourself from psychic attacks of disembodied spirits who may try to possess you."

I spoke these words while holding his hand, trying to relax his emotional body which was in a state of great confusion.

After a few moments of silence, I spoke. "Dr. Earl, you have brought into this life many strange karmic patterns with dynamic blocks. They began while you were a priest in Egypt. In that same life you were a Pharaoh for a very short time. You made vows to God and later to man. In both instances you misused your powers and broke your vows."

"This may have been the reason for the tragic breaking up of my marriages," he replied softly, "no one would ever believe what I have gone through. Only God alone knows how I have lived through it. My first wife was rather cold and later we were divorced. After a few years, I remarried. Again there was turmoil and my second wife committed suicide. Somehow I have always felt guilty about it. At present, I am married to a blond singer. She is a lovely person, but I don't feel we are suited to each other. Maybe it is because she is so disturbed about her daughter."

He stopped for a few minutes then continued. "I also have a strange problem. In business I am only successful if I am involved with a Jew. They have always been the ones to help me." Again he stopped, took a deep breath then asked, "Why, Maya?"

"Dr. Earl," I exclaimed, "your life pattern in these matters shows definite karmic curses. I am certain they came with you from the past. No matter whom you marry, the pattern will be the same until it is broken or purified."

"My heavens, I feel you are right," the doctor shouted with deep emotion, "I have had nothing but confusion and tragedy. I hope to God this karmic pattern can be either broken or purified. There are times when I have thought of suicide and putting an end to it all."

"No, you must never do that," I said in a positive tone of voice, "then you would have to come back and work out an even more difficult life-destiny. You are a Taurian. Your life-path is nine. This automatically gives you great healing powers and an inner longing to heal. You are a natural healer."

"Yes, Maya, I am that," he agreed, "my profession as I told you over the phone is dental surgery, but I am a minister of truth and I do give spiritual healing treatments."

"Wonderful," I said, "every time you heal another person, you are healing a cell within your own being. As you help another, you are helping yourself. Whatever you do for others will come back to you."

"Please explain more about my problem in the business world?" he asked, hesitating. "At the present time I have a Jewish partner. We are both successful but I have often wondered why I can't seem to move without their help."

After meditating for a few moments, I replied, "In the past you resented the Jewish people. Many times you were instrumental in holding them back. Now, you are held down and have to ask those that you resented for help. In this way, you are now purifying your ego."

"Thank you, Maya. God bless you and your work." He was silent and seemed to be praying, then suddenly he looked up and asked, "What do you feel about music and writing in connection with me?"

Meditating for a moment, I saw a black cloud over his head. I was hesitant to inform him of this, but then thought better of it and said,

"The curse that you brought into this life is blocking you. I believe there are two definite forces in your body. One is fighting the other and that is why you can never make the right decisions."

The doctor gave me a deep look then said, "I have written songs and also the story of my life but for some strange reason, I have not been able to publish my work. The concerned people would either die, or the manuscripts would be missing. I definitely feel there are invisible beings working against me, even though I realize man is the master of his destiny.

Thinking over what he had said, I was amazed to see how similar was his destiny path to mine. These same things had happened to me. God almighty, is this man my twin soul?

After a few moments of deep thought I exclaimed, "Yes, man is the master of his destiny but first he must lift up his consciousness and be in tune with the higher laws. Then, and only then can man on the mortal realms control his thinking and his actions."

We were both silent for several minutes, then I continued, "Don't lose faith. Some day God will give you the power to heal yourself and in time, you will be able to write and publish your songs and stories."

With a sad look, the good doctor cried out, "I hope to God you are right."

After those words he thanked me and left. I thought no more of the strange meeting until three o'clock the next morning, when I awakened to find him sitting on the foot of my bed. I cannot say whether I was completely awake or if I were in a semi-trance state, which means half-asleep and half-awake. Nevertheless, there he was.

Speaking through the mental thought he said, "Maya, I was your father in old Egypt. I was one of the High Priests. At that time it was the usual procedure to make the Cosmic marriage. Marriage of the soul and Spirit God. It was my turn to be the bridegroom and I was told to find a young virgin. I looked but could not find one suitable and then I thought of you, my beautiful fifteen-year-old virgin daughter. I spoke to my wife, your mother, but she was opposed to the idea. I believe she spoke to the queen. She, too, opposed me yet, I went on with the idea and finally the wedding rites were made. I married you."

The scene changed and I found myself arrayed in bridal clothes standing next to my handsome father, who appeared to be in his early forties.

The ritual was quite solemn. There were hundreds of priests and many others who appeared to be Masters of the Sun God. Everyone chanted, calling out to the God of Light and suddenly a golden stream of dynamic light came down on the bridal party. Yet, back of it was a dark cloud, which I knew was an evil omen.

Later, there was another ritual, a more intimate one. I felt my father and I were floating through space; going through one cycle of ecstasy to another until we were both locked into great bliss that was completely heavenly.

Throughout both rituals, I felt as if I were the bride and yet another individual who was viewing a play of life. It was most strange. At times I felt I was in the body of the bride and yet separated.

In a flash, I was back in my room lying on the bed and Dr. Earl was still sitting on the edge of the bed saying, "Later, we had our temples in the desert and were taught by the Cosmic Masters of the Sun. After so many incarnations, there is a great purpose in our meeting again, but I cannot speak of it now."

I do not recall when or how he left, but the next morning I was awakened about 6:30 and wrote down my vision. While I was in deep meditation, Dr. Earl called. "Maya, I had an urge to call you."

I did not answer. A great feeling of fear seeped through my being. He continued, "I'm afraid I awakened you."

Forcing myself to answer I replied, "No, I was not sleeping. As a matter of fact, I was contemplating about your astral visit to me early this morning."

He did not answer for a few moments then he exclaimed, "I knew something strange had happened but I did not remember what it was all about. This is the reason I called so early. Please forgive me." He quickly hung up the receiver.

The next few days I remained in a state of shock, so when Eileen Cook of Los Angeles called to invite me to give a lecture in her home, I immediately accepted the invitation. Eileen and her husband John were avid users of the Ouija board. Upon my arrival at their home, I asked if they would use the board for me.

"Oh, no, Maya, not you!" Eileen cried out looking at me as if I had suddenly gone out of my mind. "Why you have often warned us at your lectures about the dangers of using the Ouija board. I have also heard you advising many people not to use it."

"This is true, Eileen," I replied with a sad smile, "but at the moment I am desperate. I must get the answer to a problem that is disturbing me."

In a few words I informed them of what had transpired in the past few days, and then I said, "Do not be afraid, I will pray and meditate in order to contact a high Inner Master of Light."

After prayer and deep meditation, John and Eileen used the board, and I asked the question, "Why am I so afraid of Doctor Earl?"

The answer that came back was most astounding! "Do not be frightened of Pa, he will not hurt you. In time he will help you to heal yourself and he too will be healed."

The next question was, "What is the purpose of our meeting in this life?" The answer was, "God says, forgiveness will help each of us to evolve."

The third question, "Is Pa connected with my soul-mate?"

The answer this time was, "No, no, moon your polarity."

Shortly after the session with the Ouija board, a lady called me and said, "Maya, I am Mrs. Earl, Dr. Earl's third wife. My husband has told me some wonderful things about you. May I come to see you?"

"Yes, you may. I can see you tomorrow morning, but you will have to excuse me, I'm not feeling well," I replied softly.

"Oh, I'm sorry to hear that. What is the matter?" she asked with deep concern in her voice.

"I have just come back from the dentist. He tried to pull an impacted tooth with an abscess, but for some strange reason the doctor could not pull it. He even took me next door to another dentist, but he failed to pull it also."

"Oh, my dear, I am sure my husband can take it out for you. I will see you in the morning, after our session I will take you to the office." She spoke with such confidence that I, too, felt that the good doctor could pull the tooth and relieve me of the pain.

The following morning Mrs. Earl arrived, and immediately we began to talk as if we had known each other a long, long time. She was a tall, plump and very pretty woman with fair skin, blond hair and blue eyes that twinkled when she smiled, but the next moment deep fear and emotional disturbance clouded their brightness.

We finished a cup of hot tea and I suggested prayers to heal our bodies, minds and spirits. We prayed for several minutes then went into silence, while I sent light to quiet the cells in her being.

A few moments passed and I felt she was still not relaxed, so I whispered, "Mrs. Earl, let me teach you how to let go of your problems and transmute your fears."

"Thank you, Reverend Maya. I have never been able to completely relax," she said with a nod of her pretty head, "but how are you going to do this?"

"There are certain techniques of deep breathing that can help us to transmute fears." I stopped for a few seconds, then continued, "It is the breath that purifies the negative thought forms of fear and worry."

"I do worry," she said with a sad smile.

"Yes, I realize that and it has caused a block in your soul area," I explained holding her hand to release the tension, "when the inner consciousness is blocked, it is difficult for the physical body to be at peace."

We were quiet for several minutes, then I said, "Take a deep breath, hold it while you send the light-energy to your third eye, which is in the middle of your forehead; then go within and see this light going down to your solar plexus which is your real brain and also the creator of your inner world. Now, let go and take in another deep breath, this time see the light going from the top of your head down to the tip of your toes. Do this a few times and you will feel the energy pouring through your whole being."

We did the deep breathing techniques for quite a while, then sat in silence. After several minutes I said, "Mrs. Earl, you are a nine life path and so is your husband, who is vibrating on the same frequency. This number represents the outer and inner realms of physical and mental healings. You must heal yourself, then help your husband through prayer and meditation. This man is most important. He represents a finite cell of your soul consciousness. This means that you came to this life to work together as one unit. In several lifetimes, you were together. Some of those past lives were constructive, others were not."

"I feel this is right, Reverend Maya," she admitted, nodding her head with a serious look.

Again we sat in the silence while I released my conscious mind, going deeper into the subconscious areas. After a few minutes, I saw a vision which I related to her. "In Atlantis, you were a singer and also the High Priestess in one of the beautiful temples. Nearby, in another temple your present husband was studying for the priesthood. You met and fell in love at first sight. Later as your lover, he helped you to escape from the temple. No, you did not marry him. You were both killed by the temple guards. This is the reason for your dual feelings of resentment and love which have caused your emotional upset and nervous imbalance in the past year."

"This is very true," she exclaimed, "sometimes, I feel as if my husband's power overwhelms me. His sister says he is controlled by a presidio God who is fighting for supremacy."

"Yes, I do agree that your husband does have tremendous power," I remarked softly, patting her hand, "and it is not properly channelled.

You were brought in to help him. When a curse is put on two people by a religious group, it causes the souls to be bound. This compels you to return again and again in order to learn how to transmute the negative vibrations. Only with your help will he be able to lift up his consciousness, and in time you, too, will be freed. Together, you will rise up and become free; separate now, and your souls will be lost."

"Then we must solve our problems in this life!" Mrs. Earl exclaimed tearfully. "He is such a good man. So kind, so wonderful. Then in a moment, he is changed and becomes a different personality. Reverend Maya, are you sure I can handle this problem?"

"Yes, I will help you, I promise."

I thought for a moment then asked the Inner Spirit if I should confide in her? The Spirit gave me a definite "No, wait."

After a moment, I said, "The problems are karmic and they are in his aura. I know a woman who does aura cleansing."

"Oh, my dear," she cried out, "my husband is too proud. He will never consent or even admit that he needs soul purification or any other type of cleansing."

"Relax, Mrs. Earl," I whispered, "he does not have to know. This type of healing is done by absentee work. I cannot explain it to you, because it is a secret type of work. It is done by special practitioners. Believe me it works."

"Please tell me, Reverend, are these karmic cleansings very expensive?"

"Yes, they are," I replied patting her hand, "but I will pay half of the bill."

For a moment she looked puzzled, then asked, "Why are you doing this, Reverend?"

"Dr. Earl was my father in old Egypt. In that life we had a Cosmic marriage. He married me. I must help him. We have had many lifetimes together. Now, the Father has sent him to me for soul healing."

"I knew it! I knew there was some reason for his insisting that I come to see you!" she cried out excitedly. "When he returned the other day, he seemed very excited, as if there was a turmoil going on within him. I, too, feel you have many answers and I'm ready to hear them."

"Yes, my dear," I answered with a serious look. "I do have the answers for those who believe, but for those who just come to investigate me, the answers are not always good."

"This I know," she replied sadly, "if one does not believe, then there is no purpose coming to a mystic. It's in faith that gives you the power to contact the Inner Masters."

"You are right, I wish only those who are true believers to visit me. But sometimes, the Lord sends me strange people just to test me." We both smiled at these words.

"I see that, in several of your past incarnations, you sang and played the harp," I continued, "I visualize you in a beautiful garden with a happy smile on your face. This was in old Egypt."

"I do love to sing," she said perking up, "but at times, I cannot take the high notes. I became nervous only since I married him."

"It will take time for you to remove the nervous tension from your subconscious." I spoke slowly as I sent light into her inner being. "But it will happen, then your voice will be golden, and the healing rays will be brought forth to the world."

"Thank you, Father," she whispered with deep reverence.

We had a few moments of silence, then a message came through. "Mrs. Earl," I said, "there will be four marriages in your destiny. One will not be legal. But this third marriage is the most important, because of your past karma with the doctor."

For a full moment she looked at me in amazement, then asked, "Do you really think this prophecy will come true? I can't think of anyone that I will wish to marry."

"No, because you have not yet met the person." I spoke those words in a trance-like tone of voice. After that, we were both silent, then I continued. "You will one day divorce him, but for now, it is your true destiny to help him. Try to be patient and in time you will succeed."

"Believe me, Reverend Maya, the past two years have not been easy." She spoke with tears in her eyes. We both remained quiet while the tears streamed down her face. Wiping them off she continued, "Doctor has insisted that we pray together and this has helped us to overcome various problems."

"I know," I whispered patting her hand, "it never is when there is karma to be worked out."

After a few seconds of silence, another vision of a young girl appeared. She seemed to be in a large body of water struggling against the waves. I relayed this unusual vision to Mrs. Earl. At first she could not think who the young girl was then a startled look came to her face and she whispered between sobs, "My God! It is my daughter Bea. She has been a great problem to me and there were times when I felt her problems were more than I could take."

I asked for Bea's birthdate and year and it added up to a five destiny life path. Leo, the Sun Goddess with Saturn in several of her houses. This was symbolic of the door opening or closing. This girl could go down into the very depths of her consciousness, and then suddenly through meditation and prayer, rise up to be a great teacher of Truth. At the present time the door was closed, but in time her mother would open it for her. Both were fighting for the renewal of their souls.

"My dear," I said with confidence, "Bea is young. I am certain she will overcome her many problems. This is a testing period for both of you. God is teaching you to learn patience. There are many times when you completely forgot to pray or meditate. This is the reason Doctor has insisted that you pray together. With prayer all things are made perfect."

Mrs. Earl tried to speak but could not. Again we sat in silence and this time I saw a tiny old lady standing near her and Doctor. It was Mrs. Earl who appeared to be ministering to the old lady's needs. When I told this to her, she immediately exclaimed, "Oh, that is Noli. Doctor's elderly mother. She is ninety-five years old. What do you see for her?"

"There is a karmic tie between Noli, Doctor, and you." I answered speaking slowly. I wanted her to absorb what I was saying. "She was in the same temple with you when you met Doctor in Atlantis, but there was a great deal of misunderstanding. As time goes on, you will be drawn closer to Noli. She has a need that you will be able to fulfill. When the karma is completed and your souls are purified, then Noli will go on. Shortly thereafter, she will help you from the spirit side of life."

"I had wondered about that." She spoke as if in deep thought. After a moment of silence, she continued. "I had almost given up, but, thank God, I found you. Last week when my husband told me of your powers, I thought, this is just another one of his crazy ideas, but you have convinced me."

We sat in deep thought then she said, "Reverend Maya, you have no idea how much you have helped me and I am certain a whole new world will be opened up for me."

We prayed and thanked God for His love and mercy, then I said, "I will fix some lunch for you."

With a determined shake of her head, she said, "No, you won't. I will take you to my husband's office and he will relieve you of that tooth. Remember, I told you he will heal you. He can. Then we will go to lunch. I know of a very nice place near his office."

I smiled thinking, "How can I have lunch after taking out a tooth?"

But that is exactly what happened. Doctor took out the tooth and also the abscess came out perfectly whole. I must say that this man who had been my father and also my husband was a most amazing individual. God had given him many great gifts which I knew he would be able to use in the future for many, many people.

Later, they were divorced and shortly after, Doctor married a very charming lady executive. That marriage lasted for about two years, and at eighty-six years of age, he again married a very lovely lady who was closer to his age. This marriage has proved to be very happy and I am certain God has answered all of our prayers.

Just before Jack Kennedy's assassination in 1963, Jess introduced me to Vinnie, whose father and Joe Kennedy were friends and business associates.

Vinnie and I became good friends and worked together holding spiritual sessions with groups of people. One day, she asked me if I would like to meet the President. He was disturbed because he had been elected in the zero year of 1960. Lincoln had been elected and assassinated in 1860. McKinley in 1900, assassinated in 1901. All unfortunate enough to be elected in the years ending with zero. Arrangements were made for me to meet him, but he was killed before this could take place.

Everyone cried at his assassination, including myself. I was sitting at a table crying and looking out over the bay when Kennedy appeared before me fully dressed. It was the Sunday after he was killed. I looked up and there was the President standing in the doorway. He spoke without sound and said, "Do not cry for me. I am Abe Lincoln come back. Someone in my family will be president. My brother Ted should not run for president."

I wrote to Ted Kennedy and told him his brother had come through to me and said that he should not run for president. Three days later, he announced he was not a candidate. I do not take credit for this decision because I have no way of knowing if he received my letter, but I do know it was not Ted who spoke, but his brother Jack through him.

Many of you will ask, why did John F. Kennedy come to visit Maya Perez? I will explain.

JFK was a mystic and a great medium in many incarnations. As Abraham Lincoln, he studied mediums and spoke with the spirits of his friends who had passed through the veil. In this lifetime he chose the mother who had great powers and the father who instinctively knew he would someday be president. Rose, his beloved mother was a double master. Her birthday, July 22, 1890, makes her a Sun Goddess in the superconscious realm. A master builder of the subconscious and a metaphysician in her life path. This kind of power and deep mysticism is not given to one, it is earned through dynamic and intense suffering.

A close friend of mine, Marley, a socialite, met Rose Kennedy in a salon. It was a most unusual meeting of two Sun Goddesses. Marley is a Leo, so is Rose. They were sisters in the sun heaven. I'm sure their meeting was not by mere accident. It was planned by minds greater than man.

Marley looked at Rose and asked, "Are you Rose Kennedy?"

Rose did not answer. She stared at Marley with a look that said, "Oh dear, I'm captive of another one."

Marley, who is in tune with the master from other lifetimes and is adept in this life, had studied yoga's many masters, flinched as she sensed what Rose was thinking and said humbly, "You give me such an inferiority complex. How can we ever live up to what you stand for?"

Rose silently beamed at Marley like a big sister who is proud of her younger sister.

Later, one of the girls in the salon told Marley, "Rose is one of the most devout and sincere persons she had ever met."

She was the most natural vehicle for Jack Kennedy to be created in. As a great mystic, he had to pick a mother who was also a mystic and one he had known in a past lifetime. This man's power was so great that if it had been channeled, he would have become one of the greatest teachers of our time. Jesus died on a Friday and rose on a Sunday. Jack Kennedy died on a Friday and appeared before me on a Sunday.

Let me share the secret of why he came to see me on that particular day.

During the summer of 1963, when Vinnie asked me if I would like to meet the President, I immediately replied, "Yes, I would like to meet him. He was my beloved brother in another life, but does he wish to meet me?"

Vinnie looked into my eyes and answered softly, "I've asked him and he's given me permission to make the necessary arrangements. You know Jeanne Dixon and many others predicted his death because of his nomination in the zero year."

"Yes, Vinnie, I'm well aware of this prediction," I answered in a trance-like tone of voice, but we can pray and try to break the pattern which has been created through a curse."

Vinnie waited for me to explain the origination of the curse, but I remained silent. After a few moments she asked," What do you suggest we do?"

There was only one answer to her question. Prayer and sending light to the President and hope that God would help us to dissolve this extremely powerful karmic pattern. The group who set up this particular pattern were adept and knew how to reach the Sun God. This answer I knew instinctively, but did not discuss it with Vinnie.

I was sitting in my living room the day the news came over the T.V. that the President had been shot in Dallas. How could I ever forget my feelings? I was like a woman demented. I ran into my bathroom and looked into the mirror and said, "God! God! Why did this happen? Why did you do this to me?" My ego was so amazed that I could not believe that my beloved Father would refuse me my great desire. Suddenly, God in his great mercy, put his hand on my shoulder, on me, a poor deluded sinner. With his compassion, His hand on my shoulder led me back to my sofa in the living room. After pouring vibrations of peace and love into my soul, He said, "This had to happen. President Kennedy was Abraham Lincoln, come back."

I cried when I tried to reach a friend, only to find the phone out of order. Later the repair man phoned and said, "JFK is dead."

I went with Dorothey, my hairdresser, over to Dimmans to talk about the matter and have a light snack. We saw two ladies celebrating with champagne. Both of us were shocked and were ashamed to witness such wickedness.

Leaning over to me, Dorothy whispered, "How can they rejoice?"

"Please ignore the incident. It never happened. Bless it. Like Jesus, he's a great soul. He's hated because he stood for truth."

Around noon on Sunday, I received a special delivery letter from Vinnie. It contained one sentence, "And so it happened."

TWENTY-SEVEN

The Buddah

I have sat in meditation with the great Buddah.

It is a memory from my past which I shall always cherish and about which I enjoy reminiscing. It is a strange tale which began about 1965, while I was in New York city teaching courses in mysticism.

My friend, Dr. Harold Reilly, had asked whether I would be interested in visiting a yoga center with him and several friends. I agreed, and the following Sunday we set out upon a journey which was to become quite an adventure in my life.

We arrived at the center in the early afternoon and were met by Blanche DeVrees, the amazing woman in charge of the center.

I had been told that the center was very beautiful—but was totally unprepared for what I found. The house was large and the grounds were spacious and lovely. There were roses everywhere and flowers of every description in the gardens. It was a veritable paradise. Even the guest house, way in the back, was quite large.

Blanche's sister, Frankie, had been our guide. She seemed to supervise everything from the kitchen to the welfare of the many guests.

There were many places of interest at the center—especially a look-out point from which one could see the surrounding countryside for miles around. It was indeed a very beautiful place.

Dinner was served at 5 p.m. I sat to the left of our hostess, while Dr. Reilly was on her right. Jess Stearn and several others were also at this large table. Frankie sat at a smaller table with other guests.

Across from me sat Tara Singh, an Indian who was an ex-Buddhist monk. Dr. Reilly had introduced Singh to Blanche thinking he would be an asset to her center. The conversation seemed to revolve around Tara and myself. We were talking about names, and Tara had asked how I came to have the East Indian name of Maya. I explained how this had come about, adding that this was probably why I also had acquired the philosophy of the *illusion of all life*.

Tara told me he had a relative in Guyana, an aunt, who lived in the capital city of Georgetown. He had visited her a few years back, and he was thinking of going back there soon.

Later the conversation took a different turn, as I told Tara that several of my Masters were of the East. At that moment, one in particular was at our wavelength and had a message for him.

Everyone listened intently—especially Jess, Dr. Reilly, his fiancee, Betty, and D.D., his sister. Jess usually described this gift as a "cold message."

I went into a trance-like state and said, "Tara, it was wrong for you to leave your wife and two children. They are still very sad, and there are times when your wife feels quite despondent about the responsibility of raising the children alone."

I hesitated, then called his son's name, saying that he missed his father very much, and that Tara should go back home and make amends.

Tara was shocked. His countenance changed as he said, "Maya, I do not like your Masters!"

Suddenly, from out of nowhere, came a voice like thunder saying, "My Masters will destroy you!"

There was a period of embarrassed silence. Our hostess, Blanche Devrees, broke the silence by saying, "It is not in good taste to raise your voice in public. One should learn control and discipline."

I ignored the scolding as though I had not heard it, and indeed this was the case, because I was not in my body at the moment. I remained calm; I knew I had been the channel which the Master had used to give Tara this message.

After dinner, we all sat in the large living room discussing various subjects. One man, who was a jeweler, had traveled extensively and was showing us some of his precious stones. He had a black diamond, a huge emerald, a black pearl and several other stones of great value.

I was enthralled by his stories when Tara suddenly came and knelt before me saying, "Maya, please forgive me! Frankie told me you meant no harm. I did not understand that it was just your way of giving a message from your Masters."

Smiling at him, I said, "You're forgiven. Think no more of it."

By now, some of the other guests were asking for messages, but I had learned my lesson and only answered questions which were bothering them at the moment.

On the way back to New York we all got into an animated discussion about who had been right—Tara or me. Finally, Jess spoke up. "Tara was definitely wrong. Maya gave him some good advice and he refused to accept it. But I noticed later that he was asking for more!"

The next evening I was meditating in my hotel room when the phone rang. It was Tara, and he wanted to take me out for dinner. "Can you come down?" he asked, "I have an important matter that I need to discuss with you."

"Thank you, Tara," I replied, "but I have had dinner, and I am a little tired from yesterday. Give me a raincheck for another time."

"Maya," he pleaded, "I drove down here especially to see you. Please come down. I have borrowed Frankie's car and have to get it back tonight."

I remained silent as he continued, "I have some very valuable tapestries from the Buddhist temples in Tibet. The Dalai Lama brought them when he left the country. Oh, Maya dear, please come down and talk to me."

He sounded so desperate that I felt compassion for him and relented, "Very well, bring them up to my room. I will look at them."

Tara knocked at my door a few minutes later and I opened it to find him standing there with a large package under his arm. He strolled in with a satisfied smile on his face.

Opening the package, Tara showed me the most exquisite tapestries I had every seen. He said they were more than five hundred years old.

As he sat down beside me on the sofa, he explained, "I am trying to sell these for the Dalai Lama and I need help. Please ask your Masters to advise and guide me."

I felt he was sincere and replied, "I will pray for you, Tara. God can make all things possible."

Taking his hand in mine, I prayed for his success, then went into silence in order to become in tune with one of the Master Counselors on the Inner Planes.

Half an hour later, I came out of the silence saying, "Tara, I saw you driving a car. You got out and walked up a flight of stairs to an apartment. You then took out a key, opened the door and walked in. You seemed quite happy and prosperous. It was in California. Very shortly you will go there. God has shown me this vision."

He looked at me. "This is incredible! How can I go to California? I have no money. Devrees is allowing me to stay in her guest house, rent free. I do not know what to believe!" Tara spoke these words as if in total disbelief.

"Tara, you asked me to look into the Akashic Record for you, which I did, so you must believe what I have told you."

I spoke these words with great emphasis because I did not want him to negate my work.

"Oh, dear Maya, please forgive me," Tara spoke quietly, "but at the moment I feel so down-hearted. I want to believe. I'm like a man who is lost in the hot desert. I am thirsty, and suddenly I see water and must ask myself if this is reality or merely an illusion. Please be patient with me. I have gone through hell."

With deep sympathy in my heart, I held his hand and said, "Tara, when the Masters give us a message, we must have faith. It is through our faith that our desires are manifested. God's power and our will can move mountains. It is done unto us as we believe."

"Oh, my dear, I do believe, but this is all so new to me," Tara exclaimed, pressing my hand. "Long ago a Holy man in India told me that one day I would go to a far off land, and I could work miracles if I had enough faith. I have never forgotten his words, neither will I ever forget yours. Help me, Maya, help me!"

He was silent for a brief moment, then asked, "Will this car that you speak of be mine?"

I went into meditation again and the message came as before, "Yes, Tara, the car will be yours, and I do see success for your venture."

He thanked me, and for a moment we both remained quiet, then Tara spoke, "I do believe in you and I bless your wonderful Masters. Please, may I come and visit you in California?"

"Yes, Tara, you may." With these words, I gave him my address in Balboa and bade him farewell. A few days later I left for home.

In the early part of December, I received a letter from Tara postmarked Los Angeles. A friend had loaned him enough money to buy a car which he had driven to California. In the letter he said there was so much he wanted to discuss with me.

Several things my Masters had visualized for him had already happened. He gave me a telephone number to call. I dialed the number and we made an appointment for the next day around six. It was arranged that he would spend a couple of days with me in Balboa.

Tara arrived the next afternoon carrying a suitcase filled with tapestries to be left in my care.

We spoke of may things. Finally he said, "Maya, I know this may surprise you, but six days after I met you, I called my wife in London. I told her I was anxious to see her and the children. She was happy, and I felt more at peace with myself. You are right, my children are also my responsibility."

Smiling, I said, "I'm happy you made amends, Tara. Now you will be in tune with the higher Masters of Light."

Tara looked serious, then asked, "Did not the great Siddhartha Gautama leave his wife and newborn son? Why do you feel I did wrong?'

"Yes, he did," I said, "but it was his destiny to play this part on the lower conscious level. Through prayer and deep meditation, Siddhartha was able to reach the Inner Masters in order to manifest the Christ Consciousness."

Steadily, I looked at him, "You may not know this, but he will come back as the CHRIST BUDDAH. Many lifetimes later, he will come again as the son of the living God."

Tara seemed troubled by my words and he did not reply. Getting up, he walked over to the picture window. After a few moments of silent thought, he walked back to me.

"Am I to understand that Siddhartha Gautama will be the Christ Buddah, and also the son of God?"

"Yes, that is exactly what I am trying to explain to you. The same Cell will one day evolve as the Trinity. But you do not seem ready to accept this great truth. Come, I'm hungry!"

After we ate, I took Tara for a tour of the Balboa boardwalk and Funzone, which had closed for the winter. He enjoyed looking in the shop windows and walking along the edge of the water.

The next morning, Adele Latusa called. I had told her about Tara and that he was coming to spend a few days with me. She had asked to meet this ex-monk who was helping the Dalai Lama.

Holding the phone down, I asked Tara if he would like to meet her. "She is a mystic, too," I told him, "and works with the Inner Masters."

Enthusiastically he answered, "Yes, I would love to meet your friend. Tell her I will drive you over. What time do you want to go?"

I again spoke to Adele, and she invited us for lunch.

Tara expressed the hope that Adele would see him privately, which she did. I never knew what she said to him because they went for a walk in the garden while I remained inside with Dr. Latusa, who gave me a treatment.

I knew it was best for them to speak alone so as to avoid interference from other vibrations.

After Tara left, Adele and I had a long discussion over the telephone. "Your friend is a very confused and disappointed young man," she said. "He does have power, but it is not channeled correctly. I gathered he left his young wife and ran off to become a monk. There was much turmoil in the monastery, so he left."

I agreed with Adele's observations as she continued, "He is, in truth, running away from all responsibility. He cannot face life; therefore he is wandering aimlessly from place to place without a goal in life."

"Yes, I am aware of his frustrations and blocks, Adele, but I do feel it is my purpose to help him with the sale of the tapestries."

Adele told me she did believe I could help him, but she wondered if he would be appreciative of my assistance.

"I am not concerned with this, Adele. All I want to do is help him. There is a good side to Tara, you know. Did he tell you that Eleanor Roosevelt sponsored him when he came to this country?"

"No," she answered, "we only discussed the sale of the tapestries and, of course, his leaving the Buddhist order. I know this is his real problem. He is trying to make amends through helping the Dalai Lama. I understand it was Tara who sponsored the Dalai Lama's visit to India."

"Yes, he did, and now the tapestries must be sold in order for Tara and his friends to meet the expenses of his visit there. We must help them."

The week after our conversation, Adele came to see the tapestries. She examined them and exclaimed," Maya, these are worth a small fortune!" With that she telephoned her husband to come over right away.

Dr. Latusa arrived within the hour. He was amazed at the beauty and preservation of the tapestries and said, "Maya, these pieces are at least five to six hundred years old. They are exquisite! I have never seen such workmanship!"

The good doctor spoke his words slowly as if contemplating. He, as well as Adele, was wondering why Tara had left such a priceless collection of rare art in my care.

I explained that Tara was living in a small apartment and found it impossible to keep it there. He thought it best to leave it with me because he felt it would be safer in Balboa than in Los Angeles.

"This is exactly what Doctor and I were thinking," Adele said. "If anyone finds out what you have here, it could be stolen from you!"

"I am sure no one will ever know," I replied. "Neither you nor Doctor will say anything about it, and I certainly won't! Let us bless the collection and leave it in God's hands."

Just before Christmas, D.D. Reilly came out to spend a few months to study with me. She had lost her sister, Vi, in November and felt a need for a change.

D.D. knew I had seen Tara, but had no idea we had become such close friends, until I told her he would be coming down to spend Christmas with us. She was delighted and exclaimed, "Maya Doll, only you can scold a man at the dinner table and later become his best friend."

"I did not scold Tara," I protested, trying to defend myself. "I gave him a message from the Master. It was given in love and truth."

"Darling, I understand," she said coyly, "but Tara did not like your message, and you know it! I must write H.J. and tell him the latest." At these words we both enjoyed a hearty laugh.

Tara came on the 22nd of December. I had invited him down to see the boat parade. Every year, for a week before Christmas, all the boats parade up and down the Bay every night with people aboard singing Christmas carols. It is indeed a beautiful sight.

One boat, in particular, was quite large and beautifully lighted. It was called "Tara." It was a real joy for him to see his own name in lights. I don't remember if the boat won a prize, but we all thought it should.

January and February found D.D. and me working very hard. She wanted to be ordained before going back to New York in early April. Dr. B.J. Fitzgerald had given me permission to ordain her in Los Angeles.

Several times during this period, Tara called, and I would invite him to come down to meditate with D.D. and me.

In early March, he called with excitement in his voice as he said, "Maya, I think the tapestries are sold! There is a group interested in buying them for the museum in Pasadena. I will sell only with the understanding that if the Dalai Lama ever goes back to Tibet, the tapestries must be returned to him."

"Tara, I am delighted with your news! I'm sure you will get the right price for them."

"That has already been arranged," he said. "Please pray that the deal goes through. We plan to sign the papers early tomorrow morning."

"It will go through," I said, " for I can see a rainbow over your head."

I spent the rest of the day in prayer and visualizing the tapestries being sold to the right persons. That night I had a vision.

I saw myself sitting with the Great Buddah in meditation. I was sitting on his right side and we were both in the lotus position. Strange though it seems, I was tall, slim and brown as an Indian. I also appeared to be a young man around twenty years of age.

It is difficult for me to describe how I felt, except that I was floating on waves of perfect bliss. There was a tranquility which I have never experienced in this earthly life.

We tuned in and communed in silence with the higher vibrations of the universe. It was as if the whole world was one vast orchestrated Mind and everyone was in complete harmony.

Upon awakening I was chanting Ah-Oms, and for a few moments I continued to feel a wonderful peace flowing through my whole being.

Tara called the next morning to tell me that the tapestries were sold and that the deal was closed. I was happy for him.

I told Tara of my vision and he was amazed, calling it an incredible phenomenon. He came to see me later that afternoon bringing with him a piece of jewelry from India. He said it was a gift from his heart.

We then talked of the vision. Tara listened intently, then said, "Maya, it was Gautama who came through. He is grateful and wanted to show his gratitude."

This I believed. I still feel as though I have known Gautama in another life, and that I was a monk. Tara, in deep meditation, had also seen that we were both monks with the Gautama.

Over the years, I spent my winters in California and my summers in New York. It was during one of these winters, in California, that I met Ann Miller.

Ann is a movie star and a fantastic dancer. She has made many movies and stared in many stage plays.

She invited me to stay at her beautiful home in Beverly Hills. At that time I met her mother, who I saw as a beautiful soul. Not long ago her mother, who is now dead, came through to me and said, "Please tell Ann to burn a Novena for me. I did not fulfill my greater destiny. It is through Ann's prayers and meditations that I will be able to not only help her, but bring peace to the planet."

Ann brought in a spiritual problem, or I should say spiritual block, that will have to be worked on in 1991. She is a four life path. A psychological master who has come back to do a great work. Being born April 12, 1923, she is a very high soul, but there is a block there. One time, in one of her past lives, she left the Temple of Egypt and there was a condition that was sent to her that is still blocking her. She comes out and goes back into that block, back and forth. She has a Spiritual Master in her soul that blocks her. Every time she tries to go further on, she is blocked. However, in 1991 her mother will help her. Her mother has asked me to burn candles for her and in 1991, she will come back to help Ann.

1991 will be a nine-year cycle for Ann and something that has bothered her for eons of time will be transmuted. In 1992 she will come into a new era and her health will be better. She will have over come the block. I feel Ann is also a high soul and she will come forth as a teacher. She will write books that will teach people how to evolve and how to overcome their personal problems. Ann will have this block removed through her mother and a high priest in Egypt, who was once in love with her.

Ann is a very blessed soul and I am very happy to give her this message. She is what I would call a true friend.

Glenn Ford is another one of my good friends. I was also a guest in his home. Glenn is a movie star and made many, many movies.

In one life time, in Egypt, Glenn was a king. He took a high priestess out of the temple and a condition was put on him. I feel that 1991 will be the year that the power of the king, who studied psychic phenomena, will flow into his consciousness and he will become very powerful. He will then be able to open up the emotional blocks that has blocked him for a long time. I feel that books will be written about him and he will write or be connected with movie scripts that will be very important to help heal the world. He is a five life path, and he is a mercurial master who will bring great healing powers to the earth.

He was born in the higher realms of Venus, but he fell down into a depth that made him suffer emotional blocks. It can, however, be overcome by deep meditation and prayer and making a pack with his higher self.

When I talk about him, I feel his emotional blocks. These blocks are sadness that comes from taking the high priestess from the temple, which was wrong. He brought this emotional block with him from the past five incarnations. In this lifetime, he will overcome it. He will be able to rise above it. It may take two or three years for this to happen, but regardless of that, in this life he will be able to say, " I am free, I am free." He must ask forgiveness and pray and meditate and take these things seriously.

It is not good to nurture problems and keep it all within oneself. Talk about them or even write about them. Express how you feel. Get rid of your karma by "talking" it all out of your system. Confession is good for the soul.

His mother came through to me and told me this will be the year he will overcome this block. He's a good person. I stayed with him for a week and he was a wonderful host. With this condition, however, he was always very sad. I could hear his spirit say, "Why, why, why?" He wanted me to help him, but one must take these conditions seriously. Everyone must work through their karmas so as not to repeat them in another lifetime.

TWENTY-EIGHT
A Trip to Egypt Is Predicted

In the fall of 1970, I moved back to Balboa, California, to the same apartment on the Bay. In February of 1971, Jess Stearn formed a large group of his friends for the Merv Griffin television show. I was one of them, including Ann Miller, Ann Francis, Gladys Turner (Edgar Cayce's former secretary), and several others.

When Jess informed me of a very strange individual who was also to be on the show, I was hesitant. But after talking with my Spirit guide, a message came through saying, "Do not be afraid, keep praying and sending the light to the group and no harm will come to you."

On the show, Merv asked me to give Ann Miller a reading. I did, saying, "Ann the book you are writing will be published. I see success for the book and also for your work." I also saw a very bright light over her head and felt that she was about to come into something unusual. This also I relayed to her.

Merv asked Ann about the book, which he did not know she was writing, and she verified it.

Later, I was asked many questions about my work as a palmist in the nightclubs. I seemed to have become tangled in a psychic web, and felt that my answers were too revealing about the then-current politics. I also sensed that Merv was very disturbed and that the show was getting out of his hand. Therefore when Ann Miller and Ann Francis got off, I, too, did the same.

One of the men, who was connected with the show, ran up to me and asked, "Maya, why did you get off?"

"I had to," I replied, "there was some psychic interference from someone on the show."

Later, Merv informed me that he would have to cut a good part of the show out. I shook my head saying, "I understand." Because of my appearance on that show, I was asked to give a lecture in Dallas, Texas. There I met several Mind Control students. One of them, Helen Hadsell, introduced me to her good friends, Mr. and Mrs. George Morgan, who arranged for me to return to Dallas in the fall of that same year and also the following year of 1972.

It was in the Spring of 1972 that I gave a seminar for the Jose Silva Mind Control group. During the question and answer period, a lady in the group asked, "Maya, what was the most meaningful experience of psychic phenomena that you have ever had?"

After a moment of deep thought, I related the story of Queen Nefertiti's coming through to me and asking for help. When I was finished, the same lady again asked, "Do you really believe what Nefertiti said, that you will go to Egypt?"

"Yes, I believe every word," I answered smiling. "I feel Egypt has great significance for me in this lifetime."

I meditated for a moment then continued, "It is strange that you should ask me these questions, only last October, Barry Shawney, a psychic predicted that I would go to Egypt this year. If I do it will be a miracle. I do not have money, neither am I a citizen. Several years ago, I applied to become one, but whenever I am called, I am either ill or in another part of the country. I do not have a Green Card which all non-citizens must carry for identification to prove that they were legally admitted to the United States, and to top it off, I lost my passport and cannot even prove I entered the country legally."

This brought a loud clamor of applause from the group, who wished me to keep on speaking, but the time was up so my sponsor spoke for me and said that my time was over due.

At the end of the session, a rather pretty blond lady walked up to the platform, congratulated me on the lecture and said, "I am Betty Ivers, I will take you to Egypt."

With a happy smile, I exclaimed, "I accept!"

Pulling me aside she whispered, "Let's have dinner together and I will explain how it can be done."

I could feel her looking searchingly at me and felt that she was very psychic but had not been opened.

"Very well," I replied, "but some of my friends are going to have dinner with me. Sit beside me and explain the details."

I must admit that I did not take her seriously, but after she related the details and said that she was a travel agent, I felt there was some substance to her offer.

Before I left Dallas for California, Betty had informed me of her complete plan for the tour to Egypt and the Holy Lands. In order for me to go without paying, I would have to get fifteen or more people to join us. If we got thirty, then Betty, too, could go at no cost. This sounded reasonable and I immediately started to think how I could round up some of my good friends for the tour, which was to be called, MAYA'S ANTIQUITY TOUR.

Later, Betty sent me some brochures. We were to leave October 12, 1972 for Rome, Egypt, Jordan, Jerusalem and Greece. By June I would be back in New York and Betty and her friends would pick me up there to begin the tour.

The first few weeks I was not concerned about the missing passport or any other problem. I felt if God wished me to go on the tour, he would arrange everything for me. At the same time, it was important that I help with prayer and deep meditation. Therefore when I met the Reverend Carlo Bigivanti, a minister of Religious Science in North Hollywood, California, who came to hear me speak in Sherman Oaks, I immediately asked him to pray for me. Later, he suggested that I come to one of his healing groups which would be held at his church.

When Ginger Cromwell and I arrived at the church, we were both in excellent spirits. We took seats near the front so that I could hear better.

Reverend Carlo has a very soothing voice and I may have gone into deep meditation because suddenly, I felt Ginger nudging me as she whispered, "Reverend Carlo is introducing you, stand up."

Faintly I heard his voice saying, "Today we have a very special friend visiting us. She is Maya Perez, a writer, lecturer and mystic. Even thought I have only recently met her I feel as if we were friends for a long, long time. Maya asked me to pray for her, as she is leaving for a visit to Egypt and the Holy Lands. Let us all join in prayer and then sit in silence for a few minutes."

I acknowledged his introduction, then sat down in silence as he prayed with deep sincerity. "Divine Father, walk with Maya. Hold her hand and guide her as she leaves these shores. Stay with her every moment of the way and protect her as she visits foreign lands. Give her the power and the wisdom to discern what is good and what is evil."

Suddenly, I was transported to a distant land and I heard no more. I saw myself walking on the sands of the desert. Then I saw the great pyramid in Egypt. It was real. Very real. As I came out of my trance-like state, I knew it was my destiny to take the trip. I also knew that we were in the good Lord's care and that He would provide for us.

Later, while we were having coffee, I told Reverend Carlo of my vision. He listened intently as I related it, then he held my hand and said, "I too, had a vision of you in far-off lands. God has shown us both that you will take the trip. I feel very good about it."

He hesitated a moment then continued, "There is a meaningful purpose to this trip. It will open many doors for you."

I feel exactly the same," I exclaimed with a happy smile, "Thank you, Reverend Carlo, I appreciate your prayers more than you will ever know."

A few days before I left Balboa for my Spring tour, I visited Kathleen to tell her good-bye. I had mentioned over the telephone to Annette that I would be over to visit Kathleen and wished she would be there also. I felt I needed both of their blessings for my trip.

Kathleen usually served a fine lunch, but that particular day it was a banquet. There were several other friends there whom I had met before, and they all brought in a dish. Annette had brought some cake and a special chicken dish and my contribution was a bottle of wine to celebrate the happy occasion.

After lunch, Annette took me aside and said, "Maya, this is not the usual occasion of your leaving Balboa. This is a most important year for you. The journey to Egypt and the Holy Lands will open up your outer as well as your inner awareness. You were first awakened in Alexandria, Egypt. This is significant that Alexandria is your Earth Mother, meditate and think about what I have just said. It is important for you to understand the true meaning of your life and the invisible world that surround us. If it is possible for you to visit Alexandria, then by all means take the opportunity, for it will mean an even greater awareness for you."

Annette took my hand, closed her eyes and she whispered to herself, then added softly, "Maya, seven incarnations have passed since you left Egypt. I see you walking away from the sun and I can hear you say, "Oh Father, I must leave you. I go to fulfill my greater destiny. Later, I shall return for your blessings. Please walk with me. Oh, my Father, never leave me. Never turn your face away from me. I love you. Oh, my Father, I love you. Now I am ready to finish my work."

There was silence for a moment, then she continued. "Maya, I see the great sun shining down on you and I know you have been blessed."

I listened as if I were hypnotized. I knew that she spoke the truth. I did not understand all that she had said, but I believed that God had spoken to me through her and that it was a divine message.

Several days passed, then one morning while in deep meditation, I realized what this good woman had meant when she told me Alexandria, Egypt is your mother. Jesus once said, "The Earth is my mother and God is my Father." Therefore, it was in Alexandria, Egypt that my true self was first conceived. This was symbolic of the awareness of the Higher or I AM SELF opening up within the mortal consciousness.

I thought about going to Alexandria, Egypt, but no matter how long and ardently I asked for the answer, it did not come. Finally I said, "Father, if it be Thy will, let it be."

Then a message came through, "Not now, but later, after your book is published, you will visit Alexandria, Egypt." With a sense of utter peace, I thanked the Father for his message. I knew, when the time was right I will go back to the Sun, my beloved Father.

Shortly after I returned to New York, the Social Security office notified me about receiving my Social Security payments which were now due.

That night, I took the letter to bed with me and meditated about the matter. I did not know that you could get payments and still continue to work. I asked my Spirit if I should stop working and he replied, "No, do not stop. It is important for you to help your fellow man."

Again, I asked, "Will I be successful with my books?"

"Yes, in the future you will be successful. Have faith."

The next morning at the Social Security office, a very nice young man informed me that my payments were overdue and that I was entitled to a large refund of money.

"Mr. Cudihy, I am still working and intend to so do," I answered seriously.

"You can continue to work, Miss Perez," he said, looking at me closely, "but what I want to explain to you is, there is a large sum of money owed to you for 1970 and also 1971. In those years there was a mistake and you overpaid the government.

There was a moment of silence and then he said, "Do you have your income tax records here in New York?"

"No, I do not," I replied, "I will have to write my C.P.A. in California. I plan to leave for Egypt and the Holy Lands in three and a half months."

He checked some papers on his desk and excused himself. He went to the other side of the office and this gave me time to look back to the last few years when I was having trouble with the Internal Revenue about my tax. I did not understand about estimated tax and in 1967 my C.P.A., who was connected with a large firm in Long Beach, California, failed to explain the problem to me. I was supposed to pay a lump sum, then also pay that sum which was made out in four quarterly payments. I paid the quarterly payments, but failed to pay the lump sum. This caused me to be in a turmoil as letters were sent to me saying "You have not paid your tax and owe a certain sum." Then in a little while another letter would come with a different sum that I owed. This confused me very much.

After a while I went to see my C.P.A. and told him about the letter and he asked,"Did you pay your tax?"

"Of course, I did. Here are the checks," I replied.

This was strange, because he never asked to see the checks and I never thought of showing them to him.

I remember the Christmas of 1970, just a few days before, I had planned a party to watch the boat parade, when a letter came in the mail saying that my bank account was going to be taken over by the government. I was in tears when my good friend, the Reverend D.D. Reilly, who was spending the holidays with me, said, "Maya, let us enjoy the party and then worry about the matter later. I feel that you are being tested."

"I have wondered about that," I remarked quietly, "even Jesus was tested with tax problems."

I followed her advice, and we had a very lovely party. In 1971 I finally went to the Internal Revenue's office in Los Angeles and one of the clerks found the problem.

Coming our of my reverie, I heard him return and say, "Miss Perez, you will receive a check from the Internal Revenue in a few days."

"Mr. Cudihy," I exclaimed, "I am very apprehensive about accepting this money."

"But we owe it to you."

Still stubborn, I did not answer. I was thinking of all the aggravation I had received from them in the past few years. Again he excused himself and went to the other side of the office. At that point I remembered a joke I had read in one of the magazines. Two foreign diplomats were arguing about accepting aid from the USA. One diplomat said to his colleague, "I will not accept money from the Americans. My pride won't let me."

The other diplomat replied in a philosophical tone of voice, "My brother, if the amount is sufficient, I am sure that it will soothe you for the loss of your pride."

I smiled at this memory and just then Mr. Cudihy returned to see the smile on my face. He, too smiled and asked, "Will you accept the money? It will come in handy for your trip."

With a sheepish smile, I replied, "Yes."

In July of 1972, I contacted the Guyana, South America consulate, about my missing passport. There, I met Mr. Persaud, an East Indian gentleman who was the assistant Consul. He introduced me to the consul, a distinguished black man who I felt was very intuitive. His name was Mr. Saul.

The consul asked, "Where was the passport issued?"

"Barbados, British West Indies. I went to school there," I replied.

"Miss Perez," the Consul explained, "I will try to contact the Barbados consulate, in order to have them issue another passport, but I'm afraid we do not have much time."

"This I also realize and I truly appreciate your help."

The following week Mr. Persaud visited me at my apartment on 86th Street in New York City. He was very interested in my work of deep mysticism, and asked many questions about it and also my life.

"Miss Perez, why did you go to school in Barbados? Why not Guyana?" he asked, looking at me with his piercing brown eyes.

"Because of health reasons, my family made their home in Barbados. When I was thirteen, my mother took Albert, my fifteen-year-old brother, and me to the States. We remained there for a year and then we left for Barbados. It was in Barbados that I met my mystical teacher. He was a twenty-one-year-old Englishman, my beloved Francis. He taught me the power of the Psalms of the Bible. When I was seventeen, he told me that he was going to the States and I said, "I will miss you."

"No," he answered, "I will teach you how to follow me and by Christmas you will be in New York."

His prophecy was fulfilled, Two days before Christmas, at age eighteen, I was in New York. That is the passport that is missing."

"Miss Perez, it will take a long time to get a passport from Barbados, but we could give you an emergency passport."

"Thank you, Mr. Persaud," I replied with a tremor in my voice, "you have given me hope. I truly appreciate your kindness."

After that, we had a long talk about Guyana and the carnival that the natives were planning there.

TWENTY-NINE

Attending to Problems

September 15th arrived and I still had not received my Green Card or heard anything about my passport from the Guyana consulate.

I spoke to my good friend D.D. Reilly, who advised me to do something fast.

"Maya, write to Washington," she urged, "or go back to the Immigration Service. Do it Monday."

This was Saturday morning and D.D. had called to see if anything had happened. That same night Betty Ivers called me. She was concerned about the number of people who had dropped out of the tour. "Maya, several friends have written to say they cannot go. Have you anyone in California to take their places?"

"Not so far," I replied, sensing fear in her voice, "I have some friends in New York that are interested. Have they sent in their checks?"

"Yes, they have but we need many more people," she answered with a tremor in her voice.

"How about my good friend June Coulter?" I asked, "is she going?"

"Yes, she is going and also a friend of hers," Betty answered, "but how do you feel about the tour? I need to know because my office wants to cancel it."

"I feel confident about everything," I answered positively, "but if you are thinking negatively, we will have trouble. Have faith, I am certain it will work out."

"Maya, I have been trying to think positive, but let's face facts," she answered disturbed, "everyone is afraid to go to Jordan and Israel at this time. Did you read about the Jewish athletes who were killed in Germany?"

"Yes, I did. I prayed for those poor boys."

"Maya, this is a very serious situation," Betty answered with a sigh.

"I agree," I replied quietly, "but in times of trials we must pray and try to keep our thoughts positive. In this way we will be able to transmute the negative problems."

There was silence on the phone, then I continued, "Betty, I have applied for my Green Card. It should be here soon. I have also seen the Guyana consulate about my passport. If I don't receive it on time, I will have to travel on an emergency passport." This was too much for her to digest at one time.

"Oh, Maya, this is terrible," she cried out in a shocked tone of voice, "I really think we should cancel the tour. I am going against the whole office. Once before I took someone who was not a citizen, and we had trouble from the beginning to the end. Now you tell me you don't have your passport."

Silently, I started to pray and send the light to her. This may have calmed her down, for she finally said, "I do feel we will make the tour, but there are so many strange things happening. It could be the dark forces working against us."

"You are right," I remarked calmly, "and you are not helping the situation. Have you been reading the Psalms?"

"No, Maya," she answered truthfully, "I have been too busy. You have no idea what I go through in that office."

Yes, I thought smiling to myself, with your power working in reverse, anything can happen. Aloud I said, "I will pray for you because at this point you are too confused to find the right answers."

"Thank you, Maya, I will write and send you some more brochures. Keep sending the light." She then hung up.

A few minutes later, I received a call from D.D. Reilly. She wanted me to go with her to visit her brother, Dr. Reilly, in Oak Ridge, New Jersey. I was hesitant about making the trip by bus.

"Maya," she insisted, "I feel you should go over and get some of H.J's power. Call me in the morning, if you feel like going."

I promised that I would call her either way, then wished her a good night's rest.

The next morning, I woke up, as a voice from within the back of my head whispered, "Go over to H.J.'s. Something good will happen there."

I prayed and thanked the good Lord for His message, then called D.D. She was delighted at my change of heart and exclaimed, "Oh, Maya, doll! This is wonderful! My sister Ethel is also going over to H.J.'s. I'll meet you at the bus station. Ethel and I will be at the information desk."

On the bus, D.D. and I sat together and Ethel nearby. I mentioned to D.D. what had transpired to change my plans.

"D.D., I knew it was the voice of my Spirit-Guide," I spoke softly so as not to be overheard, "Something very important will happen to help us with the tour."

"I hope so, Maya, because if you don't go, I am sure Betty will cancel the tour." D.D. spoke as if she were giving me a message.

"Yes, this is true. Betty called last night. She was really upset with me for not getting my passport before this," I said with a smile, but D.D. did not think it was funny.

"Maya, you are a very clever woman, but at times you act as if you are a child," she remarked with a shrug of her shoulders. "I can't understand how you live without a passport, a Green Card or insurance. When trouble comes your way, you just take it with a smile. When it gets too low, you call the Prayer Group."

"D.D., listen to me," I answered, holding her hand, "why should I worry. If I am to go to Egypt, I will go. If not, I am quite satisfied to stay home and keep up our Mind Control classes."

We had been taking Mind Control together since August. JoAnna and Frank Gerber also had joined. We were all elated about traveling on the tour, with our minds on higher planes of consciousness.

Just then, I happened to look out the window. It had been raining and now there was a beautiful rainbow with the sun shinning down on the bus.

"Look! D.D., look at the rainbow," I exclaimed in a joyous mood, "let us make a wish and it will be manifested."

D.D. looked out at the rainbow, which was actually glorious. We held hands and made our desires for a successful trip over seas.

Shortly after we arrived at Dr. Reilly's home in Oak Ridge, I went into the kitchen to help Betty Billings, his assistant, with the lunch she was fixing, and also to inform her of our progress with the tour. Suddenly, I heard D.D's voice calling me, "Maya, Maya, Mr. DeFrancis and his family are here. His son, Frank Jr., is a very important lawyer in Washington. He can help you get your Green Card and even your citizenship. Come and meet him." D.D. seemed to sense something out of the ordinary.

I had met Mr. DeFrancis, Sr. and his charming wife, but I had never met their famous son, who I learned later was the acting attorney for the U.S.A in West Germany.

Later, Mr. DeFrancis, Jr., called me aside and asked, "What is your problem with the Immigration Service?"

"I'm going to Egypt and the Holy Lands. I need a Green Card and a passport. My passport is missing." I answered, looking up at his handsome face. He seemed sympathetic and understanding.

"Don't worry," he said, "I know the head of the Immigration Service personally. I will ask him to take care of your problem."

Before he left, Mr. DeFrancis said, "Maya, write to me tomorrow and give me all the details. I should be back in Washington by Wednesday, in the meantime, my secretary will have them."

Next day, I gathered all the papers that I had accumulated over the years with the Immigration Department and sent them on to his office.

I had thought that I would be able to get my citizenship papers before I left the country. This was confusing to Mr. DeFrancis and he called and asked, "Maya, what is it that you need? I thought you were asking for your Green Card. If so, I can get it for you, but the time is too short to get your citizenship papers. That will take several weeks or even months. I will call the Immigration people and then write to you."

This man whom I had just met was helping me out of the goodness of his heart. I was so filled with deep emotion, that all I could say was, "Thank you so very much." Later, the thought came to me, he was God in action. God had picked him to help me.

A few days later, I received a letter from Mr. DeFrancis, stating that he had contacted the head of the Immigration Service, and that I was to go down to see them.

After praying for a few minutes, I hurriedly dressed and went down to the Immigration office. I waited two hours, and was finally given my Green card.

On leaving the office, I thought, now I should go over to the Guyana consulate to see about the passport, but spirit-God indicated otherwise and I returned home. There I found a letter from the Social Security office. I quickly opened it and found two checks which amounted to one thousand and forty-six dollars. I had not expected such a large amount.

At my bank, I asked the manager if the checks were O.K. He looked at them and said, "They are bona fide Social Security checks. What do you want me to do with them?" I told him to put half in travelers checks and the rest in my savings account.

After he was through with the details, he asked, "What type of work do you do?"

"I lecture on Truth and teach how to visualize the material things we need. I am taking a tour group to Egypt and the Holy Lands in order to write a book."

After giving some instructions to a young lady, he remarked, "Speaking of visualization, I did this two years ago. I wanted to go on a vacation, but did not have the necessary cash, so I meditated about it, and in a few days the money appeared from a very odd source."

I smiled and said, "If this money had not appeared, it would have been very difficult for me to take the trip. I knew it would come in time, but did not expect two checks. At first, I thought they had made a mistake. This is why I asked if they were O.K."

"Don't worry, they don't usually make that kind of mistake," the banker said smiling, "have a good trip."

"Thank you, Mr. McGraw, It was a pleasure talking to you." Then in an afterthought, I said, "Use your visualization more often." He nodded and smiled.

Around the last week of September, D.D. Reilly and I went to the Lincoln Center in New York City to hear Dr. Jack Holland speak. He was giving a lecture for Dr. Seal, whose church at that time was located in the Lincoln Center.

Years ago, I had told Dr. Holland that he would be doing spiritual work and speaking to large audiences.

After the lecture, we all gathered outside to greet Dr. Seal, who was retiring and was hoping that Dr. Holland would consider taking his place to work in the church. Later, I heard that Dr. Holland had decided that the weather in New York was not suitable for him or his mother. They were living in San Jose, California and loved it.

As D.D. and I walked down the large stairway, we met a blond lady standing at the foot of the stairs. She came up and asked, "Did you knit this pretty dress?"

"No," I replied, "I do not have time to knit. A friend gave it to me."

A few minutes later while D.D. was speaking to an old friend, I happened to see the blond lady again. She was standing alone and I thought, she seems very familiar. I wonder where I have seen her? Without a second thought, I ran over and handed her a brochure saying, "You should come with me to Egypt."

Looking at the brochure the blond lady answered, "Yes, I would love to visit Egypt but I'm working with two lawyers and cannot leave for three weeks." With a charming smile, she continued, "My bosses would fire me."

Just then, a very attractive brown-haired lady came up and the blond said, "My name is Helene Chinsley and this is my friend Margaret. She is my sister's tenant and wished to hear Dr. Holland. My sister is ill, so I came with Margaret."

After the introductions I joined D.D., and we went across the street to a restaurant. Again, I met Helene coming out of the ladies room and I waited for her. As we walked back to her table, I asked for her birthday and year. Sitting down next to Helene, I discussed her vibrations, which to me were simply fantastic. This woman had extraordinary powers and beautiful gifts, but she was not open to the spiritual or psychic worlds.

I may have gone into an aesthetic description of Helene and her beautiful gifts, because later, I was told by Helene that she was secretly thinking, "this is some sort of numerology kick," and Margaret was wondering why she herself had not seen Helene's beautiful vibes, as she had known Helene all her life. As a matter of fact, Helene was Margaret's babysitter and they had grown up in the same area a long, long time and also lived in the same house.

The next Sunday, Dr. Jack Holland was speaking again at the music center, and again I went to hear him. This time, I was alone and so was Helene. After the lecture, we went to lunch and walked down Broadway. We talked as if we had known each other forever.

During our conversation, I advised Helene to change her name to Helena, and she remarked, "Maya, it is Helena on my birth certificate."

We both agreed that Helena would be more fitting, especially as the A gave her a new door. A new awakening in the soul.

We had lunch and after we finished eating, I noticed she was looking at me, puzzled. I asked, "What is it that you wish to know?"

After a moment of deep reflection, Helena replied, "Yes, Maya, I would like to know where we have met before and what was our connection?"

"It was in old Egypt," I replied with a bright smile, I was delighted to know that she was becoming more aware, "at the moment, I cannot say how we were related. I just know that we were very close."

I discussed the story of Queen Nefertiti coming through to me, Ben asking for help and also the strange events that followed up to the time of meeting her. Helena listened intently and seemed interested in my life and the work that I was doing.

The following Tuesday, Helena called and said, "I have some presents for you. Can I come over after work?"

I was delighted and replied, "Yes, come over and we will have dinner."

Around 6 p.m. she arrived with a large package. Inside was a very large book about Egypt, with some of the most beautiful pictures. Also a pair of lavender gloves to go with my outfit that I had worn the first time we met. Later this book was given to Bruce Hungerford, with Helena's permission. Bruce was a concert pianist and lecturer on ancient Egypt. Bruce played an important part in my life with the picture of Princess Hathor.

Around the first week of October, I called to find out if any news had come from Barbados about my passport. "No, we have not heard from them, Miss Perez," Mr. Persaud said, "but I think you should come down and speak to the consul about an emergency passport."

I agreed and immediately dressed and went down to the office. After an hour or more, the Consul told me in a very serious tone of voice,

"Miss Perez, we will issue you an emergency passport, but I am afraid you will have trouble with it in foreign countries."

"I will have to take that chance, Mr. Saul," I answered with a wry smile, "I have no other alternative. If I don't go, the tour will be cancelled, and several friends will be disappointed."

The Consul looked at me in deep thought for a few moments, then signed the paper and told me to have it notarized and bring it back to him. After doing this, I left the office saying, "Thank you, Father." Naturally, I thought everything was now in perfect order.

The next morning, I received a letter from the American Embassy stating that because I did not have a re-entry card, it was impossible for them to issue me a visa. I was advised to go down immediately to the New York Immigration Service and get the re-entry card. Then at the bottom of the letter were the words, Have a good trip. It was signed by one of the executives.

The last sentence gave me a clue that I would have the blessings of the Embassy. After getting the Green Card, I made the mistake of thinking it would take care of my problems. I was certain that my good friend Mr. Frank DeFrancis, Jr. had again called someone at the Immigration center because everyone there treated me as if I were a celebrity. I waited just a few short minutes when a gentleman came out and presented me with the card. He gave me a close appraising look.

On the 11th of October, I received my second shot and went to bed early because the next night we were leaving for the tour.

About 9 p.m. Betty Ivers called to report, "Maya, the Embassy has refused to give you the visas. They said, you did not get your re-entry card."

"I know. They wrote and told me to come down to the Immigration office and get it. I did," I replied, "oh, and I got all my visas except the Egypt one. I called them and someone spoke to me and said, it was not necessary."

"We will have to get one when we arrive in Rome," Betty said calmly.

After that, I related the story of meeting Mr. Frank DeFrancis, Jr. and how he helped me to get my Green Card and also the re-entry card. Betty was very impressed and remarked, "We need all the help we can get, Maya. I am glad that this wonderful man has helped you."

"Oh, Betty," I exclaimed excitedly, "the name Francis is most important to me. It was Francis who introduced me to the power of the Psalms in the Bible and I have been praying to Saint Francis of Assisi. He will help us."

"Prayer always helps," Betty replied philosophically, "another thing, Maya, a friend of yours called me from New York. I believe her name is Marilyn. She wants to go with us and has sent in her money, but I sensed she would not be happy with this type of tour. What do you think of her?"

I felt Betty had already made up her mind that Lynn, as I called her, was not right and it was important for me to change her mind.

Lynn lived in a very expensive apartment and had several servants. However, that should make no difference. I was certain that she would enhance the tour.

"Betty," I said, "you are partly right about Lynn, but I have already informed her that this is a cheap tour. I am sure she will make the best of it."

Those were fighting words and Betty corrected me. "Maya, we are giving a lot for very little money. I would not say the tour is cheap, but that the price is right. So far, we have twelve people and that is not enough for you to go at no cost to you. We will both have to pay."

After a moment of thought, I asked, "Betty, what do you feel is right?"

"Five hundred would be all right, Maya. That should take care of the expenses," she answered hesitantly. Later, I was informed that I would have to pay the full price.

"Betty," I replied, "I can give you some of it now." At that point I was very tired and felt if it were not for my friends, I would just cancel the tour.

"Very well, Maya, we can talk about it later," she said, sensing my hesitation. "Your cousin Renee Palmer sent in her money and D.D. Reilly sent hers. Today, I received a check from Mr. Frank and JoAnna V. Gerber. I have two couples from Fort Worth, Texas, two single ladies and your friend, June Coulter.

"I am happy June is going. She is one of my favorite people and I am sure we will have an amazing trip," I exclaimed, as my enthusiasm began to grow again.

"We will arrive at the airport at 8 a.m.," Betty answered with a lift in her voice, "see that your party arrives on time."

"Don't worry, Betty, we'll all be there."

THIRTY

First Obstacle!
My Arrival In Rome

On the 12th of October, 1972, Renee Palmer, my cousin and I arrived at Kennedy Airport, just as Marilyn Oucher and the Reverend Dorothy Dolores Reilly were emerging from another car. Shortly after Frank and JoAnna Gerber arrived from Kenneton, New Jersey.

Betty Ivers and her party were to arrive at 8 p.m. At 8:30, Frank and JoAnna went to the information desk to enquire and was told the Dallas plane would arrive at 9 p.m. One hour late. It was a few minutes after nine when Betty finally arrived and introduced us to Mr. and Mrs. Lewis White, Mr. and Mrs. Dude Paris, and Narone Firdy, all from Fort Worth, Texas. Betty had said there would be fourteen of us, but since only twelve arrived, I asked her about the other two.

"June Coulter of Dallas, and her friend, Ann England will arrive in Rome on Saturday morning," Betty answered. "June had a problem with her visas and Ann waited for her."

Just then, Betty spied the TWA agent, who had come to help her and Betty introduced him to the group.

We all gathered in one of the coffee shops with the airline agent. There Betty and I discussed my problem of travelling with an emergency passport and only one visa. The one to Jordan.

The agent read what was on the passport, which was not much, then looked at the Green Card and re-entry booklet and the vaccination card, then concluded, "I think Miss Perez can leave. I am sure she will be able to re-enter with the group. If she has trouble, get in touch with the American Embassy."

I thanked him and later told Renee that I was certain I would be allowed to leave. With her usual happy smile she remarked, "Why not! With your power Maya, you can go anywhere."

I smiled, for I too, felt that God was with me and that it was my destiny to take the tour to the Holy Lands.

Promptly at 10 p.m., the plane left for Rome and I, later, opened a bottle of champagne a friend had given me for this occasion.

Nothing unusual happened on the trip, but when we arrived in Rome on Friday the 13th of October 1972, I suddenly could not walk into the airport. Betty had to assist me. As we walked into the airport, I heard someone in the group say, It's Friday the 13th. I never thought of that, but it suddenly hit me that I was walking back into time. The time when I was given to the lions. My heart started to beat faster and faster and I became excited. Renee and Marilyn looked at me strangely, then asked, "Are you all right, Maya?"

"I smiled faintly and replied, "I feel strange and am very excited." I did not tell them my heart was beating rapidly and I felt as if I were going to faint.

Betty assisting me into the Rome airport was symbolic of our togetherness throughout the whole tour. In time of an emergency, it was Betty who stood by to give me courage.

Everyone in our group passed through the entrance as they showed their passports. When my turn came, the Rome authority glanced at my strange passport and told me to step aside. After everyone in our group had passed through, he told a guard to take me to an enclosed apartment.

Puzzled, Betty followed us asking, "What is wrong?"

Without answering, the guard led me away. Betty, however, was able to take me over to the TWA airline attendant, who looked at my passport and said, "This passport is not in order. We will have to hold Miss Perez until 5 o'clock, when we can contact the American Embassy."

Betty and I consulted another TWA attendant who confirmed that nothing could be done until the American Embassy was contacted.

When the tour agent in Rome unexpectedly came through the gate, Betty explained our problem to him, but he, too, was unable to help me. I was left alone at the airport.

Since I had a long time to wait, I found a seat behind a post and started to pray and meditate over the situation. After awhile, I remembered the words Annette had spoken. Maya, in Rome you and I were thrown to the lions. Again, I was in the power of the Roman authorities. This was a past karmic pattern that was being played over. If I panicked, it would only make matters worse for me. Only prayer and deep meditation will help me to lift up my consciousness.

Quietly, I began to pour out my thoughts to God, "Inner Spirit, God of Light—I need your help. Give me the power and wisdom in order to transmute this negative problem into good. Out of the nothingness it came and into the nothingness it must be dissolved. Oh, my God! Why am I left alone in a strange land, away from my home? Oh, God, help me, for with YOU all things are made perfect. Without YOU, nothing ever was, nothing could be. Give me the answer, God. I must know why I am left here?"

The answer came clearly from within, "It is important to your destiny for you to be here. Your world is facing many great problems. You must become aware of the importance of this trip and the need for peace in your world."

Suddenly, a great feeling of peace filled my heart. I was delighted that God was still with me. The negative forces would not conquer me after all.

As I continued to meditate, I received another message, "Have some lunch. It will relax and nourish you."

I went upstairs to the restaurant and was seated next to a tall distinguished German. I surmised that he was a diplomat in Rome on special business.

We discussed the menu and decided to take what he had selected, spaghetti with a special sauce. He also informed me of the amount that I should pay and what to give the waiter.

After lunch, I went back to the main lounge and sat next to a young East Indian woman holding a tiny baby. We had arrived together on the same TWA flight. After introducing ourselves, She explained that she had missed her plane connection to India. She was living in Long Island, New York, with her husband, who was studying in the States. She was going home to India to visit her mother and family who wished to see the new baby girl.

"When is your next plane connection?" I asked, looking down at the baby sleeping in the bassinet.

"Not until 10 o'clock tomorrow morning," she answered with a sad smile.

"Oh, you are not going to spend a day and night here in this lounge with a young baby?" I exclaimed.

"Yes, I'm not allowed to leave the airport," she replied sadly, "I'm not worried about myself and the baby, but about my family in India. They will have to go several miles to meet me and I have no way of informing them. They don't have a phone and it will take a long time for a cable to reach them."

My heart went out to this young girl, alone in a strange airport with a young baby. Silently, I blessed her and thought, out of evil comes much good. This prayer also would transmute the evil situation that was sent into my own subconscious, preventing it from happening to me.

Changing the subject, I asked, "Is there anything I can do for you?"

With a smile, she answered, "Yes, I would like to eat something and get some milk for the baby. Can you mind the baby until I get back?"

"I would be happy to take care of the baby for you," I replied smiling, "up the stairs, you will find the restaurant. Some lunch will help you relax."

A short while after she left, the baby woke up and began to cry. A young couple sitting nearby asked, "Are you the child's grandmother?"

"No, I'm not the grandmother," I answered and explained the mother's predicament.

The woman asked if she could pick up the baby, but this did not help, so I took her back. In her bassinet, I found a pacifier which seemed to satisfy her for a few moments. After awhile, she spat it out and continued to cry at the top of her lungs.

A young East Indian man dressed as a Catholic priest sat down in the next seat. He, too, tried to soothe the baby, but she kept on crying. Luckily the mother finally arrived and relieved me of my charge.

The priest introduced himself as Father Abraham from India. His dark skin shone like satin and his teeth were white and unnaturally even. He was about five feet seven or eight inches tall with a round, cherubic face. He was not what one would call handsome but his vibrations were beautiful. I could feel rays of peace and love emanating from his aura. I knew he was truly a man of God in many past lifetimes.

Father may have sensed my thoughts, for he smiled and asked, "Where are you from?"

"New York," I answered, "I am with a group of people from the States. We are on our way to Egypt and the Holy Lands, but my passport is not in order. I have to wait until five o'clock when the Immigration authority here can contact the American Embassy.

He then asked, "Are you American?"

"No, Father," I answered smiling, "that is the problem. I'm from Guyana, South America. I'm travelling on an emergency passport."

"Oh, that is most interesting!" he exclaimed, "I have friends in Guyana. Some day I plan to visit that part of the world."

"My home is very interesting," I remarked, "half of the population in Guyana are East Indians. I often say at my lectures that I did not have to go to India for illumination, India came to me.'

We both laughed. Then he said, "So you are a lecturer. What are your subjects?"

I handed him a brochure, which he read and said, "So you were born with a veil? We call it a caul. The wise men of India say, it's a lucky child who comes into the world with a caul."

Laughing at his remark I said, "That is exactly what the midwife said and I believe it."

"Yes," he said pensively, "some people are born under a lucky star. Others bring great trials and tribulations into this life. The good Lord knows best."

After those words we were both silent, and I mused over the vibrations of this wonderful man of God. I felt he had passed through several incarnations where he had evolved to the various Gods of the East, and now, he was ready to work out his karma and evolve to the glorious Masters of the West. How wonderful and glorious are the works of the Father who guides us through the many waters of Life.

Looking deep into his eyes, I asked, "Please tell me about yourself."

"I have been a priest for sixteen years," he answered as if his thoughts were still far away, "we have had Catholic priests for many generations in my family. We were originally from Cana."

I did not know where he meant when he said Cana, so asked, "Do you mean Canna?"

"No, Cana," he replied, then continued, "this is my first mission tour of India and I have come to Rome for the blessings of the Pope. I'm on my way to Ireland to try and bring peace between the North and the South.

He spoke with such humbleness and sincerity that I felt it was God's will and that he would be directed by the Masters of Light.

Closing my eyes, I said, "Father, may it be the will of God to Let light shine upon you throughout your journey and may the Masters of Light direct you at all time."

As I spoke, a great peace flowed into my being, I knew God had answered my desires.

The priest closed his eyes and silently we communed together. He then gave me a blessing and said, "God bless you, Maya Perez. If you ever come to India, look me up. Here is my card. Good-bye."

Around 2:30 p.m., a tall slim man with strange slanted eyes sat next to me in the same seat the priest had just vacated. He began to read an English newspaper. He did not look like an American, and I knew he was not English. Occasionally, he would glance at me, but I did not wish to speak as I felt he had a strange weird power. At that time, I did not understand my premonition of fear for him. The strange man wore dark glasses, but I could see that the expression of his eyes were unnatural.

Looking directly at me, he asked, "Are you in trouble?"

I nodded and he continued, "I noticed you have been sitting here since early this morning." He spoke with a slight accent, and peered at me with his deep penetrating eyes as if trying to read my soul.

"Yes, I have come from the States on my way to Egypt and the Holy Lands but I have a problem with my passport," I answered, a bit surprised. This man with the strange eyes and weird inner powers disturbed me, so I continued to read my book.

After a few minutes, he remarked, "I have travelled all over the world, but this is the only airport that is always on strike or being renovated."

This was true, as the airport was in a state of confusion. It was being repaired but no workers were to be seen.

"My name is Mr. Ben Osato. I'm Canadian," my strange acquaintance said, "I have travelled extensively throughout the world and am aware of passport problems. I believe I can help you." He spoke with sincerity, so I took out my passport and showed it to him. After several moments of intense study, he said, "Miss Perez, your passport is not in order. It says 'via Rome.' This is a small, rather minor error, but the Immigration officials here in Rome are very strict about things like this. After you leave this airport, you will not have any trouble."

He was quite convincing and I believed him. This man, whom I had just met, was to give me a true message. Yet, I felt an evil power emanating from him as he spoke, and I felt as if he had put a spell over me.

Quietly I thanked him and we sat in silence while I asked God what connection he had with me in the past. The answer came back, "Ask him his birthday and year. You will know."

Without a second thought, I asked, "What is your birthday and year?"

"August 7, 1922. Are you an astrologer?" he asked, smiling at me skeptically.

"I am a cosmic astrologer. I get the birthday and year then send it to the subconscious inner Masters, who do the work for me," I replied looking at him and saying to myself, ah, he is a Sun child. We were brother and sister in another lifetime.

"Now that you know my birthday and year, what do you get for me?" Ben asked still smiling as if thinking, what can a birthday tell.

"You are an eleven path in this lifetime. As a Leo, you are a Sun God, but you are also two people in your body. One being is unselfish and wants to help the world, and the other is completely selfish and wants only to get power for self."

I stopped suddenly. Ben was looking at me in utter astonishment. After a tense silence, he asked, "Who will win, the good being or the selfish one?"

I was about to say something, warning him to wake up and pray, when a demonic being appeared in his face. My words froze on my tongue. I tried to speak but could not, for his true personality had appeared to the surface and I was helpless before this dynamic Being of evil powers that had possessed the mortal soul of this man who had been my brother.

I sat there like a log. Even if my life had depended on it, I could not answer. He may have felt my confusion, for he asked, "Why are you going to Egypt and the Holy Lands?"

With a great effort, I replied, "I am writing a book and would like to see these places." I handed him my brochure to read. After a few minutes, he gave me back the brochure.

Now, it was his turn to be silent, and immediately, I knew he had something to hide. He was afraid of anyone who could look into his soul. He claimed to be Canadian, but he looked more Japanese or else his eyes were made up to look that way. I could not release the feeling of evil that he had given to me, nor forget the demon that had appeared on his face.

I soon excused myself and went to the rest room where I could be alone. I felt the need for prayer and the cleansing of my spirit. God, I cannot take any more of these negative and strange tests. If you are teaching me, then please give me less in smaller doses. These weird experiences are too many and too fast for me to transmute. The answer was to pray for this man. He needs your help.

I cried for a few minutes, then washed my face and put on some more make-up. After that, I returned to the lounge. The strange man was standing at the far end of it and I hid behind a large post. There were many times throughout my life that I have felt like becoming invisible. This was one of them. After a few minutes, Ben walked away and I continued to pray and send him the light.

Later, I felt relieved and walked back to my seat. The young woman from India was still there and the baby was quiet.

I got out my Psalm book and started to read some psalms and a beautiful feeling of peace came through to me.

(Later in Egypt, I happened to see a newspaper lying on a table which was written in English. It was the *Egyptian Gazette*. Thursday, October 19, 1972 it reported on the front page, the assassination of a Jordanian man. The murdered man was a member of the Fatah group, caught in a hail of 12 pistol shots. It happened on Monday night, October 16th, as the man was entering his apartment elevator. It was theorized by the police that he was possibly killed by rival, radical Fatah group. His killer was a tall, slim man with strange eyes that looked slanted. The paper also stated the man left the airport during the early hours of October 23rd, rented a car and later met a couple in Rome. Again I sent light to this man who was lost in the pit of darkness.)

At four-thirty, a message came though. Go to the airport officials, show them your credentials. All is well.

I got my passport, my re-entry booklet, my Green Card and my brochure with my picture and information stating that I was the head of the group traveling to Egypt and the Holy Lands. At the Immigration room, I handed all my information to an official that had just come on duty.

He glanced first at the brochure, then at the other information. Then said, "Miss Perez, go back to your seat. After I have contacted the American Embassy, I will call you."

Shortly after 5 p.m., the official came out and beckoned to me. I walked over and he handed me my papers saying, "I have spoken to the American Embassy and they say you are writing a book. Your passport is not in order. It says "via Rome", but because the American Embassy says you are a nice person, I will allow you to join your friends. Have a nice visit in Rome."

He kissed me on one cheek, then on the other. I returned his kiss and again he kissed me on both cheeks and took me outside, asking, "Where is your luggage?"

"It has gone on with my friends to the hotel."

"Let us be sure," he said calling out to an attendant, "Please take good care of Miss Perez and see if her luggage is still here."

The luggage had gone on. I went over and exchanged some money, then took a cab into Rome.

On the way in, I saw a very large familiar-looking building. Suddenly, I had a cold feeling as it came into full view. I asked the cab driver, "What is that large building?" But he did not speak English and kept silent. Again I asked him, "Please tell me what is that large building?" This time he looked back and said something I did not understand. I fell back limp and thought, oh, my God I am going to faint. I knew the building meant something that was important to me. Silently, I called out to God asking for his help. After a few minutes I felt better.

I arrived at the hotel but the feeling of depression lingered. It was as if a great fear was hanging over my head. I was weighed down. Without any reason, I began to cry as if my heart would break. I could not stop crying. One hour passed, but my heart was still beating very fast. I cried out, "What is wrong, God? Oh have mercy on my soul. Save me God for the waters have come into my world. Give me the answer, God. Why do I feel so terrible?"

I looked at the clock, it was a few minutes before midnight. After a few moments, I went to the next room where D.D. was sleeping peacefully. I returned to my room and tried to sleep but only dosed off, then woke up with a feeling I had dreamed something terrible, but could not remember what it was. I knew it was a disaster. Again, I got up and looked in the living room to see if Renee and Marilyn had returned. No, they had not and it was almost 2 a.m. I thought, oh, God, please don't let anything happen to them. These girls are in my care. I am responsible for their safety. Dear God, please protect them."

I tried to relax, but could not. Again, I started to weep. I felt my heart was breaking. After awhile my tears subsided and I sat motionless in the living room until Renee and Lynn returned and saw that I was upset.

"Renee and Lynn, I'm so happy you are back. I had a terrible nightmare, but I can't seem to recall what it was all about. I thought you were in danger. Thank God, you are both safe."

Both Renee and Lynn looked at me in astonishment. They had never seen me so disturbed. I was still very emotional but could not help myself. Renee was too shocked to answer me. It was Lynn who said, "Maya, we were walking around looking at the shops. The streets are bright and wonderful. It is not like New York. Rome is like New York used to be."

I was silent. How could I explain my feelings about the nightmare? These girls would not understand. Lynn followed me into my room and asked, "Maya, would you mind if I shared this room with Renee? We are both compatible. You and D.D. are on the same wave length. Please do this for me?"

"Of course, Lynn, I will move my things into D.D's room," I replied trying to smile, "I'm sorry I disturbed you and Renee with my nightmare."

It was not until I had returned to the United States that a mystical friend in meditation found out that I had gone back in time and relived the days and nights when I was sentenced to death by the Romans. This was the only answer to my unusual experience that first night in Rome.

At another meditation session, I found out who the man was that was connected with my sentence. He was twenty-five years old and I, fifteen. The night before my death this man told me, I could be saved if I told the Roman officials that I was a Jewess and not Christian. My answer was, "I am a Christian and I will die a Christian. In this lifetime, I have met this man and he has been very good to me. He once saved my life."

The next morning, Betty Ivers and I went to the Egyptian Embassy. Betty wanted me to have my Egyptian visa, which I had failed to get.

When we arrived at the Embassy, we were told to take a seat as the Consul was expected shortly. We sat for a few minutes in an alcove, then joined a group of people who were sitting in a large waiting room.

Betty and I sat with some people in chairs close to the wall. Several young men and women were seated around a large table discussing their reasons for being at the embassy.

I kept watching one young man who returned my stares. I was trying to remember where I had seen him before, but could not recall. After a few minutes, I asked him, "Do you remember me?'

"Yes, I do, and was wondering where I had met you." he replied coming over and sitting in a vacant chair next to me. Betty was also interested in him, but kept quiet while he introduced himself and told his story of why he was at the Embassy.

"My name is Moustafa Hassan," he said smiling, "Are you American?" Betty explained that she was but that I was South American and was accompanying her with a group of friends, "We are going to Egypt and the Holy Lands. Maya Perez has lost her passport. She is travelling on an emergency passport, so she did not get her visa in New York for Egypt. We are here for that purpose."

"I am also here for a passport," Moustafa remarked, "someone came into my apartment and stole it and some money. I am studying business law here in Rome."

Moustafa spoke perfect English and also several foreign languages. I knew he was a very important person in his homeland and asked what his name, Moustafa, meant.

"It means chosen one," he answered, looking at me with his deep set eyes. Then he asked, "Are you a numerologist?"

"Yes," I replied, "I'm interested in both numerology and astrology." He seemed very interested.

"Ah, what does my birthdate and year mean?" he asked with a happy expectant look, "I was born on November 8, 1941."

"You are a mystic and you have known both Buddha and Christ. you are one of the children Jesus blessed. You are vibrating on my frequency. We are both mystics and our life path is seven." I thought for a moment, then continued, "You can do my work, for your future destiny is to help others."

"What should I study?" he asked excitedly.

"You should study the various religions and philosophies of life," I answered, touching his hand for better vibrations, "then combine them in order to help mankind. You have been a priest, a monk, a doctor, a lawyer, and a great diplomat and ruler in your past incarnations. This is why you were given the name, Moustafa, for you are indeed a chosen one. Someday, you will realize your true destiny in this lifetime. When you do, you will again be the great diplomat and will help your country, and also many nations will praise you. We have worked together in several past lifetimes, and we will work together again."

"All the things that you have mentioned, I know I can do," the young man answered seriously, "I have powers that are most unusual and have seen several of my past lives in visions. There was one where I was a doctor, another was a statesman and a diplomat."

"Moustafa, I knew you when you were the doctor and the statesman," I remarked with a smile, "within you are the powers of these great men, who are now your thought forms. Later, many visions will be unfolded. In time, you will be able to control the outer as well as the inner worlds."

"I believe you," he said putting his hand to his heart. "Something within me says, you speak true words. I know it here in my heart."

By now everyone in the room was watching us and several were asking if I could speak to them, but Betty whispered that the Consul had arrived and that I should make it short.

Betty told the Consul that I was writing a book on Egypt. Shaking my hand he asked, "Would you be so kind as to send me a copy when it is finished?" I promised and we left, but not without Moustafa, who insisted that we take the streetcar with him.

Finally, Betty said, that we should get off at the next stop, and my friend Moustafa asked if I had something else to say to him.

"Moustafa," I said hurriedly, "remember to pray for one day you will be very important to the whole world." I don't know if he understood my message for he seemed a little bit confused. It may have been because we were leaving so quickly.

After lunch our group took a tour of Ancient Rome, the Catacombs and the ancient Appian Way. We visited the tomb of Cecilia Metalla, a saint who was poisoned. Her murderers could not kill her so they cut off her head. You could actually see where the head was cut off. Immediately, I recalled what Nefertiti had told me about her death, "Maya, they could not kill me with poison so my head was cut off. This is why my body has never been found."

I felt faint and for a moment held on to June Coulter, who said, "Maya, I can't stand this! Let's get out of here." We hurried out trying to keep close to Father Kooma, who was our guide for that tour.

Outside, we found several East Indian priests who were anxious to speak with Father Kooma. June and I felt Father Kooma's vibrations were extremely high, so we too, gathered around him and I asked the Father if he would please bless me.

The good priest gazed searchingly at me for a moment, then said, "You remind me of the American mystic, Joan."

I remained silent, but June exclaimed, "Oh, you mean Jean."

Then I said, "Father, I wish to be like Jesus."

"Ah, you want to be better," he said looking at me, as if he were trying to find the true personality within. After those words, he gave me a dynamic prayer and blessed me, which sent electric vibrations all around the group.

One of the Indian priests saw the cross I was wearing, which was six inches long and had been hand-carved by Mexicans. I prized it very much as it was given to me with love. Later I lost it. The Indian priest asked, "Do you belong to an Eastern order? What is the name?"

"I belong to the Universal Church of the Master. It is in California, " I answered softly, as I was still feeling the energy from Father Kooma seeping through my whole being.

June later said, "I wish I had the courage to ask that wonderful Father for a blessing too."

That night we went to a nightclub where dinner was served during the show. Betty Ivers sat next to me and whispered, "Maya, I'm having trouble with the hotel manager. He wants to take our rooms with the bath. You may have to move to another room."

I was shocked and felt the maitre 'd and the waiters were not pleased with our group for not tipping them.

"Betty, this is dreadful. I'm afraid D.D., Renee and Lynn are not going to like this."

"I know, but what can I do?" Betty asked in a despondent tone. Just then the show started, so nothing more was said.

When we arrived at the hotel, the desk clerk handed me a notice to move to another room. I looked at the notice and handed it back to the clerk, saying, "We leave the hotel at seven-thirty and won't be back until midnight. Please tell this to the manager."

I spoke softly, but positively. The clerk did not argue. Instead, he put the notice back into the box and left.

The next morning D.D., Renee and I went down to the lobby around seven. We were going on an all-day tour with Frank and JoAnna Gerber. Since it was too early for me to have breakfast, I went out to the street. I found Frank standing in front of the hotel. He was looking up in the sky and seemed to be in a state of semi-trance. As he looked off into the horizon, he said, "The manager of this hotel is going to have a lot of trouble. He is wrong to ask us for our room."

I sensed it was the inner voice of Frank speaking and asked, "How do you know this?"

"Maya, since I have taken Mind Control, I feel and see many strange things long before they happen," Frank replied, still speaking as if in trance, "I know that my power has started to open. Call it ESP or psychic phenomena, but whatever it is, I'm certain this man will pay a big price for his actions."

"I feel the same way, but I'm praying for the manager because it's his help that is making the trouble, and he is in the middle," I said quickly, for just then, I saw the bus coming to pick us up. I ran back into the hotel to call JoAnna, Renee and D.D. and we left on the bus.

The tour took us to Naples, Pompei, and Sorrento by deluxe motor coach. We left Rome at 7:15 a.m., then rode south through scenic and historical sights of the Roman compagna.

From afar, we saw the historic Abbey of Monte Casino, which was perched on a hill. In Naples, we saw the castle of Anjou, the beautiful harbor and the fantastic Via Caraccio. The view from Mount Vesuvius was unbelievable and so was the Bay of Naples.

In Pompei, we saw the famous ruins, then explored the lovely resort of Sorrento.

It was midnight when we returned to our hotel. I was undressing when Renee came to my room and excitedly said, "Betty Ivers and Marilyn are over at the police station. They had an argument with the bartender and the hotel manager called the police. He also said that Betty was to give up her room immediately. Now, she is in a tiny room without a bath."

D.D.Reilly was in the bathroom but heard our conversation and asked, Renee, "who told you this?"

"Oh, June Coulter. I met her in the lobby and she gave me the news," Renee answered laughing, "We missed all the excitement."

At that moment, however, Lynn came in and told us what had happened. "The manager rented some of the rooms to another group, who came in and looked, and the rooms were not to their liking. They immediately called other hotels and left. It was like Grand Central station. The cabs were pulling up depositing people and shortly after were pulling up and taking them away.

I looked over at D.D., but she remained silent, so I spoke to Renee and Lynn. "The whole group should have tipped the waiters."

"Maya, dear, that is not the problem," Lynn exclaimed emphatically, "Betty told us the tips for the waiters were included in the tour. She intends to pay for the service, but there has been a misunderstanding."

"It has been a misunderstanding all around," I said yawning, "however, these things cannot be avoided, especially when one does not speak the language."

No one said anything, so I asked, "Lynn, why were you and Betty at the police station?"

"Maya," she replied hesitatingly, "after the rooms were taken away, Betty, another couple and I went down the bar for a drink. The bartender was gone a long time, so we helped ourselves. When he came back we offered to pay him but he called the manager, who then called the police."

D.D. and I were shocked, but we said nothing. After a few moments of complete silence, Renee and Lynn left and I asked D.D. to pray with me for success and happiness for the group.

The next morning Monday, October 16th, we were free to poke around the shops until 2 p.m., when we were picked up and taken to the airport for Cairo, Egypt.

We got up too late for breakfast, so we dressed and went out to a nearby restaurant for lunch. I had invited D.D. to be my guest but when I looked for my traveler's check book, I found that I had lost it. Becoming excited, I looked all around thinking I had dropped it on the floor. A lady sitting next to me may have misunderstood my fears. With angry looks, she hurriedly paid her bill and left. When we arrived back to the hotel, we found the checks on the dresser. D.D. had paid for the lunch, so I reimbursed her and all was well.

At one o'clock we all met downstairs in the lobby. The manager was back of the desk. He looked very subdued. Everything was calm. I felt as if the storm had passed over and now there was peace.

I looked over at Betty Ivers, who was speaking with the manager, and he was smiling. It was all so very strange. I wondered what had transpired during the morning to bring about this sudden change of personalities. Then I thought, it may have been all a dream and the nightmare part is over. Thank God.

THIRTY-ONE
Egypt and Home

Promptly at 2 p.m., we left the hotel for Cairo, Egypt. On the plane Betty Ivers told me the rest of the story.

"Maya, I have never seen such a change in anyone. The manager was in utter despair, and he actually apologized to me when I paid the bill and I gave him extra for the waiters and maids. He said, after this weekend he was going to sell the hotel. It was too much for him. I really feel sorry for him."

"Betty, you and I have had several karmic experiences that were not good. We have been re-living some of our past incarnations. It is a play-back."

I spoke these words with complete conviction and also felt the truth of my words. "Rome has the highest vibrations and also the lowest. We were both connected with all of these people in our past lives. We came here under very negative aspects. At the airport Friday, the 13th, I was told that when I left Rome everything would be all right. I feel this is true and I'm very happy to be gone from there."

"I hope you are right," Betty said with a sad smile, "Maya, if this keeps up, I, too, will have to change my business."

I thought, not your business, but aloud I said, "I see a change. It's for the better." She smiled and I continued, "Betty, God is good. He will open doors for you."

"I believe you, Maya," she whispered, still smiling, "maybe it is because you say nice things, or that I feel you are telling me the truth. Anyway, I am grateful for your good news. I must make a success of this tour."

Smiling, I replied, "You will Betty. Remember, you are an eight path in this lifetime. This is the path of kings and queens who controlled the great material Masters. Eight has the power to overcome all trials of finances, as it rules everything in connection with the material world. However, there is a secret about this number. If you worry, it could put you into a double material prison. Never worry, read the Psalms of the Holy Bible, and all will be as God ordained it in the beginning."

"Oh, Maya, please help me to stop worrying," Betty asked with tears in her deep blue eyes. "This is one of my great hang-ups. I worry about every little thing. It has always been like this with me."

I could not answer for I, too, had tears in my eyes, so I patted her hand and sat in the silence.

Our guide in Cairo, Egypt, whose name was Muhammad, met us at the airport and took us in a big limousine to the El Bog Hotel. Muhammad's aura was blue with flecks of purple. He had healing powers and I knew he could help many people, as well as make money for himself. He was forever twirling a small string of beads, which, he informed me, were called worry beads. These beads reminded me of the rosary that Catholics held while praying.

Cairo, Egypt was different from Rome. Here, I was welcomed as a sister. One man at the airport insisted that he knew me. Of course, it was from another lifetime, but I did not try to explain this to him.

That night, we went to a nightclub to celebrate Lynn's birthday which fell on October 16th. Muhammad sat between Lynn and me. I remember him saying, "Maya, these beads are guaranteed to prevent illness, even heart attacks, avoid suicides, ward off evil conditions, prevent divorce, relax nerves, relieve tension, keep you from getting angry and even make you happy."

Marking the effect of his words on me, he continued, "These beads can make you successful."

"Muhammad, you speak like both a psychologist and practitioner," I remarked laughing. Yet, I marvelled at his powers of faith and positive thinking. I thought, we need more people like him.

"My mother is psychic. I often take groups to her home and she will study them, then give everyone a message." He spoke softly, so as not to be overheard. "Yes, my mother is truly blessed with the gift of forecasting the future. She told me things that happened almost immediately."

Lynn had overheard our conversation and asked if she could have a consultation with his mother. Muhammad explained that his mother was not feeling well and that she lived out of the city.

Muhammad was a Moslem who understood the power of persistent prayer. He was very sincere and used the beads to balance his emotions when he had problems he could not handle. This dynamic individual was also an eight path. He was a free and awakened soul. Later, I learned that Muhammad was a very wealthy man who owned several business ventures, including a restaurant and night club that had been in his family for many years.

The next morning, Tuesday, we got up at 6 a.m., had breakfast by seven and were ready to start out shortly after eight. Our first project in Cairo was to visit the Church of Abu Sarge, which is called Saint Sargus Church. This church is considered to be the oldest of its kind in Egypt, and was presided over by the Reverend Gabriel G. Bestavres.

Our guide for that morning was Sultan Mahmoud. It was he who assisted Muhammad when there were early morning tours. Mahmoud introduced the group to Reverend Bestavres, whose aura was gold with dark brown specks. This is the aura of an illumined Master come back to fulfill a great purpose but at the moment the good priest was seeped in sorrow and tribulations that he was not giving to the Spirit within. Like many religious souls this good priest felt he should be crucified and carry the cross forever, not remembering the words of Jesus, "*Let the spirit within carry your burdens.*"

This priest intrigued me and I asked his birthdate and year. It was April 5, 1939, which came to a four path, the prison number. An individual born in that cycle has been blocked in another life, his purpose here is to inflate the empty vessels, give power to others in order to renew his vibrations. I did not feel it was my duty to inform him of this so just said, "Reverend Bestavres, you are a four life path. This is the destiny of a very high soul come back to fulfill and overcome many strange problems." At this point I took his hand and gave him some power.

"You are very right," he answered sadly, "I have a daughter Madaline, born January 6, 1970. she was born with a most difficult ailment. I am afraid that the doctors have given up her case."

Quickly, I analyzed the child's birthday and year, then sent it to the subconscious for the answers before I spoke.

"This child is a six life path, the teacher. She came to teach you and your wife lessons of patience and understanding, also to pray and forgive yourself in order to reach the inner planes where dynamic Masters of wisdom and healing are located. Through contacting these great angels of illumination, you will not only heal yourself but many others."

Secretly, I felt Madaline's ailment came from a feeling of guilt within the parents, therefore it was difficult for the doctors to analyze it. Many high souls have had the cosmic marriage. This creates guilt feelings deep within them.

"Yes, I have felt my daughter's ailment was a test for my wife and myself," he answered, "I know God can work miracles and I believe He will heal my daughter."

The priest thanked me and asked the group to pray for his daughter. After blessing us, he told the story of his church.

This church is supposed to be built on the site where the Virgin Mary, Joseph and the babe, Jesus stayed during their flight into Egypt."

He showed us the stairway which led to the basement where they were said to have lived. The good priest explained that the church was separated into three parts and divided by twelve pillars, on each of which there was an icon representing one of the Apostles. Byzantine scenes embellished some pillars. One of the pillars was constructed differently from the rest and unpainted on the top. It did not have a cross. This signified Judas, who betrayed our Lord. We saw a screen of fantastic beauty which contained ebony panels with inlays of ivory, dating from the eleventh century.

The vibrations of the church fascinated me. Several friends in the group told me later that they felt a very high presence and sublime peace in the church.

Reverend Bestavres wrote a small book about the church, in which he states that in 451 A.D., the Coptic church was divided into two groups, each supporting the side of their belief in the nature of Christ.

After leaving the Coptic church, the group went next door to the Ben Ezra Synagogue. Mahmoud introduced us to Rabbi Nathan, who was standing at the entrance of the temple. His aura was dark white with specks of grey, indicating that the good Rabbi was a Master who had come back to illumine the world. However, he was unusually depressed and his temple was in need of repairs. This was natural, for money-energy does not flow to depressed individuals.

His depression was later verified by his birthpath. It was June 19, 1911, representing the one path and the one in the soul. I told him, "You have been a teacher, organizer and creative master in several of your past incarnations, but confusion and jealousy surrounds your present organization."

The good Rabbi stared at me for a moment then exclaimed, "You are right, there is a lot of jealousy around me."

Upon the request of Mahmoud, the rabbi then gave us the history of his Temple.

"This synagogue is built on the land where Moses lived and prayed. El Hakrizi calls it the Angel Gabriel's church. We are different in our religious ideas, yet we love one another as one family. We remember that we pray to one God. This is the oldest part of Cairo, and we are surrounded by twenty-nine Mosques and more than twenty churches. We have 10,000 Copts, 133,000 Muhammadans, and forty-two or more Jewish families; we are all united in God."

He showed us the Moses Atlas called the Miracle Rock or Jeremiah's tomb, the Arabesque ceiling built in 1115 A.D. of Christ, the Guenizah place, the wooden clock with Kofic writing referring to the visit of Amro Ibu El' Ass who came to old Egypt, a drawing of seven Branched candelabra on deer skin, and the spring (Hilva), 900 years old which dated with the Synagogue.

After taking us through the Synagogue, Rabbi Nathan gave us a blessing. Then he took a large candelabra with seven candles, lit them and gave several of us a special mystical rite.

I had gone in a semi-trance state and as I came out I saw the Rabbi had thrown the prayer shawl around Renee's shoulders. He was giving her a holy and very special blessing.

Later, she asked me to go up on the roof of the temple to see the view. Several others followed us.

We took some pictures, then the Rabbi took me over to the far corner of the roof and asked, "What do you teach?"

Looking off at the vast expanse of land, I answered, "I teach people how to purify their inner consciousness in order to visualize and create a new way of life."

"How is that done?' he asked thoughtfully.

"It is done with breath and thought. As we take in a deep breath and send light to the solar plexus, this purifies the thought patterns that we have unconsciously created in this life and also in the past. These negative patterns can become entities which block our progress. I know you feel blocked and you do not realize that you are doing it to yourself."

The good Rabbi smiled and asked, "How am I blocking myself?"

I thought for a moment, then answered, "Through allowing yourself to become depressed and staying depressed. When I feel depressed, I read the Psalms of the Holy bible. You are one life path, the Master organizer come back to learn and also to teach divine Truths to those who come into your vibrations. It is not by accident that your temple is next to a world-famous church where Joseph, Mary and the babe, Jesus stayed."

"All that you have said is quite true," he answered pensively, "I am an organizer. I have done much work since I took over this synagogue, but I would like to do more. I feel blocked, which has confused and made me depressed many times. The Synagogue needs to be re-built and a lot of other things done. I would like to have the answers in order to do these things."

"You will, but first, you must remove the karmic block that is holding you back," I said philosophically.

"You are right. Something is holding me back," he exclaimed excitedly. "I usually start to do something, and then it gets blocked and I can't seem to go ahead. Not long ago, I said to my wife, "It must be the devil." She laughed, but I feel there is actually a Being that is persecuting me."

"I feel the same way, but I never give up. I keep right on praying for right action. If I get too disturbed, then I call the prayer group to pray for me."

Suddenly, as a message came through, I looked at him in astonishment and asked, "Rabbi Nathan, do you pray for yourself?"

A strange look came over his face and he replied, "No, I am too busy praying for everybody else. I often forget myself."

"Then pray for yourself," I suggested, thinking, the good Rabbi is trying to save everybody, but he is forgetting himself, the most important person in his world. Saint Paul had said, "Physician heal thyself."

Just then Betty Ivers arrived and said, "Maya, we are ready to leave for the Egyptian Museum."

At the museum we saw a complete collection of Pharaoh antiquities and the fabulous treasures of King Tut-Ankh Amon.

Later that afternoon, Muhammad arranged a boat trip on the Nile for me and several friends. At the time, I had no idea that this trip would clarify Muhammad's connection with me in ancient Egypt. As we arrived at the dock, I overheard Muhammad and one of the boatmen speaking. I did not understand their words, as they were speaking Egyptian, but Muhammad was twirling his worry beads very fast. He wanted the man to take us for a ride in his boat, but the man was hesitating because his motor was not working. Muhammad won the argument, but unfortunately, the motor still would not work, so for two or more hours we drifted within the radius of a quarter mile from the dock.

I felt that we were waiting for something wonderful to happen. Since I was tired from the excitement of the morning, I took off my shoes and laid in the back seat of the boat with my feet hanging over the side in the cool water. I closed my eyes and went into a semi-trance. Several times I awakened to see that we had drifted to the other side of the river into the weeds. Then the boatman with a long stick would push us out into deeper water. After an hour of this, a surprising thing happened. I found myself in an entirely different boat which was much larger and had several boatmen with large oars vigorously rowing the boat. I was not surprised at all. It seemed very natural for me to be there relaxing in the cool breeze of the Nile River. Looking around, I saw many people sitting in various parts of the boat, but one man who sat in the middle of the boat drew my attention. He was dressed in a silver robe trimmed in gold, and on his head he wore a strange headgear. It was Muhammad. In the vision I knew Muhammad was a very important government official of the Pharaoh. A trusted minister of the country. Still nothing seemed unusual. It was very natural for me to be there in the boat with

Muhammad sitting in regal style, surrounded with beautiful women and men all magnificently robed.

I woke up and we were back at the dock where Muhammad was waiting for us with a smile. He said, "Maya, you had your boat ride, but it did not take you too far."

Later, I saw him speaking to the boatman, smiling and slapping him on the back gaily. Then I realized his worry beads did work miracles. Muhammad was not the least bit angry, even though the boatman had caused him to lose money. It was Frank Gerber who told me Muhammad had refused to take money for the boat ride.

That evening we attended the sound and light spectacular at the Pyramid of Giza. We heard the Sphinx, Cheops and other voices of the pyramids speak to us of their history throughout the ages. It was an unforgettable experience.

After the lecture, we were taken to Muhammad's restaurant for dinner and a show. The food was quite exotic and the native girls danced very beautifully. I enjoyed it, but we had been up since 6 a.m. and suddenly I fell asleep. I woke up in a different place and Nefertiti was there sitting beside me. After a moment of silence she said, "Maya, I have waited a long time for your visit. There are many things I must tell you, but there is not much time. Before you leave the Holy Lands you will have many strange experiences. In every one there will be a lesson. Study these lessons and you will become very wise. Remember, Maya, whenever you are in great trouble call on me. I will send my helpers to you. Always think of the sun and visualize light beaming into your soul. God be with you, my sister, may you live forever in His peace. Good-bye for now."

I woke up to find the lights on and D.D. was telling me to wake up. Later in the hotel room, I related my vision to D.D. and she said, "Maya, I knew you were in one of your trances."

THIRTY-TWO

Luxor and Problems

We arrived in Luxor before noon and were met at the airport by our guide, Fathi Salib. He took us to the Winter Palace. It was a large luxurious hotel.

D.D. Reilly was delighted with our very large and beautiful room. It had a balcony overlooking the Nile River.

"This is a lovely hotel, Maya," D.D. remarked with a nod of her pretty head. "I feel Betty is on the ball. Did you finally convince her to meditate and read the Psalms?"

"Yes, I suppose she had received the message by now," I answered shaking my head. "I explained to Betty about the light and also that I would help her on the trip, if she would do her part. This tour has certainly started off dreadfully."

"I agree," D.D. said, "but she must be following your advice because everything seems to be changed for the better."

We were standing on the terrace and D.D. went back into the room, but I continued watching the crowds going into the boats on the river. This place fascinated me. I felt as if I belonged in Luxor. It was my true home. That morning when we arrived at the airport, Betty Ivers showed our brochure to the Immigration attendant. He read it and then said to me, "Welcome back home. We are happy to have you here."

This made me very happy. Now, I knew that the Valley of Kings and Queens of ancient Egypt was once my home.

I was interrupted momentarily by D. D.'s voice. "Come Maya, we are expected in the dining room before two."

As if someone else were speaking, I heard myself say, "I'm not ready D.D., please go on and I will follow shortly." I had gone into another realm of consciousness and did not wish to be disturbed. When I did return to my earthly realm, I felt elated and vibrant.

Entering the dining room, I saw it was filled with many people of all colors and nationalities. My group was seated next to a large group of happy and radiant French people. Betty Ivers beckoned to me to take a vacant seat next to her.

"How do you like your room?" she asked with a bright smile.

"I love it, Betty, and so does D.D.," I replied, "she feels that you are now meditating and reading the Psalms."

"I am reading the ones you prescribed," she replied speaking softly, "I think they are working."

"I know they are," I remarked, pressing her hand gently, then asked, "Where are we going later this afternoon?"

"We are going on a very special tour," she answered, "we will take carriages to the temples of Amin-Ra in Karnak, also Amun, Nut and Khons. After that, we will walk down the avenue of Ram Sphinxes, the obelisk of Queen Hatshepsut and the sacred lake."

Just then Renee, my cousin, flitted over to our table and said, "Guess what? We will have to drink wine with every meal. They don't have bottled water here in the hotel."

Egyptian water, we discovered later, was to play a big part in our lives. Bending over me, Renee continued, "I have to take good care of you girls. Maya, you are my cousin and Betty is my roommate. How about a glass of wine for both of you?"

Betty nodded, and Renee tripped back to her table and brought over a large bottle of wine. While pouring some in my glass, it spilt, and she said, "Ooops. Don't worry, there is plenty more over at our table and the next. Frank is drinking water. He said it's too hot and early in the day for wine, but D.D. and I bought a large bottle. Lynn and Norene also bought a large bottle and JoAnna has a bottle. The maitre'd said they are expecting bottled water tomorrow, so today we shall live and be happy."

"Renee, just give me a small glass. I too, think it's too early for wine," I exclaimed, as she poured a large glass and it overflowed.

"Drink the wine, Maya, we want happy spirits here," Renee said laughing, "They will all be high."

At that moment, she spied the handsome maitre'd who had come to her table with more wine in a bucket of ice. With a hurried kiss on my cheek she left.

At 4 p.m., our guide Fathi Salib met us in the hotel lobby. JoAnna and Frank were missing, so we went outside to wait while Betty paged their room.

Large crowds were walking around the hotel garden and street. It was a gay and happy atmosphere that would have provided a setting for a movie.

D.D. Reilly, Lynn, Norene, and Renee were buying straw hats so I bought one too. Shortly after, JoAnna and Frank arrived and we all got into carriages and started on our first tour in Luxor.

D.D., Renee and I took a carriage together. We were all bubbling over with excitement when D.D. happened to look in her handbag and found her traveller's checkbook missing. Crying out very loud, she said, "Maya, Renee, stop the carriage. I must go back to the hotel. I have lost my checkbook, the traveller's checkbook!"

"Try and be calm, D.D.," I said, "It's too late to go back. I, too, thought I had lost my traveller's checkbook while we were in Rome. Remember how disturbed I was, but later it was found in the hotel room."

My words only made her more disturbed. "Oh, no, Maya, I must return to the hotel. Stop the carriage, I'm going back to New York!" She shouted to the driver who stopped the carriage and looked around to see what the American lady was shouting about.

While the driver was still waiting for further orders, a native photographer snapped our pictures. This may have had a positive effect on the strange condition. Suddenly, Renee said, "D.D. listen to Maya. I feel it is a condition. Remember the same thing happened to Lynn and also to Maya in Rome, but everything turned out all right. We should go on."

The driver must have understood, he told his horse to go and we hastened to catch up with our party.

While walking amidst the ruins of the temples, I began to get some messages, as if someone were speaking through me. *You lost your traveller's checkbook a few hours before leaving Rome. it was a symbol that you had come to the end of a karmic condition. Now, D.D. has lost her checkbook a few hours after arriving in Luxor. This, too, is a symbol of a karmic experience that must be played back. You were first opened in Alexandria, but it is in the area of Luxor that you became great and experienced many strange and difficult problems. These patterns must be transmuted by prayer and meditation now. D.D. has sensed it from the unconscious level and wished to leave before these traumatic events occur. All will be well.*

Immediately, I felt better as I joined the rest of our group who were admiring the tall buildings and statues which were almost in ruins. I felt a sense of awe for these marvelous works of the great Pharaohs in ancient Egypt.

We saw the streets lined with images of animals with human heads and hands. Symbolic of the animal nature of man blending into the mortal. There were Pharaohs with their queens and children. We saw their gods of stone, some crumbling on the ground and others still standing up in the sky. We walked where the great and the lowly walked, sometimes happy and other times sad.

Later, I saw Frank Gerber sitting on a large rock. JoAnna, his wife was standing nearby. I was shocked to see a grayish mist around Frank. I started to walk over to him when our guide announced, "We are now going to see the sacred lake."

The lake was quite small. At first it reminded me of a swimming pool, then it evoked a memory from the past. I saw myself swimming in the clear waters of the lake. Several young girls were there, some swimming and others just sitting on cushions around the side of the lake. We were all dressed in short robes of blue, purple, silver and gold.

The beautiful vision remained with me for several minutes before disappearing.

That night Frank and JoAnna did not come down to dinner. It was Renee who informed me that Frank was very ill, and JoAnna had called the doctor.

"By the way, did D.D. find her checkbook?" Renee asked.

"Yes, it was in the room," I replied, "but she does not wish to speak about it. She feels it is a condition she has picked up." After a moment's hesitation, I continued. "But I know it's a karmic pattern that has to be played out. Unless she continues to pray and meditate, this condition could last for several years."

"Oh, she does look strange," Renee whispered. "Here, take some wine. Let us get back our happy spirits. You don't look very happy."

"No, I'm not happy," I answered, "I feel we are in for some very evil experiences. I saw a grey mist around Frank this afternoon and now he is ill. Renee, I am very concerned."

"Take some wine, Maya," Renee insisted, "it will help you overcome the evil vibes."

"I don't care for red wine," I said petulantly, "I plan to pray a long time tonight before going to bed."

"Maya, you will become ill if you drink this water," Renee shouted, by now, exasperated by my refusal to take the wine. "JoAnna has a vision of the water, and I feel that it is cursed."

Just at that moment Betty entered the dining room and sat down at our table and the argument between Renee and me was discontinued.

"Have a glass of wine, Betty," Renee said, trying to life our spirits. Betty looked as if she were disturbed, and I sensed it was because of Frank's illness.

"I'll buy a bottle of white wine, Renee," I said, "Betty and I like it better."

Betty nodded and smiled, and Renee asked the waiter if he could call the maitre'd who was speaking with some people at the next table near D.D's. I glanced at D.D. and wondered why she was so quiet. It looked as if she were under a spell. In a few moments the maitre'd came over to our table and Betty asked if the bottled water had arrived.

"No, Madam, but we expect it by tomorrow morning," he answered speaking to Betty, but looking down at Renee as if enchanted. Renee and he talked a few moments about his trip that he was planning. He had a friend who owned a restaurant in the United States. It was located on Long Island and it was definite that he would come in a year or two if all went well.

We forgot all about the wine, and later I felt thirsty after such a hot day. I blessed the water and drank a whole glass. After dinner, I stopped by to visit JoAnna and Frank. I rapped on their door and JoAnna looked out and whispered, "Frank is sleeping. The doctor gave him some pills and told me to keep him on a liquid diet." Taking the lock off, she softly stepped out into the hall. "Maya, I'm sure it was the water Frank drank at lunch." I had a vision last night of a glass of water with a cross on it. I told Frank of the vision and warned him not to drink the water. I feel there is a spiritual condition in the water in Egypt."

"Renee feels the same way and warned me not to drink it," I exclaimed, "but I was thirsty and drank some."

"Well, let us hope it won't affect you, Maya," JoAnna answered with a serious look, "I would not want you to be ill like Frank."

"Oh, I blessed the water," I remarked with a smile, "now I'm going up to my room and read the Psalms and meditate. I'll pray for Frank. I am sure the evil will go away."

"Thank you, Maya, good-night and pleasant dreams," JoAnna said closing the door and I walked up the one flight to my room.

The next morning I woke up a few minutes to six. I was disturbed. I had had a vision but could not remember it, yet it left me with a feeling of great apprehension.

D.D. was still sleeping, so I took a bath and went out on the balcony to meditate. I knew my dream was significant and that it was important for me to remember what it was all about. Something was about to happen, my dream was an omen of things to come.

Every time I tried to reach into my inner consciousness, I experienced great fear and for the first time in my life, I could not pray. After a while, I started to read the Bible, when D.D. called me.

"Maya, dear, get dressed, we have to be in the dining room at 7:45 and it's now 7:15. She looked at me and asked, "Maya, what is wrong? You look as if you are in another land."

My voice suddenly returned and I replied, "I have had a vision and it is disturbing me. D.D. I must get the answer before I leave the room. Please go down, I will follow in a little while."

After she left, I don't know how long I sat there, but finally the voice from the back of my head said, "This is the time. Have no fear. All is well."

I thanked God, got up and dressed hurriedly and went down to the dining room. There I found only three or four of my group. After a hot cup of coffee, I joined the rest of the group who were waiting with Betty and our guide Fathi Salib, in the hotel lobby. Fathi was a little taller than our Cairo guide, Muhammad Mordash. Both had the same coloring; curly black hair, charm, spoke several languages and were trained in diplomatic matters.

Muhammad had learned his lessons in several past lives where he advised kings and queens, and now he was using them for business and everyday affairs. Fathi, who had the bearing of a priest, was not at all interested in making a lot of money or becoming powerful. He was a Christian. Muhammad was Moslem. Fathi was single. Muhammad was married with a family. Both had mothers living and were very attractive sons.

The afternoon before, I had seen Fathi's aura change from brown to bright gold with flecks of white and blue. I had thought this man has a great spiritual power. In time, he will reach the plane of consciousness where he had been very illumined, but he needs help.

Our group walked down to the dock and embarked on a large felucca. This is the type of barge that was used in ancient times. We were crossing the Nile river to the temples and resting places of the queens and kings.

On the boat Fathi said to me, "Betty tells me that you are a mystic and were with queen Nefertiti in a past life. What do you see for me?"

I asked him for his birthdate and year and with a smile he answered," November 18, 1935. His birthdate and year added to an 11.

"Fathi, you have been a philosopher, priest, healer and scribe in several lifetimes, but fears and doubts have kept you from evolving to higher planes of consciousness. It has not kept you from making money. I see much wealth and later even much more. In one life you had been the head of a great temple and many people of great wealth and power came to see and ask for your advice. Later, you misused your powers and this is why you are blocked now."

With a sad look he said, "I believe you."

Frank and JoAnna sat apart from the group on the boat. He looked very ill, so I silently prayed and sent him light. I knew Frank had had a karmic past with one of the great kings and he was sad as he returned to his old home.

On the other side of the Nile, we took a large bus to the resting place of Queen Hatshepsut and other queens. The tomb appeared like a palace instead of a resting place for the dead. I thought, people of ancient times lived their lives preparing for death, instead of making the world a better one, helping their fellow men to fulfill their highest destiny.

As Fathi was telling the stories of the various queens, again I could see his aura changing. He said, "We are now in the great temple of

Queen Hatshepsut. It was she who had this temple built. It was discovered in 1892, but it was not until 1893 when they started excavating it. This great queen was the only wife of Pharaoh Thotmes 11. After his death, his queen assumed the perogative of a Pharaoh and even wore a beard. It has been said that she was the princess who adopted Moses after she found him in the bulrushes near the Nile River. There is much mystery surrounding the birth of Moses. Let's hope that some day the complete story will be known."

This concept of Moses' adoption by Hatshepsut is also written in the King James Bible.

Some of the temple's rooms appeared to be well taken care of, as if the original good spirits were still protecting them, but others were almost in ruins. Later we came to Queen Tye's room, which was almost in ruins. She was the aunt and also mother-in-law of our beloved Nefertiti. I knew there was much karma between Tye and me. As I looked around the room, I suddenly felt hands were attempting to clutch me. I was choking. Quickly, I ran outside and sat on a large stone in the bright sunlight. After a few minutes. I felt better and thought, how strange. She must have been an enemy of mine in ancient time. I prayed for her and sent light to the temple.

Next, we travelled to the Valley of the Kings to see the tomb of King Tut and others. There we descended steps which led to several small hallways that opened into tombs. Although King Tut's was the smallest of the tombs, it is one of the most famous because of the treasures discovered in it. Fathi informed us that in 1922 the contents of the tomb moved to the Egyptian Museum.

I looked down at King Tut's mummy in the middle sarcophagus and thought, there he is, the man that I had seen in my early morning vision. As I looked, I felt drawn to go nearer and look at him. Stepping down, I first looked around at the beautiful decorations which vividly portrayed religious scenes on the walls.

I was suddenly drawn to the side of the coffin. Cold chills and fear began to run through my body. I became giddy and felt faint. Renee and another man helped me to walk out of the room. Renee said, "Maya, you looked as if you were possessed while you were watching King Tut's mummy."

When we emerged from the tomb, I sat on the steps and waited for the rest of the group. JoAnna came out and I asked her how Frank was feeling.

"He is very ill," she replied sadly, "I hope we don't have to return home. He is at the restaurant around the corner, resting."

"I will go and join him. We can both pray for good health," I said, "I feel quite weak. It's as if I have picked up a condition."

"I'm so sorry to hear this. Do try to take care of yourself," JoAnna remarked, looking at me thoughtfully.

As I walked over to the restaurant, I thought, "This is my vision. King Tut's face is the one I saw in my dream. A chill swept through my whole being as I recalled his face. I pondered over the matter, since I had had a karmic experience with Queen Nefertiti; therefore I must have known her son-in-law who later became the famed King Tut.

Frank was sitting in the far corner of the restaurant looking very ill and sad.

"Frank," I said simply, "I wish to pray and mediate with you."

With a faint smile he held out his hand to me and said, "Thank you, Maya,"

I sat down and we prayed, then sat in silence. After awhile, Frank seemed to be stronger and he remarked, "Maya, it is as if something is dying within me. I have never felt so ill."

"I too, felt weirdly ill while I was in Tut's tomb, Frank. It was as if something were trying to reach out to me. This morning, I had a dream but I could not remember it until I entered that awful tomb."

Frank, who had been lying across two chairs, then sat up and said, "Maya, that was where all my strength left me. Strange that you should feel the same way in that tomb."

"No, it's not strange." I answered, "I am certain that both of us lived in the time of Nefertiti. This is why you and JoAnna came on the tour with me. We had to relive old experiences and pray in order to transmute the thought forms within our souls. With prayer and meditation we can purify the evil conditions." Again we prayed.

That afternoon the dining room was even more colorful than the day before. I walked in with Renee and she then saw her friend, Arlene. Arlene had come with another tour leader, who had brought her mother and a small group to Egypt on their way to the Holy Land. I had met Arlene's mother at the hotel in Cairo, so I asked, "How is your mother? Is she with you?"

"No, my mother is very ill. I had to leave her at the El Borge Hotel where we met you"

This was certainly a coincidence that we came to the same hotel in Cairo and met Renee. I did not know she had planned this tour.

"Nothing is an accident. Everything is planned by higher angels," I remarked with a smile.

"I believe that. Mother and I are helped by them," Arlene said, "two years after Mother lost a close friend, she dreamed that this friend had said she would help mother. Now, we are very lucky. Mother buys stocks and they are always the right ones. Renee tells me that you are psychic, Maya. Are you lucky at gambling or with the stock market?"

"Long ago I played the horses, but now I have learned to visualize the things that I need. Sometimes answers came through a friend or money will be brought to me for my needs," I answered. "This trip was offered to me by a stranger who came to one of my lectures."

"That is fantastic!" Arlene exclaimed excitedly. "This is how I am able to travel around the world. Mother gets the money and away we go. She is so good to me."

Remembering that her mother had informed me Arlene did not wish to leave home and her wealthy gentleman friend, but had made the trip to please her mother, I said, "You are good to her, so it goes both ways."

That afternoon we visited the ruins of the Karmak temples near the hotel. I did not enjoy the tour since my head felt light and my stomach was nauseated. Later that night, I joined Betty Ivers and another lady in the dining room.

"What happened to you, Maya?" Betty asked, "June told me you were not feeling well. Are you all right now?"

"No, Betty, I am very dizzy and nauseated," I replied shivering, "I feel too ill to go with you on the boat ride tonight."

"Order some hot soup. I'll get some pills at the desk," Betty replied, leaving me with her friend who ordered the soup for me.

A few minutes later, I walked to the desk, but felt my knees give way. The manager took my arm and told the desk clerk to help him carry me upstairs. When they opened the door to my room, a great wind swept through blowing things all about. It was like a hurricane. I sat on the bed while they closed the balcony doors and straightened things out. Then the manager gave me some pills and said, "Mrs. Gerber sent these pills for you. Take two or three now and go to sleep. By morning you will be feeling much better."

After the men left, I felt nauseated and tried to get up but fell back on the bed. I tried sending the light to myself while praying out loud, but still I remained very ill. I must have been praying for two or more hours when suddenly the power came back. I went to the bathroom where I regurgitated. Then I took three more pills and went back to bed.

I must have dozed off, for sometime after midnight I head voices in the room. It was D.D. and Renee, but I could not wake up. Then I heard D.D. regurgitating in the bathroom. I sat up in bed and asked, "What is wrong, D.D.?"

Renee came over and whispered, "She is ill. If she doesn't get better by morning, we may have to leave her here in Luxor."

"I am very ill," I replied, lying back on the bed, "I hope I feel better by morning, too."

"It's the water, Maya," Renee insisted shaking her pretty head, "I still believe the water has been cursed."

The next morning D.D. woke up saying, "God, I was never so ill in all my life, and you slept all through it Maya."

Smiling faintly, I replied, "I was very ill too, D.D."

"Oh, Maya, you were just out from a sleeping pill," D.D. remarked getting up and going to the bathroom.

I remained silent and began my meditation. That morning we left Luxor at 10:30 a.m., via Cairo for Amman, Jordan.

THIRTY-THREE
Jordan and Jerusalem

It was Saturday, October 21st when we left Luxor for Amman, Jordan, via Cairo, Egypt. Our hotel was the Philadelphia in Amman. The official language in Amman is Arabic, but English is the second. This made it easy for the group to communicate with the natives.

The Philadelphia Hotel, where we stayed, was a lovely building, although some of the rooms were not kept in repair. Curious about this, I asked the maid why this was so. She explained that no matter how much the manager tried to fix the hotel, it was always in need of repair.

As she spoke, I saw a dark haze over her and knew that the hotel was under continuing negative vibrations. I thought of the airport in Rome that was always on strike and was at all times in a state of repair. That situation was political. Here was a similar situation, where spiritual people were always praying, yet conditions were being sent in to block them.

Looking deep into the maid's eyes, I said, "I know you are a Christian. I also know that you pray constantly, but you do hold resentful thoughts for certain groups of people and unconsciously send them negative vibrations."

She began to cry and said, "Oh, Madame, I really love everybody. I don't believe that I am sending out evil thoughts."

"I realize this, but you are doing it unconsciously," I replied, feeling sorry for the woman who did not understand the philosophy of thoughts coming back to the sender.

"Let me explain. Start to pray for everyone today, no matter who they are. Even if you think they are trying to hurt you, then pray more. Also send them light. The light that you send them will in time come back to you as energy. This energy will help you to lift up your consciousness and in time, your so-called enemies, will realize that their own negative thoughts are returning back to them."

"I don't understand why I must pray for my enemies. I love everybody," she replied, looking at me with a smile.

I considered her statement, then said, "But you really don't like Jews."

Resentfully, she answered, "Are you Jewish?"

"No, I'm a Christian, but my inner spirit tells me we are all Jewish." I answered gently taking her hand in mine.

"How is that?" she asked, with a puzzled look.

"Would you care to have me explain my philosophy?'

"Yes, please do."

"First there is our Heavenly Father-Mother god, which represents the sea of all consciousness. Then there is Adam, who represents a Planet in world consciousness or atom within the Father. This atom is divided in two. Adam-Positive and Eve-negative, or let us say Sun and Moon. After millions of light years the Sun and Moon became Abraham and Sarah, who created the twelve tribes of Israel. Also Abraham and Hagar created the Arab tribes. Today, we represent both the tribes of Israel and the tribes of Egypt."

I stopped for a moment to consider the effect of my words upon her, then continued.

"All humans have three brains. The first is the conscious mind. It has seven planes of consciousness and is connected to the physical body. Each plane has its own master on that level. In the Bible this is referred to as 'The Key.'

"Next we have the subconscious mind. This great mind is in the solar plexus. It also has seven planes of consciousness connected to the mental body. Each of these planes also has its own master on that level. The Bible refers to it as 'The Door.'

"The third brain is in the head of your true self. The 'I Am.' This brain has seven planes of consciousness with a mast on each level— Lord Gods. The Bible refers to this dynamic mind as 'The Power.' Our purpose in life is to unite these three minds-worlds through prayer and sending light and praise to our higher worlds. When these minds-worlds are united, this is referred to in the Holy Bible as 'The Trinity. Three Persons In One.'

I stopped speaking and the woman said, "I never heard of such a philosophy. Where did you get it?"

"From the Holy Bible," I answered patting her hand, "but I must get dressed now. My friends are waiting for me. We leave for Jerusalem later today." Presenting her with a gift, I bade her good-bye.

We visited an old castle high up on a hill in Amman, then went sight-seeing around the ancient town. We visited two churches and later stopped at Mount Nebo en route to Jerusalem by bus.

We were taken to the border of Jerusalem by a driver who was the young boy actor in the movie "Lawrence of Arabia." In the film, the boy died in the desert. He received over forty thousand dollars for that movie. We all enjoyed hearing him describe the making of the movie.

Our driver did not have a permit to cross the border to Jerusalem, so he stopped the bus at the Allenby Bridge. There, we waited for two or more hours for the bus from Jerusalem. Soldiers with bayonets came to investigate why we were going to Jerusalem.

When the bus did arrive, it was not Adel, our guide, but a relief driver who informed us that Adel's wife was ill.

We arrived at the immigration center in Jerusalem. Everyone was permitted through the door except me. A very nice man took me into a private room and asked several questions, then said, "It's all right, Miss Perez, even through your passport is not in order, we will allow you to visit our country."

I thanked him and joined Betty, who told me that in the future we will not show my passport but use the re-entry card. This we should have done when we left Rome.

Shortly after that, I saw Betty speaking to a very charming man whose aura was deep purple, flecked with black. Large holes showed in his aortic field. I knew he had the gift of discerning the secrets of the mortal hearts and could even look into their souls. Betty introduced him as Lewis, our relief guide. He seemed interested in me and said, "I would like to speak with you in private later."

I felt drawn to this man and wanted to protect him. "Yes," I replied, "I will talk with you before I leave Jerusalem."

"I would like that very much," he answered softly. I could feel the pathos in his voice and knew that he was a very troubled soul.

Our hotel in Jerusalem for that night was the National Hotel, in the heart of the old city. We did not arrive until after 3 p.m., but the manager, a very charming man, kept the dining room open for us to have lunch.

Coming out of the dining room, I recognized the manager standing at the door with a very tall distinguished-looking man, and I was introduced to him as the owner of the hotel. I shook hands with the handsome man and said, "You have great healing powers."

"Thank you, Miss Perez, I'm a doctor," he answered, looking at me with deep interest.

There were some seats at the entrance and the doctor guided me over to one of them, then sat down beside me. We discussed my group tour when I suddenly stated, "Your power would be much greater if you were not so depressed."

"I am Dr. George Habash. How can I help being depressed when my country is taken away and my people thrown out of their homes and are starving?"

I touched his hand saying, "I'm sorry."

There was complete silence then he asked, "What do you think of the Jews coming back to Jerusalem?"

Again, I touched his hand with deep sympathy and asked, "Don't you believe in the prophecies of the Holy Bible?"

With a startled look, he replied, "Yes, I do, but what has prophecy to do with our homes being taken away and our property destroyed?"

I did not know at that time how his property was being destroyed, but later Betty informed me that evil individuals were checking in at the hotel, then leaving the water running while they checked out. Many of the rooms were flooded, even the one that Betty stayed in was wet and the furniture damaged.

Several minutes elapsed before I spoke. "These are the last days. It is the destiny of our world that the Jews return home to Jerusalem. This is symbolic of man returning back to God. We must all unite and live as brothers and sisters. This is our test to prove that we are truly the children of God. If we are, then, we will share our homes with these people who have been wandering from land to land."

"Please, believe me, Miss. Perez," he exclaimed, "we have tried very hard to be fair but every time something comes up to destroy our faith."

"I understand," I answered, "yet, God is using these people to teach us lessons of patience. This is our big test. We must not fail."

Silently I thought, Sarah's curse on Hagar is truly working. The children of Abraham will not have peace until they have learned to love their brothers and sisters.

Just then Renee and Lynn came up and I introduced them to the doctor. Neither of them realized that he was the great Dr. George Habash.

After the introductions, it was Renee who said, "Maya, we are ready to leave. Betty is waiting for you in the lobby."

Very quickly, I bade the good doctor good-bye and left. Only twenty minutes I had spent in his company, but many years have passed and I have not forgotten to pray and send him light.

We were on our way to Saint Anne's church, which is also known as the church of the Holy Sepulcher. Lewis was our guide for that afternoon and part of the next day. As he spoke of the various stations of the cross of Jesus, I could see a sheet of pure gold surrounding his whole being. This man had done great works in the higher heavens, but for the moment he had forgotten his true identity. He was a lost soul and at times he would sink down into the pit of his consciousness.

At the first station of the cross, Lewis explained the condemnation of our Lord. I asked my higher self, what is the meaning of Jesus being crucified?"

The message returned very clear: the crucifixion of Christ is the symbol of the death of man's lower self, making possible the transition back to God's consciousness.

At the second station, I was inspired to pray harder. This was where Jesus was made to bear the cross. The message said: this is the time in Man's destiny when he must face himself and bear the cross of his wrong doings to himself and his world.

At the third station where the Lord fell, I was given this truth: This represents where man fell from the higher planes of consciousness and lost the wisdom and help of the Higher Self. Man had now become weak and has to call on the Inner Angels for spiritual help.

The fourth station where Jesus met his sorrowing mother, represented where man meets his soulmate through life's journey and realizes that he is bringing sorrow to his loved ones.

It was also explained to me that each one of us had three soulmates. For Jesus, it was John the beloved who represented his higher soulmate, then Mary, his mother and Mary Magdalene who represented the soulmate for the physical self.

The fifth station where Jesus was helped by the Cyrenian, is the symbol of man praying inwardly and is helped by God's ministering Angels in his hour of great need.

At the sixth station, Veronica wiped the face of Jesus. This showed that man walking through life, has leaned the many lessons of controlling his emotions. Thus, his negative self, as woman has now become his divine angel of mercy.

The seventh station of the cross, where Jesus fell for the second time, is where man has reached the seventh plane of the conscious mind and he is now at the bottom of the subconscious and is too weak to journey up. Through meditation and prayer, however, man is able to call on the Masters of the Inner Realms for strength.

At the eighth station, where Jesus met the sorrowing women, here the soul consciousness meets the feminine realms of his inner-being. The realm of great love and mercy. Jesus had made great progress; therefore, he was not afraid to die. As they wept for him in his hour of desperation, Jesus said, *"Weep not for me , but for your children. "* He meant the sons of man who are still sleeping unaware of their true divine purpose on earth.

At the ninth station, Jesus fell for the third time. Here man is persecuted by his negative vibrations, representing the end of his journey here in the lower planes.

The tenth station, where Jesus is stripped of his garments, represents how he has thrown off his outer-earthly garments and is now ready to begin his journey within. Man came from within the Mind of God, and it is through this inner door that he will make his transition back to the Father-Mother's Mind to *the universal sea of all consciousness.*

At the eleventh station, Jesus was nailed to the cross. This represented Jesus-Man as a complete symbol. Here he is put between his negative Self and his positive lower Self. The thief crucified with Jesus, who did not believe, represented the conscious negative and material world of man. The other thief, who believed, represented the subconscious and positive soul of man; the United World.

At the twelfth station, Jesus died to man's lower self. The first hour on the cross Jesus sees his lower self throughout his many incarnations, and his agony is unbearable. At the second hour, he abandoned the lower world and at the third he yields his weightless body up to God as a sacrifice for all mankind.

At the thirteenth station, Jesus was removed from the cross by his two disciples, Joseph and Nicodemus, who gave him to his sorrowing mother. Mary represents the lower self of Eve, who in time will heal all mankind. It was woman, who is the symbol of man's negative self, that was the vessel Satan, the law maker used to make man fall. Now woman will be the vessel God will use to uplift man.

At the fourteenth station, Jesus, the spiritual symbol of Adam, who came to open the inner doors for all mankind and will come again to open the Divine doors for those who are ready. He said, "*I am the way and the life. No man cometh to the Father but through Me.*" He was speaking of Adam, who is our true Divine Self.

After the message at the fourteenth station of the cross, there was complete silence, then a strange feeling of excitement seeped through my whole being. I knew something important was about to happen. I prayed and asked the Lord for enlightenment.

I remembered a vision that I had had several years ago. I saw myself coming out of the sea. I was crying. On shore was a tall, handsome man standing with outstretched hands. I ran over to him and he embraced me asking, "What is it that you wish?"

"I wish to be like Jesus," I replied, wiping the tears from my face.

With a serious look on his face, he answered, " That would take many years. It took Jesus thirteen years to fulfill his mission in this life. He left home at twelve and went to live with the Masters of the far East and at age twenty-five, he came back to see his mother. From twenty-five to thirty, those were the five lost years. At age thirty to thirty-three, he fulfilled his mission."

Looking deep into his eyes I answered, "Couldn't you rush up my training?"

He did not answer, instead he took me up a long flight of stairs and introduced me to another man who seemed to be his assistant.

For a few minutes they stood aside and spoke, but without sound, yet, I was able to understand what they were saying.

The assistant looked over to me and asked, "What do we need her for?'

"We need more doctors," the head doctor replied, "I would like you to give her a chance."

With a nod of his head, the assistant took me inside a small room and showed me a woman who was lying on a bed. I was told to give her a treatment, but I had to wait for my uniform.

At this point, I seemed to have gone into a semi-trance, for the uniform was in the other room, but I could not seem to have the power to go and get it. It may have been minutes or even hours when I finally felt I should give the treatment without the uniform. I took off my dress and my underclothes were white and clean.

As I started to give the treatment a call came in that the next patient was ready for her treatment. I replied saying, "I have just started with the first patient, the next person will have to wait."

At that point in the vision, I woke up with a great feeling that I had passed the test. I did not know how or what I had passed but I felt good.

Later in meditation, I asked for the answer to my vision. The answer was, " You were sincere with the first. You did not leave her for the second. This is symbolic that you will be sincere and loving to all people. Your work will be in a God-like and wonderful manner."

I wondered why this vision had appeared before me and I asked for the answer.

After praying for quite awhile, I saw Renee going into the church and I followed, still asking God to illuminate me.

The Church of the Holy Sepulcher is built over the site where our Lord Jesus was crucified. I stood outside of the Sepulcher where Jesus was placed after he was taken from the cross. Silently, but fervently, I prayed for a new spirit, one that would give me the wisdom and power I needed to overcome the world of matter.

Many people were entering the Holy Sepulcher, I saw a priest coming out and asked him, "Father, where is the spot Jesus was crucified?"

"You are standing on it," the good priest replied as he passed by. In a trance-like state, I looked up and saw Jesus on the cross and suddenly felt something turn in my solar plexus, and a moan came from within my innermost being, as if a child turned and moaned. I tried to call out, but only strange moans came out. I began to fall, someone took my arm and I was led to the back of the church where three priests were praying on the altar.

As I walked between D.D. and Lewis, one of our guides, it seemed as if another being outside of me was observing the whole event. I saw Lewis signal to the three priests and pointed to the back where the ladies room was. One of the priests nodded and we were given permission to go to the restroom. It was D.D. who took me inside while Lewis waited like the big brother I had known in several past incarnations.

I regurgitated and some white murky water came up. I felt like a pregnant woman who had just broken the water, only it came up through my mouth.

After that, I felt a little better and was taken back to the room where the priests were still praying, and was given a seat next to D.D. and Lewis who stayed with us.

I learned that the priest who informed me where Jesus was crucified was Father Francisco. He brought over another priest, who looked closely at me. They went back to the altar and discussed me. It was strange because I was sitting at the other end of the large room, yet, I could hear what they were saying. I heard Father Francisco say, "She had had a spiritual manifestation."

The other priest who appeared taller asked, "How do you know?"

Father Francisco replied, "Just a few minutes before she was brought in here, she asked me where our Lord was crucified. I told her, right where you are standing."

The other priest shook his head and they continued to pray for me. Later Father Francisco brought over another priest. He appeared to be older and a more illumined individual. This priest also looked strangely at me and they left. Shortly after, the older priest brought me some lemon tea, for it seemed to give me a miraculous feeling of energy pouring all through my whole being.

It may have been two or more hours that I was there in the room, I cannot say. As we were leaving, I asked Father Francisco if he would give me a special blessing. He took my arm and led me out into the Church of the Holy Sepulcher. We had to bend down to get in. My cousin Renee was standing nearby and followed us into the Sepulcher. She asked Father Francisco for a blessing and he blessed us both.

As we came out of the grotto, D.D. held me by one arm and Lewis the other. I was still rather weak, so we took a cab to the hotel.

It was around 7 p.m., the dinner hour, but I did not wish to eat. D.D. and Lewis took me up to my room and put me to bed.

I did not know it at the time, but Lewis sat outside the door while D.D. gave me a therapy treatment.

I may have dozed off while she was giving me the treatment, for I seemed to be in a dream state and heard a voice speaking. Then D.D. leaned over the bed and said, "Maya, the manager of the hotel is here. He would like to bring Dr. George Habash up to see you."

"No, no, D.D. I don't need a doctor. I need prayers," I replied softly. At the same time I looked up and saw the manager staring down at me. He had pushed his way in and Lewis was unable to stop his entry.

Again, I said, "I don't need a doctor. I am not physically ill."

Still staring down at me the man exclaimed, "But, Miss Perez, Dr. Habash is concerned about you. He would like to come up and visit with you."

"But I'm not ill. Please let me sleep."

Still persisting, the man cried out, "But Miss Perez, he is a great man!"

I did not answer. What could I say? I had just seen the greatest man of all times. I turned over and went back to sleep.

The next morning, D.D. told me that the manager left the room with a puzzled look on his face, and shaking his head.

While I was getting dressed D.D. exclaimed, "Maya, you look great this morning. Last night, I was worried about you. After dinner, Lewis came up to see how you were. When he saw you sleeping so peacefully, he said, "D.D. she is out of her body. Why, she is scarcely breathing. Lewis would like to learn how to give therapy treatments. He feels he has healing hands."

"I am sure he has," I replied, "but frankly, D.D., he has to make up his mind what he wants to do with his life. His destiny path is great, but at present there is a dark cloud over him. Maybe later it will change."

"He is very unhappy. His wife is very ill and may need an operation. Maya, what can we do for him?" D.D. asked sadly.

"We can pray for him," I said with a nod of my head, " if he has faith and truly believes, I am certain God will give him a new lease on life but first, Lewis will have to make some sacrifices."

"I am sure that he believes, but look at what is happening to these people. Everything is going to ruins."

"Did Betty tell you what is happening?" D.D. cried out sounding angry.

"Yes, she did," I answered quietly, trying to calm her. "Evil people are coming in and flooding the rooms and then walking off without paying their bills."

Our morning tour took us to the pool of Bethesda, then to King Solomon's temple and on to the Dome of the Rock on Mr. Moriah. After that, we visited the all inspiring Al Acqsa Mosque and the Wailing Wall.

After lunch we visited several churches in the old city. Jerusalem has some of the most beautiful churches that I have ever seen.

Later, we returned to the Church of the Holy Sepulcher, St. Ann's Church where I had become ill the day before. I saw Father Francisco giving a special mass to a large crowd of people. When he was finished I walked over to him and thanked him for his prayers. I was not sure he remembered me,as I felt different, more vibrant and alive. I was renewed with energy from the Inner planes. The good father was most kind.

As we were leaving the church, Lewis entered. He ran over and gave me a big hug asking, "How are you, Maya?"

With a happy smile, I replied, "My spiritual ailment has left me feeling wonderful."

"I knew you had a spiritual manifestation, and today proves it," he exclaimed standing off at arm's length and smiling down at me, "you could not have been so ill and get better this fast, unless it was a spiritual ailment."

"Thank you, Lewis," I answered with deep feelings, "I appreciate all that you and D.D. have done for me."

"Maya, we had to!" he said seriously, "It was not by accident that D.D. and I were close to you when you became ill. There was a great reason, even greater than we now think. Later you will be shown why this happened."

"I believe this. I also believe that I have given birth to a spiritual child." I spoke these words with great conviction.

"That is most amazing," he answered in a hushed tone of voice, as if afraid to speak out loud.

That night, the group went sightseeing, but I remained in the hotel. I was still feeling the after-effects of my strange ailment of the night before.

The next morning, we were to get up around 6 a.m. to drive through the country, and that evening after dinner go to a nightclub.

After breakfast, Adel, our guide, took us in a large bus up to the Mount of Olives, where we saw a beautiful view of Jerusalem.

After that we went to the Garden of Gethsemane and visited the Church of All Nations, Gordon's Tomb, and then proceeded to Mount

Zion and also the Tomb of David. Later, we went on to Bethlehem and visited the Basilica of the Nativity, the Birthplace of Jesus. We saw the manger, Grotto of St. Jerome and the Crusader's Cloister.

On the way to Jericho, we visited the village of Lazarus and the house of Mary and Martha, with a glimpse of the good Samaritan's Inn as we passed by.

In Jericho, we stopped at Elisha's fountain and drank the water, which was said to have healing qualities. As we were leaving, we saw a man sitting at the front desk with a large bowl in front of him. His demeanor was so sad and drawn that we all passed him by. One woman, in our group, stopped and gave him something. It was D.D.

On the way out, D.D. called me aside and said, "Maya, I feel terrible. Someone has given me a condition."

"Did you stop at the front desk?" I asked looking at her aura, which had suddenly changed to a dark grey.

"Yes, I did. Everyone passed the man at the desk. I felt sorry for him, so stopped and was about to put something in his bowl, when he tried to grab it, I pulled it back and left."

"Then go back and give him the money," I whispered, "or he will hurt you."

"You think he has that power?" she asked with awe in her voice.

"Yes, D.D., he has. Go back and all will be well."

"I don't want to," she cried out stubbornly.

"But, you must!" I insisted impatiently. "This man has very negative thoughts, which are in the form of demons. As you came into his vibrations one of the thought forms possessed you."

Reluctantly, she left and gave the man the money. After she came back, we prayed and the condition left her.

Early Wednesday morning, I had a vision of Lewis giving me a book with some information. I could not remember the details of the dream, but felt it was important for me to speak with him.

Shortly after 8 a.m., he called. D.D. answered the phone and spoke abruptly to him.

I whispered, "Speak nice to him, D.D., he has some information for me. Ask him to meet us for lunch. I will treat."

Changing her tone of voice, D.D. said, "Lewis, Maya wants you to meet us for lunch. She will be our hostess but we both need hair-do's and manicures. Do you know of a reliable salon?"

After a few minutes of conversation, D.D. said, "He will pick us up in front of the hotel at noon and take us to a good salon."

"Thank you, D.D., " I said smiling happily, and getting the clothes together that I was about to wear. I related my dream to D.D. and said, "It's important for us to see and speak with him today."

"I had a vision also," D.D. remarked, "I saw Rameses II. He seemed to be someone I had known long ago. He said to me, "Keep water in your mouth, and I will guide your steps." She was quiet for a moment, then continued, "I can't imagine what it means."

"I know what it means," I replied, silently thanking Rameses for his help. "It means that Lewis and I must speak together while you keep silent."

"Oh, that makes sense," she exclaimed with a wide-eyed look. "Maya, we will find out what he does."

"Yes, we will," I answered quickly, "but I am sure you have already guessed."

"I don't know anything! All these people are acting so strangely They look like the cat that swallowed the mouse."

Just then Renee called on the phone. D.D. answered and they conversed for a few minutes. Then D.D. said, "One of the ladies in our group has not returned from the nightclub. Betty is quite worried. Maya, what should we do about the matter?"

"There is nothing we can do except pray. Let us pray, D.D."

After we were finished, we both felt that the light had appeared. We knew that this was a sign that our good friend would be safe.

Promptly at noon, Lewis arrived with a cab and escorted us to a beautiful salon. Later, we walked to an Arabian restaurant. I had informed Lewis I wished to eat some Arabian food. The restaurant was one flight up, and Lewis introduced the owner to us. He had known him for several years.

After we had eaten, Lewis asked, "What do you see for me, Maya?"

Without hesitation I replied, "I see a dark cloud over you. It is the symbol of destruction and sometimes death."

I cannot remember ever having answered someone so strangely. D.D. looked at me in utter surprise, but remained silent.

"I believe you," Lewis answered sadly. Bending over he showed me a silver plate in the back of his head.

"This is from an automobile accident. "This is why I don't drive." He was quiet for a brief moment then continued, "Only God knows why I lived."

"You lived because God has a special work for you to do. There are two alternatives; either you get out of Israel or you are to fulfill God's divine purpose."

I spoke with deep sincerity. He was destined to work with the higher angels or in time, he would be destroyed.

"Maya, I cannot leave Jerusalem. My work is here, I cannot run away. This would be madness." He stopped , bent down and opened a brief case, then took out some little booklets and gave them to me.

I glanced at the cover, on it were little children looking hungry and forlorn. I handed one to D.D. She took it with a knowing look. This was my vision that had come to pass.

Lewis continued to speak, "These children in Jordan are hungry. Many of them do not have homes. I must stay here and help them."

"Lewis, I'm not over-emphasizing your danger. It is very great."

Looking deep into his soul, I continued, "This veil of darkness that covers your whole being, means death and sometimes devastation. Of course, if you are involved in areas that are dangerous, then you know what I mean. I know in your heart you wish to do good works. Your destiny could either be very great or else you and many of your relatives and friends could be destroyed."

He gazed at me intently but did not speak and I continued, "If you pray sincerely and ask God to forgive you, I am sure that in time, you will be able to save many people. Not only their lives, but their souls could be released. You could teach them how to manifest their great desires. Food and everything that you need will be given to you. You could bring peace to both Jew and Arab. These are conditions that were sent out from Sarah to Hagar. This is why the Jews and Arabs are fighting to this day and will continue until these curses are transmuted. Only then will peace be on the earth. It is up to us to put love where there is hate. We must not only save the Holy Land, but our whole world. This is our divine purpose. Lewis, this is the message God gave me for you."

"Maya, strange that you should say these words to me! I'm half-Jewish and half-Arab. My mother was a Jewess and my father an Arab. Several years before Mother passed on, she became a Christian. Maya, she was beautiful. I feel she is with me, especially when I'm in great danger and need help." Lewis spoke with tears in his eyes.

"Lewis, we must not forget, the first Christians were Jews. Jesus, the most beautiful man, was a Jew. He is our Lord and Master. As we pray to Him, then we will have power to overcome the evils of the material world. Pray for your mother. This will give her the power to come through to help you with your problems."

After giving him this message, I was silent for a few moments, then continued. "Lewis, I see a legal problem It has to do with some money that you owe."

"Yes, I owe the Israel government some tax money. I have not been successful in my project and my wife has been ill."

Suddenly, he pulled back as if he had been shot and cried out in an angry tone of voice, " Why am I telling you all this? Who are you?"

Quietly but firmly I answered, "God wants me to help you. This is why you are telling me your problems. I am your sister from another life."

Reassured by my words, he said, "Maya, for a moment, I was afraid of you. There have been so many pressures lately, I sometimes am afraid of my own shadow."

"If you pray, meditate and read some Psalms, every morning and night, you would have no reason to fear anyone." I spoke these words while sending him light to the inner planes of his consciousness.

"You will have problems because you are fighting life. Every thought that you think is how you are going to conquer your so-called enemies. Why don't you think of peace and endeavor to help your brothers and sisters? Remember the "great" Hitler? He was one-eighth Jewish and German. He was ashamed of his fine Jewish heritage and also because he was born out of wedlock; he hated life. His hatred was so intense that he not only destroyed himself, but Germany as well. You, too, could be great, but if you harbor destructive thoughts, then you will not only destroy yourself, but Jerusalem and Jordan as well."

"All that you say is true and I believe you. But Maya, I have tried to help my mother's people, but it seems as if the whole world is against them." Lewis said these words in a whisper, as if afraid to be overheard.

"They need spiritual help," I answered softly.

"I realize that, but every time I get friendly, something bad happens to me," Lewis remarked looking at his watch, then asked, "Do you have time to hear a true story?"

I looked at D.D. , who was listening to every word intently, but had kept silent throughout our whole conversation. With her silent permission, I said, "Yes we have time," thinking his story was an excuse for helping the Jews.

"Some time back, I met a very beautiful blond Jewish girl. She was radiant and inspired to do fantastic things. She was like my mother, both beautiful and good. I told her since my own mother was Jewish, we had something in common. About a week after we met, she asked me to meet her after work. I was to wait on the street and she would drive us to where we were going. When I arrived at the appointed time, I found Sari sitting in a car with a man that she introduced as her cousin from out of town. As I got in the car, I sensed immediately that something was wrong. Yuri, the cousin, did not enter into our conversation; instead he just kept driving as if we had to get some place in a hurry. I asked them where we were going but she said, "It's a secret." I thought, this is not right. These people are secret agents, not my friends. I had met them at 10 p.m., now it was close to midnight, and we were still driving. When we finally arrived at a bar way out in the desert, it was a few minutes after midnight. As we got out of the car, something inside of me said, careful, or you will not live to see morning.

"Inside there were only two customers and the bartender, who looked as if he had been drinking. Quickly, I said, 'Hello, this is my birthday. The drinks are on me.'

"I pulled out a large bill and smiled at Sari and Yuri. They looked surprised and Sari said to Yuri, 'This is his birthday.'

"I ordered Scotch but poured it into a flower pot when no one was looking. Sari and Yuri drank brandy. Two o'clock was closing time but we three left around 2:30 a.m. Both of them were drunk. Since Yuri could not drive, I drove the car with them sleeping in the back seat. I took them to the spot where they had picked me up, then I went home. I was happy to be in my own bed and thanked God for saving my life. I often get premonitions about the future. In one vivid dream, recently, I was out on the desert with a group of people that were supposed to be my friends. All at once they turned on me like mad dogs and I ran for my life. I stopped by a high wall, too high to climb over and heard myself say, 'Oh Lord, save me. Help me! Help me!' Suddenly I was lifted over the wall. What do you get from this dream, Maya?" Lewis asked looking at me with piercing eyes.

I thought for a moment and answered, "The mad people are your own negative thought demons and the wall is the symbol of the Jews, who cannot be overcome except by prayers."

"Maya, I will do my best to help both Jews and Arabs. Please pray for me."

"D.D. and I have been praying for you. We also send you lots of light," I said looking at D.D., who nodded her head.

"You have been very kind to me. What can I do for you?" he asked, looking solemnly at both D.D. and me.

After a moment of thought, I answered, "Protect our group and see that we leave Jerusalem safely."

"Have you had a problem?" he asked with a look of surprise at both D.D. and me.

"Nothing specific," I replied, "but certain premonitions foretold danger for the group. Betty and I have advised them not to get too friendly with strangers, but they are out to have a good time. They pay no attention to us. They only laugh and go on their merry way. Betty worries constantly about the image of the group."

"One of your group did not come back to the hotel last night," Lewis remarked seriously.

I was shocked at his statement and D.D's eyes showed her surprise, but she kept quiet.

"How do you know that, Lewis?" I asked still staring at him.

"It is my duty to know what goes on here," he answered. "The lady went off with a couple, but I am certain she will be all right."

"How is it that you have more information than we do?" I asked. "You must have been in the club last night."

"I was," Lewis replied smiling, "I was up on the balcony overlooking the floor show and saw everything that went on." Just then the owner came with the check. After paying it, we left.

In the bright sunlight outside, I still felt downhearted and Lewis said, "Maya, don't worry about the welfare of the group. I will see that they are safe. Also tell Betty not to worry about the group's image, it was cracked before it got here."

D.D. laughed, but I kept a straight face. If anything happened to our group, both Betty and I would be held responsible.

Renee met us in the hotel lobby and accompanied us to our room. I knew she had important news to tell us.

As soon as the door was closed, D.D. could not contain herself any longer. She asked, "What happened, Renee?"

"Our missing lady returned," she answered, then waited to measure the effect of her words upon us. "She is in a state of shock and is sleeping now."

"Well," D.D. said, "since the group's image is broken now, maybe Betty will relax and stop worrying."

THIRTY-FOUR

Nefertiti, Moses and the Babe

Nothing unusual happened that night and the next morning we left in a large bus to travel through Jerusalem. Our guide for the tour was Adel. He was just the opposite to Lewis, very sad and appeared to be overwhelmed by his problems. Adel was a Moslem. Very religious and strict. He also spoke several languages and was quite illumined.

We drove to Nablus, where we visited the Samaritan Synagogue and saw the old precious Pentateuch manuscript scroll. As we left there, our bus drove us to the burial site of John the Baptist. We were going in the same direction and we were all happy to drive with those wonderful, happy people. They sang songs and someone in the group played a musical instrument. It was truly lovely and I felt lifted up to greater heights of ecstasy. At our next stop we waited for Adel who had to get the bus fixed.

We proceeded on to Tiberias, where we took a boat ride on the Sea of Galilee. Never have I ever felt so peaceful. It was as if I had gone back to the days of Jesus when he walked on the water.

Our hotel in Tiberias was Gubermann's. It was a lovely place over-looking the Sea of Galilee. It was quite new and had been owned by a Jewish company that had gone bankrupt, and the government had taken over the hotel.

After eating dinner in that fantastic hotel, I could see why it had gone bankrupt. I have never seen so much food. It was as if the government also wanted to go bankrupt.

That evening after dinner, several people in the group went out to see the sights, but I stayed in the hotel. Shortly after 10 p.m., I went up to my room and slept soundly and did not hear D.D. come in. She was still my roommate.

It may have been around 2 a.m. when I woke up to find the room flooded with a soft bluish light, which looked like iridescent lighting. The whole room was illuminated.

I looked over at D.D. sleeping on her bed, then sat up to see where the lights were coming from. Oh, I thought, it must be the moon. However, when I got up and opened the large windows and curtains, I did not see the moon. Instead I saw a great star glistening out of the sky.

At first, I thought the star was a plane, but it was not moving. Then I thought, it was a spaceship and wondered if I should wake D.D.

I tried to turn back into the room, but a dynamic force turned me around and I found that I could not move.

Out of the star appeared two Beings, one was Queen Nefertiti and the other, instinctively I knew it was Moses. They were holding a child whose face was so beautiful that I immediately recognized him as the young Messiah. This was He, that the Holy Bible had prophesied would come. This was a great God Spirit.

I stared at this phenomenon for a long time as if hypnotized. Suddenly Nefertiti stepped forth out of the great star with the young God-Child. There were golden rays swirling around her and the child as they floated down to me. I was completely overcome and felt a strange power lifting me up to meet them.

Back of Nefertiti and the God-Child in a blue haze stood Moses. He was smiling as he said, "Do not be afraid."

Nefertiti in her soft melodious voice spoke, "Beloved Maya, we are here to tell you of the wonders that are about to be manifested in your earth, which will soon be blessed in order to receive the holy angels which the Father will send down to take over the bodies of blessed souls. Those who are ready to receive them will be given pure and holy spirits.

"Strange events shall come to pass, which may take months, even years to transpire. As the sands of time drift through the creative currents of life, many will be taken over by the powers of darkness. Diseases not yet known to man will consume the flesh. Those who are pure in thought and deeds will be given the power to heal and illumine these sick souls.

"Only those who are spiritually illumined will be given the power to lift up their consciousness in order to receive the gifts of healing, and be used as channels.

"Egypt will be the open door for all mankind to go within and seek wisdom that will be needed to make the journey back to the consciousness of our Divine Father-Mother God.

"The priests of old Egypt and Jerusalem shall return, but on a higher level, and the melody of Life shall be harmonious.

First we must gather in our powers for the wars between the forces of darkness and light."

The voice stopped speaking and I looked up at the sky and saw that it glistened as if it were pure gold, and I wondered what was going to happen next.

I may have gone deeper into a trance-like state, for suddenly I was transported back into time and I saw a strange scene being enacted before my very eyes. I was standing on the side of a large room and saw a party of women coming down the street. In front was a young girl who appeared to be about fifteen or sixteen. I knew she was the Princess Hatshepsut, daughter of the ruling Pharaoh. I also knew that her father had sent her on a most important mission.

The young princess whispered to her maids to wait, then she ran down to the river and quickly glanced around as if looking for something special. Over to the side of the river she spied some bulrushes and immediately went over and investigated them. In the bulrush was a small basket with a child sleeping in it. It was Moses.

She picked up the basket and the young child cried out. It was then I heard the princess say, "You are my brother and a Jew. My father has no other son but you. One day, you could be the ruling Pharaoh but with God's help, I shall stop it."

Just then, I happened to look over at a clump of trees, behind them stood another girl. I knew she was the Jewish sister of the baby. Looking out from behind the trees the young Jewish girl whispered to herself, "Oh, I shall go and tell my mother the Babe is safe. Soon she must go to the palace and seek the job as nurse-maid to her son, who will one day be the ruling Prince. Ah! Who knows, he may even be the ruling Pharaoh." With these thoughts she chuckled, then ran to inform her mother that all was well.

Quickly, the scene changed. I saw myself floating over Jerusalem and it was on fire. I knew a bomb had gone off and I saw hundreds of people running for their lives.

Up in the sky a fiery cross stretched out for many, many miles. Some parts of the cross was bright red and some were like pure gold.

From within the back of my head the mysterious voice spoke, "The cross is the symbol of Man's awareness. On the lower realms, men must be taught through bloodshed and sorrow, but as he transcends up, then he will be taught through the golden rule of life. The higher you evolve, the more sensitive and awakened you will become. Some like yourself, will be so highly in tune that they will feel the danger and sorrow of their loved ones, even at a great distance.

"Life is like a beautiful melody and the tunes can be changed in a moment. Therefore it is important to keep in perfect harmony with the stream of all life.

"If and when you feel inharmonious, then sit down and go into the silence. meditate and ask God to send you an angel to help you transmute the evil vibrations.

"If you are aware of those who are in danger, then send the light to yourself. This light will help you transmute and purify the evil thought forms that are working against you. In the late twentieth century, ailments that are strange and weird will take over the flesh. Man will not be able to cure them with the usual methods. Only with light from the inner consciousness will they be cured. Have no fear, know that your angel self will give you the answers to all difficult problems.

"Your body is in the earth, the living temple of God. The higher you evolve, the higher and more powerful will be your God-self.

"As you come down the many steps of life, you created many beings. Each one on a lower vibration than the last. Now, that you are ready to return up the Inner stairway of the Soul, you will bear these various creations and they will live in your soul. In time, they will be your teachers and will guide you through the many paths of your mortal destiny.

"You will not stop evolving until you have reached God-head, and even then, you will go on to a greater heights. There is no end to the immortal and heavenly heights."

Just then, I realized I was back in my room looking up at the star which was even brighter than before.

Again the voice spoke, and this time it was Nefertiti who spoke, "Maya," she said, "there will be a new avatar who will come down to earth within the next twenty years. it will be this Child-God that I hold in my arms. I'm the mother and Moses is the father. Only those who have loved and glorified the Christ in their hearts shall see Him. He is Jesus who will come back in the Spiritual Form. This shall be a gift from God's love and light to all mankind who have glorified and created the Christ within."

Just then I thought, where is your husband? Before I could finish the thought, Nefertiti gave me a deep look and replied, "Maya, you know where he is. He hated his Jewish brothers and sisters. Therefore, he came back as a Jew. Remember, my sister, we must love all mankind. Also, we must endeavor to understand all religions. No religion is complete. Each one has a tiny essence of truth. It is up to you to find that essence, then put it all together in order to create the whole."

She stopped speaking, and then I looked up into the sky and saw that the cross had disappeared.

After a few seconds, she spoke again, "The mystery of all creation will be revealed and man shall walk the earth as gods. The earth and all thereof shall be blessed for a thousand years. The light from our divine Father's consciousness shall absorb all evil, and darkness shall be no more."

Friday, October 27th, we left Tiberias in the large bus with Adel as our guide. It was quite early when I got up, but D.D. had already left with our guide. I quickly dressed and followed her down to the dining room where the whole group was enjoying an amazing breakfast, which I thought was more like a feast.

Strange as it may seem, I did not discuss my fantastic vision with either D.D. or Renee. It was as if I thought they would think me completely mad.

Immediately after breakfast, we left for Nazareth and then continued on to Canna of Galilee and the Port of Haifa to visit the Bahai Temple and its famous Persian gardens, Elijah's Cave, the Carmelite Monastery and Mount Carmel.

After Carmel we stopped for a light snack and then continued along the seashore highway of Caesarea and along the Valley of Hefer and the Plains of Sharon to Tel Aviv.

Our hotel in Tel Aviv was owned by a very nice Jewish man. We had arrived after 8 p.m., and he had kept the dining room open for our group. The owner came and sat down at my table. D.D. and Renee were seated at the same table. We were enjoying our conversation with the owner and his wife when suddenly, I saw him watching a table at the far end of the room. It was occupied by our guide and two of the ladies in our group. With them were three strange-looking men.

The owner seemed very disturbed and he and his wife got up and left. I sensed he knew who the three men were. As I looked over at the table, I saw a dark cloud swirl over the table and I whispered to the girls, "Something is wrong at that table where our guide is sitting with the three men and the girls from our group. I see a very dark cloud over them."

It was Renee who informed me the next morning at breakfast that the owner had locked the door and the guide with the two ladies had to practically knock down the door in order to be admitted back into the hotel. Later, when I got back to the States, one of the ladies confessed that she had had an argument with one of the strangers and told him she had seen his picture on television and that he was a very evil man. It was our guide who had to stop the man from injuring her. I asked her why she had done this? Her reply was, "I was stupid."

Saturday, October 28th, we flew into Athens, Greece. Our hotel was the Astor, which is directly opposite the Parthenon. I did not realize the significance until I went down to the dining room before the others arrived and sat down at the large table at the far corner of the room. The window faced the Parthenon.

It may have been five or ten minutes when suddenly the lights came on. I felt it was important for me to be alone at the table in order to view the sight alone.

I immediately went into a state of trance for I saw myself as the High Priestess in a temple on the top of the Parthenon. There were days of joy and sorrow, but the joy was much more than the sorrow. I could see myself walking in a beautiful garden that surrounded the temple and many young and beautiful girls were singing and enjoying themselves. I knew that was a happy life.

I do not recall how long I stayed in the trance but suddenly the lights went out and I was back at the table with Renee saying, "Maya, are you all right?"

Later, I related the vision to Renee and she said, "Greece is wonderful. The vibes are perfect."

Sunday was a day of fun and festivals and many of us strolled along the streets and relaxed in the beautiful atmosphere.

Monday, we went on a cruise to Aegina, Poros and Hydra on the beautiful Aegean Sea. it was truly delightful and I enjoyed every moment of our stay in Greece.

Tuesday morning, after breakfast, we departed from Athens via Rome to New York.

In Rome, we were delayed for several hours as there was one strike after the other. Finally we left and arrived in New York late that evening. I believe it was around 9 p.m. I must say, I was very happy to be home in beautiful New York.

The next morning, November first, I called Helena Chinsley to report about the tour. She came that evening to my apartment on East 86th Street. During the course of our conversation, I invited her to spend the Christmas holidays with me to see the boats that were decorated every Christmas. A week before Christmas Eve many boats sail every night in Balboa, California.

THIRTY-FIVE

Princess
Sin Hathor Yuen

T wo days after I arrived in New York, Betty Billings, now Mrs. H. J. Reilly, called and said, "Maya, Dr. Reilly would like you to come and spend a few days with us here in New Jersey." I was delighted and immediately said, "yes."

I was told that Edgar Cayce had said Dr. Reilly was one of the gladiators in the Roman arena and was connected with many Christian deaths. Therefore, in this life he was destined to heal the many people that he had injured; and also, that he would work to the very moment of his death.

One day, while sitting in his kitchen, I suddenly saw a glimpse of this experience and cried out, "H.J., I know why you are so good to me."

The good doctor must have known also, because he got up and left the kitchen. I never referred to the experience again.

There is much karma between us. H.J. is a Taurus, and I a Leo with Taurus rising.

A few days after I was there, the doctor and Betty asked if I remembered Ellen Morrison Mann? I replied, "Yes, I remember the name, but could not place her."

It was H. J. that said, "Maya, I would like you to go to Virginia Beach and get some colonics and massages at the A.R.E. Center."

I was quite surprised, and of course being a Leo with Taurus rising, I immediately rejected his kind offer saying, "Now, H. J., I need to get back to Balboa, California and find an apartment. My landlady has rented the one I had for several years. It's already late in the season and all the winter rentals will be gone."

"Maya," the good doctor insisted, "you are not well. D.D. has told me that you were ill in Jerusalem. I feel that you should get these treatments. Ellen Morrison Mann, from Atlanta, Georgia, has invited you to be her guest. You helped her some time back and she would like to show you her appreciation."

Well, after many more talks with H. J. and Betty Billings, I did go to Virginia Beach and truly loved it. Ellen was extremely nice, and through her, I met several friends who are still my good friends.

I arrived back in Balboa the 30th of November and December 1st went out to look for a two-bedroom apartment with two baths and completely furnished. When I asked the real estate agent to find it for me, she looked at me in shock and exclaimed, "Miss Perez, this is December first and all the winter rentals are gone. I may be able to find you a one-bedroom, but not two."

After looking through some papers she said, "I think I have one here for you."

I sat and prayed while she made the call, then she said, "There is a two-bedroom apartment a couple of blocks down the road. Go and look at it."

Later I confessed to the agent that I had stood on the corner and asked the Holy Spirit to find me the right place.

The apartment was perfect and I invited a friend to come and share it with me, as Helena could not come that winter. That whole winter seemed to be like a magical time. Everything that I desired just seemed to flow right in to me. It was absolutely amazing.

In June of 1973, I arrived back in New York and a few days later called Helena. She was delighted that I was back and said, "Now, Maya, we will meditate and find out the connection we had in the past. I feel that it was very important."

"O.K. Helena, we will get together and do some work."

I had tried to meditate with Helena several times, but always felt I was blocked. I could never tune into her subconscious. She had thought that it was strange. So did it.

A week after I came back to New York, my cousin Renee brought over some pictures that she had taken in Egypt. I was happy to see them until I saw one. It was of a young girl that was quite pregnant. I looked at the picture and asked Renee, "Who is that young girl? I don't remember her."

Renee laughed and pulled the picture out of my hand saying, "Don't you know who she is, Maya?"

Renee never takes anything seriously, so nonchalantly said, "That is you. That's the way the picture came out." With that she laughed as if quite amused. By this time I was angry and said, "I'll smack you Renee. What have you done to my picture?"

"I really don't know, that's the way the picture came out," she replied seriously.

We talked about the strange picture, then looked through the rest and found another, different print that was also of me, pregnant. It was certainly strange, but there was no way that we could find out what had happened so we just felt that it was a strange phenomenon of the film.

In July, Helena called and said, "Maya, I met a woman on the subway. It was a strange meeting. We just started talking and she informed me that the A.R.E. was giving a lecture this month. It will be on old Egypt. The lecturer's name is Bruce Hungerford, and he is also a concert pianist. How would you like to go? It will be on East 49th Street."

"No, Helena," I replied impatiently, "I just came back from Egypt. I have seen all there is to see and hear."

Well, a few days later, Dr. H. J. Reilly also called and said, "Maya, I feel that you should go and hear Bruce Hungerford who is speaking in New York tomorrow. His subject is on old Egypt."

Again, I replied, "H. J., I have seen Egypt and heard lots of lectures on this subject."

"But Maya," he insisted, "Betty and I may go. I feel it will be very interesting. You should hear this man. He is a wonderful speaker and a very knowledgeable person."

"Very well, H. J., I'll think about it," I replied, not at all interested in another lecture on old Egypt.

The next afternoon, I had two cancellations, so had nothing to do. Therefore, I called Helena and told her that I was free to accompany her to the lecture.

When we arrived at the hall, I introduced Helena and myself to Bruce Hungerford, then informed him that Dr. Reilly and his assistant Betty Billings were unable to come. They had called me just before I left home.

Nothing unusual happened until the very last part of the lecture, where Bruce showed a picture of the Sphinx. I looked at the picture and could not believe my eyes. There was a picture of my own face.

Excitedly, I held Helena's hand and whispered, "That is me! Helena, that Princess is me!"

Of course, by this time Helena had gotten accustomed to my strange outbursts and did not pay too much attention to what I had just said. Not getting any response from her, I ran over to Bruce Hungerford, who was speaking to a very important Egyptian diplomat. Taking hold of Bruce's arm, I asked, "Who is that Princess, Bruce?"

He looked at me in surprise and I continued, "That Princess is me, Bruce!"

Well, one can imagine the shocked looks that I got from both men. The Egyptian may have thought that I had suddenly gone insane, but I paid no attention to him. I pulled out the picture of me as the pregnant lady that I had been carrying in my purse and showed it to Bruce. He looked at it and then gave it to the diplomat who looked at it and then gave me a piercing look.

Again I asked," "Who is that Princess, Bruce?"

Still looking at me strangely, he replied, "She is the Princess Sin Hathor Yuen. She is the Princess of the Little Kingdom."

Later, Helena and some friends went to a coffee shop to have a snack, but I could not eat. All I could think of was, that Princess is me. She is me!

The next morning, I woke up about 6 a.m. and was still excited about the fantastic experience. I prayed for an hour and then sat in the silence. Suddenly, I heard a voice from the back of my head saying excitedly, "Maya, Maya, I am you. You are the Princess that modelled for the Sphinx, and Helena was your most trusted hand-maiden.

That was all, and then this Being jumped into my body. Oh, dear Lord, never have I ever felt anything like this. The only way I can explain what I felt is to say, it was like a mother having her first child. A child that she had longed for and now, it was manifested. I cried for joy and could not stop crying.

Later, I called Helena and told her what had happened She, too was excited. So many times in the past few months, she had asked, "Maya, what is the connection between us in the past? How were we related?"

Now we knew. We knew.

Bruce Hungerford must have been impressed by the picture of the pregnant lady. A few days later, after that dramatic incident, he called and asked if he could come over. He wished to speak to me.

When he arrived, we talked of the picture and I told him of my experience the next morning. I also told him of my two dreams of taking care of a very tiny baby, and that I had taken some warm clothing and a blanket for the baby.

He listened intently while I spoke, then remained quiet for a few minutes before asking, "Maya, what is your analysis of the pregnancy and your dreams of the tiny baby?"

I thought for a few moments then replied, "Bruce, I know we bear spirit beings, which are the thought forms we have created in former life times. This was told to me by Nefertiti."

"That is very interesting, Maya, are you writing about your experiences?"

"Yes."

"That is most interesting. I'll buy a copy of your book. Let me know when it is out."

We were both quiet, then he said, "Maya, I would like to talk to you about some business problem."

"Very well, Bruce, but first, let us pray and meditate in order to call in the spirit guides."

During the meditation, I saw a woman standing back of him. The aura around her was quite red, and her demeanor was most hateful.

I informed Bruce of this and he said, "Maya, I know who this woman is. I believe she has followed me from many past lifetimes. I may have rejected her in one of my past lives and for this she has returned to block me. Only God knows what I have gone through with this problem."

"Bruce, try not to be depressed. If so, you may open up the inner doors which will give her the power to destroy you. Pray and send light. In this way, you will purify the karmic patterns."

"Maya, I feel this problem will have to wait. Possibly in another lifetime I'll be able to handle it."

"No, Bruce, do it now," I cried out in a shocked tone of voice.

He did not reply. Instead he got up and walked over to the window and looked out to the back of the houses on 87th Street and said, "Maya, I have some friends who live back of you."

I wondered why he had suddenly changed the subject of our conversation, but said nothing. After a few minutes he came back and sat down, saying, "Maya, I have been teaching a young boy. He seems to have a promising future. What do you see for him?"

"Do you know his birthday and year?" I asked.

"No, I do not," he replied shaking his head.

After a few moments of thought, I answered, "This young boy has a great gift. I believe, he has a master in his subconscious body, but he will have to pray and go deep into meditation to awaken the great spirit that lies sleeping within his soul. I feel this will happen."

"Thank you, Maya. You have helped me more than you will ever know."

It was Bruce who sent his sister, Paulina Hungerford Clouston to me. The first time I saw her, I knew we had worked together and would work together again. She was separated from her husband, and I believe, divorced. Paulina had been both mother and father to Kate, her young daughter who was at that time in her early twenties. At the moment, the great problem was what Kate was going to do with her life.

I suggested that we pray and put the matter into God's loving care. After the prayers she seemed more relaxed so I said, "We will go into deep meditation and find out what God has in store for you, Paulina."

Paulina was working for a British organization, and had been there for fifteen years. Nevertheless, after the meditation, I looked at her vibrations and could see dynamic blue lights coming from within her subconscious mind. I knew that she had healing powers and said, "Why are you working as a secretary, Paulina? You are a metaphysician and a true healer. Leave this job and get into a healing type of work."

With a look of astonishment she replied, "Maya, I have been helping an elderly lady. She is the mother of one of my friends."

"Then get a full-time job as a practical nurse," I exclaimed, "this is your true calling."

We talked of many other things and then she left. I did not see her for another year, but when I arrived back in New York, she called and asked if she could bring her mother to see me. I agreed and a few days later, she came in with a very distinguished white-haired lady .

Try as I could, nothing seemed to come up for this elderly lady. As the reading continued, I would look over at Paulina and say something. Finally I cried out, "Paulina, a master is standing behind you. He tells me that he is unhappy about the change."

She stared at me for a moment then said, "Maya, you told me to leave my job and work full time with someone that needs my care. Well, I did leave my job after fifteen years, and they paid me five thousand dollars severance pay. Now, I'm with Grace, a friend who has cancer. It's a night and day job, Maya, I don't know how long I will be able to stand the pressures. "

I thought for a moment. It was now August, a message came through which said, "Stay on the job. By November Grace will pass over and by March of next year, you will be free. The little house and the property around it will be left to you."

"Oh, dear, this is very sad news," Paulina whispered, as if to herself, "but if by March of next year I'm free, I will come to California and bring you back in my car."

I thanked her and did not hear anything more until late November, when she called and said sadly, "Maya, your prophecy came true. My best friend passed around the early part of this month and left me the house and the property. If, as you have predicted, I'll be free in March, then I will definitely come and drive you back to the East Coast"

In February, she called and announced that she would be in Balboa, California by the early part of March. Two weeks later we left California and Paulina had an urge to stop at the Grand Canyon to see the wonderful sights. I remember when we arrived in Arizona, I felt happy and elated, even though it was snowing in this northern area. I said to Paulina, "I believe this will be the place for my center." We wrote to Alfred DeCarlo to ask him about it. It was as if I knew that Arizona would one day be my winter home.

When we arrived at the Grand Canyon, it was snowing and the roads were all blocked, but we were lucky the big snow did not come until the day after we had arrived.

The next morning, Paulina came to the room and announced, "Maya, I have a gift for you. We are going down the Canyon tomorrow, it will be a two-day tour and we will go on mules."

I was apprehensive, but did not feel I should chicken out, therefore I agreed to go on this venture. At lunchtime, the guides were all in the dining room and I informed them that I was going on the tour the next day. I also told them that I had never been on a horse.

One of the guides put his hat on my head and said, "Don't worry, little lady, we will give you our best mule, Lucky."

The next morning we bundled up warmly because it was still cold. Snow was still on the ground. I looked over at a tall gentleman who was bundled up in a long black cape. He looked like one of the mystery men in the movies. I asked him, "Are you one of the guides?"

With a serious look he replied, "No, Madam, I am one of your fellow nuts."

His answer caused me to be even more apprehensive, so as I got on Lucky, I was so nervous that my foot would not stay in the stirrup.

I called out to the guide and he came and fixed the problem. Then we were off, or so I thought, because Lucky took a few steps and put his foot right over the edge of the Canyon. I have to explain that the path leading down into the canyon is on a narrow ledge only a few feet wide. It's a four mile mule ride down into the canyon, most of it on a narrow ledge with a view that seems miles straight down to the bottom.

When Lucky's foot slid over the side, I was never so scared in all my life and I leaned back so that if Lucky went over the edge, I would fall to the ground. I heard the guide say, "Lady, sit up straight."

I paid no attention. I was in a state of shock. The guide quickly came over and guided Lucky back to safety, and I just as quickly got off.

I don't know how I had the common sense to go to Paulina and ask for the key to the car trunk where all our clothes and belongings were. It must have been my other self. She gave me the key and the guide handed me my lunch.

I ran back to the hotel and told the travel agent what had happened. After a full minute of total silence, he asked, "Where is the lunch?" I handed it to him and he returned the seventy dollars for the tour.

I went back to my room, but it was already taken and I had to wait for another room. Not having anything to do, I went to the dining room, where I met some Australians and they invited me to join their party.

I am positive that if I had gone down the canyon, that I would have had a heart attack. Lucky was a very sensitive and wise mule. He knew that I was unable to take the crucial trip and therefore, he did what he felt was right. Thank God for Lucky.

In August of 1976, Fathi Salib called me, saying, "Maya, I'm in New York. Can I come over to see you?"

Fathi was one of my favorite people and I was happy to hear he was in the States.

"Oh, yes, Fathi," I replied, "I'm very happy to hear your voice. Do come over."

When he arrived, we talked of his mother, who was ailing, and that the doctors in Luxor, Egypt had given her just a short time to live. We prayed for her and then meditated and visualized the light around her. After we were through he said, "Maya, I would like to get married and have an heir to carry on my name. Will you pray with me for these desires of my heart to be manifested?"

I nodded and again we prayed. During the meditation, I saw a star over his head. I knew this was the symbol of great success and the fulfillment of his great desires.

Fathi had met an American girl and was hoping that she would be the one he would marry and have a child with.

I felt that this girl was right for him, and that she would bear a child for him. He thanked me, then asked, "How about you? Are you still dreaming of the baby?"

"Yes, the visions are still recurring," I replied, "they are always the same. The tiny baby is crying and I am taking clothes and food for it."

He listened, then took out some scarabs and a tiny silver spoon from a briefcase, saying, "Maya, do not tell this to anyone, but these scarabs are blessed and the spoon is also. The scarabs will bring you blessed experiences and the spoon will help you to feed the spirit."

I thanked him for the gifts , and thought no more about the matter, until a few months later when I realized the visions had stopped completely and my happy spirit was back again.

I believed, as Fathi did, that the spirits did not eat the food, but took the essence of the food for power to fulfill their spirit destinies. On the higher realms the spirits were fed by our prayers.

In 1978, his desires were manifested, but this was only after the passing of his beloved mother.

Another incident occurred that same year. In September Bruce Hungerford called and said, "Maya, I have returned from England. It was a very difficult trip. I need some prayers, can I come over?'

"Of course, Bruce," I replied, "come over at 5 p.m."

I was doing some typing and did not realize it was past 6 p.m. when I stopped and wondered why Bruce had not kept his appointment.

The next morning, he called and said, "Maya, I was at your door and rang the bell for half an hour. What happened?"

"Bruce, I was typing. Why didn't you call me on the phone? I'm sorry but you can come over this afternoon. I'll leave the door open."

After I hung up, I meditated about the matter, and was told by my spirit that Bruce is blocked by a very wicked individual. He needed help or he would go down into the pit.

When he arrived, his aura was completely black. We prayed. As we prayed, I asked the Holy Spirit to forgive Bruce and to help him to forgive himself and his world. I was careful not to mention the evil individual. I knew he could not handle that situation.

We sat in the silence for quite a while, suddenly Bruce got up and exclaimed, "My God, help me!" Then he walked over to the window and looked out of it for several minutes. I kept on praying and quietly asked God to heal his soul. I felt he was filled with deep emotions and did not wish me to see his despair.

After a while, he came back and sat down and I spoke, "Bruce, we must transmute this evil karma."

"Maya, please believe me. God knows how I have tired but I just can't seem to be able to break through the darkness. Maybe, in another lifetime, I'll be able to handle it. Yes, it will have to wait for another time."

I tried to speak, but no words came, then he asked, "Maya, do you think I'll live a long time?"

"Bruce, why do you ask me such a question? It is as if you would like to end it all." I spoke these words while remembering my own desires to die.

"Yes," he replied, "I would gladly welcome death."

"Bruce, do you have time to listen to my story?" I asked, thinking maybe the story would change his thoughts.

I asked if he would care for a cup of tea and he nodded. After I gave him the tea and took a cup for myself, I told him the story of my great desire to die, and how Dr. H. J. Reilly saved my life. Bruce listened to my story and said, "That is a very interesting story, Maya. I, too, have felt life was not worth living and like myself, I have certainly felt trapped."

"Bruce, many people feel the same way as you and I, but we must remember, life is a school and we must not fail. We must live and conquer the forces of darkness."

"I know you are right, Maya," he said taking my hand in his, "please pray for me. I need it very much."

In October of that same year, I received a letter from Paulina. Kate was getting married shortly. "Maya, all these two people can talk about is their marriage plans. They don't go beyond the marriage into the future. I can't understand them."

I had never given Kate a consultation. She never asked for one. I had met her several times and always thought, how beautiful she is. She is almost like an angel with her blond hair and beautiful complexion. The news of the wedding gave me a strange feeling, yet, I could not tell why I was concerned.

In February of 1977, I received a letter from Helena saying, "Maya, I just read in the newspaper that Bruce Hungerford, his mother, niece and her husband were all killed in an auto accident."

I walked home from the post office saying, "Oh, God, oh God. No, this cannot be. What will Paulina do, oh, my God, how will she survive this terrible tragedy?"

Later, I learned that Paulina had taken it very well. I suppose she went into a state of shock and was not really conscious of what had happened. The man who caused the accident was coming back from his retirement party. Paulina forgave him and did not care to prosecute him. She got a small amount of money from the insurance company and later built a large home in Connecticut.

I was not surprised to hear of Bruce's death, but I was very surprised to hear about that of his niece and her young husband. About the mother, I remembered I could not see anything for her. And at the time I had felt that her life span was at an end.

THIRTY-SIX
My Brother Cecil, Reincarnated

Francis had been in my thoughts, many times, over the years, and in 1974 I felt that he had died. I had a vision, I dreamed I was in Barbados and it was a beautiful moonlit night.

I went to a house and a lady came to the door. I asked for Francis and she answered, "He is ill."

"I am May and I have come to heal him," I patiently replied.

She left me and went back into the house. When she returned she said, "He is too ill to see you. Come back another time."

As I walked away, I thought, "I will never see him again." I never did.

After the dream, I went to Barbados, with three friends, to find out what had happened to him. I felt I had to know. So many years had passed and I did want to know.

I arrived in Barbados in April and contacted his wife, Mrs. Lord. She was most kind. He had died on New Year's eve of 1974. It was the same year I felt he had died, the one in which I had had the vision. She was the woman I had seen in my vision when I went to heal Francis.

All through the years, the spirit of Francis has guided me up the stairway back to God. It was he who inspired me to write about the Psalms and he gave me the interpretations and power of the Psalms. May God bless his soul now and always.

A few years later, in 1979, my dear sister Clarice passed away. She had acquired her own hotel in 1950, in New Haven, Connecticut, and she left me a hundred thousand dollars in her will. I shared this money with the rest of my family.

She was the second sister to pass on. Dear Cecily had died in 1950 and Albert in 1962. I miss them all and my prayers are with them.

I was in Atlanta in 1979, giving readings at my friend Ellen's home, when I spoke to a girl named Carol. When she gave me her husband's birthdate, I became very excited. Ecstatic is a better word.

"Carol, Carol, " I cried, "I know this man! I know him! He is connected to me in my lifetime!"

Carol went home and called her husband, Richard. She told him to leave his job and hurry home. This he did. When he heard my voice on the phone, he started to cry. He couldn't stop crying.

Carol called Ellen and said, "Ellen, Richard must see Maya."

"Maya is leaving tomorrow on a one o'clock flight so come around about ten o'clock, he can see Maya then," Ellen answered.

In the morning I started praying. "Who is Richard?" I asked God and the spirit said, "He is your brother Cecil, who named you Maya."

When I saw Richard for the first time, I held out my arms and he held out his. I said, "You are my brother Cecil."

He answered, "Yes, I know."

That same year, Carol, Richard, another lady and I went to England. We rented a car and drove all over, visiting the places connected with King Arthur. We came to Stonehenge and I said a prayer because the Druid Priests had put a spell over Richard and me. We prayed about it.

We see each other at least once a year and I firmly believe that my brother Cecil has reincarnated into Richard.

The following year, in 1980 I met Teddy's stepson by his last wife. I told him to tell Teddy that I had forgiven him. Some time later, Teddy passed over into the spirit world.

THIRTY-SEVEN

Predictions

In meditation, the following came though to me from my spirits:

Many more problems have started for Saddam Hussein. He is in great trouble and he will ask Gorbachev for help. Saddam will go within and talk to the God-force and it is the God-force who will help turn him around from his evil ways. Yes, I say Saddam and Gorbachev will bring total peace to the earth. Yeltsin is going to make Gorbachev humble. He is a good man and will give Gorbachev balance.

Israel will have to give back the land to the Palestinians or Tel Aviv will be totally destroyed.

The trouble between the Jews and Arabs began in a past life when Sarah threw Hagar out of Jerusalem. (Book of Genesis). It was while I was in meditation that I saw Hagar's God sending negative vibrations to Israel. Hagar's God put a condition on Israel. This condition must now be transmuted through forgiveness by both Israel and the Arab nation. (What came through to me in meditation is not in the Bible. I meditated on chapter 21, 9th to the 21st verse, in the book of Genesis.)

Richard Nixon will be involved, when he asks forgiveness. Nixon was a top Rabbi in the days of Jesus. He was a friend of Jesus, but he hid behind the trees at the time of the crucifixion. For this he brought great feelings of guilt into this lifetime. Because of this guilt he gave up the tapes. Giving them up was for his soul to revolve back to God. He will again help this planet.

I see Vice President Quayle as a great soul, but he is still not opened up. So far President Bush is doing all the work; in time, Quayle will come forth as an amazing soul. He is an inner soul that needs our help. What's amazing is he may one day be President.

Russia is still full of anger, because of what she went through over the years, but as the people pray and meditate, great miracles will be manifested. Gorbachev is one of the greatest souls that I have ever met. In time he will speak to Saddam, who will listen, and peace will come to the planet. Gorbachev must pray and ask forgiveness. In one of my past lives I was connected with Peter, the Great. This is how I came to give Gorbachev the message, "You will one day be the top power in your country."

Last year Rabbi Meir Kahane was shot. The assassin was an Arab. I asked God, "What is in store for this Rabbi?" God answered and said,

"This Rabbi will in a very short time be conceived in the womb of an Arab woman and a Jewish father. The boy will be great at the age of five. He will begin to help the Arabs. Yes, in ten years the war between the Jews and the Arabs will begin to abate, and their world will become more peaceful. Many strange and evil situations will have passed. Jerusalem will be bombed, but man must pray for out of evil will come good. As mankind kneels down and asks forgiveness, light will flow onto the Earth.

We must pray for Jerusalem and the Palestinians to have peace. I see President Bush in great danger before his term is over.

The planet is being lifted up by mortals through our faith and through all our faith in God, mortals will become immortals. We will be given wisdom and knowledge to open up the door to immortality.

THIRTY-EIGHT
And Now in Closing

When I look back over my life I can understand now what old lady Douglas said to me, the day I was hanging onto her gate, about me doing her work. She was a spiritual advisor and helped people with their problems. The people did not understand this power that she had, and thought she was a witch. She knew I had the same power.

The native Hindu healer, that my dear father and stepmother took me to and who told me I had great work to do, she also knew.

Then there was Bacchus, who said I would lead many people back to God.

Many unhappy experiences happened to me before I fully understood what my true destiny in life was. A destiny to devote my life to helping people and leading them back to God and this is what I finally did, and still do.

I devote my life to helping people with "readings" and giving them advice. If they believe in my psychic powers than they can be helped, and those who do not, of course, I cannot help.

Reading palms, in those exclusive clubs, was the fad in those days and the clubs needed to entertain their customers. I read palms because it was expected of me, but my inner spirits always came through with the answers and eventually I discarded palms and cards because all I needed was the person's birthdate.

With this date, my inner master comes through and tells me everything that I need to know about that person and how to advise him or her.

People come to me from all over the United States for "readings." I even do a great many by mail. All I need is their birthday and the date of birth of their loved ones, because our lives are all intertwined.

I support myself with donations and live a simple life. Like Jesus, I own nothing. HE takes care of me with what little I need.

You may or may not believe in reincarnation. There are a great many mysteries in life that mankind does not understand, but the curiosity of man is opening up and the day will come when the answers will be understood by all because the consciousness of man is rising up to new heights.

This year 1991, I will celebrate my eighty-sixth birthday. My life is just as busy today as it has always been. I spend my summers on the

East coast, never knowing which state I will be in, depending on where my work takes me.

Just a few days ago I was deeply disturbed over something a member of my family had told me and as I sat in quiet meditation, a vision came through to me from Yuri Andropov. He said, " *Many centuries ago on this earth, Michael was called Peter and men called him great. In heaven he was called Michael. As he prays and meditates, the Michael power will flow to him and in time a great work will be fulfilled. The countries that stay with him will be blessed by the Holy Spirit.*

"It is through our work, prayers and meditation that we are able to lift up our consciousness to the Master of Light. As we pray and meditate, we will be lifted up to a higher plane of consciousness. In time the Michael power will flow down to us."

It was a strange vision and I truly believe Edgar Cayce's prediction, just before he died, that Russia will be the hope of the world for freedom. Communism is coming to its end and peace will flow.

It has been my dream to establish a non-profit center for the purpose of fulfilling our true destiny as Jesus fulfilled his. This is what I am striving for today. This was given to me, one day, when I was in deep meditation.

Perfect Truth is the Root of the God Consciousness. Christianity is the Root of Truth. Judaism is the Root of Christianity. Moslem religion is the Root of Judaism.

Now when the ungodly nations invade this inner root, it will in time surround them like the tentacles of the octopus, and all mankind shall be joined together as brothers and sisters of the light of the living God, and we shall love one another as God loves us.

I now spend my winters in wonderful sunny Arizona. My phone rings constantly from people all over the United States seeking my help. My life has been both strange and mysterious, but God set my path when I was born.

May God walk with me and all mankind up the spiritual stairway of the soul into paradise and heaven.

A Word From Terry A. Latterman

I met the Reverend Maya Perez through a friend who had met Maya at a New Year's party at Jess Stearn's house in California.

My friend spoke to me about a "reading" that she had had, and my curiosity got the best of me. I sent Maya a donation with my date of birth. I also included birthdates of my immediate family. A couple of weeks later I received a one-hour tape that astounded me. There was personal information on that tape that no one knew about, except myself. It was a beautiful reading, enough to open my curiosity about this woman and the psychic world.

When Maya came to Arizona for a week to visit my friend, we were introduced at the airport. I was intrigued to meet this women, who had sent me a tape of my innermost sad and unhappy experiences—experiences before my marriage.

The minute she climbed into my son's van, she looked deep into my husband's eyes and asked, "Why are you so depressed?" I was shocked to say the least. Depressed? I looked at my husband because I was startled at even the thought. He had not given me any indication that he was depressed. If he was he did not show it.

My husband, however, did not deny it. He answered her quietly and said, "Yes, I am somewhat."

"Somewhat? You are very depressed," She announced emphatically, "we'll have to talk about it later."

He was indeed depressed because of a circulation problem in his legs, a hernia, and other ailments. These problems have been corrected since that first encounter.

Does anyone ever wonder where psychics get this ability to foretell the future and the past lives of an individual? A great deal of research has been done by writers, especially by her good friend Jess Stearn, himself a writer of many books (which she predicted that he would become, long before he considered this occupation). Can there be an answer when God is involved?

Maya Perez is in the same world as Edgar Cayce, Jeanne Dixon, and numerous other famous psychics—a world of mystery that is not as yet understood by mankind.

I took Maya to a doctor and also to an ear specialist for a check-up. They were hilarious experiences because she scrutinizes everyone she comes in contact with, and she has a natural curiosity and genuine concern about everyone.

During the initial examination at the medical doctor's office, she studied him carefully; then she took the unsuspecting doctor by surprise. Poking him in his stomach with her finger she announced, "You don't pray." The startled doctor was speechless. It took a few minutes before he shook his head and admitted to this. Maya looked deep into his eyes and said, "You look like your mother. She was a religious women and prayed all the time. What is your birthdate?" He gave her the date, and she proceeded to tell him that he was a very nervous man. He needed to pray, and then all his problems would be solved.

As we walked out, she commented, "Poor man is a nervous wreck. He has lots of problems."

Our trip to the ear specialist proved to be just as interesting. Before the visit was over she revealed many things about the doctor. Personal information that left him astounded. She was very pleased with both men, and informed them they were good doctors. Her opinion helped lessen their shock.

I learn a great deal about people through her. I had one of my business acquaintances meet me at her apartment one day, for the main purpose of getting her opinion of him. He arrived ahead of me, and they had been visiting for a few minutes before I arrived. I was delighted of course. Maya immediately sensed that he was very psychic and was afraid of it. He then admitted to some strange experiences, and she informed him that he had to meet me in order for me to help him in business. She informed him that he looked like his mother, and proceeded to tell him about his parents. He admitted that what she said was true. When he left, she told me he was loaded with money. It was all right to continue my doing business with him. He was a good man. If he was not, she would have been quite vocal about it. She is emphatic about her concern when her predictions denotes danger.

She phoned me one evening and excitedly announced, "It just came through to me that Mark is thinking of committing suicide." She was referring to a member of my family who was having tremendous problems with his ex-wife. I phoned him immediately and related her phone call, and had a long conversation with him, which luckily helped. He is fine now and his problems are being slowly resolved, but I know she was right about her premonition. Many things come through to her in her prayer sessions about people who are going through difficult times. She knows what problems one is experiencing, and along with her advice, she urges one to pray and meditate.

Everyone adores Maya. She receives daily phone calls from people all over the United States. She also has people come from all over the U.S. to visit her for private readings. She is fortunate that the apartment complex that she lives in will rent furnished rooms to out-of-state guests. This is convenient for everyone, because her residences, in Arizona, change each winter. Maya supports herself with donations. Her mission in life is to help people. She prays daily. She starts her prayers by reading the Psalms—especially her favorites: 1, 4, 8, 40, and 91.

Her one goal now is to open a center which she has named "Center For The Christ and God Realization." It has been her dream for many years to establish a non-profit center for the purpose of fulfilling our true destiny as Jesus fulfilled His. She said the Blessed Mother has told her that we will not have peace until Russia is converted. Even as I write this, Russia is opening up her churches.

To be in Maya's presence is truly an experience. I've spend many a happy day with her. I especially love our prayer sessions. These are a must before or after our day begins. Holding hands we go deep into meditation. Everyone joins in. During these sessions her thoughts go deep and interesting information comes forth. She casually announces good and bad predictions, especially about personal matters. Problems that I, or anyone else present, may consider to be private. These are the sessions that astound me, because she will reveal situations that have actually happened in my life and the lives of others who are seated in the prayer session.

"Your mother-in-law is here, Terry," she announced one day, "and she asks your forgiveness for her cruelty to you. She is truly sorry and wants you to pray for her. It didn't matter who her son married, she would have given his wife a hard time." Then she proceeded to describe my mother-in-law's height, the color of her hair, and the fact that she was quite heavy in weight. All true. She has been deceased for twelve years and was a mean and cruel woman. Maya made it easy for me to forgive her and pray for her.

Maya's advice, "Pray for your enemies and you will heal a cell in your body." I found it difficult to do this but found that she is right. Praying for those who wish you harm, or give you problems, does prevent them from succeeding.

I've changed the names of some of the people in this book for obvious reasons. But everything in this book happened to the Reverend

Maya Perez. It is a book about a psychic's extraordinary experience in this world, a world we still do not fully understand.